Humanizing Hell!

The individuals named in this search for justice are not dragged into a nuclear dock, to be browbeaten and pilloried for their part in the tidal wave of nuclear violence poised to engulf them and all of us. Their responsibility for violated law and abuse of power is spelled out, but so is the complicity of each of us. It is only by spelling things out that we can, together, start afresh.

This book is dedicated to you, who value life enough to protect it from vandals.

GEORGE DELF's background was in education and politics
before he became a specialist in international law on war. He
has written two previous books and is now heading the
campaign INLAW fighting for the enforcement of international law.

Humanizing Hell!

THE LAW V. NUCLEAR WEAPONS

by
GEORGE DELF

HAMISH HAMILTON
London

Permission to quote from published material is gratefully acknowledged to
the author's estate and Chatto & Windus for an extract from *Nuremberg* by
Peter Calvocoressi; to Greenwood Press, USA, for *Law, Soldiers and
Combat* by Peter Karsten; to Macmillan for *Independence and Deterrence* by
M. Gowing; to Quadrangle Books, New York, for *Nuremberg and Vietnam*
by Telford Taylor; and to Sweet & Maxwell for Schwarzenberger's *The
Legality of Nuclear Weapons*.

First published in Great Britain 1985
by Hamish Hamilton Ltd
Garden House 57–59 Long Acre London WC2E 9JZ

Copyright © 1985 by George Delf

British Library Cataloguing in Publication Data

Delf, George
   Humanizing hell!: the law v. nuclear weapons
   1. Nuclear weapons (International law)
   I. Title
   341.6'3   JX5133.A7
   ISBN 0–241–11593–0

Typeset by Computape (Pickering) Ltd
Printed and bound in Great Britain by
Richard Clay (The Chaucer Press) Ltd, Bungay, Suffolk

Contents

Foreword

'Justice cannot be approximated if the hope of its perfect
realization does not generate a sublime madness in the soul.
Nothing but such madness will do battle with malignant
power and "spiritual wickedness in high places". The illusion
is dangerous because it encourages terrible fanaticisms. It
must therefore be brought under the control of reason'
– Reinhold Niebuhr

This book is not about dreams of human potential, but about a
man-made nightmare which threatens to drag down civilization to
nuclear death. It is about two-faced authority, which conceals a
murderous dagger behind a smiling face. It is about our desperate
need to restore integrity to minimum universal laws, a struggle
made doubly hard by our own complicity in crime. It is a search for
sane landmarks in a mad world where the incineration of cities is
equated with defence. It is a citizen's indictment of criminal
power.

'Remember,' goes a Bengali saying, 'that when you stalk a
man-eating tiger it is also stalking you.' To write this indictment of
crime in high places is to reflect on my own part in it. The
grotesque 'balance of terror', a competition in nuclear pesticide, is
the product of minds whose inner balance is severely disturbed.
We share that imbalance. The agents of nuclear terror, our chosen
leaders, present it as regrettable but necessary, lawful, patriotic.
They lie. It violates not just the essence of the laws of armed
conflict, which insist on restraint, but the inner springs of feeling
which give life to the law.

George Orwell and Franz Kafka watch over our shoulder as we
seek a path out of this labyrinth of deception. Their insight will
help us see through the criminalized logic which presents the law as
an optional icing on the international cake, something to be
swallowed only when convenient. The Nuremberg Trial of
1945–46 gives the lie to such distortion. Nazi war criminals claimed

that the law did not concern war. They found out that it did. Many were hanged or imprisoned. The law was enforced, against mass murder and 'total war'. But it was half-justice, aimed only at one set of criminals. By denying Allied complicity in war crimes we robbed the law of universal meaning. The wildly escalating malignancy of cold war weaponry is the price we continue to pay for this evasion.

The law is now confined by its guardians to one extremity of our collective mind, while across the schizophrenic abyss looms the dark shadow of mass murder and extinction. The first step in restoring coherence to fragmented law is to recognize the huge scope of the problem. How did we come to dig what may well be our grave? It has been dug over centuries by an incoherent idealism. While our rhetoric flies higher and higher, mocking rational thought with feverish visions, our actions give the lie to such nonsense. Both nuclear champions claim to promote values of the utmost importance, and both defend them with weapons which undermine the fragile structure of civilization, life and law.

Our arms race is a descent into hell, down into a nightmare darkness pervaded by private and official lies. People who live in such depths of despair, as we do, are very close to extinction. It is an age of senility, when the meanderings of a King Lear pass for leadership and wisdom. Senility is an addiction to nonsense, when unlived belief finally parts company with experience. Our leaders have their brief moments of clarity, as do all madmen, when they denounce as 'utter madness' the arms race which they fuel on our behalf. But at the next moment paranoia holds a gun to their heads and they urge more missiles, more submarines, more money, more trust, more haste. They apply the brake with their tongues as their feet press down the accelerator.

It is the purpose of this book to confront carefully the extent of our present home in hell; to absorb darkness in watchful eyes until the outlines around us become clearer; to search gingerly for a path out of this dead end; to take each step with care, neither boasting of its value nor cursing its limits; to take back the powers stolen by a parasitic élite; to begin the slow formulation of a new language and perspective designed for single, co-operating minds rather than mobs; to recapture law from the nuclear *mafia* and restore it to its natural place, in courts of justice where each of us is judge.

Such simple path-finding will seem wildly ambitious to those who have lost heart. Lives stifled by evasion and denial are not easily re-awakened. But the distance is short between despair and hope. The gap can be closed.

A book of this kind, then, is the most and the least of things. Its scope is as large as the horizon, because it seeks to throw out the rubbish of corrupt authority, its crumbling institutions and Hollywood fantasies. All these stand condemned by the law and by that final judge, personal experience. Only when we have cleared space for ourselves can we begin to re-make civilization, on the foundations of just law and mutual respect. A simple task demanding all our co-operative energy.

Acknowledgments

To swim against the current of convention is heavy going, when the support of others counts for much. My warm thanks, first, go to Susan Jeffers for her encouragement at a time when this book was still a pipe-dream.

The transition from typescript to print was smoothed by the expert and thoughtful guidance of Julian Evans, whose faith and critical understanding are much appreciated.

My largest debt, in terms of her consistent, patient encouragement over many months, followed by untold hours of careful correction, is owed to Pauline Slater. Whatever the book is worth owes much to her insight and humour.

My two sons, Simon and Jason, provided the best possible incentive to write a book which aims at a fully human life beyond our nuclear death cell. Their creative optimism is evidence enough that humanity is capable of reaching that goal.

Chapter One

Our Nuclear Nightmare

'And now I'm locked inside
The savage keep, the grim rectangular tower
From which the fanatic neighbour-hater scowls;
There all is emptiness and dirt and envy,
Dry rubbish of a life in anguish guarded
By mad and watchful eyes'
– 'The Journey Back', Edwin Muir

'The humanizing of war! You might as well talk of the
humanizing of hell!'
– Admiral Sir John Fisher, during the Hague Conference on
the laws of war, 1899

Stripped of its pomp and play-acting, jargon and cant, law is the hard floor of civilization. Without its even surface, upon which all citizens may walk securely, there is nothing but neurotic anxiety. Civilized law is a common denominator of common sense, a social bond which permits each person to live uniquely and at peace. It is not passed down from on high but grows naturally out of ordinary human need and perception. Murder is not a crime because we are told it is, but because we know it is. 'Thou shalt not kill' is present in the human bloodstream, felt in heart and mind, in every part of the world.

But when a civilization decays this hard surface crumbles, leaving the citizen uncertain, distrustful, afraid. Daylight confidence gives way to the nightmare of arbitrary power. We become like the child who discovers that a parent is out to exploit trust. In modern civilization, East and West, just law has receded to the surface of life, leaving at the core false law, a cheap imitation dressed correctly but lacking in feeling and devoid of justice. The usurper offers no reassurance to the citizen on matters of war and peace, acting at the beck and call of power. This con-law feeds on and incites apathy and despair.

When at last, impatient with the failure of conventional peace-making, I explored the relation of law to nuclear weapons, I discovered far more than I was looking for. It was a revelation of disaster, of a spiritual and cultural dry-rot eating its way through the foundations of modern life. I had expected to find half-baked, inadequate laws which tolerate the crimes they deserve. My low expectations, I soon learned, were reflections of my own gloom. I had been conditioned to expect little from a legal system long adapted to policies of threatened mass murder. The law had failed to check the nuclear monster during the years since Nuremberg. It could not be worth much. Or so I supposed. I was wrong.

As I read through the laws of armed conflict, formulated during this century, I felt like an archaeologist who has dug down through rotting vegetation and debris to hit upon the stone floor of an ancient temple. At The Hague in the first years of the century, at Geneva and Nuremberg, the world's governments had pledged to contain military violence within a legal straitjacket. Undefended targets must not be attacked, attacks must be limited to military targets, and even fighting between armies must not cause excessive suffering. Above all, mass destruction and indiscriminate attacks on non-combatants are outlawed. Specially protected persons include women, children, the elderly, sick and wounded, and prisoners of war.

There is room for argument about the peripheral meaning of these laws. What is clear is a binding legal commitment on the part of nations to refrain from the worst excesses of war. Better still, it is not just a pact between remote governments but has a binding effect on individuals. The Nuremberg trials underlined the fact that war crimes can be, and have been, committed by citizens as well as soldiers.

The British Manual of Military Law, I soon found, spells out the laws which regulate military life. Most are concerned with internal discipline, including such weighty matters as the right of a soldier to refuse an order to take part in amateur dramatics. But hidden among its solemn pages is a section which describes military obligation to international law. This responsibility is taken very seriously and offenders are warned that punishment will be severe. Britain's Royal Military Academy, at Sandhurst, teaches its aspiring officers that 'it is the policy of the UK Government to comply' with these laws. Non-combatants, it warns, must not be attacked.

I felt a rising sense of anger as the full meaning of these laws sank in. It is not laws which are at fault, imperfect though they are, but governments and nations which allow them to moulder and decay. Nearly two generations of nuclear corruption have spread a tangled web of deceit across the plain surface of these laws of humane restraint. Lawyers, it seems, like those of Nazi Germany, have connived willingly at the prostitution of their calling. They, with a handful of exceptions, have followed the voice of money and power, not law. In so doing they have fooled the general public, who imagine that such a well-favoured professional group must know what it is doing.

If it were only the legal profession at the heart of this corruption the problem might be solved without too much difficulty. But it is evident that the rift between the law and nuclear security systems runs deep, through modern civilization. Like most people, I was brought up and trained to honour and obey the prevailing system of values, not to challenge it.

Crime, like any other activity, becomes a part of normality if repeated often enough without challenge. The bombing of Dresden in 1945 by the RAF, which killed more than one hundred thousand people, mostly refugees, women and children, was just-ified and rationalized by the British without reference to the law. It was said to bring the end of the war closer and must therefore be right. The same rationale served to justify the atomic bombing of Hiroshima and Nagasaki. The end, it appeared, justified the means.

It became clear to me that the prosecution of leading Nazis at Nuremberg had a criminal side-effect. By excluding Allied war crimes from legal scrutiny, all Allied war action became, by implication, lawful. The deliberate bombing of cities, denounced by the whole world community as criminal in 1938, had by this sleight of the victor's mind become absorbed into normal war behaviour. Far from re-assessing city-bombing in the light of existing law, post-war governments of East and West soon engaged in a competition to build bigger and better missiles of mass destruction. Crime had become law, con-law, the law of necessity invoked by every gangster in history. Because they devalue human life to the level of insect pest, nuclear threats of mass murder are the very essence of criminal corruption. Even if never carried out, such threats impose a dead weight on feeling and justice, corrup-ting law like a *mafia* conspiracy. No human being half-sensitive to the pain of others can plan to exterminate millions of strangers, no matter what the provocation. Just law does not meet bad behaviour with worse.

My mind reeled as it struggled to grasp the full enormity of this disaster. In earlier days I had clung to the notion that at least the peace movements understood the problem posed by nuclear weapons. But as I examined more closely the legal implications of nuclear defence systems I saw that peace movements have become to an alarming extent an integral part of the nightmare they denounce. By insisting on the moral and political objections to nuclear weapons, without reference to their criminal status, the peace movements have obscured rather than exposed the core of the problem.

I had long been puzzled by the fact that peace movements in all countries seemed to be forever on the defensive, in terms of the law. In Britain, activists were constantly charged with breaches of the peace, obstruction and other minor offences, resulting in small fines and short prison sentences. It was as if an unruly puppy were kept in check with an occasional jerk of the lead. The aim of their protest, nuclear weapons, did not figure in court, except perhaps as the disregarded part of a defence speech. Whenever a judge in Britain contemplated the nuclear issue, a rare event, he would dismiss it with a solemn incantation of 'Crown prerogative'.

When at last, in 1983, the British peace movement began to take an interest in the law and nuclear weapons it seemed there might be a breakthrough in campaign strategy. It appeared that at last the Government was to be challenged at its most vulnerable point, on the law. But these hopes were naïve. Far from grasping the radical implications of an exposure of Government illegality on such a fundamental issue, the peace leadership saw it as no more than another tactic to add to several others. They seemed to imagine that the addition of various often contradictory objections to weapons of mass murder would result in a sum of argument the Government could not refute.

Such a childish trust in the value of rational argument betrayed a wilfully unrealistic understanding of the workings of Government and the roots of nuclear strategy. The machinery of mass murder is not engineered and maintained by reason. It is a by-product of bitter, degrading experience, of suffering and killing, of hideous cruelty sweetened by patriotism. It is the expression of a collective poison which paralyzes feeling and hope, choking the human spirit with guilt. To contemplate, coldly, the murder of entire cities requires a mind in the last stages of sensory decay. It is immune to positive reason, except where everyday trivia are concerned. It can manage mortgages and work routines, perhaps, but not matters of global life and death. But fear of crime may penetrate such a mind, arresting destructive tendencies. Or so I thought.

The peace movement's limitations on this issue were made clear to me one day in 1983, when I took a train to the Campaign for Nuclear Disarmament's annual conference at Sheffield in Northern England. I had been invited to attend a press conference on the issue of nuclear policies and their legal status. As requested, I had drafted a short press statement, which stated simply that according to international laws then in force, all forms of mass destruction are illegal. Therefore, current threats to destroy 'enemy' cities with nuclear weapons are a gross violation of the law. The Government was therefore charged with conspiracy to commit war crimes.

Such a statement, I felt, was merely the first obvious step in a campaign to attack the nerve centre of nuclear annihilation. It would require continuing action and initiative of the highest order if it were to reverse the most destructive tide in history. But when the General Secretary of CND read this statement, which we were to present jointly, he refused to sign it. By then we were barely two hours away from the press conference. In the company of a lawyer friend, the Secretary and I met in a quiet corner of the conference hall. When I pressed for an explanation of his rejection of the statement, I was told that the conference had not approved it. He refused to discuss the obvious point, that he had earlier been willing to issue a press statement without specific conference approval. I suggested he could make an emergency intervention at the conference, read out the statement and ask for conference support. I would accept their decision, whatever it might be.

This too was rejected. I was overcome by the absurdity of our situation. How could the peace movement make serious use of the law while refusing to declare its outright rejection of illegal policies? Pressed further, the Secretary's final comment was: 'What if *The Times* comes out tomorrow with headlines proclaiming CND's accusations that the Government is conspiring to commit war crimes?' I looked at him in disbelief. Such an eventuality, it seemed to me, was exactly what was wanted. The whole issue of Government illegality would then be at the centre of public debate and controversy. It was not to be. The press conference was cancelled. There were no headlines next day, no public debate, just a few paragraphs on an inside page outlining various CND conference decisions.

I soon found that a majority of the peace movement share this largely passive response. It is a deceptive passivity. Not lack of concern or belief but a reluctance to look beneath the surface of the problem, to identify deep-seated emotional obstacles, to explore complex issues requiring energetic criticism and initiative. Peace is wanted, but on the cheap. Normal life takes precedence.

When I travelled to many parts of Britain, visiting local peace groups and talking to them about the law, I was impressed by their quiet interest and concern. They accepted that the law is a neglected campaigning issue which requires attention. But it was also clear that they were for the most part as inhibited as the CND Secretary on the issue. They sensed that serious opposition to Government illegality must involve a radical shift in personal as well as campaigning behaviour and thought. Like a show-jumping horse confronted with an unexpectedly high fence, they balked at the challenge.

The personal nature of this problem was well expressed by three young solicitors at a meeting in Chesterfield, not far from Sheffield. It was all very well for me to live on the dole and give my time to the problem, they said at a miners' club after the meeting, but what would happen to their jobs and their mortgages if they treated the issue of nuclear illegality as a full-time challenge touching the foundations of life? The problem, I told them, does not exist for their convenience. It exists in its own right and each of us must judge what response is most effective. If the response does not measure up to the problem, I suggested, it is frivolous. They were intelligent, thoughtful young people and I felt sympathy for them. They were victims, not architects, of our nuclear nightmare. But there is no cheap, easy escape.

The peace movement, then, is finding the law a bitter pill to swallow. It is as easy as it is futile to denounce nuclear illegality and do nothing about it. Government policy may be wrapped in pretty thoughts but it is rooted in primitive and brutal traditions fed on the blood of two world wars. It may hear but it will not listen to sermonizing. It has an answer for everything. Only the most specific, exact and personal indictment of crime, spelling out the actions to be taken, can hope to penetrate to the heart of this conspiracy.

The peace movement's complicity in this nightmare of deception made me think long and hard. Often, it seemed impossible to find a way out of our self-imposed dead end. Perhaps the human race was indeed a misbegotten species which had betrayed evolution and deserved extinction. The dodo and the dinosaur had committed lesser sins before they vanished. I was tempted to turn my back on this mad flirtation with death and enjoy nature at its simplest and most beautiful. Sanity still hovers in fresh air. To watch a dragon-fly on a summer's day, a shimmering dart of blue above clear water, is a luxury beyond price. To rescue the law from its dusty exile and unite it with such natural life is a task to daunt the bravest.

Bruised by the agents of peace, what of the law's own middle-men, the lawyers and judges? Meeting with them was another sharp lesson in the mad logic of nuclear realism. At university, I had regarded law students with disdain. Their use of language was enough to arouse suspicion. The world's most flexible language was stripped and gutted, the dead words propped up in a cemetery of pomp. Even the youngest of the students embraced old age, dressing up in ceremonial garb to feed off the weak, poor and crooked. It seemed no more than a pretentious *mafia* of 'learned friends' and 'm'luds'. I could never understand what all that had to do with justice, the most elusive of virtues.

To find myself immersed in the law, against all my inclinations, is therefore a shock. To meet its exponents was a suitable punishment, no doubt, for earlier contempt of court. It was not that they were rude or unfriendly. They were not. It was their closed system of thought, a professional closed shop, which grated. They were accustomed to public acceptance of their splendid and profitable isolation. My intrusion into their remote kingdom provoked an immediate disturbance.

My first encounter was with a retired professor of international law. Not any professor but the leading expert, Professor Georg Schwarzenberger, author of many works of renown. I tracked him down to his retirement home near London and he was gracious enough to answer my many questions, most of which must have seemed to him of an irritating simplicity. I wanted to know, for example, why laws against mass destruction had been, and were being, so casually swept aside by the nuclear powers. He gave me his writings on the subject, which I read with care. He spelled out the many paths by which governments, including ours, evade the obvious and embrace the devious. There are always loop-holes, it seems, for those in power who are able to keep a prying public at arm's length. Every scrap of vitality had been squeezed from the law at Nuremberg, where there had been a determination to convict the Nazis. But those same laws, strengthened since then, had been struck down in the nuclear era by a mysterious paralysis. They hung limply in the church of official righteousness, like battleflags from long ago. The law was not dead, simply fading away in the glare of nuclear weaponry.

Professor Schwarzenberger agreed wearily that this was so. But he suggested that it was no use pretending that power did not dictate world policy. In the presence of such realism, I felt like an apprentice Saint George stalking his first dragon, filled with heroic dreams and armed with a paper sword. Stung a little, perhaps, by my innocent enthusiasm, the professor reminded me that he too was unhappy with Government policy. But governments would not be diverted, I concluded, by quiet professors, even when well-informed, eloquent and waspish.

It was next the turn of the lawyers. I met with a group of them at an early planning discussion of the London-based Lawyers for Nuclear Disarmament. It took place in the Temple, in central London, a cloistered place reeking of Oxford and Cambridge. In the university manner, names were painted at the foot of staircases. I was fully conscious of my status as the only non-lawyer present. Should I be suitably meek and attentive, or take them on at their own game? There was no need to answer this question because I found that there were only two people present who knew much about the laws of armed conflict. I was one of them. Very few lawyers, it is clear, learn much about international law during their training. Of the few who do, most head for a well-upholstered academic career, the kind of people least likely to rock the boat of convention. It is a macabre irony. Lawyers are willingly insulated from the laws of war.

At first, this encounter seemed hopeful. There was a determination to inform the public about the laws which prohibit mass destruction. Pamphlets would be published and meetings held. But as time went by and I read the pamphlets and attended the meetings, the early promise faded like the laws themselves.

Nuclear policies were denounced but there was always a vital element missing. There is something incongruous about lawyers who spend their working week concerned with routine crime, and a few spare hours arguing against mass murder and the destruction of civilization. It is as if a passenger on the *Titanic* had spied an iceberg ahead but was saving the news until after dinner. The priorities are back to front, as perverse as those which paralyze the peace movement itself. Are we all mad or just exhausted?

The ambivalence of lawyers is no fantasy. It has been confirmed over and over again. One example overshadowed the others. CND had agreed, in 1983, to publish my leaflets warning British and American military personnel of their responsibility to avoid war crimes and obey the law. But first they wanted to check the contents with a friendly firm of solicitors, whose leading partner writes articles in the liberal press in support of international law.

In May, after several weeks, a letter was sent to CND by a partner of this firm, stating that 'there is no doubt at all that distributing or attempting to distribute this leaflet to members of the Armed Forces would constitute an offence under Section 1 of the Incitement to Disaffection Act, 1934. The maximum penalties are two years. . . . ' Moreover, the letter went on, the 'mere possession of this leaflet . . . is an offence in itself'. CND was advised to send back all existing copies of the leaflets to their author, 'as their presence in a CND office could easily be misunderstood'. CND duly refused to print them.

I checked the passage in the Incitement to Disaffection Act. It was brief and to the point: 'If any person maliciously and advisedly endeavours to seduce any member of His Majesty's forces from his duty of allegiance to His Majesty, he shall be guilty of an offence under this Act'. The Act had been designed to ward off the encroachment of Marxist and other political influences. But the whole aim and content of the offending leaflet consisted of a warning to obey the law. To prosecute it would involve an Alice-in-Wonderland case that soldiers must be protected from such seductive and malicious advice. Not only would such a prosecution invite ridicule, it would be a public exhibition of the Government's own perversion of the law.

So we went ahead and printed the leaflets on our own account. Thousands were duly circulated at many military bases, including the home of the British Army, Aldershot, where they attracted front-page attention in the local newspaper. At the time of writing, more than one year later, there have been no prosecutions. During this time it has become evident that Government policy is still to keep the flattest of low profiles on this embarrassing issue.

How is it possible, I wondered, for trained lawyers to give such poor advice on such an issue? They are not bound by official rationalization of nuclear weaponry and consider the latter illegal. Yet they had failed to appreciate Government vulnerability on the issue and exaggerated the literal meaning of the Act in question. They had put two and two together and made five. Passive CND acceptance of such dubious advice compounded the error. No wonder the peace movements of the twentieth century have so conspicuously failed to halt lawless violence.

A further and common reflection of this inertia appears in the tendency of even the least conservative lawyers to shroud the law in a veil of mystery, beyond the reach of common sense. What appears in black and white is seldom what it appears to be, except when convenient. Always, there are hidden meanings lurking behind the obvious, available like highwaymen to rob passers-by. The important Protocol 1, agreed at Geneva in 1977, which binds nations to protect non-combatants and outlaw mass destruction, is one such example.

The British and American Governments were alone in adding a reservation to this Protocol, which they themselves had helped to formulate, specifically excluding nuclear weapons from its scope. They thus achieved the spectacular feat of swearing fidelity to principles of minimum civilized restraint in war, except when they chose to use nuclear weapons of mass murder. But behind this exercise in the grotesque lies an even more nightmarish twist of logic. Various academic legal experts, even those sympathetic to the peace movement and hostile to nuclear weaponry, have solemnly gone on record as stating that the Additional Protocol 1 cannot be held to concern nuclear weapons because it was made known during the discussion stages of these laws that they did not touch nuclear weapons.

The Government's scandalous part in this attempted fraud will be examined later. It is the response of the legal fraternity which concerns us here. To accept as legally valid, background discussions which do not appear in the final document, is at best misleading and at worst dishonest. It is as if a law specifically banning murder were to be held not to apply to millionaires or dustmen because this was 'generally understood' during the preparatory stages of the law. For lawyers to connive at this calculated deception is to play games with principles affecting the lives of millions.

Superior to lawyers stand the magistrates and judges, the men (and a few women) appointed to safeguard the law at every level. Wolves in sheepskin, I used to think. But I had always nursed a secret hope that these remote beings did indeed have the best interests of justice at heart. During the summer of 1982, for the first time, I witnessed three of them at close quarters. The experience was revealing.

At a small town in East Anglia, a magistrate was trying several peace activists for minor offences at a nearby military base. I was invited as an expert witness to explain how nuclear weapons violate the law. I had barely finished a brief statement when the prosecuting solicitor rose to announce that international law did not apply in British courts, as if it were some sort of foreign infection. The chief magistrate nodded, clearly relieved, and declared that I would not be allowed to undergo cross-examination by the defence. I must leave the court.

The appeal against conviction of two of the accused at that trial duly took place some weeks later, at a Crown Court in Peterborough. Once again, I was asked to appear on their behalf. This time I wrote out a four-page statement, detailing the various laws which together comprise a strong indictment of any form of mass destruction. When the judge learned of my presence he asked to see the written statement. He then told me to leave the court while all present, including police witnesses, lawyers and defendants read the statement. I was then called back into court. Addressing me with the solemn finality which is the hallmark of unassailable authority, he said that I could not be cross-examined and must leave the court. When I asked if he would tell me why, he replied, curtly, no.

I learned afterwards that during the reading of the statement the judge had commented that he would not allow the court to be used for political propaganda. He made no reference to the laws detailed in the statement. On the third occasion I was the defendant in a civil case concerning family property. Here the judge quickly discovered that he and I had one thing in common, our university. This led to a number of private and humorous asides during my presence on the witness stand, unintelligible to everyone else in court. The result, a partial victory for an elderly relative, proved, if nothing else, that age as a bond is superior to education.

These three cases taught me a number of lessons. Two of them concerned matters of life and death, the fate of an entire civilization, perhaps of life itself. Yet both had squeezed out this primary issue in favour of petty arguments about who had obstructed whom. Both courts had refused to take into account my efforts to help the defence presentation by citing relevant laws to which our society is committed. There had been a concerted and effective move to trivialize the issues and motives involved. Laws which are adequate to convict Nazi war criminals were tossed aside as irrelevant. Quotations from the laws themselves had been dismissed, without explanation, as 'political'.

The third case concerned a minor dispute about the use of a semi-derelict outbuilding. It had occupied the attention of a judge, various lawyers and a dozen witnesses, during two days. I had been allowed almost three hours to explain my case and reply to questions. The judge had been utterly bored, most of the time, by a public exhibition of family pique, but also polite, often friendly. The contrast was striking, and depressing.

As our campaign to enforce these minimum laws of military restraint developed I was to discover that this early experience of the law was entirely typical. Our much vaunted British justice, with its scarlet robes and archaic machinery, is a pygmy charade in the context of nuclear confrontation. The rituals of the courts in this respect are little better than the scratching for fleas of an old baboon, under the gaze of a hungry lion. Or to relate it more directly to recent experience, it is as if a court near Auschwitz were to focus on the highway infringements of people objecting to gas ovens.

The schizoid quality of law enforcement, part precision, part nightmare obscurity, is not simply the effect of a second-rate legal system and judiciary. It is the reflection of a generalized defect of cultural awareness and responsibility, nowhere better exemplified than in the behaviour of Government. It is the Government, after all, which appoints the judges from the tiny pond of customary privilege which guarantees their narrow perspective. It is the Government which has direct access to public communications, setting the tone and leaving unspoken what it considers unspeakable.

It is the Government, not just this one but all of them since Hiroshima, which has promoted without shame the supreme lie, that to threaten death and destruction of untold millions is a form of defence which complies with the law. It is the Government, as I soon discovered, which outdoes Kafka's imagination in its capacity to confuse and deceive. To make out of the simplest truth a complex, lifeless wreckage is a devilish art which is second nature to modern government and its patronizing agents.

Asked to explain how laws, which state clearly that mass destruction in any form is a crime, can be squared with policies which threaten extermination, the Government tells us something else. It says that its policies are entirely defensive, that nuclear weapons have kept the peace and are not forbidden specifically by any international convention. It does not answer the question. Its replies have the shoddy veneer of an old-time American teamster leader announcing to the press that he has been elected by free and democratic vote. It is hard to know how to react. By smiling or reaching for the handcuffs?

The Government should remember what one of its own defence experts had to say on the matter. Julian Critchley, MP, Vice-Chairman of the Conservative Party Defence Committee, said: 'It requires something of a revolution for British Ministers and defence officials to abandon the objectives of population extermination. For the traditional objective of the British "nuclear deterrent", Chevaline included, has all along been Moscow, as the evidence given to the defence committee of the House of Commons makes clear.'[1]

The essence of official evasion on such a vital issue is expert camouflage. Never speak to a member of the public face to face. A lofty remoteness is vital. Such evasion is itself a gross affront to the law, which requires honest personal responsibility. At first I was angry and upset when I received letters from the country's leading legal and political authorities which answered what was not asked,

[1] *Guardian*, 5 March 1984.

or shuffled my letter to yet another remote figure. But after many such exchanges I know what to expect. When I read the words 'I am instructed to . . . ' I know that the writer is aspiring to the safe haven of total anonymity, an Ariel in pin-stripes, His Master's Voice, the perfect criminal who cannot be caught because he does not exist, except on paper. The climax of such an exchange was reached one day when a colleague received a letter from the Foreign Office, announcing that he was responding to a letter sent by her to the Queen, which had been sent on to him, and that the answer to it could be found in a letter which had been sent six months earlier to me in reply to my letter to the Attorney-General about other related matters.

But there exists somewhere in everyone, however deeply hidden, an instinctive recognition of truth. Occasionally a slim blade of grass pierces the concrete. I once came upon a Cabinet Minister on a pay-train in Suffolk. I went to sit beside him and for half an hour we talked about the Government's nuclear policies. He would have preferred to talk about anything else, but was polite. The chance was too good to miss. There was no 'minion' to be 'instructed', no convenient reply to fish out of its slot, regardless of relevance. For a few precious minutes he was trapped in the open, just an ordinary human being obliged to behave like one. I explained my objection to threats of mass murder and he listened gravely. For a moment he stared out of the window at the passing fields. 'I agree, the whole thing is crazy,' he murmured. I had barely stored this rare confession in my memory when he realized his mistake and added: 'But of course we have to have them, unfortunately.'

Such a brief recognition of the lunatic wilderness into which we have strayed is like a peep-hole in a maximum security prison. Through it can be glimpsed another larger, saner world, until the lid snaps shut and colour vanishes from our cell. A Minister of Defence in the British Government told Parliament: 'The present arms race is utter madness.'[1] A month earlier, in the same place, he had said: 'We believe that the nuclear arms race is madness.'[2] But such an admission is itself madness when it is accompanied by continuing and voluntary mad action. It is no better than the admission of an alcoholic, as he drains another bottle, that drinking

[1] *The Times*, 20 May 1981.
[2] *The Times*, 15 April 1981.

is suicidal. The Minister of Defence is stating that the security of our society, and of modern industrial civilization, is founded on a vastly complex, expensive process which is mad. This mad process, according to him, cannot be reversed except with the full agreement of the other asylum bully who is equally mad. Otherwise we must continue along our mad track.

Occasionally these flashes of Government insight are supplemented by a fuller analysis. That maverick logician of British conservatism, Enoch Powell, enjoys dissecting the follies around him. He attacked his Government's identification with the American nightmare: 'It is, in the strictest terms, Manichean. It divides the world into two monoliths – the goodies and the baddies, the East and the West, even the free and the enslaved. It is a nightmarish distortion of reality. Indeed, to call it a distortion is too complimentary to it. It is a view of the world which this country cannot possibly share, or can share only at its own greatest peril.'[1]

Enoch Powell went on to suggest that the defence debate was not so much about technology or military strategy but about Britain trying to 'rediscover its true self'. Any nation in pawn to weapons of mass murder and competitions in madness could not be further removed from its true self, that open country of the spirit where each person accepts and expresses a responsibility for life and its laws. But to diagnose an illness is one thing, to cure it another.

Testing the scope of our nuclear nightmare I examined the response of education. Far from preparing me to comprehend the nature of our modern madness, my own education had induced me, with bribes and threats, to accept and exploit it. Was it still the same, or was there a new breed of teachers able to present and demonstrate a saner reality? Of course not. What I found, and what anyone can find who cares to look, is a system of learning which still glorifies and idolizes memory, depersonalized information, obedience and tidiness. The rewards still go to the well adapted rather than creative. To be docile is good. To be clever and docile is better. There is a token concern to alleviate some of the world's worst injustices. Enough to soothe the conscience and prepare for a lifetime of spare-time good works. Not enough to effect a cure which might shift the balance or change the rules. The law must be obeyed, but not laws which recognize the human race as one.

[1] *Guardian*, 9 March 1981.

To lift ourselves by our own bootstraps out of our collective and personal madness will require an education far beyond the stilted dreams of teachers content to offer children a drip-feed of orthodoxy. Children, it is evident, are well aware of the nuclear threat overhanging their lives. They also know that this doom-laden shadow is swollen by the same adults who denounce it. The nuclear nightmare is a part of the hidden curriculum, a by-product of robotic obedience. To shake off such a nightmare requires an act of intelligent, humane, uncompromising rebellion. What is most vital to education at this time is most repressed.

To solve this problem and assert new standards of sanity and natural justice will require many changes, some of which will be explored later. What is clearly inadequate, however, is the injection of a token 'peace studies' programme which denies that school orthodoxy is itself an integral part of international anarchy. To offer vegetarian options at a cannibal college merely serves to legitimize a human diet. Something more radical is required if deep-rooted habits are to be altered. Restrictive tolerance is not enough.

Another sponsor of our nightmare is the Christian church. Again, the words of religion flatter to deceive, expressing a commitment to peace and just law which turns out to be no more supportive than a punctured life-belt. During the heyday of anti-nuclear protests in the early sixties, I wrote to the Archbishop of Canterbury, asking why he did not speak out against threats of mass murder which contradict the most basic Christian beliefs. He replied at length, explaining carefully how deeply he was appalled and disturbed by nuclear weapons. They did indeed negate Christ's message of love and hope. But, he concluded sadly, we have to live with current reality, which includes governments committed to such weapons. It would take time to create a Christian climate of opinion. Until then we must endure this difficult problem.

The Archbishop was not alone in his ability to have his stake and burn it. With brave exceptions, the established church is a public relations branch of the establishment, wringing its hands, or its bells, when appropriate. The average man-in-the-pew, not surprisingly, soon adapts to such convenient excuses. It was not until many years later that I began to understand the nature of this problem. One afternoon, I visited Canterbury Cathedral. Its huge, dark bulk weighed down on me. Such excess of stone oppressed rather than uplifted. As I wandered around the interior I stopped to read the inscriptions on the monuments.

With one or two exceptions those commemorated were men, mostly young, who died fighting for their country in many parts of the world, in East, West and South Africa, and West Indies, India and the Far East, in North America and in Europe. The observer was clearly expected to accept at face value this tribute to heroism around the globe. But why? To die in another country, in defence of one's own, reflects an aggressive belief that the other country is a simple extension of one's own. What would the English think of Russian or Chinese monuments to those who had died in England in defence of their remote homeland? These long dead British heroes had not just died but killed for their country. Why do we go on playing this inflated game of imperial pride? Is it not time to assume an adult grasp of human limits as well as powers? To value fully the diversity of life on earth, to live and let live, requires, paradoxically, close attention to home. Only when the place where we happen to live becomes fully human in its variety and scope can we afford to laugh away the nightmare of 'foreign devils' and respect their right to live. It is not an abstract problem. I was a child of the British Raj in India.

Outside the cathedral walls, in a remote corner of the grounds, I found a cherry tree planted in memory of the atomic bombing of Hiroshima. It seemed somehow a true reflection of our church that peace graced a part of the exterior, while inside was a glorification of war. So when an Archbishop of Canterbury says, in Dresden, that the arms race is 'madness'[1] it is as well to remember that his church is well and truly wedded to the State which promotes such madness. We have a church which preaches love yet cannot bring itself to uphold without reservation the law against mass murder in war. Our nuclear nightmare is composed of many such contradictions.

And what of the military part in this story? My father was a professional soldier. Like many of his generation he countered the vicious economic insecurity of his time by embracing the welfare state of army life. Far from wanting to win glory by killing enemies, he hated violence and sought refuge in military routine.

[1] *Daily Telegraph*, 14 November 1983.

He exchanged his soul, or most of it, for a mess of khaki pottage, and by the time nuclear weapons arrived on the scene he could only shrug helplessly. 'Wars,' he told me, 'will only stop when soldiers refuse to fight.' Which is true, but of little relevance today when it would be a giant step merely to guarantee minimum standards of international law. It is not sainthood which is needed from today's soldiers but a simple commitment to the bottom line of civilization. It is too easy to evade the good by pointing to an improbable best.

According to military law, our armed forces are bound to obey the laws of war, on penalty of severe punishment. The basic requirement that helpless people should never be shot at, bombed, burned or poisoned, is supposed to be known to every serviceman and woman. The Government is bound by the terms of international law to inform its armed forces and the public about the law. But the truth is very different, as we shall see later. During my national service in the British Army, first as a gunner and then a parachutist and junior officer, I never heard a word about these laws. But I knew that disobedience would lead to a court-martial. Nuclear weaponry was in its infancy and we manned our regiment in West Germany, a few miles from the Soviet Army, in the expectation that war would result in all-out violence.

Many years later, when waiting in a court-house corridor to appear as witness in one of the cases already mentioned, I spent an hour or so discussing military law with a fellow witness. He was an RAF squadron-leader responsible for the designated Cruise missile base at Molesworth, not far from Cambridge. An affable man, he admitted without shame that he was unaware of international law and its relevance to his work. When I reminded him that at Nuremberg these laws had resulted in the hanging or life imprisonment of many Nazi war criminals, he just shrugged. All that was in the past, he implied. His Government would protect him from any wrath to come.

Military evasion of the law concerning this issue is similar to that found throughout our society. It was well illustrated at a public meeting on the subject which I addressed in 1984, at York. I quoted the Law Notes used for the training of young officers at the Royal Military Academy, Sandhurst. These state categorically that non-combatants must never be attacked, and that 'it is the policy of the UK Government to comply' with these laws. After the meeting I was approached by a member of the audience. He was an officer and legal expert who taught law at the British Army's Staff College. He agreed with what I had said and confessed that nuclear weapons and mass destruction do not figure in his classes. He uses the Sandhurst Law Notes and there is no mention of the word 'nuclear'. Thus, considerable legal training is given to officers of all ranks, and the essence of international law governing warfare imposes an outright prohibition on indiscriminate mass destruction, yet these elements remain disconnected, while British defence strategy is based on weapons of mass destruction. The bridge does not meet in the middle.

As we move closer to the core of our nightmare, this apparent fragmentation of thought and behaviour becomes even more alarming. We enter the inner sanctum of our own disorientation. Confessions do not cure, but they sometimes reveal, as can be seen from this introductory paragraph of a London *Times* editorial entitled 'Thinking the Unthinkable': 'The main basis of nuclear deterrence until now has been the belief that nuclear war would inevitably be suicidal but that an opponent might just believe in our willingness to commit suicide if sufficiently provoked. President Nixon summed it up when he said (approximately) that for deterrence to be effective it was necessary for the Russians to believe that we might be mad.'[1]

A society or civilization which treats profound issues of life and death on this level of deception is without doubt mad. Not raving mad in the old-fashioned sense of the word. Few if any of our leaders actually foam at the mouth or tear their hair out. Our madness is an affair of winter rather than high summer. Frost has penetrated our souls as it does dead plants, causing a cold fragmentation of feeling, thought and action. On issues of life and death the mind has become a calculator, adept at manipulating numbers and controlling organizations and machines. Feeling has drained away, forced down beyond contact with this busy, dead-and-alive surface life. Such feeling as survives, mainly among the young, is not connected to the elaborate network of cold and calculating organization which is our nuclear caricature of life.

Where is the source of this disorientation? One immediate source is the Nazi experience, and our response to it. There was a tendency to regard the worst Nazi atrocities as the work of

---

[1] *The Times*, 17 August 1982.

monsters, but when confronted in court they were seen to be embarrassingly ordinary. Embarrassing, because they were so like us in almost every respect. Had we killed the devil, only to discover a twin? Five psychiatrists examined Adolf Eichmann, the administrator of the extermination programme, prior to his trial at Jerusalem. They found him entirely sane, full of worthy sentiment about family and friends.

Faced with this reflection in the mirror, and denied the illusion of believing evil to inhabit only the enemy, we do the next best thing to evade responsibility for war crimes. We use history as a mechanism to distance ourselves. By isolating the horror of war in a specific and limited time frame we sit back in the hope that years will do the rest. Each year the problem seems to become more remote and thus de-fused. But does it?

Published studies of the Nuremberg war crimes trials, of which there are many, some very recent, serve as one important means of fixing in the past the scene of the crime. They aid and abet our conspiracy to keep the Nazi experience at arm's length, by focusing in detail on Nazi crime and Allied prosecution, while the writers inhabit a safe, neutral observation platform. By exaggerating Nazi evil they caricature virtue in current society, which in turn fuels our nightmare of fragmented deception. A Jewish writer of German background, George Steiner, has a more perceptive grasp of the situation. The climate of modern life, he declares, is one of 'political cant, oppression, torture, lunatic armaments, social deprivation and ecological destruction'. This situation, he goes on, 'is, in some sense, a posthumous triumph of such systematic inhumanities as those of Stalinism and of Nazism. It is my conviction that we are accomplices to that which leaves us indifferent'.[1]

But the problem is not even simply one of action or inertia. Our nuclear fragmentation of mind and feeling allows us to cross borders when convenient, between one perception of reality and another. We adopt psychological frames of reference to match the mood of the moment, discarding them as rapidly. The Nazi criminals were quick-change artists, too. One moment they would be prodding naked women and children into gas ovens with bayonets. The next, they would weep tears at a concert of classical music.

We are blood relatives of such disintegration. A nuclear missile

[1] *The Times*, 27 March 1982.

operator, acting in our name, is as ready to obliterate a million people as eat a hamburger. A robotic psychopath one moment, a good father the next. Prime ministers and presidents are no better. There is no greater value than human dignity, they tell us often enough, supported by the law. What is more, no minister is above this law. Yet they are equally happy to tell us that in the event of war they would be willing to promote the murder of whole cities. The Nazis were defeated and punished, yet we sponsor the most total concept of total war ever conceived.

The Nazi Propaganda Minister, Goebbels, said, 'Even if we lose, we shall win, for our ideals will have penetrated the hearts of our enemies'. He was right. We won, and lost. Massive, unrestrained violence stopped one war, staining our peace with blood. Our own self-imposed propaganda machine, euphemistically referred to sometimes as a 'free press', is yet another integral part of the nightmare. While the more primitive organs dispense a crude war-chant, as if nuclear war were a brief flurry of blood and broken bones among savages, the so-called quality papers pick their way through the asylum, expert in the art of sitting down when the music stops. They fill their columns with the mumbo-jumbo of missile-counting, strategic planning and cost equations, made palatable with a sauce of even-handed rationalization. Lacking any genuine integrity, their split mind accommodates itself easily to disparate views, the resultant stew being palmed off as evidence of democratic free thinking. The notion that threats to kill millions might amount to gross criminality is entirely incompatible with such professional dithering. It would require not only an implied admission of past and present guilt but even worse, a new perspective on the law, sanity, everyday behaviour and future action. A mind held together by a contradictory jumble of fears, illusions, habit and self-righteousness can only survive in a vacuum. The slightest puff of fresh air will send it crashing. Readers weaned on this musty diet fear change as much as editors. Nightmares, like asylums, tend to be self-perpetuating.

But it is not just in the grand forum of nuclear annihilation that such fragmentation is evident. A former inmate of Auschwitz, Kitty Hart, eventually reached England after the war, to be met at Dover by her uncle. 'The moment we got in his car,' she wrote, 'he staggered us by saying firmly: "Before we go off to Birmingham there's one thing I must make quite clear. On no account are you to talk about the things that have happened to you. Not in my house. I don't want my girls upset. And I don't want to know".[1] Everybody, she discovered, wanted to talk about their war experiences, but the inner touchstone of evil was taboo and must stay hidden.

Kitty Hart was not fooled by a surface normality. She saw all around her in England signs of concentration camp behaviour: 'Everyone I have met since the war slots in my mind into an Auschwitz setting. I know within a few minutes who they would have been and how they would have behaved. . . . There may not be the same undisguised physical brutality in our contemporary surroundings, but the pattern is the same: personal viciousness, greed for power, love of manipulation and humiliation. How do men get and hold the most coveted jobs in big firms? By starting as "trusties" and trampling over others on their way to the top. . . . You may even be privileged to eat with the SS and use their washroom if you're truly dedicated to the cause.'[2]

Not many people fight over a hunk of bread any more but in the office skyscraper there is a war going on just the same, 'steady attrition covered by a veneer of artificial politeness. Nobody gets physically beaten up, tortured or murdered, but often there is what you might call a slow campaign against life. This breed of killers prefers scheming in an atmosphere of polite treachery rather than speaking malice out loud. But the greed, malice and power lust are at the heart of it just the same.'[3]

As Kitty Hart implies, our small circle of everyday normality, like a clearing in the jungle of our minds, does not and cannot dispel the nuclear nightmare around us. Denial is an escape, not an answer. We have tried to shut out our worst fears, at the expense of our feelings. As Ronald Laing, a creative psychiatrist of Celtic intuition, wrote of the nuclear threat, 'let no one suppose that this madness exists only somewhere in the night or day sky where our birds of death hover in the stratosphere. It exists in the interstices of our most intimate and personal moments.[4]

'Only by the most outrageous violation of ourselves,' he said, 'have we achieved our capacity to live in relative adjustment to a

---

[1] Kitty Hart, *Return to Auschwitz*, London 1981.
[2] Ibid.
[3] Ibid.
[4] Ronald Laing, *The Politics of Experience*, New York 1967.

civilization apparently driven to its own destruction. . . . If we can stop destroying ourselves we may stop destroying others.'[1]

Full-scale nuclear war would be the end of a civilization, perhaps of a species or of life itself. But before it can take place we must endure an interior dissolution of mind and spirit which will eventually make the final bang superfluous. We live today at an advanced stage of this nightmare decay, our powers of reason and our commitment to just law hijacked by imitation sanity and bogus law.

Clear spirits have pointed to this nightmare: 'We behave as though we have been hexed by the bomb – put under a spell. . . . It is as though we have become passive, fascinated spectators of the slowly unfolding nuclear tragedy.' So said Dr Nicholas Humphrey, a Cambridge university lecturer, during his BBC Bronowski memorial lecture.[2] He quoted a former US Ambassador to the Soviet Union, Professor George Kennan, speaking in Washington that year: 'We have gone on piling weapon upon weapon, missile upon missile . . . like the victims of some sort of hypnotism, like men in a dream, like lemmings heading for the seas.'[3]

Confronted with this nightmare within my own family and my own mind, the ultimate experience of each of us, I have discovered at least one negative truth. To describe and define this all-engulfing problem may have some potential value, but without creative action such analysis is little better than mockery. The victims of Auschwitz knew in detail the vile hell they inhabited. But they could not escape. The children enveloped in the flames and crashing buildings of Dresden and Hiroshima had a split-second education in modern violence. But they could not act on it. Even our own leaders, political, military, legal, religious, cultural, strapped as they are to the chariot of nuclear suicide, occasionally confess insanity. But without taking steps to discover a path out of our asylum we might as well go silently to our deaths. Passive confession is as useless and pathetic as if a herd of cattle were to plod towards the abattoir, murmuring to each other, 'I told you so.'

We cannot hope to escape from our asylum until we have admitted that the nuclear nightmare exists, not just out there in Washington or Moscow, but in and around us, staining normality.

[1] Ibid.
[2] *Listener*, 29 October 1981.
[3] Ibid.

There are no experts in the art of picking asylum locks, but we can learn as we go. If and when we reach the point where everyone on this Earth feels an inner commitment to enforce the law against mass murder in all its forms, we will know that at last we are out in the fresh air. We will have arrived at the very first stage of creating a just world society, the foundation stone of a post-nuclear civilization.

Such a commitment will knock the emotional, political, military, and legal keystone out of the asylum's structure. A simple, firm refusal to kill defenceless people will render obsolete not just a major part of the military machine, conventional as well as nuclear, but the corrupt basis of modern centralized power. When ordinary people discover the power to judge life and death on their own terms, there is an immediate need for social reforms to reflect this democratic reality. In a lawless era such as ours, to affirm the law on such a basic issue is to initiate radical change.

To write or even to read a book on such an elusive, complex, political, personal process is hard work. The minds which seek new life and law are the same minds which are subservient to death. Nagging doubt will shadow every hesitant step. Our thoughts will be mocked by a sense of futility. We will frequently despair. Who are we, after all, to try to redeem a corrupt and decaying civilization? There is always someone better qualified to take up such a burden. But we are each our own expert, if we accept the challenge.

This book insists that a 'Nuremberg trial' take place before rather than after a nuclear war, for obvious reasons. The law must be used to restrain and neutralize the threat of mass murder. It is preventive law or nothing. This pre-war 'trial' must apply to every law-breaker with impartial weight. No nuclear threat of mass murder is better or worse than another. Each is an absolute, lunatic crime. Beside such a stark fact, political ideologies are dancing shadows on a cave wall.

Chapter Two

A Sense of Direction

'A million zeros joined together do not, unfortunately, add up
to one. Ultimately everything depends on the quality of the
individual, but our fatally short-sighted age thinks only in
terms of large numbers and mass organizations, though one
would think that the world had seen more than enough of
what a well-disciplined mob can do in the hands of a single
madman'
– C. G. Jung

'And you are past. Remember then,
Fix deep within your dreaming head
Year, hour or endless moment when
You reached and crossed the Bridge of Dread'
'The Bridge of Dread' – Edwin Muir

Our glance at the nuclear nightmare which enshrouds modern life
has indicated something of the enormous scope of the problem
facing anyone determined to explore the way to a minimum sanity.
The law, specifically the law which prohibits any form of mass
destruction, has been used here as a touchstone of our pre-
dicament. The law condemning mass murder has been turned
inside out by the nuclear powers, presenting us with a disaster of
unique magnitude. Many governments in the past have turned into
cancerous power centres, perverting law, justice and common
sense to suit destructive ends. But never have such governments
had the power to drag the human race down with them, before the
advent of nuclear weapons of mass destruction. We stand at the
end of a highway of violence. A dead end.

As we have seen, breaking the law at this primary level is far
more than a legal problem requiring court action. Mass murder is
not the option of a sane person, or of a sane government or
civilization. It is the culmination of a long and accelerating degeneration, not just of commitment to the law but of human relationships, perspectives on life and death, work patterns and every

major human activity. Most radical of all, the kind of thought and corruption of feeling which underlies such lawlessness reflects a mental landscape bare of signposts. Language itself is a double agent paid well to pervert the law. Yet we have no choice but to use the same words in planning survival which have been so cynically debauched during past decades.

At such a time of cultural confusion we have no real choice but to fall back on our own personal experience and that of others. Problems, ideas and options must be discussed in terms of individual experience and responsibility. This is not easy. We have grown up in an age of 'objective truth', that bogus short-cut to reality which has been so wantonly misused by those in authority. Every variety of quack expert, in every industrial nation, has waved the magic wand of 'objective truth' to keep the ignorant masses, us, in our place. Professional groups, including lawyers, have made stacks of golden hay while this artificial sun shone. Common sense and natural justice are silenced by appeal to 'objective' authority.

To counter such manipulation of language and experience by offering alternative 'objective truth' merely compounds the problem. Beggars on foot who challenge horsemen are quickly whipped into place. Even if the beggar wins, everybody loses. The beggar becomes the horseman, armed with the same whip. Nothing has changed.

To meet the debased legal currency of modern nuclear government with nothing but another version of the law, spelled out in conventional jargon, is to play the fool, as if Dresden, Auschwitz and Hiroshima had never happened. We live in a dark nightmarish age, more lost than the one which declared the self-evident norms of the law of armed conflict. We have been swept down a foul-smelling river and are tainted.

So our goal in this book is limited yet ambitious, because we aim to rediscover the hard floor of civilization, a just law which respects life and prohibits any form of mass murder. Finding that law is easy. Enforcing it is the challenge. We could not even find the energy to set out on such a quest if we did not know that within even the most dispirited, greedy human being is a sense of crime and its meaning, however well hidden. Better still, we know that every government which relies on nuclear weapons relies too on the law, miserable caricature though the latter has become in the service of power. Our path will lead, if it is true, to the gates of offending authority.

There is no place for refinements of ambition in this crisis. We live in a cultural ruin and need a firm floor and sound roof, not a palace. We are not building utopia. Despite this, people will accuse us of romantic idealism, because they know only the grey realism of the concentration camp. For them, life is bounded by the barbed wire and searchlights of nuclear orthodoxy. That is their reality. Even the possibility of a larger reality casts doubt on their fantasy prison freedom and must therefore be branded unrealistic. Yet one day, like the prisoners of Beethoven's *Fidelio*, they may be led into daylight. They will not lead. They may follow.

Ours is a simple aim, then, like fresh air, clean water and enough food. Not the flowering of a great civilization but the planting of its seed. At a moment of chaos and disillusion disguised as busy normality, such an act is ambitious enough. It is an act of faith in the integrity of life, especially ours. Along the way, we will try to relate problems to people, not to inflated landscapes of theory and history. We will fall into bad habits, no doubt, but not for long. There is no shortage of men and women, some dead, some alive, to help us along. They have a lot to tell us.

At the Treblinka death camp in Poland, where the Nazis murdered hundreds of thousands of Jews, there was a miraculous transformation. Towards the end of the war it was decided, suddenly, to close down the camp and move the carnage elsewhere. Bulldozers moved in. Grass was laid above the vast burial ground. A farmer was installed, in a new farmhouse, with his family and a guaranteed income. He was told to act as if nothing odd had ever taken place.

With our cold historical surveys and stone monuments we have done much the same to the millions killed in two world wars. But far from keeping those sad ghosts at bay, we will welcome them as companions. It is their unrequited pain which will warn us when we stray off course. We will remember them, every step of the way. They will be offered something more than sentimental remorse. A positive anger and specific proposals.

We will not accept the law as defined by lawyers and judges, a theatrical event for experts, but as a basis of everyday life. We will examine the law and the way university professors explain it, in case they do it less than justice. We will try to understand what role the media plays in this equation. Are they mediating fact or fiction, stale truth or fresh? Do their rare articles and programmes on this issue warn? Or fawn?

And what of the sailors, soldiers, and airmen? Their relation to minimum law is vital yet paradoxical. Obedience is their profession, yet they are told to refuse illegal orders, on pain of severe punishment. They are presented with an image of military behaviour which conforms to lawful restraint. But their training is also geared to a computerized plan of nuclear war. How do they respond to such contradictory discipline?

It is a Government, or rather its individual members, which imposes such a policy of confusion. It is they who preach the superior values of our society at one moment, and in the same breath describe our defence policy in terms of 'population extermination'. They are the heirs of the official killing of this century, the mass murder which for so long has been presented as patriotism, and which now overshadows us. One by one, how do they interpret this political, legal yet personal problem?

At Nuremberg, after the Second World War, it was made plain that ministers of government were subject to the laws of war, like everyone else. Yet politicians, when they become members of a government, tend to behave like the back legs of a pantomime donkey, active but irresponsible when it suits them. Our efforts to pierce official camouflage and locate the responsible individual have been consistently blocked by tactics of evasion. We will examine this abuse of power.

We will try to minimize the risk of self-righteousness. 'Physician, heal thyself!' is an appropriate warning. We may discover new perspectives but we all share common roots. We will examine the role of the peace movement in this breakdown of the law, with the same critical energy as we devote to the agents of nuclear government. The peace movements of the twentieth century have an impressive record of failure. Are they, behind all the sound and fury, merely play-actors, secretly adapted to their secondary role and well content with it? It can often be easier, and more convenient, to lose than to win. That possibility is more than intriguing. It is embarrassing. I am part of that peace movement, implicated in its experience.

One part of that question concerns the special role of women. During most of the twentieth century there have been women's groups fighting to prevent war, but during the early 1980s they reached a new intensity of purpose. Determination to obstruct nuclear policies makes some women more aggressive, and adventurous. The drawing-room politeness of earlier days has vanished as thousands of women have learned the meaning of confrontation with authority. A sometimes sexist, anti-male element among the women has become vocal, demanding revenge for past and present wrongs. But what has this new energy achieved, as far as war and peace are concerned? In particular, what is the relation of these women to the issue of the law and nuclear weapons?

If we can find a path out of our nightmare it will be constructed from the experience of these varied people, and our response to it. You will certainly disagree with some of this story, perhaps with most of it. What matters is that your response gives you the insight to discover your own best path. We may meet one day. Anyone who writes a book on such an important yet provocative theme deserves whatever he gets. Authors too often behave like cats, bringing in a dead mouse to lay at the reader's feet. They imagine that before a book can be written its subject must be caught, killed and dissected. I have tried another way, to bring in the subject alive.

Chapter Three

The Professor's Tale

'Barbarism prevailed on the very ground of Christian
humanism, of Renaissance culture and classic rationalism'
– George Steiner

'I have seen corruption boil and bubble
Till it o'errun the stew; laws for all faults,
But faults so countenanc'd that the strong statutes
Stand like the forfeits in a barber's shop,
As much in mock as mark.'
– *Measure for Measure*, William Shakespeare

Lawyers and judges do not spring, fully gowned, from the brow of
modern society. They are hatched at law schools, nurtured with
care by professors and coached in courtroom arts. These professors, like their students, deserve our attention. Are they, like other
specialists, an integral part of our nuclear nightmare? It is what
they teach and how they teach it that must concern us. Do they
stand in the way of minimum world law, or do they promote it?

Such questions would be absurd in a rational society. The job of
a professor of law is to teach and promote the law. It should be
self-evident, then, that professors of law teach and promote laws
which restrain warfare and prohibit all forms of mass destruction
and murder. It should be, but it is not. Nazi Germany may jolt our
memories. 'National Socialist law,' says Dr J. P. Stern, a refugee
from Nazi rule, 'is not, as the law is in Dickens, "an ass" . . . it is, as
Hitler unwittingly suggests, itself criminal. It is the exercise of
objective-seeming power in support of purely arbitrary and subjective decisions. . . .'[1]

Nazi law retained a rational face, but its strings were pulled on
matters of national importance by Hitler. '*Adolphe légalité*', the
French called it. But just as Hitler could not have moved a single
Jew into a concentration camp without willing hands, so his

[1] J. P. Stern, *Hitler, the Führer & the People*, London 1975.

perversion of the law required willing minds. German law schools were among Europe's best, yet their products became agents of national crime. Germany's most brilliant international lawyer, Carl Schmidt, according to Dr Stern, was among the Nazis' most enthusiastic supporters in 1933, at the start of their reign of terror. 'Yet however much Hitler abused and humiliated the lawyers, believing that he could do without them altogether, they could always be relied upon to provide the rationale of their own debasement?'[1]

The strength of Hitler's contempt for lawyers reflected both insight into their weakness of character and awareness that just law can be a dangerous opponent of arbitrary power. 'Nobody,' he said during one of his monologues in his war-time headquarters, the *Wolfschanze* (wolf's lair), 'is more akin to the criminal than the lawyer, and also as regards their international character there is no difference between them'.[2]

The law schools of Germany produced lawyers and judges willing to mediate the law on behalf of the Government, even the Government of Hitler. They were not obviously wicked people. As Dr Stern observed: 'These men . . . are not Chicago shysters. They are ponderous professional men of the Central European middle classes, scholarly and intellectual, heirs to a tradition of literal-mindedness rather than fairness, but also of honesty, thoughtfulness and integrity. How . . . can such men put their minds at the service of so primitive, so transparently arbitrary a conception of law and legality?'[3]

Nazi perversion of law, as far as our own legal system and its professors are concerned, proves only that such corruption is possible in a modern, twentieth-century state. The example and the warning are clear. Policies of nuclear mass destruction are the next of kin to Nazi 'total war' concepts and Allied city-bombing. International law during this century, from the Hague Conventions of 1899 and 1907 to the Nuremberg trials and the Additional Protocol of Geneva, 1977, are clear enough in direction and detail. They are designed to restrict warfare to a contest between military forces only, to limit the extent of that warfare and to prohibit attacks on non-combatants. Throughout history, in all parts of the

[1] Ibid.
[2] Ibid.
[3] Ibid.

world, there is evidence of such efforts to contain violence, most often expressed through custom rather than written law. In an age of nuclear weapons this law is light above our dark pit. It reflects a minimum sanity which gives direction to our struggle to climb out.

Far from exposing official evasion of humanitarian law, and issuing a sharp and detailed warning to Government, backed by a refusal to co-operate further with criminal policies, our law schools pay almost no attention to the law as it concerns the survival of civilization. The rationale for such evasion is the 'weakness' of laws which governments can ignore. As if an epidemic of murder in a city were to provide the excuse for disbanding the courts and police force. What lies behind this problem is something even more disturbing and closely related to the Nazi experience. The effect of law school policy is to allow governments to pursue the arms race in a legal vacuum. Robbery is the subject of minute legal attention and dispute, while the fate of life on Earth is left to the whims of men and women who admit their power contest is mad. Hitler would feel at home. Law enforcement and its absence mirror a schizoid culture.

A major incentive to continue this bias in the teaching of law is money and status. The handful of law students who make international law their main concern have narrow career prospects. Their employers will be mostly governments or law schools. Wrangling over sea-bed mineral rights and such things is a major area of international legal dispute. So the majority of Western law students opt for the gilded path to fame and fortune, by way of lucrative disputes on familiar ground, at home. They are taught how to make the most of the opportunities presented by the prevailing power structure and legal system. Far from criticizing national norms, self-interest ensures they identify with them. Those few lawyers who oppose the ruling caste tend to do so for political rather than legal reasons.

Professors of international law, with few exceptions, fit happily into this scheme of things. They are the poor relations of the legal fraternity, but wear the faintly superior air of the family member who opts for a life of academic purity while more primitive brothers and sisters plunge into a golden trough. Far from stretching their minds to match the challenge of international security, they reduce the problem to suit themselves. It is much easier to surround oneself with fragments of dissected law than to apply it forcefully to a problem which engulfs all life. The indifference of governments to their art may irritate, but has its compensations. To be left alone, undisturbed, is attractive to those of a passive nature. Authority has little to fear from such people.

How is it that the law has become so inward-looking, more parasitic than creative? Like much else, the laws of armed conflict have become detached from their natural roots in ordinary everyday consciousness and behaviour. Before looking more closely at the work of our professors, it is useful to examine the roots.

Although the laws of armed conflict can be traced back to the earliest times, it is generally considered that their modern interpretation owes most to the thinking of a Dutchman of the seventeenth century, Hugo Grotius. His most famous work, *De Jure Belli ac Pacis* ('About the Law of War and Peace'), was published in 1625, during a war lasting eighty years between the United Provinces and Spain. In this book Grotius expresses his view that sovereign states have a right to exist and develop their different character, but within the framework of a law of nations based on the needs of civilized survival. Not law imposed by a superior power but one which flows naturally from common human experience, a natural law. In the words of the historian Michael Howard: 'Grotius virtually created the framework of thinking about international relations, about war and peace, within which consciously or unconsciously we still function.'[1]

Grotius was revolted by the war raging around him in Western Europe. 'I saw prevailing throughout the Christian world a licence in making war of which even barbarous nations would have been ashamed; recourse was had to arms for slight reasons, or for no reason, and when arms were once taken up, all reverence for divine and human law was thrown away; just as if men were thenceforth authorized to commit all crimes without restraint.'[2]

Almost three hundred years separate us from that time, yet in terms of our own commitment to the law upheld by Grotius, the clock has stopped. Howard recognises something of this stalemate. 'By the 1950s,' he writes,' the international order appeared to rest on nothing more substantial than what a leading American

[1] Michael Howard, *War in European History*, Oxford 1976.
[2] Hugo Grotius, *De Jure Belli ac Pacis*, 1625.

strategic analyst, Albert Wohlstetter, termed "a delicate balance of terror".[1]

Like so many academics, Howard speaks a static truth. Ensconced in the cosy wasp's nest of Oxford University it is easy, even obligatory, to cast doubt on outside behaviour. But without remedial action even the sharpest insights mock their author. Our nuclear 'balance of terror' is nothing if not rooted in the blinkered logic of established power, and there is no university more devoted to such power than Oxford. Thought without action becomes a sour guilt. Students fed on such inertia become adapted and addicted to it, their energy diverted into narrow self-interest, making them spectators at their own execution.

The master of a Cambridge college, a celebrated historian, was not amused to be asked why the university did not pay more attention to the pervasive threat of nuclear destruction. He warned loftily against 'the tyranny of the contemporary'. The rough water of mid-stream is not for academics. Better watch the dead than risk contamination by the living is the safety-first motto of the university. To teach law in such an environment is to breed trouble. Positive law must protect life, not handcuff itself to the logic of obedience, however refined.

The German thinker, Immanuel Kant, reflected on the natural human impulse to impose law on the chaos of war: 'In view of the evil nature of man which can be observed in the free relations between nations, it is surprising that the word *law* has not been entirely banned from the politics of war. . . . This homage which every state renders to the concept of the law (at least in words) seems to prove that there exists in man a greater moral quality (though at present a dormant one) to try and master the evil element in him. . . .'[2]

A nineteenth-century American, Emerson, warned his generation not to mistake the uniform of the law for its content: 'I think there never was a people so choked and stultified by forms. We adore the forms of law, instead of making them vehicles of wisdom and justice. Language has lost its meaning in the universal cant. . . . The judges give cowardly interpretations to the law, in direct opposition to the known foundations of all law, that every immoral

---

[1] Op. cit.
[2] Immanuel Kant, *Zum ewigen Frieden* ('Perpetual Peace'), 1795.

statute is void.'[1] He looks over our shoulder.

Of all Americans, Henry Thoreau insists most emphatically on the law's roots in personal responsibility. Governments and lawyers tend to downgrade this fragile yet vital process. 'The lawyer's truth,' he wrote in his essay on civil disobedience, 'is not truth, but consistency, or a consistent expediency.'[2]

Closer to our own times the law, like a dead fish, has tended to rot from the head. Nobody was more alert to the smell than Franz Kafka. He sensed Nazi crime invading with a cockroach stealth. His spirit wilted before this horror, but he knew there is a remedy. 'The power of the human scream,' he wrote, 'is so great that it will smash all the iron laws decreed against man.'[3]

These perceptive people have known what most academics ignore, that life's centre of gravity is to be found within each person, and that everything else is secondary. Too many of those who teach law genuflect before this fact while promoting by example and precept a craven allegiance to established power. Treachery is not too strong a term for such sleight of mind, because our law is filtered through their teaching and they are well rewarded. Such casuistry continues to paralyze each generation of law students.

It is the false god of objective truth which seduces our professors. By inflating rationalism they devalue more personal sources of truth, thus becoming vulnerable to government and social conformity. Whatever the latest forms of government, in Hermann Hesse's words, these professors 'can be expected to kowtow to the new regime as spinelessly as yesterday they bowed down to princes and altars'.[4]

Carl Jung is another witness at this indictment of academic myopia. He knew very well that life is less like a cardboard cut-out puzzle than a river in which we swim, float or drown. We are only detached when dead. He acknowledged that modern intellect 'has developed almost to perfection the capacity of the bird of prey to espy the tiniest mouse from the greatest height, yet the pull of the earth drags it down. . . .'[5] Once this sharp intellect dares to look

[1] Estey and Hunter (ed.), *Violence*, Boston 1971.
[2] Henry Thoreau, *Walden*, New York 1980.
[3] Quoted by Romain Gary in Estey and Hunter, op. cit.
[4] Hermann Hesse, *If the War Goes On*, London 1972.
[5] Carl Jung, *Collected Works Vol. II*, London 1968.

within, the individual 'falls into the throes of a daemonic rebirth, beset with unknown terrors and dangers and menaced by deluding mirages in a labyrinth of error. The worst of all fates threatens the venturer: mute, abysmal loneliness in the age he calls his own.'[1]

Such natural confusion tends to undermine an objective, manmade reality, reducing the expert to the status of fellow explorer. It is not surprising that in such a cultural environment few professors of law (or of anything else) dare to base their teachings on such shifting sand. Far from introducing their students to the rich soil of experience from which the law has grown, they present it as an elaborate game of criminal snakes and golden ladders, where the climbers are always lawyers. The fastest climbers are the quickest witted, those whose grasp of justice is the lightest. With such shallow loyalties it is not surprising that few lawyers resist political oppression, or any sustained government pressure.

Just as in a nightmare, when running is confounded by leaden feet, so the teaching of law means well while delivering little. The medium too often negates the message. To describe a murder which took place one hundred years ago in the street outside, for example, it may be enough to assemble the relevant details and put them in order. But if the murder is taking place now, such an approach is inappropriate. It will paralyze rather than incite counter-action. Laws which are dissected and reassembled in professors' notebooks are skeleton laws, disconnected from meaning and purpose. Justice, the application of law to a problem is a by-product of personal as well as social commitment. Personal commitment entails personal risk, the risk of causing offence to the powers that be. Professors of law seldom take such risks. By objectifying the law they distance themselves from it, teaching a pale reflection of pale life.

The professors whom I met during my exploration were infuriating people. They endured my persistence with quiet patience, carefully explaining their assessment of the law and nuclear weapons. But as soon as I reached out gratefully to accept a cogent statement it would be withdrawn, or so amended as to neutralize its meaning. They reminded me of deep-sea fish in the Pacific Ocean which tend to explode when raised to low surface pressures. Or the caged animal which paces to the bars and then retraces its steps.

[1] Ibid.

One who was helpful, within these limits, was Professor Schwarzenberger, retired after many years as one of the world's leading authorities on international law. He offered me valuable advice and information. It was soon apparent that he considered the nuclear arms race to be a violation of the law. It was, he said, a 'competition in cosmic irresponsibility'.[1] I was heartened by this graphic comment, but disappointed to find no hint as to how this irresponsibility might be ended. Once again, reason had outstripped action, rationalizing rather than dispelling the nuclear nightmare. I sensed a weary disdain for politics and politicians, not a burning sense of injustice.

Professor Schwarzenberger tries manfully to fit the monster of nuclear weaponry into a suit of international law, but seems unsure as to whether the monster is too fat or the suit too small. 'The laws and customs of war,' he says, 'embody a broad consensus on the avoidance of unnecessary cruelty, protection of non-combatants and the civilian population, and exemption of non-military objectives from intentional attack.'[2]

In the same article he touches on the poisonous dimension of nuclear weapons. In European civilization, as in most others, poison has long been regarded with particular revulsion. 'Judged by the text of the laws and customs of war,' he concludes, 'a common denominator of the triad of biological, chemical and nuclear weapons is apparent. Their use conflicts with the reason behind the prohibitions in international customary law and the Hague Conventions of 1899 and 1907 on the use of poison and poisoned arms. They are an affront to human dignity beyond any of the horrors associated with other forms of warfare and fall far below the minimum standard of civilization as incorporated in these rules.'[3]

These comments, which summarize the main intention of international law, mark a slight advance on his earlier writings on this issue. Soon after the development of the first British atomic and hydrogen bombs, he wrote about their legal implications. He stressed that a sense of common humanity is itself a powerful law-creating process, the fertile ground, so to speak, in which

[1] George Schwarzenberger, *The Legality of Nuclear Weapons*, London 1958.
[2] *Wig and Gavel*, April 1982.
[3] Ibid. The Geneva Gas Protocol of 1925 reinforced this general prohibition against poisoned weapons.

specific laws can grow. He refers to the use made at the Nuremberg trials of this underlying sense of the 'elementary dictates of humanity', and of the reference by the International Court at The Hague to 'elementary considerations of humanity, even more exacting in peace than war'.[1] The preamble to conventions relating to war, which declare their purpose, are also part of this process.

Within limits, 'these preambles would also illustrate how non-legal considerations and standards of conduct of a high formative potency, such as postulates of individual and international morality or the standard of civilization, can be received legitimately and "above the counter" into international law'.[2] He also mentions the celebrated de Martens clause which appears in the preamble to the Hague Conventions of 1899 and 1907. De Martens was a Belgian who was part of the Czar of Russia's legal team at The Hague. The clause he successfully promoted was a positive attempt to anticipate the invention of weapons of warfare, such as nuclear missiles, whose characteristics might seem to render the new laws out of date. Certain basic principles must, he said, be kept intact. These are the 'principles of the law of nations, as they result from the usages established among civilized peoples, from the laws of humanity, and the dictates of the public conscience'.[3]

As if sensing a dramatic expansion of military killing power, these law-makers imposed certain minimum standards. Their choice of language may be dull, but they offer us an important check on militarism gone mad, if we choose to use it. It is therefore shocking to read Professor Schwarzenberger's opinion that, despite these declarations of principle, 'it appears impossible to discover any automatic limitation of the freedom of the subjects of international law to possess, test or use nuclear weapons'.[4] Such a statement leaves the implication that the killing of city populations *can* be reconciled with the law's most basic principles.

Professor Schwarzenberger goes on to examine legal protection of non-combatants. Again, pessimism darkens his thoughts. From the St Petersburg Declaration of 1868 to the Hague Conventions of 1899 and 1907, and the Geneva Conventions of 1949, laws have

[1] Corfu Channel case, 1949.
[2] Schwarzenberger, op. cit.
[3] J. B. Scott, *The Hague Conventions and Declarations of 1899 and 1907*, London 1915.
[4] Op. cit.

been formulated which restrict warfare to military targets and protect non-combatants. According to the first of these, the 'only legitimate object which States should endeavour to accomplish during war is to weaken the military forces of the enemy'.[1] This is the thread of essential law which runs through the carnage of this century, surfacing today in such statements as that of the Royal Military Academy, Sandhurst, which warns British officers: 'A distinction must be drawn between combatants and non-combatants. The former are permitted to take part in hostilities, whereas the latter are not; the former may be attacked, while the latter are protected from attack.'

Since the Hague Conventions, long-range artillery, missiles and airplanes have brought the whole of enemy territory under attack. 'The practice of belligerent States in the Second World War,' Professor Schwarzenberger tells us, 'and the trends in post-1945 treaties suggest that the immunity of the civilian population from intentional attack is reaching vanishing point.'[2] By enlarging the definition of a military target to include anything and everything, he suggests, modern nuclear states try to get away, literally, with murder.

He points to the slide in legal standards which took place during the Second World War, in which the British slid as rapidly as anyone. The British Directive on Air Warfare of 29 October 1942, approved by the Committee of the International Red Cross, prohibited the intentional bombing of civilian populations. This conformed with the essential nature and aim of the law. But there was a sting in the tail. These limitations, declared the directive, did not apply any longer to the territories of Germany, Italy or Japan. 'Consequent upon the enemy's adoption of a campaign of unrestricted air warfare,' it said, 'the Cabinet have authorized a bombing policy which includes the attack on enemy morale.'[3]

If hypocrisy is the homage paid by vice to virtue, then euphemisms are the homage paid by crime to the law. By morale was meant the inhabitants of enemy cities. This policy of unrestricted revenge was confirmed the following year at Casablanca, when the Allied Combined Chiefs of Staff issued a policy statement on the bombing of Germany from the UK. The aim, it declared, was 'the

[1] Ibid.
[2] Ibid.
[3] Ibid.

progressive destruction and dislocation of the German military, industrial and economic system, and the undermining of the morale of the German people to a point where their capacity for armed resistance is fatally weakened'.[1] The way was open for total war, and cynical manipulation of the law.

Instead of exposing the extreme risk to our survival posed by such a degeneration of standards, Professor Schwarzenberger catalogues the decline with a shrug: 'it must now be regarded as understood in governmental and military quarters that the scope of legitimate objects of warfare is considerably wider than combatants and includes somewhat indefinite categories of civilians engaged in war work. Moreover, legitimate target areas are no longer limited to military objectives, even if these are understood in a very liberal sense, but extend to centres of communication, large industrial and administrative establishments of any kind and any area likely to become important for the conduct of the war. Thus, at present, the principle of the protection of the enemy civilian population appears to apply at the most in favour of a residue of persons who fulfil two conditions. They must not be connected with the war effort and be remote from enemy target areas.'[2]

This, he concludes gloomily, 'marks what little remains of a border line between legitimate warfare and complete relapse into the barbarism of total war'. Like a despondent child clutching a melting ice-cream, he describes what little is left of the law in the nuclear era. If, he tells us, a ten-megaton nuclear bomb is dropped, destructive power five times greater than that of all the bombs dropped on Germany during World War Two, this would probably kill and poison even the small residue of the population protected by law. It would thus amount to 'an illegal form of warfare and the commission of a war crime in the technical sense of the term'.[3] There is, after all, a dribble of law at the bottom of the cornet, but hardly enough to worry the nuclear powers.

What must concern us here is not so much the bloodless manner in which Professor Schwarzenberger describes the erosion of the law but the fact that it typifies a civilization which is losing vitality and hope. There is no anger at a systematic corruption of minimum laws, no demand for urgent renewal, no proposals for

[1] Craven and Gate, *The Army Air Forces in World War Two Vol. II*, London.
[2] Op. cit.
[3] Ibid.

action, only a tired shake of the head. This anaemic posture contrasts sharply with the view of a seventeenth-century jurist, Gentili, who wrote against the use of poison in war, 'because war, a contest between men, through these facts is made a struggle of demons'.[1] Perhaps it is the demons who have sapped our strength, ensuring listless apathy. But Professor Schwarzenberger does at least assert that the Geneva Gas Protocol of 1925 is declaratory of international customary law, and thus binding on all States, whether signatories or not.

The professor offers law students, and us, an interpretation of the laws of war which is thin gruel rather than main course. Like many professional guardians of the law, he seems to take his cue from governments rather than first principles.

It is hardly surprising that law students fed on this diet of ifs, buts and maybes turn out to be reflections of the same doubting vision. The humane essence of international law quickly disappears in such a ground mist, surviving only as a vague phantom in panelled studies.

Professor Ian Brownlie QC, of Oxford University, offers his own variations on this theme. In 1983 he gave an address on the subject of 'The Legal Status of Nuclear Weapons in International Law'. It is an urbane review of the problem. He points out that the nuclear powers assert that nuclear weapons and nuclear deterrence are legal, while accepting the validity of the laws of war. He quotes from the British Manual of Military Law, which states: 'There is no rule of international law dealing specifically with the use of nuclear weapons. Their use, therefore, is governed by the general principles laid down in this chapter.'

Professor Brownlie tells us that there are three main principles embodied in the British Manual of Military Law. The first permits the use of force to compel the enemy's surrender. The second is the principle of humanity, which forbids violence which is beyond the needs of warfare. The third principle concerns chivalry, or a certain minimum respect for the enemy.

He declares his own position on the issue of nuclear weapons: 'The use of nuclear weapons, and more particularly of thermonuclear weapons delivered by rocket, is in most conceivable situations illegal under the existing laws of war which rest on generally

[1] Gentili, *De Jure Belli Libri Tres*, Book II, 1612.

accepted customary rules and on conventions relating to laws of war which are generally regarded as stating the customary law and are thus binding on all States.'[1]

A major reason for this view is a belief that 'the use of nuclear weapons on any appreciable scale would involve a refusal to distinguish between combatants and non-combatants and military objectives from other targets'.[2]

Professor Brownlie asserts that the Geneva Protocol of 1925 is a further indictment of the use of nuclear weapons. Their use would amount to 'crimes against humanity', as defined by the Agreement on Military Trials of 1945, which provided the policy framework for the Nuremberg Trial. The Convention for the Prevention and Punishment of Genocide, of 1948, would also, in his opinion, be relevant. But this Convention requires an 'intent to destroy in whole or in part a national, ethnical, racial or religious group as such'. The wording of this sentence makes its application to nuclear weapons problematic. The enormous scale of nuclear destruction renders distinction of any kind difficult if not impossible. Nuclear war is an ocean which swallows individual rivers of destruction.

He points out that fall-out from nuclear explosion would drift over neutral States, thus violating the Hague principles ('The territory of neutral powers is inviolable', Hague Convention, 1907, Concerning the Rights and Duties of Neutral Powers and Persons in War on Land, Part 1). This, he says, 'is generally accepted as a statement of general international law'[3] and thus binding on all states, whether or not signatories.

Professor Brownlie punctures the official defence of the legal status of nuclear weapons. Radiation is not simply a secondary effect of nuclear weapons but an integral part of their threat. To claim, as nuclear governments have done, that the indiscriminate bombing of World War Two went unpunished and must therefore imply legitimacy, is a false argument. Such logic can have the support of gangsters alone. As far as reprisals are concerned, these are governed by the principle of proportionality, and can never justify wholesale disregard of the law. The Geneva Conventions of 1949 make it clear that the laws governing the treatment of civilian

[1] Ian Brownlie, 'The Legal Status of Nuclear Weapons in International Law'.
[2] Ibid.
[3] Loc. cit.

prisoners and the sick and wounded must apply 'in all circumstances' (Article 1, General Civilian Prisoners and Sick and
Wounded Convention, 1949).

He refers to the claim of manuals of military law that 'the use of
nuclear weapons is lawful provided that the laws of war are
applied'.[1] This could be so, he suggests, if attacks are confined to
'vessels in mid-ocean, army brigades in deserts and the base on the
Greenland Icecap along with the destruction of missiles on the
fringes of space'.[2] Yet such exceptional targets, he suggests,
confirm rather than disprove the illegality of nuclear weapons. The
deterrent theory relies on massive retaliation and the destruction of
cities.

The customary aspect of international law and war, a vital
element, lends weight to the indictment of nuclear weapons.
United Nations resolutions are law-making in the sense that they
are a sensitive indicator of world opinion and the development of
public conscience. Professor Brownlie cites in particular a General
Assembly resolution of 1961 as having an important bearing on the
legality issue:

> The General Assembly, mindful of its responsibility under the
> Charter of the UN in the maintenance of international peace and
> security; gravely concerned that, while negotiations on dis-
> armament have not so far achieved satisfactory results, the
> armaments race particularly in the nuclear and thermo-nuclear
> fields has reached a dangerous stage requiring all possible pre-
> cautionary measures to protect humanity and its civilization
> from the hazard of nuclear and thermo-nuclear catastrophe;
> recalling that the use of weapons of mass destruction causing
> unnecessary human suffering was in the past prohibited as being
> contrary to the laws of humanity and to the principles of
> international law by international declarations and binding
> agreements such as the Declaration of St Petersburg of 1868, the
> Declaration of the Brussels Conference of 1874, the Conventions
> of the Hague Peace Conference of 1899 and 1907 and the Geneva
> Protocol of 1925 to which the majority of nations are still parties;
> believing that the use of weapons of mass destruction such as
> nuclear and thermo-nuclear weapons is a direct negation of the

[1] Loc. cit.
[2] Ibid.

high ideals and objectives which the United Nations has been
established to achieve for the protection of succeeding generations from the scourge of war and for the preservation and
promotion of their cultures; declares that:

a) *The use of nuclear and thermo-nuclear weapons is contrary to the
spirit, letter and aims of the UN and, as such, a direct violation of
the Charter of the UN.*

b) *The use of nuclear and thermo-nuclear weapons would exceed
even the scope of war and cause indiscriminate suffering and
destruction to mankind and civilization, and, as such, is contrary
to the rules of international law and to the laws of humanity.*

c) *The use of nuclear and thermo-nuclear weapons is in a war
directed not against an enemy or enemies alone but also against
mankind in general.*

d) *Any State using nuclear or thermo-nuclear weapons is to be
considered to violate the Charter of the United Nations to act
contrary to the laws of humanity and to commit a crime against
mankind and its civilization.*[1]

Out of 101 states, 55 voted in support of the resolution, 20 against
and 26 abstained. In assessing this breakdown of voting, Professor
Brownlie points out that several of the abstentions sprang from a
desire to have such a resolution incorporated within disarmament
negotiations, not from hostility. With very few exceptions,
members did not challenge the legal content of the resolution.
'Exceptionally,' he says, 'the United States representative argued
that the UN Charter placed no limitation on the type of weapon
which could be used.'[2] No resolution is perfect and this one refers
to the Declaration of the Brussels Conference of 1874, which was
not ratified by any State. But there can be no doubt that the content
of the resolution is directly in line with the development of
international law during the preceding century.

Professor Brownlie fails to relate this event to his own country,
Britain. He does not mention the fact that Britain, along with the
United States and France, voted against the resolution while the
USSR voted for it. The role of the Western nuclear powers is thus
presented obliquely, without the kind of close examination which
might reflect uncomfortably on the nature of British society, of

[1] Author's italics.
[2] Loc. cit.

which Oxford University is such an integral part. The Macmillan Government of that time justified its negative attitude by claiming that such statements of principle achieve nothing, are manipulated for propaganda purposes, and that only substantive agreements backed by on-site verification can achieve nuclear disarmament.

Such a response, much in evidence in the 1980s, needs to be exposed for the facile fraud it is. British Governments during this century have not been shy in making declarations of principle when it suited them. Such declarations are always used for propaganda purposes, if by that is meant publicity favourable to the Governments concerned. Only by taking such declarations seriously and following them up with concrete proposals for action can their true value be assessed. To evade the first part of this process and claim an interest in verifiable agreements is cynicism. To imagine that any modern State will permit detailed on-site inspection by an overtly hostile power is fanciful. No neutral state, even, could be trusted to fulfil such a sensitive role. The British, American and French Governments of the 1960s regarded nuclear weapons as an ace in their defence pack, essential to counter 'the Soviet hordes'.

By ignoring such practical political factors, Professor Brownlie goes far to neutralize the effect of his conclusion that 'in any readily foreseeable inter-state conflict these weapons will involve mass destruction, violation of existing legal standards and the infliction of unnecessary suffering'.[1] As is common in the largely passive world of academic study, where ideas are less an inspiration for action than its substitute, Professor Brownlie draws in his horns when he encounters the brick wall of today: 'Another conclusion which may not be good to hear, but I am afraid it is a part of the picture, is that the possession of nuclear weapons *as such*, apart from any treaty provision – is not illegal. Perhaps it should be, but it isn't so far.'[2]

What is given with the left hand is taken back with the right. This statement, that possession of nuclear weapons 'is not illegal' is breathtaking in its dogmatic self-confidence. Not a word of explanation is offered, not a single objection noticed. The professor has spoken. We are expected to take note. But the terrain which escapes his attention is as vast as it is vital.

[1] Ibid.
[2] Ibid.

The law, no less than common sense, takes note of preparation to commit crime. Possession of nuclear weapons is certainly no more neutral a fact than possession by a citizen of a machine-gun. Nobody has licensed nuclear weapons, except their owners. At Nuremberg, conspiracy to commit crimes was adjudged criminal. Nuclear weapons are maintained in order to threaten an enemy with mass murder, not as ornaments. To claim blandly that threats to commit the most monstrous crime in history are 'not illegal' is to make the law a jackass.

Further, at Nuremberg it was held that international law applies to every individual, regardless of status. To train individuals to aim nuclear weapons at coded targets, as is the case today, is to train them in mass murder. At Nuremberg and elsewhere in Germany, ordinary businessmen were charged with war crimes and some executed. They had supplied extermination camps with such products as crematorium ovens. All denied knowledge of intended use of their product. Most were found guilty. And as Professor Brownlie knows well, the law is presumed to make sense. Laws which can only be applied after a nuclear war are by definition senseless. At Nuremberg the law was applied with energy and commitment. We have slid far down the slope of illegality since then. Only pre-nuclear war enforcement of law makes sense. Anything less is frivolous. To absolve the nuclear threat of any legal sanction is a mockery of the law.

Professor Brownlie completes an intellectual conjuring trick by concluding that even if the rabbit of nuclear illegality could be drawn from the hat, so what? 'Just supposing,' he says, 'having looked at the matter, just supposing it turned out that the use of nuclear weapons was lawful, one would still presumably oppose them and I think that when enthusiasts and laymen pick up law they sometimes pick it up rather as a sort of new religion and separate it from common sense. Presumably we are against the use of nuclear weapons because it is wrong, not because it is illegal. Supposing they were lawful, so what?' The trouble with most of us, he says, is that we 'treat the law as though it is a thing in itself divorced from other values and it isn't'.[1]

The logic of these comments explains why the law and nuclear weapons have drifted so far apart, especially in our universities. To

[1] Ibid.

propose the possibility that the law might allow the use of nuclear weapons is to propose a law bankrupt of minimal morality, implying a moribund culture. Such a supposition, coming from someone living and working in one of the world's most prestigious academic institutions, is misleading. It is Professor Brownlie, not we laymen, who separates the law from common-sense morality. Anyone with a real commitment to civilization will assume the law prohibits anything which is self-evidently wrong and immoral.

Most alarming of all in Professor Brownlie's statement is a lack of comprehension of the role law and crime play in the mind and life of the citizen. We retain a sense of crime and justice at a largely subconscious level of emotion and instinct. We do not say 'so what?' when a murderer strikes next door, or in our own home. We feel an immediate identification with the law. It, common sense, fear, morality and justice become a dynamic whole. Can we afford to treat nuclear mass murder and its threat as anything less?

The effect of Professor Brownlie's talk is to intrigue, stimulate and disillusion, a common enough sequence. He says, in effect, that the law condemns nuclear weapons, to some extent, but that even if it did not it would not matter much. An effect of this reasoning is to ensure that no further demands are put on Professor Brownlie. He prefers to be left alone with his private version of the law, a model for classroom use, polished and useless. He is wrong. The law is of the utmost importance in reining in the nuclear monster because it is grounded in elementary morality. To teach students otherwise is to obstruct the law.

More positively assertive on this issue than either Professor Schwarzenberger or Professor Brownlie is Professor Griffith of the London School of Economics. We are armed today, he says, with weapons 'that will admit of no discrimination, no distinctions, no humanity at all'.[1] He draws attention to the 20th International Conference of the Red Cross in Vienna, 1965, which reaffirmed four major principles of international law:

1. That the right of opponents to adopt means of injuring the enemy was not unlimited,
2. That it was prohibited to launch attacks against civilian populations as such,

[1] Gwyn Prins (ed.), *The Choice: Nuclear Weapons versus Security*, London 1984.

3. That distinction had to be made between combatants and civilians, and
4. That the general principles of the Law of War applied to nuclear and similar weapons.'[1]

Professor Griffith concludes that 'on the assumption that the use of nuclear weapons would be illegal, any preparation to use them would be a criminal conspiracy'.[2]

To brand as criminals the agents of nuclear deterrence is strong stuff. But strong language is like strong law. Without equally strong enforcement it is apt to expose impotence. To huff and puff without blowing the house down can be embarrassing. Professor Griffith deserves respect for his firm assertion of nuclear illegality. But where is the recognition that a criminal defence policy reflects a criminal society and a conspiracy to commit crime which corrupts every social institution, including the London School of Economics? Such a crisis of legality cannot be countered by written statements alone, however firm, in a context of collusive normality.

Colonel Professor Gerald Draper, of the University of Sussex, is considerably less inspiring. Appearing in a BBC World Service report on 'The Rules of War' in January 1984, Professor Draper started by making sensible comments about the relevance of customary law. Japan could not opt out of the Hague Convention protecting prisoners of war because it had not signed the treaty, he said. By the Second World War this law had become customary and thus binding on all states. 'Humanitarianism,' he said, 'is written large into the existing customary law of war and the conventional law of war.' (Conventional here means derived from treaties and conventions.) Professor Draper then engaged the issue of nuclear possession and threat. He described the allegation that British possession of nuclear weapons violates the law as, in legal terms, 'a non-starter'. His interviewer meekly accepted this assertion and asked: 'Can the policy of nuclear deterrence – a situation where peace is maintained through a balance of terror – though it may be strictly legal, be justified in moral terms?'

To which Professor Draper replied: 'Deterrence is a very important factor in keeping the peace. The law of war, therefore – far from outlawing the retention of nuclear weapons – should in no

---

[1] Ibid.
[2] Ibid.

way move in and try to forbid that. If I'm asked in moral terms, I would say that anything that helps to keep major nations from engaging in armed conflict is morally desirable, even if it means having in one's territory weapons of a capacity to destroy never hitherto known in the history of mankind.'

What had become of 'humanitarianism'? Genghis Khan or Hitler would have agreed with him. This statement is as frank an assertion of the right of the end to justify the means as can have been heard on the BBC for many a year. Such a belief would leave the law with nothing to do until after the event, when there would be no law. Dr Barry Paskins, of King's College, London University, refuted Professor Draper by declaring that it is immoral and illegal to intend to murder people, as well as to carry out the threat. The BBC interviewer compounded the confusion by stating that 'the laws of war are really no more than the lowest level of moral consensus that can be achieved by nations'. This Freudian confession disguised what we must assume was his intention, to describe the laws of war as the highest common denominator possible.

This particular discussion concluded on a note of customary paralysis, when Dr Adam Roberts, of Oxford University, said that a bridge must be built between deterrence and morality, 'and the construction of bridges is a very difficult and delicate task'. Especially when the bridge-builders are skilled only in equivocation. As with so many public discussions on this issue, this broadcast was as useful as adulterated penicillin. To debate the issue of mass murder as a rational option is to distort and deny its true significance. The programme's producer, when challenged later, replied in characteristic BBC fashion: 'On such a sensitive and contentious issue we felt it only right to leave it to the listener to hear both points of view and form his or her own judgment accordingly.'[1]

It is a mark of the academic mind to reduce all issues, no matter how elusive or engulfing, to the level where detached, objective discussion irons out inconvenient and disturbing peaks or troughs of feeling and fact. Reason too easily becomes traitor to itself. Just as Auschwitz, Dresden and Hiroshima imposed an experience of violence which floods reason in a tidal wave of blood, so the consequent nuclear nightmare continues to defy reason and mock

---

[1] Letter to the author from Derek Blizzard, 26 January 1984.

our feeble attempts to grasp its meaning. The BBC broadcast was just another half-hearted attempt to wrap the problem in legal options. The listener was invited to take his or her pick. A choice between weak interpretations of weak law. A caricature both of choice and law.

At a time like ours, when reason has become divorced from experience to an alarming extent, academic lawyers are inclined to lose sight of the common-sense meaning of law-making and law enforcement. Thus, in the case of the vitally important Additional Protocol 1, signed at Geneva in 1977, the plain language of the final document is too plain for many of them. This Protocol, agreed after years of discussion under the auspices of the International Committee of the Red Cross, sets out to strengthen protection for non-combatants in war.

Article 12 states that medical units 'shall not be the object of attack'. Article 35 states that 'in any armed conflict, the right of the Parties to the conflict to choose methods or means of warfare is not unlimited'. It further states that 'it is prohibited to employ weapons . . . of a nature to cause superfluous injury or unnecessary suffering'. It is forbidden to employ means of warfare 'which are intended, or may be expected, to cause widespread, long-term and severe damage to the natural environment'.

Article 48 states a basic rule: 'In order to ensure respect for and protection of the civilian population and civilian objects, the Parties to the conflict shall at all times distinguish between the civilian population and combatants . . . and accordingly shall direct their operation only against military objectives'. Article 51 states that 'indiscriminate attacks are prohibited', and adds that 'attacks against the civilian population by way of reprisals are prohibited'. Article 77 states that 'children shall be the object of special respect'. Article 85 states that violations of these laws are war crimes, and Article 87 states that it is the 'duty of commanders' to 'prevent' and 'suppress' such violations of the law.

Such basic principles stem from the main source of international law and war, a simple sense of common humanity in a shared world. Yet such is our nightmare confusion of values that even this straightforward good sense is bewitched by nuclear paranoia, serviced by a compliant intelligentsia. The British and United States Governments signed this Protocol, and were alone in adding a reservation that they had signed on the understanding that nuclear weapons remained outside the scope of the Protocol. In the words of the British reservation: 'The new rules introduced by the Protocol are not intended to have any effect on and do not regulate or prohibit the use of nuclear weapons.'

This particular cynicism will be examined more closely later. What concerns us here is the response of the academic lawyers. With few exceptions they not only noted the reservation without surprise or disgust, but were content to accept as relevant in law the preparatory discussions which preceded the Protocol. In the words of Dr Perry Robinson, of the University of Sussex Science Policy Research Unit, 'The Geneva Diplomatic Conference succeeded in producing the two Additional Protocols only because it was generally accepted that any new law it created would place no restrictions on weapons per se of a kind that would in any way inhibit continued possession of nuclear weapons.'

All the British Government was doing with its reservation, Dr Perry Robinson went on, was 'making that understanding explicit.'[1]

Dr Hampson, of the School of Law, University of Essex, wrote in similar vein: 'It [the UK] emphasized throughout the negotiations and upon signature that the Protocols did not affect in any way whatsoever the legal position regarding the possession, deployment or use of nuclear weapons.'[2] A West German, Dr Eibe H. Riedel, of the Institute for International Law at the University of Kiel, was even more explicit: 'The question of nuclear weapons was expressly excluded from the Geneva Conference by consensus right at the beginning.... Moreover, it was clear to the International Committee of the Red Cross, as well as to most Western and Eastern States, that this whole question raised issues far too complex to be included in the Geneva Conventions' Revision. Inclusion might have jeopardized the whole project. Needless to say, there are writers who disregard these facts and who tend to belittle the *travaux préparatoires*, but this certainly does not have the support of the respective governments. All this shows is that while it is highly desirable to find solutions to the burning questions of weapons of mass destruction, it amounts to wishful thinking to translate legitimate desires into legal obligations when the necessary consent of states is sadly lacking. Although I do not

[1] Letter to author dated 7 January 1982.
[2] Letter to Martin Howard dated 14 May 1984.

know, I believe that this probably represents the German position on the issue, but no formal statements to that effect have as yet been made.'[1]

To accept these expert opinions is to swallow whole the nightmare logic of nuclear government. A character in a Kafka novel would feel at home in a culture which boldly proclaims laws stating that 'the Parties to the conflict shall at all times distinguish between the civilian population and combatants', and then adds, as an afterthought, that the law-makers agreed that 'at all times' does not mean at all times but only those times when weapons of mass destruction are not needed. Governments of all kinds have a long and grisly record of such deceit, but what is striking here is the docile manner in which academic legal experts have colluded. They do not even point out the irrelevance of the UK and US reservation if indeed it was so 'clear' to all concerned that the laws excluded nuclear weapons. They do not expose the attempted perversion of law which results when the law, plainly written, is contradicted by unwritten 'understandings'.

When intelligent, well-paid and supposedly independent experts seem to align themselves with official deception on an issue of such fundamental importance, doubts must arise about the health of society as a whole. Worst and most alarming, the three experts quoted are supportive of moves to abolish nuclear weapons. They are not hard-line hawks. When such people offer deferential support to devious official policies it is hardly surprising that the public remains highly sceptical of the value of the law in preventing war. When intelligent people undermine their own beliefs there is always a reason, however unconscious. By stressing the dominant role of background discussion the experts confirm their own superior status as people with inside knowledge, out of reach of the ordinary citizen. Those in authority, even in universities, have a vested interest in stressing the scarcity value of their knowledge. They are an exclusive priesthood which is nothing if not exclusive.

Perhaps we get the law we deserve. 'Law has been growing in popularity recently,' according to a leading British newspaper. 'It is a very socially okay subject – you hardly ever get a working-class law student. Oxford and Cambridge remain pre-eminent. . . .'[2] It is

---

[1] Letter to author dated 8 November 1982.
[2] *Observer*, 12 September 1982.

evident that the popularity is related to that part of law which fosters selective wealth rather than peace on earth.

All is not entirely anaemic on the legal academic scene, thankfully. Someone who believes that the plain language interpretation of the law is more than 'wishful thinking' is Professor Richard Falk, of Princeton University, USA. I first heard him at the Nuremberg Tribunal of February 1983, organised by the West German Green party to assess the legal status of nuclear weapons. The Tribunal's expert witnesses mostly veered between over-ripe moralizing and dry legalism. But when Professor Falk spoke, the audience immediately sensed a rare combination of knowledge and feeling.

The earlier Nuremberg war crimes trials, he said, could be called the 'Nuremberg Promise', that 'the rules and principles that were being used to judge the responsibilities of the defeated countries would in the future serve as a guideline for all countries in the world'. But that promise, he went on, 'has been decisively broken, and nowhere has it been more powerfully broken than in relation to nuclear weapons and nuclear doctrines governing the use of these weapons of mass destruction'.

He was expressing a familiar American tradition of citizen's rights when he told his audience: 'It becomes essential that the citizens of the world use their own authority to uphold and give content to the idea that no leaders, no governments are above the law of war ... the content of the law at Nuremberg was that not only political leaders but all people in society, whether they be members of the armed forces, or workers in scientific establishments, or in business or merely tax-payers, that all these individuals have a right to insist that international law is upheld by their governments. It is a continuing crime against people to fail to uphold these minimum standards, and individual responsibility requires that those who occupy positions of influence in society have an obligation to withdraw from their complicity in the arms race and the preparation for nuclear war.'

'Everyone,' he warned, 'has a right and duty to say no to illegal State policy. And it is very important that this is understood not as disobeying the law – on the contrary, it is the enforcement of law to refuse to be an accomplice to preparation for nuclear war.' Early American democrats like Waldo Emerson and Henry Thoreau would have applauded such sentiments. He repeated that the 'supreme crime that has been committed against the peoples of the world has been the arrogance of State power that would use nuclear weapons against cities as weapons of war'.

In his view the boundaries imposed by international law are vital, and 'it is ironic that now for the first time the Rand Corporation in the United States [a private corporation which conducts research for, among others, US Government departments] has issued a report which draws dramatic attention to the fact that US foreign policy has been consistently violating international law when it comes to nuclear weapons strategy'. The Rand report asserts that MAD (Mutual Assured Destruction) is an illegal policy: 'no competent international lawyer,' Professor Falk continued, 'would question the conclusion that the policies being pursued by the nuclear powers violate the most fundamental respect for and minimal perceptions of international law. They violate them by threatening poisoned weapons of untold magnitude. They violate them by ignoring neutral rights. They violate them by making no distinction between civilian and military targets. They violate them by inflicting cruel and inhuman injury ... and they violate them by proposing grossly disproportionate means to accomplish limited military objectives.'

He insisted that these laws are 'embodied not only in the laws of war and international treaties but have been confirmed in a number of ways, by UN General Asssembly resolutions that have repeatedly put the consensus of the governments of the world behind this interpretation of international law. They have furthermore been confirmed by the only judicial body ever to pronounce on these questions, the Japanese Tokyo District Court, 1955, [which] concluded, with the help of three independent international law experts, that the attacks on Hiroshima and Nagasaki violated international law in decisive respects.'

Professor Falk concluded by stating that 'the time has come to found a movement of political action that will impose international law standards on the nuclear powers and bring the people of the world some hope of peace and justice.'

At last an academic expert on the laws of war had dared to apply the common sense meaning of the law to the essence of the nuclear problem, not in tones of anxious hair-splitting but with urgent conviction. But careful, I warned myself. Forthright statements are good, a great deal better than the usual drizzle, but what about action to follow the thought? I reminded myself that senile yet sophisticated societies are adept at neutralizing even the finest pronouncements. Professor Falk is not alone in finding it easier to talk and write than act. But he suggested one important course of action. 'It would be entirely appropriate, legally and technically for a single neutral State, or a group of neutral States, to initiate an action at the International Court of Justice at The Hague, asking for the suspension of all reliance on nuclear weapons in any context. The grounds for this would be that unless the nuclear arms race is stopped at this point there will be no opportunity in the aftermath. We can't wait until the crime has been committed.... It would be an extremely constructive act to give the International Court the chance to distinguish itself as a growing institution by upholding and developing international law.'

Such an initiative would indeed be constructive, despite the limitations of the Court. Nations may reject its decisions, but this usually attracts widespread condemnation. There are signs that such a move may take place, due to rising anxiety among non-aligned powers at the irresponsible and illegal behaviour of nuclear States.

It is good to welcome a positive affirmation of the law on this issue. Most professors of law are trapped between distorting mirrors which reflect the lie that all is well in the wider world, the preserve of responsible governments. This frees them to focus on more normal, conventional problems. This comforting delusion is reinforced by a cast of mind which mediates the law as an objective body of knowledge, as remote from personal experience as it is from the nuclear nightmare. George Steiner, a perceptive thinker of Jewish origin, knows very well how such complementary delusions foster hellish acts like the holocaust: 'it is precisely the "objectivity", the moral neutrality in which the sciences rejoice and attain their brilliant community of effort, that bar them from final relevance. Science may have given tools and insane pretences of rationality to those who devised mass murder. It tells us scarcely anything of their motives, a topic on which Aeschylus or Dante would be worth hearing.'[1]

Our law schools have become the servants of this objectivity. They lack the depth of personal awareness and commitment

[1] George Steiner, *Language and Silence*, New York 1967.

which can grasp the law's simplicity. They sell their students short and act as unwitting midwives of our nightmare.

George Steiner pays tribute to the perception of Kafka: 'he heard the jargon of death growling loud inside the European vulgate. Not in any vague, allegoric sense, but with exact prophesy.... He understood, as if the bush had burned for him again, that a great inhumanity was lying in wait for modern man, and that parts of language would serve it and be made base in the process....'[1]

'Kafka,' he said, 'prophesied the actual forms of that disaster of Western humanism which Nietzsche and Kierkegaard had seen like an uncertain blackness on the horizon.' Our professors of law have still not confronted that disaster. They and their universities are a part of the 'core of Europe' from which the 'ultimate of political barbarism grew'[2], and grows.

'Barbarism,' writes Steiner, 'prevailed on the very ground of Christian humanism, of Renaissance culture and classic rationalism. We know that some of the men who devised and administered Auschwitz had been taught to read Shakespeare and Goethe, and continued to do so.'[3]

The law was not proof against barbarism in Nazi Germany, nor is it proof against nuclear barbarism today. In a madhouse, madness must first be understood before reason can get a word in edgeways. 'In Treblinka,' says Steiner, 'with its incessant assembly line of death and technology of mass disposal, with its fake railway station and Teutonic village, with its dogs trained to attack men's private parts and its official Jewish marriages, life had reached a pitch of extreme insanity.'[4]

So it had. But we have reached yet another, higher pitch. The fake jollity of Treblinka has swollen and multiplied until we are all part of it. There were thousands in those prettified extermination camps, where death was a lottery. The whole of modern industrial civilization is now a nuclear death camp, with extermination waiting in the wings. Even Kafka could not imagine the refinements of our nuclear nightmare. We elect the camp commandants in the name of democracy, and willingly pay for the weapons which will kill us all, this year, next year, some time, never? We

[1] Ibid.
[2] Ibid.
[3] Ibid.
[4] Ibid.

encourage our professors of law to haggle solemnly over 'reservations' and 'understandings', while we strive to adapt to the nightmare's peculiar demands. Even if we are brave enough to denounce
this normal lunacy we do it so that we are scarcely inconvenienced.
The denouncers are absorbed by what they denounce. The bandits
of Corsica used to complain of intruders, 'their shadow takes away
our sunlight'. We have given away our sunlight, pretending that
the shadow of the bomb is part of life, a rational, lawful option.

In the context of this deception our professors of law, for all their
knowledge, are fooling around in a darkened basement, lit by dim
objective night-lights. They can do better. They must do much
better, if they are not to remain a major part of the problem. Their
students must be taught that law belongs to people, not people to
law. They must learn that crime originates in the highest, seeping
down to the lowest, not the other way round. It is time for the
preening, play-acting and money-grubbing to stop, and for world-
wide law enforcement to start.

Chapter Four

The Lawyer's Tale

'Since when has the civilized world accepted the principle that
the temporary immunity of the criminal not only deprives the
law of its binding force but legalizes the crime?'
– Sir Hartley Shawcross QC, at Nuremberg

'The Advocates did not dare even grumble. For although even
the pettiest Advocate might be to some extent capable of
analyzing the things in the Court, it never occurred to the
Advocates that they should suggest or insist on any
improvements in the system'
– *The Trial*, Franz Kafka

During a childhood spent in India, in the shadow of the Himalayas,
I sometimes watched the antics of mountain bears, taken from
house to house by their captors to earn a few coins by their tricks. I
watched, wide-eyed, their strange, agile, yet humiliating parade.
There was a menace in the circus act of those animals.

Observing lawyers in court today I have some of the same sense
of embarrassment, tinged with anger. How is it that such agility of
mind serves justice with so little dignity and so much posturing?
The uniform, mannerisms and eccentric speech provide a theatrical
show, certainly, but what is it all worth? The effect is to distance
the citizen from justice. He becomes a spectator at his own trial.
The court is too often a scene of intimidation rather than justice. Is
the failure of the law to impose limits on our nuclear madness due
in part to this legalistic showmanship? It is hard for a circus to serve
a serious purpose.

Perhaps the most creative of all English lawyers, Francis Bacon,
was well aware of the law's need for strong natural roots. Too many
lawyers, in his view, 'have no freedom of opinion, but as it were
talk in bonds'.[1] The people best able to formulate law, he thought,
'are statesmen, who best understand the conditions of civil society,

[1] C. D. Bowen, *Francis Bacon*, Boston 1963.

welfare of the people, natural equity, customs of nations, and different forms of government; and who may therefore determine laws by the rules and principles both of natural equity and policy'. Laws, which are 'severed from the grounds of nature, manners and policy are like wall flowers, which, though they grow high upon the crests of states, yet they have no deep roots.'[1]

There were, in the sixteenth-century England of Bacon's time, two streams of law which still co-exist in our nuclear era. The first is common law, which embraces trial by jury and the slow accumulation of judicial precedent. The second, continental and Roman, is impatient with slow methods, relying on a centralized paternalism which prefers written principles to experience. The first risks entanglement in its own contradictions, while the latter is vulnerable to arbitrary power. Bacon's rare, creative mind preferred the second trend but was broad enough in scope to make good use of both. His humane vision is singularly absent from our courts today.

The lawyer, despite high-income status and close association with power, attracts more fear than respect. In our fragmented, nervous tribe he is a medicine-man, muttering strange incantations and liable to invoke punishment. According to the Chief Justice of the United States, American lawyers are 'near the bottom of the barrel' in public esteem.[2] In his annual address to the American Bar Association he accused lawyers of 'absurd' lawsuits, abuse of legal procedures and 'spectacular' rises in fees. The legal profession, he said, is 'so mesmerized with the stimulation of the court-room contest' that it has failed to explore cheaper and more effective ways of settling disputes. He had no need to remind his audience that an American President, Nixon, had demonstrated a lawyer's contempt for the law at least as spectacular as its rising costs.

In Britain, where lawyers are only slightly less pervasive, the situation is if anything worse, thanks to professional mysteries designed to keep the public in ignorance and at bay. Lawyers are not confined to companies and courts but have invaded parliament in numbers, more than one hundred of them having been elected Members of Parliament,[3] among them the Prime Minister,

[1] Ibid.
[2] *Daily Telegraph*, 14 February 1984.
[3] 111, according to the *Guardian*, 17 December 1983.

Foreign Secretary, Home Secretary, Education Secretary and Environment Secretary. If Francis Bacon was right, it might have been hoped that these lawyer ministers would bring a new dimension of wisdom to the law. Or they might simply apply the restricted vision of their legal training.

At a time when four million British citizens are without work it is disturbing to find that a leading lawyer, appearing at a public inquest, can earn £164 per hour, or a total of £32,237,[1] for a single case. If the law is the highest common denominator of public morality, then it is a debased law which depends on the vastly expensive expertise of a tiny élite of professional lawyers. An English Bar Council survey revealed that the top ten per cent of Queen's Counsel lawyers, working in specialist fields, earned an average of £133,600 in 1982/3,[2] far more than the Prime Minister. The average earnings for all barristers (court lawyers) was £17,700, more than twice the average national income. As a conservative British newspaper put it: 'The cost of going to law remains ... incredibly high. Justice cannot be seen to be fair when it is out of the reach of at least a third of the population – those neither rich enough to risk the very roofs over their heads on legal action, nor poor enough to qualify for legal aid.'[3]

In an atmosphere such as this, when the devil has already taken the hindmost millions and few can aspire to be millionaires, it is not surprising that it is a rare lawyer who dares venture into the legal no-man's-land of nuclear weapons. Training, social convention, private accountants and friends are all against such quixotic adventures. Lawyers are in no doubt that judiciary and government, whatever their public claims to independence, are a common law husband and wife team, very hard to beat. One appoints the other and the other absolves the one, with only a rare lapse of loyalty, quickly forgiven in a common cause.

When a lawyer does dip a toe in this murky water it is usually in such a way that a diplomatic retreat is always available. One such attempt was made by a British lawyer, Mark Benney, who questioned the refusal of British courts to explore the underlying law-affirming intentions of peace protesters who break minor laws

[1] *Daily Telegraph*, 31 December 1983.
[2] *Guardian*, 1 December 1983.
[3] *Daily Express*, 8 December 1983.

at nuclear bases.[1] He quotes an American, John Rawls, and his 'A Theory of Justice.' John Rawls cites the example of a 'non-violent, conscientious yet political act contrary to law usually done with the aim of bringing about a change in the law or policies of the government'. Such an act, he suggests, invokes 'the commonly shared conception of justice that underlies the political order'. It expresses a 'fidelity to law' and appeals to 'the fundamental political principles of a democratic regime'.

Such an initiative, according to Rawls and Benney, deserves to be reviewed by the highest courts of the land, in the widest context of the law; not dismissed with a petty counter-accusation. 'As an illustration,' says Mark Benney, 'the argument that the commission of summary offences at Greenham Common air base is reasonably necessary to prevent a breach of the Genocide Act by the United States or the United Kingdom Government has not been determined by an appellate court. It may be that it is unlikely to succeed; but the point is that this argument, which is based on the "self-help" provisions in Section 3 of the Criminal Law Act, 1967, has been left unresolved.'

Civil disobedience of this kind, says Rawls, is a force for stability in a democratic society, and an expression of 'fidelity to law'. Mark Benney agrees. But there is a weakness in this approach which makes it largely irrelevant to such a fundamental issue as nuclear weapons and threats of mass destruction. Nuclear deterrence is not an aberration of government, an absent-minded act out of character with usual good behaviour. If it were, it might be reasonable to expect the law to right itself, so to speak, with the help of an enlightened court of appeal of wise judges. But nuclear deterrence is a deadly outgrowth of the Nazi 'total war' mentality. Like a plague bacillus it has spread steadily throughout the mind and sinews of society, subverting what was once healthy.

To confront a nightmare as if it were a dream is not just to fail but to play devil's advocate. It compounds the problem while pretending to solve it, and it is a mark of the liberal lawyer today that appeals are made to sweet reason when the latter has been taken hostage by darker forces. In Mark Benney's case the flaws which paralyze his argument are common. First, he works within a legal system which colludes with official evasion of the laws restraining

[1] *Guardian*, 23 July 1984.

military violence. His mild rebuke to this system is a polite rap on the knuckles which cannot hope to disturb such deeply ingrained abuse of authority. Second, his article appears in a liberal newspaper which has a long record of collusion, in terms of the law, with Government defence policy. Mark Benney, again, alludes to this briefly in the mildest way, and then only obliquely, by reference to the Sarah Tisdall case in 1984 (the *Guardian* contributed to the incrimination of Sarah Tisdall by handing back leaked documents to the Government).

Worst of all, by focusing on 'civil disobedience' and 'conscience' as the mainspring of protest, he by-passes the main crime of government, that it is violating existing law. Missing such a large target owes something to a professional situation which imposes pressure to think, write and act within narrow channels. Despite his good intentions he ends by offering such weak opposition to the nuclear nightmare that it emerges, by contrast, in even darker colours. Yet another paper dart is fired off at the nuclear monster.

But there are a few signs of restiveness among British lawyers. They rarely take part in public protest, but the stop-and-search powers of the Police and Criminal Evidence Bill, 1984, provoked several hundred to picket police stations and courts. Solicitors were joined by 'doctors, church leaders, students, lecturers and trade unionists on picket lines in Birmingham, Leicester, Liverpool, Sheffield, Oxford, Brighton, Bradford, Nottingham, Reading and Derby'.[1] Even the governing body of England and Wales' 41,000 solicitors had the veil lifted on its antiquated methods. Described by one observer as 'the most effective example of a restrictive trade union,'[2] the Law Society's handling of a complaint against one of its leading members was described by its own inquiry in damning terms: 'We have found administrative failures, mistakes, wrong decisions, errors of judgment, failures in communication, high-handedness and insensitivity on a scale that must have done great harm to the Law Society.'

Such chronic administrative failure stems from a basic lack of vision in the legal profession. When rationality develops at the expense of feeling and imagination there is inevitably a loss of balance in personal and professional life. Major realities, like the nuclear threat, are caricatured and diminished. A matter of life and

[1] *Guardian*, 14 January 1984.
[2] Blake Baker in the *Daily Telegraph*, 23 December 1983.

death is drained of vitality by the legal mind so that the corpse can be dissected safely. Primary distortion of reality on this scale can result in compensatory projection of repressed feeling on to such scapegoat figures as prostitutes and petty gangsters.

In a public prosecution of obscene videos, an American cult terror film, *Nightmares in a Damaged Brain*, was described by the prosecution lawyer as 'glorifying and encouraging violence'. He went on to claim that 'in the firm submission of the prosecution, obscenity is not confined to sexual matters. It also embraces extreme forms of violence.'[1] Such a statement was made without a hint of irony, or any sign of recognition that the legal profession and society itself base their security on threats to commit the most horrendous violence in history. Such is the schizoid character of most lawyers that they are adapted to an institutionalized double-think. Responsible, privileged citizens at one level of social convention, and irresponsible yes-men at another. Violent nightmares are not confined to damaged brains in video nasties but extend their obscene shadow across the whole spectrum of social behaviour.

To claim in this context of confusion that there is such a thing as 'the complete professional independence of barristers' which is 'a vital ingredient of our legal system'[2] is yet another strand in our nightmare, a fiction designed to stifle doubt and reform. The very opposite is true. Our lawyers cannot function in the way they do without extreme dependence on both the legal system and the social system which tolerates it. But it is possible to be 'bounded in a nutshell' and still count oneself a 'King of infinite space'. Once separated from reality, belief becomes capable of any folly.

The rationalist fantasy life of the British legal profession probably owes something to Britain's relative isolation from direct experience of horror. In Nazi Germany lawyers had a harsher time of it. Hitler's frequently expressed contempt for lawyers stemmed in part from his awareness of their dependence on power and money. He knew they would eat out of his hand and they did. Most of them. But there were a few brave souls who could recognize crime as such whatever its origins and however many guns it carried. Their sad fate reminds us that in a murderous age humanitarian law is more expensive than most of us know.

Hans von Dohnanyi was thirty-one when Hitler came to power,

[1] *Daily Telegraph*, 2 February 1984.
[2] Nigel Seed, a London barrister, in the *Guardian*, 12 March 1984.

and worked at the Reich Ministry of Justice in the Department of International Law. He became private secretary to several Ministers of Justice, thus acquiring personal insight into the working of Nazi law. After the Reichstag fire he tried to organize a public inquiry by the German judges into the growing reign of terror. He was thwarted and realized that only active resistance could succeed. He kept a secret record of the crimes committed by the Nazi regime. He became a part of Military Intelligence at the outbreak of World War Two, and helped to co-ordinate an abortive assassination attempt on Hitler. He was arrested by the Gestapo in 1943 and is believed to have died on 8 April 1945, in Sachsenhausen concentration camp.[1]

Joseph Wirmer said at his trial before the so-called People's Court and its deranged President, Freisler: 'If I am hanged, Herr President, then you will be the one who is afraid, not I.' He was sentenced to death on 8 September 1944 for complicity in the attempt on Hitler's life of 20 July, and hanged the same day.

He was a lawyer of rare perception and courage. On 1 May 1933 he heard the broadcast of Hitler's speech at Tempelhof, Berlin. It was Hitler's first public speech since assuming power and thousands were carried away by his oratory, including several of Joseph Wirmer's friends. 'I shall be Hitler's enemy,' he told them, knowing that the whole basis of his life and profession were under threat.

His brother wrote of him: 'He believed he could best retain his independence in the practice of his profession as a solicitor, although the rigid rules and regulations were an anathema to him and an outrage to his feeling for individual responsibility. For all his legal training and inclination, he regarded laws which took no account of facts or circumstances as so much nonsense; the thesis "autoritas non veritas facit legem" (authority not truth makes the law), he dismissed as Jesus dismissed the tempter in the desert, and he was in the end deeply convinced that law must emerge from the order established by historical evolution, and must itself and by that virtue continually evolve. He thus believed that by defeating the formal law introduced by a dictatorship he was in fact serving on a much higher plane the cause of justice to which he had dedicated his life. The fact that Freisler attacked him with par-

---

[1] Annedore Leber, *Conscience in Revolt*, New York 1957.

ticular venom was a sure sign that the regime regarded him as one of its most dangerous enemies, and therefore as one to be eliminated. Just as they had thrown him out of the *Rechtswahrerbund* (Nazi "Guardians of Justice"), years before, for his fearless defence of victims of racial persecution.'[1]

Klaus Bonhoeffer was forty-four when he was shot by the SS on the night of the 22/23 April 1945, as the Russians were entering Berlin. He had worked as a lawyer for the German airline Lufthansa, and had visited many parts of the world. The human and social implications of the law were his main interest and he wrote a thesis on the basis of law, in which he challenged the legality of totalitarian power. He became involved with resistance groups, which included his more famous theologian brother, Dieter. He was arrested and sentenced to death by the People's Court on 2 February 1945. In a farewell letter to his children he wrote: 'don't imagine the main purpose of education to be the high position for which it may fit you; the main purpose is the individual dignity and freedom which it can bestow'. He told them: 'ask a lot of yourselves and your friends'. He asked a lot of himself.[2]

Rudiger Schleicher was shot by the SS at the same time as Klaus Bonhoeffer, after months held in chains. He was an expert in aviation law and was warned repeatedly by his superiors for intervening on behalf of Jews and concentration camp prisoners. In 1939 he refused a court-martial case because he would not help convict someone whose actions he approved. In 1942, at the height of the war, he made a public speech on 'Right and Law', the publication of which was banned. He became involved in the July 1944 coup attempt and was arrested.

Karl Friedrich Goerdeler was condemned to death on 7 September 1944 and executed on 2 February 1945, after torture. He was a former mayor of Leipzig and became convinced that the 'laws of nature and of God' would ensure the eventual collapse of a regime founded on 'financial folly, economic compulsion, political terror, lawlessness and amorality'. He sent a secret circular to many German generals in March 1943. 'It is no good whitewashing the facts or burying our conscience,' he told them, 'for that will not absolve us from the duty of averting this disaster before it is too late.' The war must end, and 'if the government of the day stands in

[1] Ibid.
[2] Ibid.

the way, the government must fall, as governments have fallen throughout history'. He asked how a decent people 'can put up with such an unbearable system for so long? The explanation is simple: only because all infringements of justice and decency are protected by secrecy and terrorism.'[1]

'The German people,' he told the generals, 'should be told out loud of what they already know and discuss in secret, of the consequences of incompetent military leadership, of the excess of corruption and of the countless crimes, which are quite incompatible with honour. They should then be asked to declare in public whether they are prepared to defend this state of affairs, and which of them can justify it. I guarantee that no one in the world, not even a born criminal, would publicly associate himself with such a criminal system.'[2]

After the murder of these brave Germans, after Auschwitz and Dresden and Hiroshima, and after forty years of nuclear terror, we live in a brighter, wealthier yet more gruesome landscape. There is no ranting Hitler to tease atavistic instincts, nor a black-uniformed SS to boast of crime. Those features of hell are hidden from sight because we have no need of them. The brutal meaning of nuclear weapons is locked in the cellars of our mind, with only a polite façade on view. History's vilest weapons are an 'insurance policy', the final solution of a suicidal civilization.

How many of today's lawyers can read the signs of our times, the meaning behind the official hand-outs? Educated in a surface interpretation of the law, can they be trusted to detect endemic corruption? Of the German lawyers who rejected Nazi law, none was more perceptive than Ewald von Kleist. He was arrested during the first days of Hitler's reign, in 1931, and again after the July 1944 plot. He was beheaded on 9 April 1945.

Ewald von Kleist published a pamphlet in 1932 in which he rejected without compromise the politics of National Socialism: 'Now a new faith is rammed down our throats; we are asked to believe that National Socialism and Hitler, and they alone, have power to bring us joy and salvation; a belief which demands a fantastic quota of gullibility ... National Socialism is purely destructive and gives itself away at every turn. Fanatical party members feel no loyalty but to the Party itself . . . . Officials neglect

---

[1] Ibid.
[2] Ibid.

their normal duties and, in short, the basic principles of both private and public life are destroyed . . . .

'It is not merely a question of the open National Socialist agitation, which breaks all bounds for sheer unscrupulous provocation . . . but the whispering campaign is even more vicious . . . [the notion that] National Socialism is a respectable national movement which happens to have a few passing defects, an attitude which we have condoned, has placed our whole future in jeopardy; and it will take all our strength to avert the danger . . . . This lunacy must be exposed.'[1]

Just before his execution he wrote: 'Who is the greater, who has achieved more for humanity, Caesar, or a simple, conscientious genuine working man, whose whole life has been an example of faith? I think it is the working man. I think it is worth thinking about.'[2] Ewald von Kleist did not look at the present in terms of the past. He saw it for what it was. And it would be folly to examine our nuclear era in terms of Nazi conditions. The stage props of nuclear apocalypse are quite different.

The brief lives of those Germans flicker like candles in this gruesome century, reminding us that all lawyers are not undercover agents of authority. They were few, they failed, they were snuffed out in the storm. Yet their example remains to mock those today who choose a blind conformity. And it is as well to remember that in Britain and the United States there were no lawyers who spoke out against their Governments' law-breaking bombing assaults on enemy non-combatants, in Hamburg, Dresden, Hiroshima and Nagasaki. They, like their societies, were swept along in a tide of vengeance.

As if shocked by their own wantonness, as much as by the manifest barbarism of their opponents, the Allies enforced the laws of war at Nuremberg in 1945–46 with high-minded severity. Twenty-two leading Nazis were prosecuted for crimes against peace and humanity, and war crimes. Twelve were sentenced to death and the others imprisoned or acquitted. Like an alcoholic who wakes to a brief moment of self-awareness, our industrial civilization affirmed its commitment to the rule of law in world society. Like most such moments of remission it was genuine and

[1] Ibid.
[2] Ibid.

short-lived. We live today in the lengthening shadow of that imperfect monument to world justice.

What was the lawyer's role in that achievement? It was, on the whole, positive, eloquent, often creative. Followed by a relapse into the trivial subservience of today. When midnight struck in post-war Europe, the golden court of Nuremberg became once more a pumpkin stage for mercenary lawyers, as anxious to bully their victims as please their paymasters.

No lawyer at the Nuremberg Trial was more eloquent than the American prosecutor, Justice Robert Jackson. He was the kind of man who regards history as something to be made rather than remembered. Some months before the main trial began, in June 1945, he wrote a report for President Truman: 'In untroubled times, progress towards an effective rule of law in the international community is slow indeed. Inertia rests more heavily upon the society of nations than upon any other society. Now we stand at one of those rare moments when the thoughts and institutions and habits of the world have been shaken by the impact of World War on the lives of countless millions. Such occasions rarely come and quickly pass. We are put under a heavy responsibility to see that our behaviour during this unsettled period will direct the world's thought towards a firmer enforcement of the laws of international conduct, so as to make wars less attractive to those who have governments and the destinies of peoples in their power.'

His British counterpart at the trial, Sir David Maxwell Fyfe, said of him later: 'In the truest sense of the word he was a romantic of the law. For him, the vocation of the lawyer left behind dull huckstering and pettifogging things. It caught the full wind of the traditions of natural justice, reason and human rights.'[1] In 1941 Jackson had told the American Bar Association: 'We may be certain that we do less injustice by the worst processes of the law than would be done by the best use of violence.'[2] He refused to accept the evasive doctrine that those in power escape the law, and quoted Lord Chief Justice Coke's warning to King James I: 'A King is still under God and the Law.' The bloody ruins of Europe were to be redeemed by a determined enforcement of civilization's minimum laws.

Jackson's opening address to the court still rings true in our

[1] Obituary in *Stanford Law Review*, California 1955.
[2] Telford Taylor in *Columbia Law Review*, Vol. 55, 1955.

nuclear era: 'The wrongs which we seek to condemn and punish have been so calculated, so malignant and so devastating, that civilization cannot tolerate their being ignored, because it cannot survive their being repeated .... The common sense of mankind demands that law shall not stop with the punishment of petty crimes by little people. It must also reach men who possess themselves of great power and make deliberate and concerted use of it to set in motion evils which leave no home in the world untouched .... What makes this inquest significant is that these prisoners represent sinister influences that will lurk in the world long after their bodies have returned to dust.'[1]

He was not interested, he told the court, in 'abstract speculations' and 'legalistic theories .... We must never forget,' he warned, 'that the record on which we judge these defendants today is the record on which history will judge us tomorrow. To pass these defendants a poisoned chalice is to put it to our lips as well.' Jackson continued: 'When I say that we do not ask for convictions unless we prove crimes, I do not mean mere technical or incidental transgression of international conventions. We charge guilt on planned and intended conduct that involves moral as well as legal wrong .... It is their abnormal and inhuman conduct which brings them to this bar .... It is true that the Germans have taught us the horrors of modern warfare, but the ruin that lies from the Rhine to the Danube shows that we, like our Allies, have not been dull pupils.'

He indicted the modern desk-murderer: 'These defendants were men of station and rank which does not soil its own hands with blood. They were men who knew how to use lesser men as tools.' And Nazi party membership, he said, 'in effect amounted to an abdication of personal intelligence and moral responsibility ... an idolatry and self-surrender more Oriental than Western'. He was not to know that very soon there would be operatives of many nationalities trained to fire weapons of nuclear mass destruction. Jackson referred sarcastically to the criminal side-effects of European imperialism, with its 'foul doctrine', contrary to the teaching of Hugo Grotius and other international law scholars, that all wars are legitimate. 'Does it take these men by surprise,' he asked, 'that murder is treated as a crime?' By 'multi-

[1] HMSO, *Trial of Major German War Criminals*, 1946.

plying this crime by a million' it did not become a 'legally innocent act.'[1]

Attempts to 'give war-making a complete immunity from accountability to law' were 'intolerable . . . . Plain people,' he said, 'with their earthy common sense, revolted at such fictions and legalisms so contrary to ethical principles and demanded checks on war immunities.' Jackson had no inkling that within ten years legal restraints on war would have been violated to such an extent that annual nuclear bombing competitions of Britain's largest cities would take place between the USAF and RAF, with a silver cup awarded to the aircrew which 'destroyed' these cities most accurately.

Jackson reminded the Nazi defendants that Hitler had never repealed Article 54 of the Weimar Constitution, which stated that 'the generally accepted rules of International Law are to be considered as binding integral parts of the law of the German Reich'. International law grew, as did the common law, by means of government decisions designed to use settled principles to meet new circumstances. Individual responsibility, he declared, lies at the heart of these laws: 'The idea that a State, any more than a corporation, commits crimes, is a fiction. Crimes always are committed only by persons . . . . Modern civilization puts unlimited weapons of destruction in the hands of men. It cannot tolerate so vast an area of legal irresponsibility. The Charter recognizes that one who has committed criminal acts may not take refuge in superior orders nor in the doctrine that his crimes were acts of State . . . .'[2]

Jackson was acutely aware of the fragile nature of the Tribunal's task: 'This trial represents mankind's desperate effort to apply the discipline of the law' to statesmen and those in power. 'The real complaining party at your bar is Civilization,' he said. 'The refuge of the defendants can be only their hope that International Law will lag so far behind the moral sense of mankind that conduct which is crime in the moral sense must be regarded as innocent in law.'

Finally came an appeal to ordinary common sense: 'Civilization asks whether law is so laggard as to be utterly helpless to deal with crimes of this magnitude by criminals of this order of importance. It does not expect that you can make war impossible. It does expect

[1] Ibid.
[2] Ibid.

that your juridical action will put the forces of International Law, its prospects, its prohibitions and, most of all, its sanctions, on the side of peace, so that men and women of goodwill in all countries, may have "leave to live by no man's leave, underneath the law".[1]

This American lawyer's eloquence and humane promotion of the law has been reported and admired in the many books about this famous trial. Yet not one of the authors draws attention to the sobering fact that Jackson's vision pierces the distorted logic of our own time. It is more convenient to freeze history, with Nazis for ever convicted and Allies acquitted.

In his concluding speech for the prosecution, Jackson reaffirmed his vision of the law as civilization's last hope: 'Two world wars have left a legacy of dead which number more than all the armies engaged in any war that made ancient and medieval history. No half-century ever witnessed slaughter on such a scale .... If we cannot eliminate the causes and prevent the repetition of these barbaric events, it is not an irresponsible prophecy to say that this twentieth century may yet succeed in bringing the doom of civilization.'[2]

The defence tried to show that the Tribunal was inventing rather than applying the law, but Jackson refuted this: 'As an International Military Tribunal, it rises above the provincial and transient, and seeks guidance not only from International Law but also from the basic principles of jurisprudence, which are assumptions of civilization and which long have found embodiment in the codes of all nations.' And he touched another nerve which is still alive: 'The charge requires examination of a criminal policy, not of a multitude of isolated, unplanned or disputed crimes.'

He exposed the deterioration in military conduct which the Nazis accelerated, and which continues today: 'The orders for the treatment of Soviet prisoners of war were so ruthless that Admiral Canaris [Head of military intelligence], pointing out that they would "result in arbitrary mistreatments and killings", protested to the OKW against them as breaches of International Law. The reply of Keitel [Chief of Staff] was unambiguous. He said: 'The objections arise from the military conception of chivalrous warfare!

---

[1] Ibid.
[2] *International Military Tribunal Vol. XIX*. All quoted material up to p. 79 comes from this source unless another source is indicated.

This is the destruction of an ideology! Therefore I approve and back the measures".'

Keitel was later hanged. The military leaders of East and West justify nuclear threats of mass extermination in much the same way today, and remain free.

The defendants, Jackson told the court, 'meet this overwhelming case, some by admitting a limited responsibility, some by putting the blame on others, and some by taking the position, in effect, that while there have been enormous crimes there are no criminals'. And in the light of today's arms race it is good to be reminded of the Nazi defendants' claim ' "to be sure we were building guns. But not to shoot. They were only to give us weight in negotiating." At its best this argument amounts to a contention that the military forces were intended for blackmail, not for battles.'

He ridiculed the defence of helplessness: 'These men destroyed free government in Germany and now plead to be excused from responsibility because they became slaves. They are in the position of the boy of fiction who murdered his father and mother and then pleaded for leniency because he was an orphan.' There was no stand on principle or law: 'Nowhere do we find a single instance where any one of the defendants stood up against the rest and said: "This thing is wrong and I will not take part in it".'

Jackson reminded the court that International Law has its roots in the law of every town and city: 'In all our countries, when, perhaps in the heat of passion or for other motives which impair restraint, some individual is killed, the murder becomes a sensation, our compassion is aroused, nor do we rest until the criminal is punished and the rule of law is vindicated. Shall we do less when not one but on the lowest computation twelve million men, women and children are done to death?'

He quoted Lord Acton: 'The greatest crime is homicide. The accomplice is no better than the assassin: the theorist is the worst.'

Justice Jackson's energetic, imaginative grasp of the law reminds us that such a thing is possible. It is a living measurement of the abject gap which separates the modern lawyer from nuclear reality. If the other Nuremberg prosecuting lawyers did not quite live up to his eloquence, many of them played admirable supporting roles. Two other American prosecuting lawyers, Dodd and Telford Taylor, made a valuable contribution. Dodd understood the conceptual paralysis which results from crime on a huge scale: 'Our mental processes are conditioned by our whole experience of living. We shudder at one bestial murder, we shrink from a few disgusting crimes, but when confronted with mass horror we find ourselves groping for adequate reaction. We simply cannot comprehend six million murders.'

He touched on the sinister ability of soldiers to kill in cold blood, with psychopathic absence of feeling: 'These were the men who sat on the edge of anti-tank ditches, cigarette in mouth, calmly shooting their naked victims in the back of the neck with their machine-guns. These were the men who, according to their own corpse accountants, murdered some two million men, women and children.'

And Dodd addresses us as well as the court when he deals with a Nazi assassination plot: 'This was white-collar homicide, custom-built for deceit, starched up with foreign office formality, bearing the cold sheen of Kaltenbrunner's SD and Gestapo, and supported and sustained by the outwardly respectable yoke of the professional army.' These tactics of murder live on, magnified a millionfold by nuclear weaponry.

Telford Taylor examined the German armed forces in terms of international law: 'The record is replete with testimony by or about commanders-in-chief who openly disagreed with Hitler on tactical matters, and who, as a result of such disagreements, were retired or allowed to resign. I note in passing that the record is notably barren of evidence that any commander-in-chief openly disagreed with Hitler so decisively on the issuance of orders which violated the laws of war, or who forced his retirement on account of these orders.

'The uncontested fact is,' he went on, 'that the Supreme Command of the Wehrmacht, under instructions from Hitler as its commander-in-chief, issued various orders which flagrantly contravened the rules of war. These included the orders for the shooting of commandos and political commissars, the orders to "pacify" the occupied territories of the Soviet Union by spreading terror, and others.'

Military killing becomes murder when it violates the law of war: 'We must not forget that to kill a defenceless prisoner of war is not only a violation of the rules of war. It is murder. And murder is not the less murder whether there is one victim, or fifty-five ... or

Ohlendorf's ninety thousand . . . . We have heard so much of mass extermination that we are likely to forget that simple murder is a capital offence. The laws of all civilized nations require that a man may go to some lengths to avoid associating himself with murder, whether as an accomplice or an accessory or co-conspirator . . . . Under German military law, a subordinate is liable to punishment for obeying the order of a superior if the subordinate knows that the order requires the commission of a general or a military crime.'

As with the West today, the main focus of Nazi policy was the Soviet Union. Telford Taylor told the court: 'On the Eastern front, the callous indifference of the German warlords to violations of the laws of war and to mass suffering and death produced results equally criminal and, because on a grander scale, far more horrible. The atrocities . . . were of such staggering enormity that they rather tax the power of comprehension. Why did all these things happen? Analysis will show, I believe, that this was not simple madness and bloodlust. On the contrary, there was both method and purpose. These atrocities occurred as the result of carefully calculated orders and directives.'

Telford Taylor examined the legal limits of military obedience: 'Is it really too much to ask that the commanders-in-chief should have refused to obey these orders? As soldiers they were bound to obey their supreme commander, but their own law and code says that it is the duty of every soldier to refuse to obey orders which he knows to be criminal. This is hard for the ordinary soldier acting under pistol-point orders from his lieutenant. It is far less difficult for the commander-in-chief, who is expected to be mature, educated, accustomed to responsibility and disciplined to be steady and unflinching when put to the test. Under their own law and according to the traditions they are so shameless as still to vaunt, the leaders were in duty bound to reject these orders. Their failure caused suffering and death to hundreds and thousands; their failure resulted directly in countless murders and other brutal crimes; and they, far more than the soldiers whom these orders led into crime, are the real criminals.'

As Telford Taylor put it: 'He who touches filth is not excused because he holds his nose.' He was aware that something was at stake in the Nuremberg Trial which extended far beyond that historical episode: 'something big and evil and durable . . . something older than anyone here . . . something that is not yet dead and that cannot be killed by a rifle or a hangman's noose. For nine months this courtroom has been a world of gas chambers, mountains of corpses, human-skin lamp-shades, shrunken skulls, freezing experiments, and bank vaults filled with gold teeth. It is vital to the conscience of the world that all the participants in these enormities shall be brought to justice. But these exhibits, gruesome as they are, do not lie at the heart of this case. Little will be gained by shaking the poisoned fruit from the tree. It is much harder to dig the tree up by the roots, but only this will, in the long run, do much good . . . . Militarism inevitably leads to cynical and wicked disregard of the rights of others and of the very elements of civilization.'

Telford Taylor, of all the lawyers at Nuremberg, was apprehensive about the future: 'German militarism, if it comes again, will not necessarily reappear under the aegis of Nazism. The German militarists will tie themselves to any man or party that offers expectation of a revival of German armed might. They will calculate deliberately and coldly. They will not be deterred by fanatical ideologies or hideous practices; they will take crime in their stride to reach the goal of German power and terror.'

He knew that modern war overlaps crime. 'This was not war,' he said, 'it was crime. This was not soldiering; it was savagery.'

Telford Taylor was to learn more of the poisoned tree of militarism, in the example of Vietnam. What he did not realize was that future militarism would become a more sophisticated plague, able to dispense with jackboots and bullying in favour of the soft sell. Denial and falsification of pain and power had been nurtured in the poisoned culture of the extermination camp, later to spread through modern industrial society in the form of a sanitized nuclear defence policy presented and accepted as 'insurance'. The final solution had grown up, to become the final insurance.

Our nuclear callousness echoes the accusation of the Soviet prosecution lawyer at Nuremberg, General Rudenko, when he quoted 'the instruction of . . . the defendant Keitel, of 16 September 1941, in which he ordered the German troops to "bear in mind that in the countries which are concerned, human life is absolutely of no value and that intimidating action is only effective by resorting to unusual cruelty"'. Such barbaric logic is now enshrined in a 'balance of terror' and its ever-present threat of extermination.

The British contribution to the prosecution case at Nuremberg was effective in its way, though less ambitious than the American. Sir Hartley Shawcross led the British team. According to Airey Neave, then a young legal officer and later a Conservative MP who would be assassinated by the IRA in a London bombing, 'Shaw-cross poured elegant scorn on these military men who had had no stomach for revolt. He tore into the rotten defences of the Nazi politicans like an avenging fury .... "These are our laws," he cried, "let them prevail".'[1]

Shawcross, like the others, has given us definitions of the law and its scope which are as instructive today as they were damning then: 'Every one of these men knew of these plans at one stage or another in their development. Every one of these men acquiesced in this technique, knowing full well what it must represent in terms of human life. How can any one of them now say he was not a party to common murder in its most ruthless form?' He tied the law which binds the citizen to that which limits government: 'Just as the individual is answerable for the common law exercise of his right of self-defence, so the State is answerable if it abuses its discretion, if it transforms "self-defence" into an instrument of conquest and lawlessness ....'

In the light of today's refusal of the courts to take serious note of international law his views on the matter are interesting: 'In England and the United States our courts invariably act on the view that the accepted customary rules of the Law of Nations are binding upon the subject and the citizen, and the position is essentially the same in most countries.'

As the Attorney-General of a British Government his statement has added meaning. And he confirmed the primary value of international law: 'If international law is to be applied at all, it must be superior to State law in this respect, that it must consider the legality of what is done by international and not by State tests.'

To those who pretend that the rules of war lack force because they were formulated before modern development of weaponry, he said: 'It is true that the lawyers and statesmen who, at The Hague and elsewhere in days gone by, built up the code of rules and the established customs by which the world has sought to mitigate the

---

[1] Airey Neave, *Nuremberg*, London 1978.

brutality of war and to protect from its extreme harshness those who were passive non-combatants, never dreamed of such wholesale and widespread slaughter. But murder does not cease to be murder merely because the victims are multiplied ten millionfold. Crimes do not cease to be criminal because they have a political motive.'

Shawcross emphasized with relentless logic the simple principles of humane behaviour which lie at the heart of the law: 'the principal war crime, in extent as in intensity, with which these men are charged is the violation of the most firmly established and least controversial of all the rules of warfare, namely, that non-combatants must not be made the direct object of hostile operations. What a mockery the Germans sought to make of the 4th Hague Convention on the laws and customs of war – a convention which merely formulated what was already a fundamental rule: "Family honour and rights, the lives of persons and private property as well as religious convictions and practices, must be respected."'

The law, he made clear, must protect life, not oppress it. He quoted the Englishman, John Westlake: 'The most distinguished of British international lawyers: "Laws are made for men and not creatures of the imagination, and they must not create or tolerate for them situations which are beyond endurance."'

The British number two was Sir David Maxwell Fyfe. He too stressed the organic, living quality of the law: 'The law is a living thing. It is not rigid and unalterable. Its purpose is to serve mankind, and it must change and grow to meet the changing needs of society. The needs of Europe today have no parallel in history.'

Our nuclear threats of extermination provide just such a parallel. Where are the lawyers of today with the common humanity and courage to speak out in this way?

As the other lawyers had done, Sir David exposed the plea of 'superior orders'. The Nazis, in his view, 'carried out orders which, on the admission of many of them, bit deep into the remnants of their conscience. They knew that they were doing what was wrong, but they now say, "*Befehl ist Befehl*" – an order is an order.'

He also quoted Shakespeare on the saturating effect of horror:

Blood and destruction shall be so in use
And dreadful objects so familiar
That mothers shall but smile when they behold
Their infants quartered with the hands of war;
All pity choked with custom of fell deeds.[1]

He concluded: 'It may be presumptuous for lawyers, who do not claim to be more than the cement of society, to speculate or even dream of what we wish to see in its place. But I give you the faith of a lawyer. Some things are surely universal: tolerance, decency, kindliness. It is because we believe that there must be a clearance before such qualities will flourish in peace that we ask you to condemn the organization of evil.'

If the lawyers of today are silent before the question of civilization's survival it may be that in them, too, pity and its protective laws are 'choked with custom of fell deeds'.

Among the many continuing ironies of the Nuremberg Trial is the role played by the German defence lawyers. Their excusing argument foreshadows what is so widely heard in today's corridors of power. There was the line that international law represents fine ideals which are, alas, no longer practical. Or, as Admiral Doenitz's lawyer, Kranzbuehler, put it: 'According to classical international law the destruction of combatants was a legal goal of war actions but not the destruction of non-combatants. In view of the development of the last war one may be doubtful whether this classical theory still has any validity.'

Dr Exner, General Jodl's defence lawyer, claimed that training, loyalty, obedience combined to make autonomous action impossible. The generals carried out 'the military preparations', but 'it was Hitler who pressed the button to set the machine in motion'. Had Jodl resisted, 'he would not actually have been shot, but his sanity would have been doubted'. And 'even if he had recognised the war as illegal', he would have been between the devil and the deep blue sea, his oath of loyalty and the pressures of the law. It was not the role of a mere soldier, even though a general, to raise 'objections based on International Law', but the 'duty of the responsible State authorities'.

Dr Steinbauer, defending Seyss-Inquart, diverted attention

[1] Mark Antony in *Julius Caesar*.

from his client's crimes by pointing to the 'many innocent war victims on the German side, women and children who have fallen victim to the terror attacks which violated International Law, in Freiburg, in Cologne, in Dresden, in Hamburg, Berlin and Vienna'. Dr Seidl's defence of the strange Rudolf Hess implied that International Law should not be applied until there was a world order 'which guarantees the indispensable rights of all nations and which assures in particular the satisfaction of the legitimate claims of every nation to a proportionate share of the material wealth of the world'. Thus international law is too good for the present, belonging either to the past or the future.

The German defence lawyers exposed, unintentionally, the curious Jekyll and Hyde quality of the law in Nazi Germany. Now you see it, now you don't. Law officers inspected concentration camps to root out corruption. SS Reserve Judge Morgen was one of them. He told the SS defence lawyer, Dr Pelckmann: 'I studied law at the Universities of Frankfurt on the Main, Rome, Berlin; at the Académie de Droit International at The Hague and the Institute for World Economy and Ocean Traffic in Kiel . . . . Before the war I was a judge at the Landgericht in Stettin . . . I had specialized in International Law . . . . '

Europe's finest legal training produced a mind capable of sniffing out financial corruption in a camp whose business was mass murder. Such schizoid behaviour is still with us, comfortably installed at the highest levels of the law, a Kafkaesque fixture, it seems, of every modern industrial State.

Even more closely entwined with today's rationalizations of crime was the assertion that defendants believed Hitler's repeated commitment to peace. Dr Servatius, defence lawyer of the Nazi leadership, quoted Hitler's speech at a Nuremberg Party Rally in 1936: 'During these long years we had no other prayer than "Lord give our people domestic peace and grant and preserve for them peace with other nations". In our generation we experienced so much of fighting that it is understandable if we long for peace . . . . We wish to care for the future of our nation's children, and to work for the future, not only to safeguard their lives but also to make them easier. So much misfortune lies behind us that we have only one request to address a merciful and benevolent Providence: spare our children what we had to suffer! We desire nothing but peace and tranquillity for our work.'[1]

Such blameless sentiments, co-existing with a will to murder and destroy, were as devilish a cocktail then as they are today. Perhaps the closest anyone came to defining this problem of sanitized evil was the defence lawyer of the Gestapo, Dr Merkel, when he quoted Goethe: "Demonocracy is a power which, though it does not oppose the moral world order, nullifies it." '[2] Looking around us today, behind a moralizing busyness lies abundant evidence of such paralysis.

Nuremberg and the other war crimes trials did indeed represent the 'rare moment' mentioned by Justice Jackson, when a major historical disruption releases a new vitality and vision. With few exceptions, the lawyers of the four prosecuting powers rose to the occasion. They were not simply enforcing international law but defending civilization itself. If the law could not encompass the huge scope of Nazi crime it would leave humanity defenceless in the face of its own murderous energies. In sharp contrast to their successors of today, these men did not plead the weakness of the law, the overriding power of the State, the helplessness of the individual, the fallen nature of mankind. They extracted every last drop of vitality from international laws which had grown dusty with disuse in diplomatic files. They stressed the common sense basis of the law, pointed to the inescapable legal duties of citizen and soldier, named murder for what it is, and gave no ground to State power. They remain a living proof that lawyers are not obliged to serve as weathercocks of privilege.

But as weathermen know, highs are followed by lows. The decline of the lawyer's role began at Nuremberg itself, in the selective angle of legal vision on display. Dr Steinbauer was right. Innocent men, women and children were killed by the tens of thousands in Allied bombing. The blind eye turned towards those crimes remained shut, slowly transforming the emphatic justice of Nuremberg into the Nuclear Cyclops of today. The Afrikaans writer, Laurens van der Post, describes this problem: 'European man is fast forgetting to balance the fixed outward stare with a questioning inward glance, and therein lies our great and growing danger.'[3]

[1] *International Military Tribunal Vol. XXII.*
[2] Ibid.
[3] Laurens van der Post, *Dark Eye in Africa*, London 1955.

We are, he warned, 'confined in a cage and threatened with annihilation by the one-eyed giant we have made of ourselves and our age'.[1] Deaf to these larger truths we have allowed the law to become gaoler instead of friend. Lawyers have colluded with this futile process.

So the roots of international law and war, carefully nurtured at Nuremberg, have been torn up and left to wither in the filing cabinets of State power. As a sop to public concern, periodic additions are made to these laws, and they are briefly paraded before the public as proof of life. But robbed of their commonsense roots they become remote, inert, a plaything for professors. Their development has become as fictitious as their worth. Lawyers have conspired to rob the law of its central strength, thus undermining their own role. They behave like a slash-and-burn peasant who slowly commits suicide by creating a wasteland.

Instead of fighting to save the law, and themselves, from decay, our lawyers prefer to turn their backs on the void separating their court-room lives from the threat of annihilation. The Genocide Convention of 1948, designed to ward off any repetition of the Jewish holocaust, deems it a crime to kill or persecute 'in whole or in part, any national, ethnical, racial or religious group'. Far from using this convention as a means of prosecuting nuclear threats of annihilation, lawyers protest that genocide requires an 'intent', and that nuclear threats are defensive and lack intent. At Nuremberg, imperfections were a spur to justice. Now they are a pretext for inaction.

Likewise, the Geneva Conventions of 1949, and the Additional Protocol 1 of 1977, fail to inspire our lawyers. All very fine, they murmur wearily, but not one of these fine laws protecting non-combatants in war makes any mention of nuclear weapons. What is more, they add, there were 'understandings' during the preparatory work on those laws which excluded nuclear weapons from their scope. So the letter of the law is not to be taken literally, because of those unwritten 'understandings'. And the spirit is dead anyway, because the most elementary principle of the law, protection of the helpless, is so selective as to be absurd. Having proved by dissection that the body of the law is indeed dead, our lawyers turn away from such unpleasant peripheral things, back to the

[1] Ibid.

courtroom jousting which is their pride and joy. Like their counterparts in Nazi Germany they know on which side their bread is buttered, and who is the chef.

As always, thankfully, there are exceptions. In Britain and the United States there are small groups of lawyers concerned to enforce minimum international laws against all forms of mass destruction. The British 'Lawyers for Nuclear Disarmament', formed in 1982, has the support of about 300 lawyers and academics, a tiny fraction of the profession. They hold that any use of nuclear weapons is illegal, and that their possession and threat may also be illegal. They publish educational pamphlets and have appeared in court on a few occasions on behalf of peace protesters. These attempts to raise issues of international law in British courts have been thwarted by a judicial response which considers any such initiatives an assault on 'Crown prerogative'. But as one lawyer, Geoffrey Bindman, has said: 'The peace movement has international law on its side and governments should not be allowed to forget it.'[1]

The weakness of this group is the same as that which affects any professional group which proposes radical reform reflecting on its own role in society. Trained to exaggerate the value of what is said and done, at the expense of what is felt and believed, lawyers become victims of their own simplistic vision. To condemn as illegal the most fundamental policy of any government, defence, is to raise basic questions about the nature of government and society, including the law and its mediators. To do this while carrying on the normal working routine of a courtroom lawyer is to ensure failure. To change the metaphor and adopt an Arab view: 'the dogs bark but the caravan moves on'.

The American counterpart of Lawyers for Nuclear Disarmament is called the Lawyers' Committee on Nuclear Policy, based in New York. Its aims and methods are similar to its British cousin, although American lawyers tend to be more outspoken. Elliot L. Meyrowitz, a lawyer and executive director of this group, is an eloquent spokesman. He points to the irony of the American legal profession's long silence on this issue, in contrast to its long tradition of involvement in social issues. He states that 'a review of the basic principles and documents of international law supports

---

[1] *Guardian*, 14 February 1983.

the conclusion that the threat or use of nuclear weapons pursuant to a doctrine of massive retaliation, mutual assured destruction, counterforce or limited nuclear war is illegal under international law'.[1]

Nuclear weapons, in his view, are 'not only incompatible with the fundamental rules of international law and prevailing morality, but also the development, possession and deployment of nuclear weapons subvert the traditions and structure of democratic society. When the essential foundation for our security rests upon a logic that has the potential for destroying our population, democracy no longer exists. The discretion to launch a nuclear war gives our political leaders a control over human destiny that no tyrant – however despotic – has ever claimed. In short, the very nature of nuclear war destroys all the values that the law obliges us to preserve.'[2]

But as usual, when it comes to remedial action, the options presented are few: meetings, seminars, articles and 'selective litigation that raises the illegality of nuclear weapons as a defence'.[3] As we have seen, tactics which assume a high degree of rationality are self-defeating in the context of a nuclear nightmare. They do not work because they do not comprehend the nature of a nuclear addiction rooted in emotional trauma. Not even the sweetest reason will make a tiger change its diet.

Tougher and more surprising is the stand taken by two American lawyers who wrote a report on the legal implications of US nuclear defence policies for the Rand Corporation, a conservative research body which acts on behalf of various Government departments.[4] This study was supported by a grant from the no less conservative Ford Foundation. Its main conclusions must suffice at this stage of our investigation. We will return to it later.

In their preface to the report, Builder and Graubard offer the following counsel: 'To those who seek the control of arms under international law, "Take care that you have not limited your theory of weapons use to that which is unlawful under international law".' And 'to those lawmakers who commit the nation to observe

---

[1] *Californian Lawyer*, Vol. II No. 4, April 1982.
[2] Ibid.
[3] Ibid.
[4] Builder and Graubard, *The International Law of Armed Conflict: Implications for the concept of Mutual Assured Destruction*, USA 1982.

international law: "Take care that you do not resort to theories of
weapons use that are contrary to international law as a basis for
rejecting otherwise reasonable efforts to acquire more discriminating and militarily effective weapons."

'The concept of Assured Destruction,' the authors warn, 'when
deliberately applied to policies for the acquisition and use of
nuclear weapons, appears to be directly opposed to the most
fundamental principles found in the international law of armed
conflict . . . . Even as a reprisal,' they say, ' . . . the concept of
Assured Destruction is prohibited if it includes deliberate attacks
on the civilian population.'[1]

Builder and Graubard describe how defence policy evolved over
the years, departing from international law 'in many small steps . . .
until we are now confronted with an enormous gulf'. 'If the basic
thrust of our policies,' they conclude, 'and the intent of international law are obviously opposed in their plain language interpretation, something is wrong which cannot be made right by theories
of possible exception'.[2]

Had this damning analysis of superpower illegality been
published under dictatorial rule, as in Nazi Germany, the authors
would have met the same brutality which stifled German legal
protests. It is a measure of the real but restricted scope of American
freedom that these two lawyers remain at large, unheeded. Once
again, the nuclear nightmare shrugs off rational exposure, because
it can depend on irrational support. Only rational action, accurately aimed, will drive away the necrophiliac fog which smothers
the law.

A tiny percentage of the legal profession in Western countries,
then, has dared to expose the illegality of nuclear weapons. Even
this small number of lawyers has done little more, so far, than bark
discreetly at its master. By continuing to ply their lucrative trade in
the courts while confining criticism to the weekend, they ensure
ineffectiveness. Their actions belie their words. They have the
imagination, some of them, to recognize the disastrous implications of illegality, but when it comes to action involving a
response as comprehensive as the problem, they are as paralyzed as
any other social group.

The two-dimensional, rationalist approach to law and peace in

[1] Ibid.
[2] Ibid.

this century has been tried and found wanting. Out of sixty-seven Nobel Peace Prize winners in the years up to 1976, including fifty-six men, three women and eight institutions, twenty have been lawyers (including the Institute of International Law).[1] Yet far from checking the nuclear arms race, the legal profession fell on its face at the hurdle after Nuremberg. It became the creature of a civilization drunk with blood and terrified by its nuclear shadow, preferring to exploit rather than uphold the law.

Yet in the gloom of our self-made dungeon, with wits both sharpened and dulled by greed and the balance of terror, our lawyer companions can contrast their sorry state with the example of those who lit the court room at Nuremberg with their humane vision of a world committed to minimum civilized law. And they can contemplate with pride and shame the example of those few German lawyers who accepted that humane law costs much more than statements of protest dashed off at weekends. As long as lawyers prefer to feed off rather than uphold the law they will continue to undermine their professional integrity by obstructing what they claim to serve.

[1] From Tony Gray, *Champions of Peace*, London 1976.

Chapter Five

The Judge's Tale

'Thieves for their robbery have authority
When judges steal themselves'
– 'Measure for Measure,' William Shakespeare

'I view with apprehension the attitude of judges who on a
mere question of construction when face to face with claims
involving the liberty of the subject show themselves more
executive-minded than the executive'
– Lord Atkin

'Judges expatiating on their impotence make a sorry sound'
– editorial in *The Times*

Judges, like governments, have a vested interest in the stability of
the State. Without this they cannot function and there will be
neither law nor order. So how do the judges stand in relation to the
force which, more than any other, threatens to destroy this stability, nuclear weapons of mass destruction? Do they seek to uphold
and enforce young and vulnerable laws of armed conflict, with the
same determined energy as drove the judges from four countries
(Great Britain, USSR, USA, France) who presided at the Nuremberg war crimes trial? Do they seek public support for laws which
are the thread upon which the life of civilization hangs?

They are accused of doing neither of these things. They, like the
professors and lawyers from whom they come, have shown during
the whole span of the nuclear era that they cannot bring themselves
to confront this challenge. Whenever the opportunity has presented itself (with the exception of the Shimoda case in Japan,
discussed in Chapter Eight), they have turned a blind eye to the law
and a deaf ear to those who sought its aid. By choosing to align
themselves on this issue with government rather than law they have
demonstrated a political allegiance which subverts their own authority and the rule of law. The judges have become agents of our

nuclear confusion, their pretensions as suspect as that of any social group which evades its main responsibilities.

This is a harsh description of a fundamental problem. When a judge cannot be trusted to uphold the law on a matter of primary importance, there is a smell of chaos. The charge against them is simple. The whole intention and direction of the laws of armed conflict, in spirit and in detail, seek to restrict and contain military violence. As authorities on this law have stated throughout the century, its essence is an outright prohibition against attacks directed at non-combatants and protected persons. Thousands of war criminals have been executed and imprisoned for violating these laws, many of them at the hands of British courts and British judges.

It would be reasonable to expect that the advent of weapons of indiscriminate mass destruction would attract the close concern and interest of men and women paid handsome salaries to enforce the law. It would be reasonable to expect from the judiciary, at the very least, a searching investigation of nuclear threats in relation to the law. As a result, they would seek the ear of government to warn of any violation of the law, actual or proposed. None of this has happened. Instead, there has been a mixture of silence and evasion. On the most important issue ever to face any civilization, its survival or annihilation, the judges have nothing to offer except the washing of hands. As guardians of the law they have a lot to answer for. Their case requires careful scrutiny.

But judges have not always been elective mutes on such matters. The post-war trials of German war criminals offered judges as well as lawyers an experience of enforcing the international laws of armed conflict. Vietnam provided a more recent example. As we have already seen, the main Nuremberg Trial of leading Nazis was living proof of the law's potency, once the will to enforce it was made plain. In the words of a conservative British journalist, Bernard Levin: 'The Nuremberg Trial, for all its limitations and for all the dashed hopes that it raised, was a true turning-point in history, the blood of the murdered millions cried from the ground for requital, and the judges of the International Military Tribunal did true deliverance make.'[1]

The Nuremberg Tribunal consisted of a panel of eight judges,

[1] *Observer*, 20 November 1983.

two from each prosecuting nation, presided over by Sir Geoffrey Lawrence. Norman Birkett was the other British judge. The relevance of Nuremberg to our nuclear age lies not so much in its surface detail as its active judicial intervention in the military behaviour of a government and its agents. The judiciary of Britain, more than most, is sensitive to the influence of legal precedent. British law is bound by past judicial decisions even more than by written statute. The experience and decisions of Nuremberg are the writing on the wall of the modern court, to be taken with the utmost seriousness.

The Nuremberg judges were given an intensive experience of duplicity and crime by a modern European State. The defendants tried on a cloak of excuses which is uncomfortably familiar today. The actions of Nazi Germany were based on self-defence; personal actions were the result of orders from higher authority; any crimes committed were the work of someone else, somewhere else; it was all Hitler's fault because only he exercised real power; and so on. As the Court complained, there were crimes but no criminals.

'It was contended for the defendants' said Maître Falco, a French judge, during the final judgment, 'that the attack upon the USSR was justified because the Soviet Union was contemplating an attack against Germany, and making preparations to that end. It is impossible to believe that this view was ever honestly entertained.'[1] Yet today, Soviet intentions are viewed by the West with hardly less suspicion.

An American judge, Biddle, made it clear in his part of the judgment that the law was not a feeble expression of wishful-thinking, a thing of shreds and patches, nor was the court's Charter a legal invention: 'The Charter is not an arbitrary exercise of power on the part of the victorious nations, but in the view of the Tribunal, we will be shown, it is the expression of International Law existing at the time of its creation; and to that extent is itself a contribution to International Law.'

He sought to emphasize the strengths of the law, not its flaws: 'In interpreting the words of the Pact [the Kellogg-Briand Pact, Paris, 1928], it must be remembered that International Law is not the product of an international legislature, and that such international agreements as the Pact of Paris have to do with general principles of

[1] *International Military Tribunal*, Vol. XXII. All quoted material up to p. 93 comes from this source unless another source is indicated.

law, and not with administrative matters of procedure. The law of war is to be found not only in treaties, but in the customs and practices of States, which gradually obtained universal recognition, and from the general principles of justice applied by jurists and practised by military courts. This law is not static, but by continual adaptation follows the needs of a changing world. Indeed, in many cases treaties do no more than express and define for more accurate reference the principles of law already existing.'

The judges of today know that the laws of armed conflict have been considerably strengthened since Nuremberg, thanks in part to the powerful and positive impetus provided by Biddle and his colleagues. It is not the law which has become static but those whose duty it is to enforce it. Enforcement of the law concerns the individual as much as the State, according to Biddle: 'It was submitted that International Law is concerned with sovereign States and provides no punishment for individuals; and further, that where the act in question is an act of State, those who carry it out are not personally responsible, but are protected by the doctrine of the sovereignty of the State. In the opinion of the Tribunal, both these submissions must be rejected. That International Law imposes duties and liabilities upon individuals as well as upon States has long been recognized. . . . Crimes against International Law are committed by men, not by abstract entities, and only by punishing individuals who commit such crimes can the provisions of International Law be enforced. . . .

'The principle of International Law,' he went on, 'which, under certain circumstances protects the representatives of a State, cannot be applied to acts which are condemned as criminal by International Law. . . . Article 7 of the Charter expressly declares: "The official position of defendants, whether as Heads of State, or responsible officials in government departments, shall not be considered as freeing them from responsibility, or mitigating punishment". . . .

'On the other hand, the very essence of the Charter is that individuals have international duties which transcend the national obligations of obedience imposed by the individual State. He who violates the laws of war cannot obtain immunity while acting in pursuance of the authority of the State if the State in authorising action moves outside its competence under International Law.'

This judgment goes to the heart of our dilemma in an age when mass destruction has been 'legitimized' by the nuclear powers. The same four states which accepted and enforced the Nuremberg judgment now seek to evade its plain logic. Far from warning their nuclear operatives to carry out 'international duties which transcend the national obligation of obedience imposed by the individual State', they are ordered to do the opposite. The humanitarian restraint of the law has been deliberately withdrawn by these nuclear powers from weapons of mass destruction. Their behaviour recalls the loyalties of the SS concentration camp guard who considers the law to be relevant to everything except his victims. Our judges have proved no more willing to draw attention to this calculated evasion of the law than were their Nazi counterparts who administered German law with meticulous care within the criminal context of Nazi rule. No greater scandal can afflict the law than this judicial indifference to its most vital principles.

The judgment deals directly with the plea of superior orders. 'The Charter,' said Biddle, 'specifically provides in Article 8: "The fact that the defendant acted pursuant to order of his Government or of a superior shall not free him from responsibility, but may be considered in mitigation of punishment."

'The provisions of this Article are in conformity with the law of all nations. That a soldier was ordered to kill or torture in violation of the International Law of war has never been regarded as a defence to such acts of brutality, though, as the Charter here provides, the order may be urged in mitigation of the punishment.'

Our judges have no reason, then, to be unaware of this principle of personal responsibility, yet they remain content to see it mocked in the operating procedures of nuclear weaponry. Repeatedly, as they must be aware, nuclear operatives have responded to questions about their apocalyptic role by asserting that it is made bearable by the fact of State responsibility. The regular psychiatric tests given to such men are premised on the absence, not presence, of personal responsibility. It is assumed, probably correctly, that no 'normal' human being can accept a personal responsibility for incinerating millions of strangers and much of the world. Judges, usually so quick to expose contradictions of logic and law, remain silent, face averted.

The Nuremberg judgment exposed the criminal implications of 'total war'. 'The evidence relating to War Crimes,' said the second American judge, Parker, 'has been overwhelming in its volume and its detail. . . . There can be no doubt that the majority of them arose from the Nazi conception of "total war", with which the aggressive wars were waged. For in this conception of "total war", the moral ideas underlying the conventions which seek to make war more humane are no longer regarded as having force or validity. Everything is made subordinate to the overmastering dictates of war. Rules, regulations, assurances and treaties all alike are of no moment; and so, freed from the restraining influence of International Law, the aggressive war is conducted by the Nazi leaders in the most barbaric way. . . . Cities and towns and villages were wantonly destroyed without military justification or necessity.'

Total war does not cease to be a crime when mass destruction becomes universal in scope.

Judge Parker quotes the 'correctly stated' interpretation of international law by the head of the German military intelligence, Admiral Canaris, when he opposed Hitler's orders to mistreat and murder Soviet prisoners of war. On 15 September 1941, the Admiral stated: 'The Geneva Convention for the treatment of prisoners of war is not binding in the relationship between Germany and the USSR [USSR was not a signatory]. Therefore only the principles of general International Law on the treatment of prisoners of war apply. Since the 18th century these have been gradually established along the lines that war captivity is neither revenge nor punishment, but solely protective custody, the only purpose of which is to prevent the prisoners of war from further participation in the war. This principle was developed in accordance with the view held by all armies that it is contrary to military tradition to kill or injure helpless people. . . .'

'To kill or injure helpless people' is still prohibited. Our judges know that this principle of military restraint is encoded in the Manuals of Military Law of all modern States. For the citizens of the West today it is salutary to note Judge Parker's final comment: 'The murder and ill-treatment of civilian populations reached its height in the treatment of the citizens of the Soviet Union and Poland.' This is not to imply that there is any modern desire for mass murder, just a blank acceptance of its possibility. The SS, too, regarded their murderous exploits as an onerous rather than satisfying duty.

One of the Soviet judges at Nuremberg, General Nikitchenko,

confirmed that international law is a process which acquires added strength from established custom. Referring to the Hague Convention, he said: 'The rules of land warfare expressed in the convention undoubtedly represented an advance over International Law at the time of their adoption. The convention expressly stated that it was an attempt "to revise the general customs and laws of war" which it thus recognized to be then existing, but by 1939 these rules laid down in the convention were recognized by all civilized nations, and were regarded as being declaratory of the laws and customs of war which are referred to in Article 6(b) of the Charter.'

As far as we know, Soviet judges today are as reluctant as ours to apply such positive reasoning to the law and nuclear weapons.

The Nuremberg judgment offers a clear view of the law and military behaviour. Many of Germany's officers, said the President of the Tribunal, Sir Geoffrey Lawrence, 'have been a disgrace to the honourable profession of arms ... many of these men have made a mockery of the soldier's oath of obedience to military orders. When it suits their defence they say they had to obey; when confronted with Hitler's brutal crimes, which are shown to have been within their general knowledge, they say they disobeyed. The truth is they actively participated in all these crimes, or sat silent and acquiescent, witnessing the commissions of crimes on a scale larger and more shocking than the world has ever had the misfortune to know.'

Not one of Sir Geoffrey's modern successors has asked the leading military figures of our nuclear States to justify their obedience to policies of threatened mass destruction. The latter may note the Soviet General Nikitchenko's observation that 'in spite of the manifest violations of international law and customs of warfare', these did not 'provoke any protest on the part of the higher staff officers.' Private conversations with middle-ranking officers of British army and air force indicate extensive ignorance of the laws of armed conflict and their history.

The Nuremberg judgment, despite its vigorous application of these laws, gives us a hint of subsequent evasion. In his judgment on Admiral Doenitz, the French judge De Vabres told the court: 'In view of all the facts proved and in particular of an order of the British Admiralty announced on the 8th May, 1940, according to which all vessels should be sunk on sight in the Skagerrak, and the answer to interrogatories by Admiral Nimitz stating that unrestricted submarine warfare was carried on in the Pacific Ocean by the United States from the first day that nation entered the war, the sentence of Doenitz is not assessed on the ground of his breaches of the International Law of submarine warfare.'

Allied law-breaking thus served to excuse Nazi crime. Selective application of the law at Nuremberg seemed necessary, even inevitable at the time. But it established a distorted vision which has grown over the years into a monumental evasion of responsibility and law.

Sir Geoffrey Lawrence, who had earlier described the trial as 'unique in the history of jurisprudence . . . and of supreme importance to millions of people all over the world',[1] later said the aim of the trial was to 'bring home to the German people and the peoples of the world the depths of infamy to which the pursuit of total warfare had brought Germany'.[2] It is the exclusive mention of Germany which undermines the principle described. Unwittingly, Sir Geoffrey handed his successors a ready excuse for dodging the universal meaning of Nuremberg. Total warfare is no less infamous when conducted by any other nation. Judges trained to apply legal principles with impartial energy are not expected to seek such excuses.

What is undeniable is that the judicial path leading from Nuremberg has been downward, into and across a black ravine and up onto a plateau of inertia. The chasm between is vast. West Germany still grapples, many years after Nuremberg, with a judiciary rooted in Nazi acquiescence. The rest of us must find ways of waking up a judiciary which has succeeded in learning only the wrong lessons from the most famous trial in history. It is their duty to assimilate, develop and apply the principles of Nuremberg, not wash their hands of them as if they were just a means of punishing Nazis.

How is it, then, that our judges have failed to learn from Nuremberg as they claim to learn from other legal precedent? The lack of a modern international criminal court to replace the Nuremberg Tribunal is no excuse. Failure to catch a criminal has never been accepted as a reason to abandon the law. Judges are capable of voicing their opinion on important legal issues, and often do, with or without appropriate courts and procedures. They

[1] Neave, op. cit.
[2] Bradley F. Smith, *Reaching Judgment at Nuremberg*, London 1977.

do not always shy away from exerting influence. Some even court publicity. They are citizens, after all, with a range of aims and opinions.

Some case studies will help to clarify this problem. Two concern nuclear weapons and the law. They all help to define judicial understanding of the 'national interest' and defence policy. The first case is known as Chandler versus the Director of Public Prosecutions (1962), and concerns a demonstration at a nuclear air base in southern England by a radical part of the peace movement known as the Committee of 100. The latter had the backing of several well known figures in British life, including Bertrand Russell.

The aim of the demonstration was to block the entrances and runway of the US Air Force base, by means of a sit-down protest. Six of the organisers were charged under the Official Secrets Act, 1911, with conspiring to incite others to violate the law 'for a purpose prejudicial to the safety or interests of the State'. It would seem logical for defendants in such a case to present their own understanding of how their actions might affect such interests. But their scope for this was severely restricted by the judge. He ruled that no evidence would be admitted which related to the ultimate purpose of the defendants in doing what was done. They were prevented from calling expert witness on the possession or use of nuclear weapons by the State, and from cross-examination of the Crown's experts on that issue. This ruling guaranteed the success of the prosecution because it left the Crown as the sole judge of what is or is not 'prejudicial to the safety or interests of the State'.

The Attorney-General, a Minister of the Government, led the prosecution and told the jury that it was not a political case. He thus sought to cloak the safety and interests of the State in a politically neutral, patriotic dress which could not be questioned. Yet it is a matter of plain fact that every government reflects distinctive values, which inevitably colour its every decision and policy. The judge accepted the Attorney-General's view of the matter, thus tipping the scales of justice against the defendants. He played a part with distinct political implications.

Despite the judge's ruling, some of the defendants managed to make telling points, in several of which were echoes of the Nuremberg Trial. Patrick Pottle asked the RAF Director of Operations at the Air Ministry, Magill: 'Air Commodore, is there any official order you cannot accept?'

Judge: Is there what?

Pottle: Is there any official order from the Government that the Air Commodore would say to himself, 'I accept orders, I am a servant of the Government, but on this particular occasion I cannot accept this order'?

Judge: He is an officer in the forces of Her Majesty.

Pottle: So actually there is no order you would not accept?

Magill: It is my duty to carry out any order that is given to me.

Pottle: Would you press the button that you know is going to annihilate millions of people?

Magill: If the circumstances so demanded it I would.

Pottle: Would you slit the throats of all the two-year-old children in this country, Air Commodore?

Judge: I think you must stop all that.

Pottle: I feel it was comparable with the effects of nuclear weapons. It was the same as saying he would press the button to explode the nuclear bomb. Have you read the summing-up of the judge at the Eichmann trial?

Judge: Where are we getting to?[1]

Pottle managed later to quote the Eichmann judge's judgment: 'The very contention of applying the defence of the act of State to the extermination of helpless people is an insult to justice'. But most of his defence was ruled irrelevant. The Air Commodore's replies and the judge's interjections indicated either a complete lack of awareness of the Nuremberg Trial judgment and the laws of war, or a wilful refusal to acknowledge them.

Another defendant, Michael Randle, tried to make use of international law in his defence. He told the court: 'There were people in Germany during the Nazi regime who were ordered to commit what have since been defined as crimes against humanity. They would have been going against the law of their country by disobeying their order. I feel they had a moral duty to disobey that order in that situation.'[2]

Again the judge revealed his ignorance of the Nuremberg principles when he said, 'As far as I can see, it means this, doesn't it, if you disagree with the law, you break it?'[3]

---

[1] Transcript of trial, Chandler v. DPP, 1962.
[2] Ibid.
[3] Ibid.

Unfortunately, from the perspective of today, Randle and his lawyer lacked a detailed grasp of international law and tended to stress the laws being broken rather than the laws they were trying to uphold. This allowed the prosecution to harp on the law-breaking of the defendants and distract attention from official violation of the law. In his closing speech the Attorney-General said of Randle: 'What he said amounted, did it not, to this: "We have decided what laws we broke, after very careful consideration . . . and where we think fit we break the law." It is really an admission of rather an astonishing character.'[1]

In his summing-up at the end of the trial, the judge said: 'If you can find it in your conscience to come to the conclusion that the purpose was not prejudicial, or if you have any reasonable doubt about the matter, then you should acquit all the accused. If on the other hand you are satisfied so that you can feel sure that the purpose was prejudicial to the safety and interests of the State, then you should convict, and you will, of course, bear in mind the evidence which Air Commodore Magill has given, and it is for you, and you alone, to say whether you accept that evidence as correct. If you do, you see, it means that the air base was an essential part of the defence of this country, and that those aeroplanes on it had a vital part to play in that defence, and that any interference with the ability of those aeroplanes to take off at any moment would seriously affect their operational effect.'[2]

The jury took four hours to reach their decision of guilty, and added a plea for leniency. The defendants were sentenced to eighteen months imprisonment, except the only woman involved, who received twelve months.

In our assessment of the judge's role in the age of nuclear weapons, what is of most concern in this case is the judge's evident acceptance of the government's assessment of the 'interests of the State' as having legal as well as political validity. His standpoint was almost the same as the Attorney-General's and he did not attempt to explore the meaning of the defendants' actions in terms of the laws used sixteen years earlier to hang and imprison the Nazi leaders.

An appeal was later heard by five Law Lords of the House of Lords, who upheld the judgment. One of them, Lord Devlin,

[1] Ibid.
[2] Ibid.

added an important qualification: 'The fact to be proved is the existence of a purpose prejudicial to the State – not a purpose which "appears to the Crown" to be prejudicial to the State. . . . There is no rule of common law that whenever questions of national security are being considered by any Court for any purpose, it is what the Crown thinks to be necessary or expedient in fact. . . . Consequently the Crown's opinion as to what is or is not prejudicial in that case is just as inadmissible as the Appellants.'[1]

This minority opinion appears to give the judiciary the responsibility of establishing what is 'in fact' prejudicial or not.

Lord Devlin had a healthy scepticism about official impartiality. 'Men can exaggerate the extent of their interests,' he said during the same appeal hearing on 12 July 1962, 'and so can the Crown. The servants of the Crown, like other men animated by the highest motives, are capable of formulating a policy *ad hoc* so as to prevent the citizen from doing something that the Crown does not want him to do. It is the duty of the Courts to be as alert now as they have always been to prevent abuse of the prerogative.' But despite this robust assertion, the case of Chandler versus the Director of Public Prosecutions remains sad evidence of the selective amnesia which has struck the British judiciary and the world at large since Nuremberg. International law, the mooring rope of civilization, had been allowed to fray while governments and the weaponry of mass destruction conspired to hold the world, and the law, to ransom. Judges did next to nothing to impede or correct this process.

It is doubly ironic, then, that Lord Devlin concluded his comments by saying: 'It is the duty of this House to see that men and women who have a creed they want to preach in no case pay any penalty for their faith – unless they have taken themselves out of the protection of the law by doing that which the law forbids.'

At Nuremberg, the defendants had pleaded that obedience to the laws of Nazi Germany absolved them from international law. They were convicted. In the Chandler case the defendants pleaded that obedience to international law absolved them from minor violations of State law. They too were convicted. It was the judge, the Government and the Air Commodore who had 'taken themselves out of the protection of the law', by their narrow interpretation of its scope and purpose.

[1] Quoted in Christopher Driver, *The Disarmers*, London 1964.

A more recent case offers further evidence of judicial distortion of the law. On 8 November 1983 Judge Mynett heard an appeal at Oxford Crown Court by eleven men and women against their conviction for obstruction of the highway outside the USAF nuclear air base at Upper Heyford, while protesting against nuclear weapons. The defendants appealed on the grounds that they were lawfully entitled to obstruct the highway. They cited the Criminal Law Act, 1967, which says in Section 3 that a person may use such force as is reasonable in the circumstances to prevent a crime. A few months after this hearing a young man stabbed a burglar who had broken into his flat. The judge in this case told the jury: 'It is clear the person involved was committing a crime, and the defendant was lawfully trying to arrest him or prevent the commission of a crime.'[1] But at Oxford, Judge Mynett rejected this defence. Before announcing his decision the judge told the appellants: 'Each member of this court is deeply conscious of the horrors that necessarily would result from a war in which nuclear weapons were used. No member of this court doubts the complete sincerity of the appellants in opposing the presence of nuclear weapons in this country.'[2]

This recognition of sincerity has become for today's judges what the touching of gloves is for boxers before a fight, a glimpse of velvet before the iron fist of the law is applied. It is a means of acknowledging and simultaneously dismissing morality. 'I accept that your beliefs are genuine, but I am not prepared to let this court be used as some sort of forum for your beliefs. I am here only to enforce the law,' said the magistrate to peace protesters arrested for a 'breach of the peace' while praying on the steps of the Ministry of Defence in London in 1984. A judge who convicted a Church of England minister in 1983 for refusing to pay tax to buy nuclear weapons, told him: 'This is a court of law, and not a court of conscience.' The moral imperative of the law, so proudly evident at Nuremberg, has dwindled to vanishing point in the eyes of our judges, as far as world responsibilities are concerned.

Judge Mynett spent the bulk of his judgment expatiating on the fact, which nobody had denied, that the highway had indeed been obstructed in the vicinity of the air base. When it came to the heart of the matter, whether there was a lawful purpose for this obstruc-

[1] *Daily Telegraph*, 5 April 1984.
[2] Appeal transcript.

tion, he dismissed the appellants' claim with scorn. It was their submission, he said, 'that the use of nuclear weapons under any circumstances whatsoever, and, indeed, probably their mere presence in this country at Upper Heyford where they might possibly be used in the event of war, was a crime. There were cited to us the Genocide Act, 1969, and various international conventions.'

Judge Mynett said that the defendants' lawyer, Owen Davies, a secretary of the Lawyers for Nuclear Disarmament group, 'did not shrink from carrying it to its logical conclusion, because if the presence of nuclear weapons in this country or their use was a crime, then, of course, those in authority, whether civil or military, would be involved in the commission of that crime. Indeed, counsel admitted that if this country were in the course of being devastated by a nuclear attack it would still be a crime to use nuclear weapons in retaliation or self-defence, even if it meant this country would lose the war, because it would be impossible to use nuclear weapons without the risk of injuring or killing innocent civilians.'[1]

This summary of the defence case was accurate, and it raised fundamental issues of law, morality and State policy at least as far-reaching as those of the Nuremberg Trial. Judge Mynett's response provides a glimpse into the mind of the English judiciary in the nuclear age: 'Had it been necessary or competent for this court to do so we should have decisively rejected this submission and the arguments made by which it was supported. In particular, we should have decided that what was taking place at Upper Heyford at the moment was not an offence under the Genocide Act. I said if it were competent for the court to have pronounced on this matter, because in my judgment the court has no power whatsoever to deal with this question. Section 3 of the Criminal Law Act, 1967, has no application.'[2]

In one short paragraph Judge Mynett sank the appellants' case, but in a manner which recalls Alice's court experience in Wonderland. The King of Hearts was no less dismissive and impatient in his role as judge: '" Consider your verdict," said the King to the jury at the start of the trial. "Not yet, not yet!" the Rabbit hastily interrupted. "There's a great deal to come before that!"' But there was no Rabbit to interrupt Judge Mynett. His tortuous logic was

---

[1] Ibid.
[2] Ibid.

heard in respectful silence. Judge Mynett ate his tarts and kept them. By stating that the court was not competent to examine the appellants' case he ruled out the need to examine and evaluate it in detail, as is normal. He thus gave himself the option of making a damning judgment without fear of counter-argument.

Alice might have known how to respond to such eccentric reasoning, but she was not in court. If Judge Mynett was not competent to evaluate a case based on international law, and had no power to do so, then two questions await an answer. By what justification did he then make a dogmatic assertion that 'had it been necessary or competent for this court to do so' he 'would have decisively rejected this submission and the arguments made by which it was supported'? Such certainty implies a high level of awareness of the law involved, but the assertion hung in the air, unsupported by legal argument. By claiming competence and non-competence he could attack without having to defend. He used his power to adopt a can-win-can't-lose posture. He was a judge playing the role of prosecutor.

The second question concerns the extraordinary fact that an appeal was heard in a court by a judge who then declared that the court was not competent to consider seriously the appellants' case, although the latter was known before the hearing was appointed. How can such a situation be anything but a deliberate decision to side-step the law?

Judge Mynett followed up his personal declaration in the time-honoured fashion of English judges, by reciting precedent. He referred to the Chandler case and its official legal interpretation that the 'disposition and armament of the armed forces was within the prerogative and exclusive discretion of the Crown, and the wisdom of the Crown's policy in exercising that discretion was not open to challenge in the courts.'[1]

He quoted one of the Law Lords who heard the Chandler appeal, Lord Reid: 'It is in my opinion clear that the disposition and armament of the armed forces are, and for centuries have been, within the exclusive discretion of the Crown and that no one can seek a legal remedy on the ground that such discretion has been wrongly exercised.' He added that defence policy may be changed by parliament but 'no one is entitled to challenge it in court'.

---

[1] Chandler v. DPP, 1962, 3 All England Reports 142.

He further quoted Lord Hodson in the same case, who referred approvingly to an even earlier statement by Lord Parker; '"Those who are responsible for the national security must be the sole judges of what the national security requires. It would be obviously undesirable that such matters should be made the subject of evidence in a court of law or otherwise discussed in public."'[1]

Having wrapped himself up snugly, so to speak, in this comforting dogma, Judge Mynett laid down the law: 'It is clear, therefore, from the passages I have cited that this court has no jurisdiction whatsoever to enquire into, still less to pronounce on the validity or use of, the deployment of nuclear weapons at the RAF base, Upper Heyford [all USAF air bases in Britain are officially known as RAF bases]. The disposition and armament of the armed forces is within the prerogative and exclusive discretion of the Crown; the correctness of that discretion cannot be challenged in a court of law . . . I conclude by saying this: the right of protest is a most valuable safeguard, but it must not be abused, and it is being abused if its exercise involves breaches of the criminal law.'[2]

Yet the meaning and effect of what Judge Mynett said was to do exactly what he said he had no power to do, pronounce on the validity of the nuclear weaponry at Upper Heyford. He declared in plain language that it was lawfully there. Further, he confirmed without qualification earlier rulings that defence policy is outside the reach of the courts. It might reasonably be assumed that in a society which boasts of its Magna Carta, it would be impossible to declare any part of society beyond the law. After all, King John was compelled to sign the Magna Carta in 1215 because of his abuse of power. Democracy has no meaning when a major area of authority is held to be outside the law.

The most astonishing feature of this hearing in Oxford is perhaps its calm violation of the law as interpreted and enforced at Nuremberg. Who can doubt that a judge in Nazi Germany would have followed the same logic as Judge Mynett in protecting the undisputable authority of the government? The Nazi defence reasoning at Nuremberg, as we have seen, made use of the same claim that governmental authority, especially in matters of military policy, could not be challenged in law and could not therefore be

[1] Ibid.
[2] Appeal transcript.

illegal. The Nuremberg judgment made it clear that no State, no leader, no agent of the State can remain outside the law of nations.

An observer of the Nuremberg Trial commented on Nazi abuse of law: 'When he (Frank) acquired the extraordinary but typically Hitlerian title of "Reich Commissioner for the Standardisation of Justice in the Länder and for the Renewal of the Legal Order" he informed German judges in 1936, "The judge has no right of review over the decisions of the Führer as embodied in a law or decree".'[1]

In the light of this scandalous, if semi-traditional distortion of the law, it is doubly objectionable to note Judge Mynett's final warning that protest must not involve breaches of the law. The nuclear nightmare becomes darker yet when judicial authority allies law with anarchic power. The judge's logic leads us in the circles of *Alice in Wonderland*: 'The judge, by the way, was the King, and as he wore his crown over his wig, he did not look at all comfortable, and it was certainly not becoming.'

As a footnote to this appeal case, there were various consequences. Far from expressing outrage at such a blatant abuse of judicial authority, the British press reported the event with little or no comment. Judge Mynett was clearly swimming in a large sea of public acquiescence. When it came to consideration of a further appeal against Mynett's decision, counsel for the appellants decided against it, on the grounds that a further negative result would create yet another negative precedent. Yet the grounds for a further appeal were clear-cut and of the greatest significance in law. The judge had deliberately disregarded the legal basis of the appellants' case.

Such timidity and defeatism among lawyers supposedly committed to the cause of international law against mass destruction is indicative of the legal profession's concern with peripheral rather than primary issues of law. The handful of lawyers who dare to oppose the general drift find it hard to sustain counter-arguments. More positive and daring were two of the appellants, Cherry Quinn and Angela Hunt. Following their own research and without professional help, they appealed to the European Commission of Human Rights at Strasbourg in the spring of 1984. They did so on the grounds that they had been denied justice in British courts,

[1] Neave, op. cit.

because their defence case had not been fully heard. Private initiatives of this kind are blades of grass in a wasteland. Judge Mynett will not see the result of their appeal, which as of this writing is still unheard. He died in 1984, on holiday in France.

This legal exclusion zone, imposed by government with the connivance of the judiciary around defence policy, extends even further, to anything in the 'national interest'. There were two events in Britain during 1983 and 1984 which highlighted this issue. Both concern official secrecy. The first involved a young clerical officer, Sarah Tisdall, who worked at the Foreign Office and gave to the *Guardian* newspaper a secret memorandum on the arrival of Cruise missiles in Britain. The *Guardian*, under Government pressure, gave back the document, thus providing evidence for Sarah Tisdall's arrest and prosecution. She was sentenced to six months imprisonment for breach of the Official Secrets Act.

Her prosecution is relevant to our inquiry into the role of judges in the nuclear age, because of the judicial response in the context of what we have already discovered. The full force of righteous indignation was directed at this young woman by the trial and appeal judges. Lord Justice Griffiths described the leak as 'a very serious threat to our national security.'[1] Lord Lane, the Lord Chief Justice, said it was 'dangerous arrogance' for anyone to 'decide for themselves which laws to obey or disobey'.[2] 'People who believe in obeying the law only when it does not conflict with their interests,' he said, 'must be reminded that they become liable to prosecution and punishment in the shape of a prison sentence.'[3]

The Sunday *Observer* was not impressed by signs of judicial outrage. 'The scandalized tone of the Appeal Court judges,' it said, was 'misplaced and disproportionate.'[4] It referred to the 'obsessive secrecy of the administrative machine'. But the British media and people strained at the gnat of official secrecy and continued to swallow the camel of official crime. Ponderous condemnation by the judges masked their own connivance with governmental evasion of the law concerning defence policy, a no-entry area of deceit which was spreading like a dark stain across British life. They protested too much their concern for 'national security', the

[1] *Daily Telegraph*, 17 December 1983.
[2] *Daily Telegraph*, 10 April 1984.
[3] *Guardian*, 10 April 1984.
[4] *Observer*, 18 December 1983.

very thing they were helping to undermine by selective application of the law.

Next came the GCHQ case, which concerned the Government's decision to ban union membership from its main communications centre in western England. Again, national security was invoked. Unions might incite strikes, it was held, and strikes would disrupt the centre's key surveillance role on a world-wide scale. At first a judge, Justice Glidewell, held on 16 July 1984 that the rules of natural justice bound the Government to consult with the unions and staff before using its prerogative powers. There was no reason in logic or principle why the exercise by a minister of a power conferred by an Order in Council should not be subject to the same scrutiny and control by the courts as would be appropriate to the exercise of the power if it had been granted by statute.[1]

Justice Glidewell, by this mild rebuke to the Government, appeared to be doing no more than telling it to retrace its steps a short distance and consult the prisoner, so to speak, before chopping off his head. But he was also lifting the lid, if only by a fraction, on the Pandora's box of national security interests. He may not have realized this, but the Court of Appeal certainly did. They sat heavily on the lid, trapping the judge's fingers. Less than a month later, on 6 August – the anniversary of the bombing of Hiroshima – the three Law Lords of the Court of Appeal delivered their judgment. The Government's action was 'clearly taken on the grounds of national security. Therefore the court was not entitled to inquire into the actions which were taken in the exercise of the Royal Prerogative.'[2]

According to the Court of Appeal, 'the ministers were sole judges of what the national security required and consequently the instruction and certificates were not subject to judicial review.' There might be some actions of the Royal Prerogative which were open to such review, but certainly not one 'which could truly be said to have been taken in the interests of national security to protect this country from its enemies or potential enemies'.[3] It was obvious that in the Court's opinion the word of the Government on this matter must be accepted as 'truly said'.

Yet another rampart had been erected in defence of the national

---

[1] Law Report in *The Times*, 17 July 1984.
[2] Law Report in *The Times*, 7 August 1984.
[3] Ibid.

interest's expanding empire, and yet another nail had been driven into the coffin of equality before the law. But before we leave this scene of judicial betrayal it is worth looking at what the Prime Minister, Margaret Thatcher, had to say on the matter during a House of Commons debate. This took place on 17 July, the day following Justice Glidewell's short-lived judgment. She said that this was not the first time that a court had declared a minister's decision invalid. 'Mr Sam Silkin, when Attorney-General,' she said, 'was told by the Master of the Rolls that he had no prerogative to suspend or dispense with the laws of England. It is right that every member of the executive must be subject to the law of the land.' And at the end of her speech she emphasized this point again: 'Every minister, every Prime Minister, is within the law and must be seen to be within the law. I wholly accept that every minister in taking action takes action in the belief that he or she is taking it within the law on the best advice.'[1]

It is a strange situation when a Prime Minister declares a willingness to obey the law at all times and in all places, while our judges offer her a limitless area of national security where the law dare not enter. Even the normally deferential *Times* newspaper, on 7 August, expressed concern at this 'total exclusion zone over so large and dark and expanding an area of official activity'. For the courts to say, declared *The Times*, that 'they have no point of entry into the whole area of the exercise of prerogative power in relation to national security, or that they are not permitted to enter (permitted by whom?) is to withdraw the protection afforded by the law in relation to a sensitive and uncomfortably large area of official business'.

The newspaper then cited the comment of another judge in an earlier case concerning national security, Lord Denning: '"In some parts of the world national security has on occasion been used as an excuse for all sorts of infringements of civil liberty. But not in England . . . Ministers here never have interfered with the liberty or freedom of movement of any individual except when it is absolutely necessary for the safety of the State." If the judges will not look into these matters, how do they know any such thing? If they will not inspect even the form and procedure surrounding prerogative decisions affecting the liberties of the subject taken in

[1] *The Times*, 18 July 1984.

the name of national security, what value have their assurances that all is well?'

Lord Denning's statement reflects the cast-iron complacency of Gilbert's patriot: 'For he himself has said it, and it's greatly to his credit, that he is an Englishman.'

As *The Times* concluded, in its untypically stern editorial, 'the three checks on the abuse of state power are a diligent Parliament, a free press, and a correct and courageous judiciary'. It was clearly difficult for the judiciary to respond effectively to matters of national security. 'All the more reason to try,' said the *Times*. 'Judges expatiating on their impotence make a sorry sound.' A 'more robust line of reasoning' was wanted. When a newspaper so largely identified with establishment thinking as *The Times* sees fit to poke the judiciary in the ribs in this way, it is evident that our judiciary are neither 'correct' nor 'courageous' when it comes to matters of national interest and security.

Why not? What is wrong with them? Are they capable of change? After all, on other issues closer to home the judiciary are outspoken, even robust. If our judges shy away from the legal implications of international violence, they show no such inhibitions when it comes to violence on the streets. The Court of Appeal had no doubt that a young Londoner was rightly convicted for 'possessing an offensive weapon in a public place'. The weapon was a flick-knife and the sentence was a suspended sentence of three months and a £100 fine: 'Once one reached the conclusion that a knife, proved to be a flick knife, necessarily was one made for the use of causing injury to the person, their Lordships' view was that that was a matter of which judicial notice could be taken and the jury directed accordingly,'[1]

Yet when criminal violence overlaps military commitment there is often a softer response. A young soldier was convicted at Norwich Crown Court on 8 March 1977, of causing grievous bodily harm to a seventeen-year-old girl, combined with indecent assault. He was sentenced to a total of three years imprisonment. The Court of Appeal changed this sentence to one of six months, suspended for a period of two years: 'It appears that this young man has an excellent record of service in the Coldstream Guards ... whose career as an excellent soldier would be completely destroyed if this sentence were allowed to stand.'[2]

[1] Law Report in *The Times*, 31 October 1983.
[2] *The Times*, 22 June 1977.

Despite this judicial deference to military needs, the Army promptly fired the soldier concerned.

Violent sexual attacks normally attract severe sentences and sharp denunciation. When a Crown Court judge at Exeter jailed a rapist for nine years he condemned the inaction of those living near the scene of the crime: 'The English habit of turning a deaf ear to what happens can lead to terrifying results.'[1] It can indeed. Peddling drugs, or 'peddling death' as one judge has called it, also attracts severe condemnation. The judiciary has a lively sense of morality, which tends to be ingrowing and selective rather than universal in scope.

Two events in 1983 offer a revealing glimpse of the judge's mind at work, a lecture delivered at Cambridge by the Lord Chief Justice, and a debate in the House of Lords on violent crime. Chief Justice Lane introduced his lecture with a reference to a brutal assault by two youths of sixteen on a woman of eighty-three. He would have expected such an assault to arouse a 'mass mobilization of determination to attack this type of crime and to defeat it. It is not that the British as a people are incapable of such action. It was capability so to act that Hitler feared most about the British as a nation.'[2]

Yet such a response was lacking today.

Why? He quoted a former Home Office Minister in answer. The British have a '"weary familiarity with crime, a fatalistic acceptance in the community, that crime on a rising scale seems inevitable, unstoppable, even unremarkable"'. Perhaps, the Chief Justice wondered, the citizen has become too far removed from such responsibilities: 'A parallel can be drawn between wars of olden times which were fought with unsophisticated weapons when every citizen would visualize himself wielding arms and doing his bit (however reluctantly) and the wars of the present day, which are fought by specialists operating systems of high technology totally beyond the ken of the ordinary citizen. We defer too much to experts in the treatment of the criminal. . . .'

'A stable family life,' he thought, lay at the root of crime prevention, but 'it is no coincidence that the crime explosion started at a time of affluence, when permissiveness ceased to be disapproved and began to become the fashion.' He ended by

[1] *Daily Telegraph*, 23 November 1983.
[2] *The Times*, 10 November 1983.

lamenting: 'Instead of encouraging youngsters to think straight, instead of making clear what is good and what is bad, society deliberately blurs those boundaries which ought above all to be clearly defined.' More public involvement was needed: 'If you disapprove of violence being used as entertainment, say so. If you disapprove of pornography in its many forms, say so.'[1]

What is remarkable about these sentiments is what is not said. An observer from outer space would never guess from such remarks that this crime wave takes place in the context of nuclear weapons systems which threaten instant death to juvenile delinquents and Lord Chief Justices alike. As this overhanging shadow is not mentioned, it must be assumed that Lord Lane considers it irrelevant. Such indifference is entirely consistent with his Court of Appeal decision of 6 August 1984, to keep the law out of matters of national security, what *The Times* referred to as 'the sorry sound' of judges 'expatiating on their impotence.'

The Nazi experience could teach him another logic. It was one of the Nuremberg defendants, Hitler's Minister of Technology, Albert Speer, who warned us of the criminal implications of a wanton technology: 'Earlier dictators ... needed highly qualified assistants, even at the lowest level, men who could think and act independently. The totalitarian system ... can dispense with them; the means of communication alone make it possible to mechanise the lower leadership. As a result of this there arises the new type of uncritical recipient of orders. We have reached only the beginning of the development. The nightmare of many a man that one day nations could be dominated by technical means was all but realized in Hitler's totalitarian system. ... Therefore the more technical the world becomes, the more necessary is the promotion of individual freedom and the individual's awareness of himself as a counter-balance.'[2]

Speer foresaw nuclear missile warfare, able to 'destroy one million people in the middle of New York in a matter of seconds. ...'

As a former minister of a highly developed armament system, it is my last duty to say the following: a new large-scale war will end with the destruction of human culture and civilization ... therefore this trial must contribute towards preventing such degenerate

[1] Ibid.
[2] *International Military Tribunal*, Vol. XXII.

wars in the future and towards establishing rules whereby humans can live together.'[1]

If a Nazi technocrat can relate the human implications of modern technology to warfare and the fate of civilization, why is this impossible for the Lord Chief Justice of a country hemmed in by nuclear weaponry?

If, as he tells us, we lack personal responsibility for crime and 'pass the buck' to remote experts, then the remedy is clearly to exert a high level of personal responsibility. Yet Lord Lane has demonstrated by word and deed that he does not apply this principle to matters of national security, where power and responsibility must be left in the hands of a tiny political clique. Courts confronted by citizens who claim that nuclear weapons are immoral and illegal are given short shrift. Men and women asked to act with fierce independence where mugging and rape are concerned are expected to revert to feudal apathy in matters of national survival.

Selective use of principle may be the normal failing of an ordinary citizen, to be greeted with irritation or indulgence according to taste. But when a nation's leading judge promotes such a selective version of morality there is something rotten in the State's inner structure. 'Lilies that fester smell far worse than weeds.' All the more ironic, then, that Lord Lane went on to dispense more half-digested morality in a House of Lords debate the following week.

'We cannot re-introduce hanging,' he said, 'may I suggest we might re-introduce conscience and the devil?'[2] What for? So that judges may lace their judgments with a thicker dose of moralizing brimstone-and-treacle? We have already seen how judges throughout the land meet opponents of nuclear weaponry with the dismissive 'this is a court of law, not of morals'. Perhaps the devil and conscience are only tolerable on one side of the judicial coin.

In the same debate the Lord Chancellor, the nation's leading law authority, added his own version of current events, linking violence with sex in the manner approved by the Chief Justice. He attacked a society 'which glorifies in hatred and violence'. Nuclear threats of mass destruction were not what was on his mind. He went on: 'If we see what we see on page three of a newspaper, or in

[1] *Ibid.*
[2] *Daily Telegraph*, 16 November 1983.

other media, let us not be altogether surprised if on page one or on page five we read the melancholy recital of homosexual murder, rapes, crimes like the Ripper's, muggings, woundings, burglaries, riots, kidnappings or child abuse, either by violence or sex.'[1]

'Page three' is a euphemism for sex, in fact usually consisting of a nude woman with a pretty face and figure. The eyes of our leading judicial authorities are as firmly fixed on such slender signs of wickedness as they are closed to the ultimate violence of national security.

The Chief Justice told his audience that some of today's television controllers 'seem to be engaged in speeding to the easy descensus to Avernus' with their violent and obscene entertainment. 'Very soon the weaker brethren,' he said, 'accept them as a norm.'[2] As we have seen, judicial failure to uphold and enforce principles affirmed at Nuremberg owes much to the personal and social inability of the modern judge to assert the law in the teeth of government power. Weaker judicial brethren have been all too ready to accept the official logic of total war as a norm, allowing the blatantly criminal and immoral machinery of nuclear murder to hide behind national security.

Whether British judges are better or worse than others is hard to say. What is undeniable is that they stem from a small highly privileged and therefore entirely untypical part of our society. Any reform becomes a monumental task. Even a Conservative Lord Chancellor, Lord Hailsham, was driven to admit to a 'growing sense of despair and exasperation at the appalling conservatism of the legal profession'.[3] According to a recent study of the politics of the judiciary by Professor John Griffith, 'in broad terms, four out of five full-time professional judges are products of public (i.e. private) schools, and of Oxford or Cambridge.'[4] Almost all of them are selected from among practising barristers. A private income is considered necessary to survive the first years of practice.

For those fortunate enough to have avoided public school education it is worth noting a few of the more obvious influences which have shaped the average judge's thought and behaviour. Most such schools in Britain are boarding, which imposes specific

[1] Ibid.
[2] Ibid.
[3] *The Times*, 16 November 1983.
[4] J. A. G. Griffith, *Politics of the Judiciary*, London 1981.

emotional pressures on the child. It is natural for a child to live within the close adult framework of mother, father, relatives and friends. Childish feelings are contained within, one hopes, a warm and loving home. As strength grows within this nest, there is a natural need to move out. The public school brutalizes this process, removing the child for periods of about three months, three times each year between the ages of thirteen and eighteen. Many have already experienced a similar process at preparatory schools, from the age of eight or even seven.

The effect is profound and long-lasting. To be moved back and forth in this way, between utterly different environments, requires the child to survive extremes of emotional pressure. Strong emotional attachment increases the stress of separation. Much better to move more easily by suppressing feelings. Such schools tend to impose a dominant standard of thought and behaviour. The school environment, by its very nature, offers the child a society composed mainly of strangers, organized by adults who may be friendly and are certainly powerful. Love is replaced by discipline, natural inclination by school goals.

Such a setting offers the child only one means of gaining reward and status – commitment to school aims – and one form of emotional support – the friendship and approval of a peer group. British public schools frequently boast of their character-building qualities. The sort of character, built by the thousand at these schools and observable in many British professions other than the judiciary, is that of someone with fierce group loyalties, strong self-discipline directed at socially approved goals, and a weak emotional base. Strong three-dimensional people can and do emerge from such places, in spite of the education rather than because of it, but the vast majority are as socially conformist and uncreative as the process requires. Judges are not alone in finding it natural to exchange the cold embrace of the *alma mater* (foster mother) for that of their Prime Minister and Sovereign.

Oxford and Cambridge serve to complete the make-up, providing intellectual cosmetics to disguise still more expertly the underlying, frightened, disoriented child. Their relaxed social environment, complemented by sharp rationality, are a terrible recipe for creative thought and action, which require maturity of feeling as well as thought, but it spawns exactly the right blend of easy-going charm and social self-confidence to perpetuate an élitist, superficial society. It is an education which sponsors rationalizations for all seasons in the service of established power.

How do I know? Because I was there, and have spent my adult life squeezing out of this velvet straitjacket. I watched at close range young men mimicking their masters, growing up to replace them, eventually, as Minister of Defence or High Court Judge. My escape was helped by the problem of nuclear weapons and the law. The hydrogen bomb provoked some academic thought, but there was a lack of emotional strength to measure up to such a monstrous affront to personal, political and legal integrity. Our judges have failed abjectly to rise to this challenge, not because they are bad or stupid, but because they are at heart emotionally immature and dependent. A Lord Chief Justice who ignores the nuclear missile in favour of the flick-knife is trapped in a small world. His mind is like that of the aborigines who greeted Captain Cook's arrival in Australia with indifference. His ship was too large to be noticed. Only when the life-boats were lowered did they spring into action, recognizing something their own size.

This assessment, it must be repeated, is not based on an ambitious notion that judges have a general duty to facilitate radical reform. That is another issue requiring other evidence. What is at stake here is much more simple and basic, whether our judges do all they can to uphold and enforce existing law. So far, as we have seen, their record in terms of laws governing international violence is dismal and disgraceful. Far from applying the law with the same vision and commitment as the judges at Nuremberg, they have deliberately and frequently evaded it. They have used government evasion of the law not as a spur to enforcement but as an excuse to turn away. Instead of making the most of the law against international crime, they have made the least of it. They have led the way in a social and legal conspiracy of silence.

'Politically, judges are parasitic,' is Professor Griffith's assessment.[1] By which he means that they naturally serve prevailing political and economic forces. But this is not the whole truth. The forces which govern judges are not simply past experience and present government, otherwise they would pay close attention to the precedent at Nuremberg. Their allegiance is to a conservative, often primitive interpretation of past and present power. In terms

[1] Op. cit.

of the declared values and laws of our society they have proved themselves partial mediators, at best.

The wonder is that such manifest inadequacy remains largely undetected, as far as society at large is concerned. Judges still inspire widespread awe and respect. They reflect in the British mind an ancient ceremonial power, combining royalty with government. They are not recognized for what they are, human beings of limited experience and insight, deserving of no more power than the rest of us. Instead, by virtue of an inflated public image, their effect is to distort rather than clarify. Wilful evasion of the legal implications of nuclear weaponry is an inevitable by-product of this escapism. Yet the public, so far, has declined every incentive to expose this sham. It has indicated a clear preference for a make-believe judiciary to match a make-believe image of life. We have made our own nightmare and must un-make it.

The tale of the British judge is a sorry one. It has its peculiar features, but the problem is no more localized than that of nuclear weapons themselves. Other countries have other judges with other features, but they have one thing in common, a boundless capacity for loyalty to established power. In the United States, for example, the judiciary shares with the executive and Congress the commanding heights of society. Occasionally there is a Supreme Court judge like William O. Douglas, whose primary allegiance is to human rather than official values, and the election of judges brings them closer to the people. But 'only occasionally' in the United States, as Professor Griffith says, 'has the power of the supreme judiciary been exercised in the positive assertion of fundamental values'.[1] US judges have shown no more willingness to challenge the legitimacy of nuclear weaponry than any others in East or West.

The judges of such countries as Italy and France sometimes appear more obviously political in character, perhaps due to the fact that they are appointed at a much younger age than in Britain, after public examinations which involve a wider social spectrum. But closer concern with policy issues has not so far been matched by independence of mind on matters of fundamental legal principle. In the Soviet Union and the communist countries, the judiciary is no less bound to the established system of power.

If law is finally to be applied to the official anarchy which

[1] Ibid.

threatens world destruction there must be radical changes in the
role of the judge and our perception of the judiciary. Judges can
help to initiate this change, by publicly investigating our current
crisis of legality and their part in it. By insisting on a high-level
review of world-wide failure to enforce the law, they can set in
motion a process which will apply positive pressure on governments. They can use their influence to speak directly to the public
on this vital issue. They can transform the seedy and suspect no-go
area of national security into a focus of legal inquiry. They can do
what they are paid and supposed to do, uphold and enforce the law
as the humane bedrock of civilized life.

But miracles are rare. No professional body of such arthritic
power ever reformed itself without intense public pressure. We
must reject entirely, with a sour smile, Lord Denning's lofty
appeal: 'Someone must be trusted. Let it be the judges.'[1] The
judges will deserve trust when they enforce the law without fear or
favour. We must insist that the judiciary becomes a reflection of
society, not wealth, and that more women must be recruited. At
present only about 5% of High Court judges in England are
women.

There can be no resolution of this problem, ultimately, until
citizens begin to assume a responsibility for understanding the
basic principles of the law and demanding their enforcement. Not
the partial responsibility advocated by the Lord Chief Justice,
directed at sex-and-violence, but responsibility for the world we
live in.

[1] In his 1980 Richard Dimbleby lecture on 'The Abuse of Power', reported in the
Observer, 29 January 1984.

Chapter Six

Soldier, Sailor, Airman – Their Tale

'Do you ever think of the millions you might kill?' the
controller of a Minuteman missile was asked. 'No, I block it
out,' he replied
– BBC Radio report, 1983.

'Distance, time and physical barriers neutralize the moral
sense . . . for the man who sits in front of a button that will
release Armageddon, depressing it has about as much
emotional force as calling for an elevator'
– 'Obedience to Authority', Stanley Milgram

Governments which evade the law can and do hide. Ministers and
civil servants make sure there is no face to face encounter with
doubt. Letters are left unanswered, or questions answered which
are not asked. Public interviews on radio or television are easily
dealt with by a verbal flurry which sounds plausible until examined. By which time the quarry has vanished. The ritual contests of
Parliament seldom do more than stir a predictable stew, confirming prejudice. And as we have seen, even the legal profession has
dodged the laws of armed conflict for many years, with little
trouble. But what about the military agents of government, the
men and women in uniform without whom no war is possible?
How do they stand today in relation to nuclear strategies and the
law? What do they care about the legal restrictions on their right to
kill?

Before investigating the behaviour of others it can be useful to
look at personal experience. My father spent his working life in the
Army. He was a man who hated violence and the sight of blood. He
joined the Army to gain a secure income. He questioned the detail
of army life but never its basic discipline and direction. Those in
power knew best, because they knew most. He knew next to
nothing about the laws of armed conflict but, as far as I know,
never committed a war crime. He did as he was told. And others

did as he told them. He did not like nuclear weapons, and did nothing about them.

I met many men like him when I became a British Army conscript. I became part of a huge, impersonal, obedient organization with no mind of its own. My training taught me many things, especially the need to do as I was told. I was based near Belsen and its concentration camp monument, in West Germany, within firing range of the Soviet Army. Nobody discussed the meaning of the war and its death camps, or the nature and purpose of the Cold War and nuclear weapons, even though we were mostly reluctant conscripts. My mind and heart seethed with anger and doubt but I said little. It was as if the army had paralyzed the part of us which takes note of life. We were shrunken heads, drained of wider meaning. Soldier ants.

Nobody in the Army told me about the laws of war enforced at Nuremberg a few years earlier, or their place in the British Manual of Military Law. As far as I was aware, military law was for military policemen to enforce, loud-mouthed men in red caps who arrested drunks at weekends outside *Gasthaus* bars. I found out how governments deliberately kept their armed forces in the dark, in terms of the law. Like most of my contemporaries I was an educated fool then, and for many years afterwards. I assumed that governments, particularly those which boast of democracy, obey their own laws. I had swallowed the convenient myth that Nazi crime was a German problem.

Today, when it comes to examining the legal status of the soldier I swallow my scorn instead. I was a potential war criminal and know it. Secretly proud to become a parachutist, only the luck of history saved me from a 'defensive' attack which would sweep away all in its path. My anger is reserved now for those in high places who exploit the young and gullible, in or out of uniform. It is these people in authority who know most, are paid most, and are safest. They owe the soldier a service of the highest quality. Above all, they owe the soldier policies which serve and protect civilized values, within the law.

So if we discover that men and women in uniform have drifted outside the law we will know where the major responsibility lies. As was laid down at Nuremberg, and is reflected in every modern State's military laws, obeying illegal orders is a crime, but there may be mitigating circumstances, such as poor education, low intelligence, military discipline and so on. When a human being is trained to obey like a robot, it can be hard not to think and act like one. The Nazi experience is a harsh warning to the military profession as well as the rest of us. Let us see how well it has been heeded, by the British, the Germans and the Americans.

The British Soldier's Tale

'We know enough if we know we are the King's men. Our
obedience to the King wipes the crime of it out of us'
– *Henry V*, William Shakespeare

'If any question why we died
Tell them – because our fathers lied'
– Rudyard Kipling

'A month ago Europe was a peaceful comity of nations; if an
Englishman killed a German, he was hanged. Now, if an
Englishman kills a German, or if a German kills an
Englishman, he is a patriot'
– Bertrand Russell, 1914

'I have never had that question before,' the RAF group-captain told me, surprised. He was the leader of an RAF Presentation Team, whose job is to tour British towns and cities with a film unit explaining and promoting RAF activities. There were five hundred invited citizens in the hall that evening in September 1984 and we watched dramatic film of military jets screaming over Europe in defence of peace. Apart from the ghoulish anti-poison suits of ground personnel there was little but the speed of the modern aircraft to distinguish these films from those of World War Two. The RAF was a defensive force, prepared to fight any aggressor. There was scarcely a hint of the nuclear dimension of this strategy.

My question was simple: 'Are there any restrictions imposed by international law on the operations of the RAF?' For a moment there was silence. He was clearly surprised and nonplussed. He thought hard. Then he asked me to explain the question, which I did. He recovered a little of his fluency and explained that the RAF is responsible to the sovereign and that the Government's job is to deal with matters of law. I quoted some lines from the Hague

Convention, 1907, which emphasize that military targets only must be attacked, not undefended towns and cities, explaining that I was reading from the Law Notes of the RAF Pilots Training College, Cranwell, sent by the Directorate of Legal Services (RAF) at the Ministry of Defence in London. He made no comment.

I had no time to add that the same document[1] quotes with approval sections of the 1949 Geneva Conventions, including the fact that signatory nations agreed to 'disseminate the text of the present conventions as widely as possible in their respective countries ... so that the principles thereof may become known to the entire population, and in particular to the armed fighting forces'. It was clear that the Group-Captain, despite his role as RAF salesman, knew nothing of these or other laws. It was particularly odd that he would be unaware of laws which might impose on him severe punishment. The document ends by citing the UK Geneva Conventions Act of 1957, by which the 1949 Conventions became ratified by Act of Parliament.

This Act, warns the document, 'provides that any person guilty of a grave breach of any of the conventions if it involve the wilful killing of a protected person shall be sentenced to life imprisonment; a person committing any other grave breach shall be liable to imprisonment not exceeding fourteen years'. A 'grave breach' is a war crime.

Other enquiries confirm that the group-captain is not alone in his ignorance. The RAF commander of a nuclear base told me two years earlier that he was unaware of the major laws governing warfare. At a public meeting at York in May 1984, I spoke about the relation of the law to nuclear weapons. After the meeting a member of the audience confirmed what I had said about the reluctance of the British armed forces to confront this aspect of military strategy. He had personal experience of the problem, being an instructor in law at the Army Staff College. The nuclear dimension, he said, was largely ignored.

A colonel of the Royal Engineers, who had helped prepare the Christmas Island test site for Britain's first hydrogen bomb explosion in the 1950s, claimed in private conversation that his job was unrestricted by any laws of war. The lower ranks of the British armed forces show even less evidence of awareness of the law. Only

[1] MOD (DLS) (RAF) Revised 1980.

at the highest level, and there only rarely, do a few faint doubts surface about nuclear policies.

Field-Marshal Lord Carver publicized his doubts. Referring to the atom-bombing of Hiroshima and Nagasaki, he wrote: 'When one considers how horrible was the destruction and suffering caused by those two, one is driven to the conclusion that the world has gone mad .... They could not possibly be used – even a small proportion of them – in any way that could be called a "continuation of policy", unless it were a policy of genocide and suicide. No wonder old and young alike protest against so-called defence policies that could result in their use.'[1]

If a field-marshal cannot make military, legal, moral sense out of his country's defence strategy, it is hardly surprising that the vast majority of military personnel dare not try. They fall back, when pressed, on patriotic clichés suitable for the days of Nelson and Wellington. Nelson, judging by his naval record, would have no difficulty recognizing Polaris missile destruction of Soviet cities as simple mass murder, totally unrelated to any sane, lawful goal of naval warfare. On one occasion, having lost a minor naval battle off the Spanish island of Tenerife, and an arm with it, he sent a keg of English beer to the Spanish Governor. In return he received a cask of Spanish wine. Warfare then was bloody, cruel, wasteful, as it always has been, but it was not a matter of indiscriminate killing of enemy populations.

It is ironic that in those days the written laws of war were few, yet the conduct of war was infinitely more restrained in ferocity and scope. To ascribe this solely to primitive weaponry would leave out of account the way of life of that time. A cursory look at Nelson's life is enough to show that mass murder of the old and sick, women and children, as a deliberate policy of State, would have revolted him. A Polaris attack on Moscow, for example, would kill, cripple or poison around two million Russian children. Yet that is what is written in small print on the reverse side of our nuclear 'insurance policy'. How is it that the crew of a Polaris submarine, outwardly proud of naval tradition, carry out an operational role of criminal lunacy without protest? They are human beings with children, families, feelings.

They, like the rest of us, live in a dream within a nightmare. A

[1] Carver, *A Policy of Peace*, London 1982.

Polaris crew is selected carefully, trained meticulously, psychologically vetted, paid well. Its purpose is ideal, to protect freedom and democracy. That is the dream which on closer inspection turns out to be the core of our nightmare. The Nazi SS were selected, trained and assessed with equal care. Only those with no police record and good education could enlist. Their professed ideal was not inferior, to defend the fatherland and German culture. And they too, until war started, seemed relatively normal. We do not judge the SS now in terms of their peace-time role, but on their murderous record in war. Are we fools that we refuse to face the declared role of a Polaris crew in war? We pay psychiatrists to examine them regularly, fearful that a madman might fire the missiles, whereas only a madman could.

Only a nightmare can boast such mad sanity. Like the SS we obey a perverted and criminal law, which commands a Polaris sailor to obey orders involving the murder of millions. If war breaks out, and according to our leaders the decision is in enemy hands, not ours, those judged especially sane and responsible will carry out the biggest crime in history, involving the murder of whole populations. Our armed forces shield themselves from this reality by claiming that war will never occur, thanks to the nuclear threat. But this is a hope, not a fact. In our dwindling area of sanity, in everyday life, people take responsibility for failure as well as success. We do sensible things to prevent fire, theft and murder, and willingly employ a fire service and a police force in case of failure. Failure, properly understood, opens the way to new thought, new action, new life. Failure which is disowned and denied leads to further disaster. Failure of the nuclear deterrent will lead to ultimate disaster, the price of ultimate irresponsibility.

No wonder the military mind is fractured, regressive. Our armed forces have been led into a dead end by a leadership which has exchanged law and restraint for the rule of unlimited fear and destruction. 'Into the valley of death', a nuclear death, we are all riding, hell-bent, as stupid as the 'six hundred' but without glamour or the excuse of ignorance.

Before examining the soldier's relationship to the law in more detail it may help to look at the military view of military madness, when the soldier can no longer function as a soldier. Not the madness of Field-Marshal Carver's 'world gone mad' but an inner breakdown of the individual mind. The Falklands war provided recent experience. The militarily insane contradict and undermine what is militarily sane, the will to fight, to kill and risk being killed. As a British Navy surgeon commander and psychiatrist, Morgan O'Connell put it, following his experience of treating mental casualties of the war: 'Yes, we indoctrinate them in the forces. Otherwise they wouldn't fight. That's why we cut their hair the same, make them wear the same uniform, make the same salute and march together. We indoctrinate them in order to enhance group cohesiveness. That's how you get people to fight.'[1]

This naval psychiatrist referred to one patient still under his care, half a year after the war. 'His illness', he said, 'is directly attributable to the war.' He described the illness as 'reactive psychosis, losing touch with reality, and a conflict of ideology . . . . He has a strong feeling that the war should never have been allowed to happen. He could never manage to identify the Argentines sufficiently as enemies. He said he'd have no problems about the Russians, but the Argentines were friends until a short time ago. He does see it was necessary for us to retake the Falklands, but he thinks the invasion itself should have been prevented.'[2]

When asked how these views could be described as a disease, the doctor-sailor replied: 'You have to remember what his job is. He's losing touch with reality. For as long as he's in this job, this conflict is a problem for him, it handicaps him.'

The key words in this exchange are 'reality' and 'illness'. Both are distorted and diminished to suit military logic. Reality in this context owes nothing to individual perception and everything to the requirements of the institution. It is the reality of the ant-heap, blind, obedient, functional. For the sailor to express his personal feeling of common humanity with the enemy is to 'lose touch with reality'. In an institutional context where one opinion and reality rule, opposition must either be crushed, physically by the firing squad, or psychologically with the weapon of illness. Madness in such a primitive, punitive context is nothing but a by-product of institutional repression. If the declared values of civilization have any meaning, it is the Royal Navy in this case which has 'lost touch with reality', breeding madness in its wake. To sell counterfeit values requires a logic and discipline to match, inciting the 'illness' it deserves. The Royal Navy continues to advertise the values

[1] *Guardian*, 1 November 1982.
[2] Ibid.

which it subverts. It seeks recruits capable of 'tolerance of your fellow men' with 'strength of character and adaptability'.[1] The young sailor's madness is the price of fraud.

Selective use of principle leads easily to selective use of the law. Much was heard of international law during the Falklands conflict, most of it concerned with the rights of prisoners of war. The leading ship of the British task force, HMS *Invincible*, broadcast programmes on the ship's closed-circuit television which explained the 'rights of prisoners of war under the Geneva Convention. Extracts from the article of war were read to remind crew of their duties and the penalties for not fulfilling them during action.'[2] A prisoner of war is protected by law precisely because he is no longer a combatant. Every combatant knows that being taken prisoner is a possibility in war, and therefore willingly demands and offers such protection. Non-combatants who have never been anything else, however, such as mothers, grandparents, children and the sick, are the core of the category known in law as 'protected persons'. Why then do combatants whose supposed function is to defend such people find it so difficult to apply to them legal standards which they are quick to claim for themselves? The sailors in *Invincible* were sticklers for law, up to a point.

British soldiers in the Falklands were no less committed to this limited version of the law. They 'did not behave cruelly by killing the wounded,' said an Argentinian soldier, Captain Hugo Robacio. 'on the contrary, many of our heroic wounded had their lives saved thanks to the help of the enemy.'[3] There is among these soldiers a schizoid vision of life and the law, a micro-reality where traditional behaviour reigns and the rule of law is more or less intact, and a macro-reality where chaos is king. The latter is a dark and forbidden continent of the soul, only rarely penetrated.

When the law is applied selectively the first casualty is the law. Soldiers whose sense of reality is confined to military logic find the complexity of civilian life hard to endure. When a British assault ship paid a goodwill visit to the Danish port of Odense, as part of a NATO exercise designed to protect Western democracy, the Royal Marines among its crew 'left a trail of blood and destruction in several bars .... One had his throat slit by colleagues .... The

[1] From recruitment advertising in British newspapers.
[2] *The Times*, 23 April 1982.
[3] *Observer*, 11 September 1983.

Marines smashed windows, tables, and each other and local inhabitants, according to police spokesmen. "I thought they were here to practice saving Denmark in time of crisis. With friends like that who needs enemies?" said Mr Joergen Petersen, owner of one of the bars left devastated.'[1]

This confusion of behaviour and thought is further complicated when the armed forces apply good paint to a rotten structure. A full-page Army advertisement extolled the role of the small British peace-keeping force in the Lebanon. It described the experience of a young officer of the Queen's Dragoon Guards: 'His briefing was intense and very much to the point. No aggression, no confrontation. No attempts at heroics.'[2] The detachment's purpose, it said, 'was to match violence and division wherever possible with calm impartiality .... In the face of violence, there's nothing so disarming as a friendly approach.' The young officer, according to the advertisement, had only the 'highest praise' for his sergeant, corporal and eight troopers: 'They all displayed skills in arbitration and conciliation that were really quite remarkable. And to a man they were restrained and level-headed in even the most difficult circumstances. To my knowledge the squadron fired not one single shot in Beirut.' Such mature principles run directly counter to the promiscuous and suicidal logic of nuclear strategy.

Very occasionally, in every army, exceptional individuals enforce their own laws of restraint. One such man was Captain William Douglas-Home, according to a fellow officer: 'From June 1944 to May 1945 I commanded, as a young lieutenant, a troop of flame-throwing tanks equipped to project napalm against German troops in Normandy and Holland. None of us, as I recall, was moved to abjure this terrible weapon, until in October 1944 Captain William Douglas-Home of my regiment refused to participate in an assault on the demoralized Germans in Brest.'[3] The Captain was tried by court-martial and sentenced to spend the rest of the war in prison.

The logic of modern war and weaponry must silence the individual voice, cutting off the law from its roots. The professional military mind is easy prey to a fantasy that the law can exist outside

[1] *Daily Telegraph*, 16 September 1983.
[2] *Observer*, 5 August 1984.
[3] *Observer*, 6 June 1982.

the individual. It has hardly evolved since the days of King
Richard III:

> Go Gentlemen, every man to his charge,
> Let not our babbling dreams affright our souls:
> For conscience is a word that cowards use,
> Devised at first to keep the strong in awe,
> Our strong arms be our conscience, swords our law.
> March on, join bravely, let us too't pell mell,
> If not to heaven, then hand in hand to hell.[1]

When I set out to explore the British armed forces and the law I
fell at the first fence – or rather, was tripped. A major library had no
copy of the *British Manual of Military Law*. The main London
branch of Her Majesty's Stationery Office, the publishers, told me
that Part Three was out of print, was being revised and there was no
date set for publication. Laws supposed by their own requirements
to reach the widest public were almost unavailable. Justice Jackson
and his colleagues at Nuremberg would not have been amused.

The situation was saved, in the end, by courtesy of the Ministry
of Defence, which sent me a photo-copy of Chapter 14 of Part
Three. The thirteen pages and thirty-five paragraphs of this
chapter comprise a detailed and concise summary of the laws of war
binding British service personnel. The only major omission is the
important Additional Protocol 1, 1977, which further strengthens
protection of non-combatants. The latter appears, however, in the
more recently published law notes of the Sandhurst military
academy. So we have, after a persistent search, an up-to-date
picture of British military law.

Chapter 14 is called 'Means of Securing Legitimate Warfare'. Its
introductory sentence sets the tone: 'Complaints of unlawful acts
and omissions alleged to have been committed by individuals or by
commanders are an almost invariable feature of warfare.'[2] It goes
on to cite as particularly relevant the Hague Conventions (1907) and
the Geneva Conventions (1949). The latter contains 'detailed provisions for the punishment of individuals' for war crimes. 'Such
responsibility is additional to, and not exclusive of, the responsibility of the Governments concerned.'[3]

---

[1] *Richard III*, Act V, sc. iii.
[2] *Manual of Military Law*, Part III, para. 617.
[3] Op. cit., para. 618.

Why bother with international law during a war? 'Because,' says the *Manual*, 'no State can afford to be wholly regardless of public and world opinion. This was apparent during the Second World War when the German authorities took elaborate security measures to ensure that no evidence of war crimes fell into the hands not only of the Allies but of neutral countries. An example of this is a teleprint signal from Field Marshal Keitel to Field Marshal Rundstedt concerning the massacre of the women and children of Oradour-sur-Glane in July 1944, by a unit of an SS Division forming part of Rundstedt's command. Keitel administered a severe rebuke to Rundstedt for failing to hold an inquiry into the massacre, as he had been ordered to do, and pointed out that German prestige had suffered considerably because no suitable reply could be issued to counteract the effects of the allegations of the Allies upon neutral and world opinion.'[1] Even Hitler's war machine could be sensitive to such an issue.

Among the 'means of securing legitimate warfare', says the *Manual*, are 'complaints lodged with the enemy and with neutral states, the mediation of the latter and punishment of war crimes'.[2] It might have added, but does not, that an even more basic means of securing legitimate warfare is a thorough training of military personnel of all ranks in relevant law. Violations of the law are not always melodramatic. Examples listed include the alleged deceptive use of Chinese clothing by Russian troops in the Russo-Japanese war in 1904, and the alleged intentional firing on the bearers of flags of truce by the French during the Franco-Prussian War of 1870–1.

'The term "war crime",' says the *Manual*, 'is the technical expression for violations of the laws of warfare, whether committed by members of the armed forces or by civilians . . . . A State may elect to punish its own nationals under the appropriate municipal laws for acts that amount to war crimes. Members of the British armed forces can be proceeded against under the relevant sections of the Army Act, 1955, for murder, manslaughter, etc.'[3] The British soldier is subject to military law but this does not shield him from ordinary criminal law. As a famous judge of the nineteenth century laid down: 'It is therefore important that the mistake

[1] Op. cit., para. 619.
[2] Op. cit., para. 620.
[3] Op. cit., para. 624.

should be corrected that an Englishman by taking upon himself the additional character of a soldier puts off any of the rights and duties of an Englishman.'[1]

The *Manual* goes on to list examples of war crimes: the causing of 'great suffering' to protected persons; mistreatment of prisoners of war, and 'extensive destruction and appropriation of property not justified by military necessity and carried out unlawfully and wantonly'.[2] In addition to these are: 'maltreatment of dead bodies; firing on undefended localities and non-military objectives; using expanding bullets or poisoned or otherwise forbidden arms or ammunition; poisoning of wells, streams, and other sources of water supply; killing without trial of spies, saboteurs, partisans and others who have committed hostile acts; bombardment of hospitals and other privileged buildings; killing of hostages; using asphyxiating, poisonous or other gases, and all analogous liquids, materials or devices; and genocide.'[3]

Such attention to detail seems almost quaint at a time of nuclear threat. But this law has its roots deep in history. Ancient Muslim laws forbid the poisoning of wells. Attacking and killing sick and helpless people did not become offensive when written into the *Manual*, but has been for centuries a crime to the civilized soldier. The *Manual* merely collates deep-rooted legal principles of restraint, echoing the convictions of Gustave Moynier, the famous Swiss jurist who presided over the first forty years of the International Committee of the Red Cross: 'What is called the "law of war" is essentially a barrier against the abuse of force, a brake put upon the unleashing of bestial passion aroused by the heat of battle; it is therefore necessary to get it into the mind and the conscience of any society willing to pursue its end by war . . . . It is an illusion to believe that last-minute preachings of moderation to men already excited by the smell of powder, will bring any worthwhile result.'[4]

The glaring and most disgraceful fact that most if not all of these laws would be violated by a nuclear attack is coyly disregarded by the *Manual*, which does not lift its angle of vision to the mushroom cloud. Its warnings may be simple and clear-cut, against 'forcing women into prostitution' or 'exposing prisoners of war to public

---

[1] Lord Mansfield, in Burdett v. Abbott (1812).
[2] Op. cit., para. 625.
[3] Op. cit., para. 626.
[4] Gustave Moynier in *Anniversaire de l'Institut de Droit International*, 1878–79.

insults or mob violence',[1] but they are legally correct, as far as they go. The principles promoted are the tiny threads of life which help to keep the nuclear death sentence suspended.

Next comes the crucial issue of the defence of superior orders, touching the most basic and dangerous contradictions of military life. Soldiers, as I know only too well, are trained to obey orders. Not trained by reason and friendly persuasion, but by threat and fear, backed by a battery of collective pressures. My ability to think for myself was not valued by the Army. It was suppressed and denounced with calculated ruthlessness. As a warning symbol, the look of a soldier must be uniform. During my basic training I received three hair-cuts in one week, due to a conjunction of routine, ceremonial parade and transfer to a new regiment. A fellow conscript and graduate of Oxford could not march properly but bounced up and down, like Jacques Tati acting M. Hulot. This drove our sergeant wild with frustration. He feared disgrace during the final passing-out parade. As we lined up smartly the latter whispered something in the clumsy graduate's ear, causing him to collapse suddenly into the sergeant's arms. He was promptly led off the parade ground and disappeared. He had been ordered to faint, in the interest of good order and military discipline.

When soldiers must assume robotic behaviour patterns, can they be expected to weigh up what is lawful or not? As the sailor with the British Falklands fleet discovered to his cost, to swim against the official current is to risk not just punishment but madness. But the problem remains. It has ancient roots. The officer who executed King Charles I was himself put to death when the monarchy was restored. 'When the command is traitorous,' said the judge, 'then the obedience to that command is also traitorous.'[2] The British and US manuals of military law of 1914 both specified the guilt of officers who gave illegal orders, but not that of obedient subordinates. It was not until World War Two that this principle evolved into the present broader interpretation.

'Obedience to the order of a government or of a superior,' says the *Manual*, 'whether military or civil, or to a national law or regulation, affords no defence to a charge of committing a war crime, but may be considered in mitigation of punishment.'[3] This

[1] Op. cit., para. 626.
[2] Axtell's case, 1660.
[3] Op. cit., para. 627.

statement is confirmed in Part One of the *Manual*: 'The command must not be contrary to English or international law and must be justified by military law.' And again: 'If a person who is bound to obey a duly constituted superior receives from the superior an order to do some act or make some omission which is manifestly illegal, he is under a legal duty to refuse to carry out the order and if he does carry it out he will be criminally responsible for what he does in doing so.'

It is illegal for an officer to order a soldier to take part in amateur dramatics. To order him to take part in the destruction of civilization is also illegal, by any reasonably interpretation of the law.

The *Manual* cites as a supporting argument Article 8 of the Charter of the Nuremberg International Military Tribunal, 8 August, 1945: 'The fact that the Defendant acted pursuant to order of his Government or of a Superior shall not free him from responsibility, but may be considered in mitigation of punishment.'[1] Article 6 of the Charter of the International Military Tribunal of Tokyo, Nuremberg's brother-in-law, adds: 'Neither the official position, at any time, of an accused, nor the fact that an accused acted pursuant to order of his Government or of a superior shall itself, be sufficient to free such accused from responsibility for any crime with which he is charged.'[2]

The *Manual* says that other countries, including Norway and France, have a similar law: 'In no case does the law of any State provide that superior orders should of themselves constitute a valid defence to a charge of a war crime.'[3]

The *Manual* cites the Nuremberg judgment as additional confirmation: 'The provisions of this Article (8) are in conformity with the law of all nations. That a soldier was ordered to kill or torture in violation of the international law of war has never been recognised as a defence to such acts of brutality . . . . The true test, which is found in varying degrees in the criminal law of most nations is not the existence of the order, but whether moral choice was in fact possible.'

Referring to the leading Nazi generals, Keitel and Jodl, the Nuremberg judgment went on: 'Superior orders, even to a soldier, cannot be considered in mitigation where crimes as shocking and

[1] Ibid.
[2] Ibid.
[3] Ibid.

extensive have been committed consciously, ruthlessly and without military excuse or justification .... Participation in such crimes as these has never been required of any soldier and he cannot now shield himself behind a mythical requirement of soldierly obedience at all costs as his excuse for commission of these crimes.' And referring to the German General Staff: 'Many of these men have made a mockery of the soldier's oath of obedience to military orders. When it suits their defence they say they had to obey; when confronted with Hitler's brutal crimes which are shown to have been within their general knowledge, they say they disobeyed. The truth is they actively participated in all these crimes or sat silent and acquiescent, witnessing the commission of crimes on a scale larger and more shocking than the world has ever had the misfortune to know. This must be said. When the facts warrant it these men must be brought to trial so that those among them who are guilty of these crimes should not escape punishment.'[1]

The *Manual* cites various war crimes trials which confirmed this judgment, among them the Belsen Trial, the Krupp Trial and the I. G. Farben Trial. It drives home the crucial importance of this primary law of individual responsibility by stating of higher ranking officers: 'Far from being irresistibly compelled to obey unlawful orders they are in a position, by a refusal to obey them, to avert or prevent their operation.'[2] There is unfortunately no evidence to suggest that higher ranking officers of the British Army fully understand these laws, and are able and willing to relate them to the threatened nuclear incineration of enemy cities. They should note, in particular, the *Manual*'s advice: 'In exceptional cases when the political or military superiors of a commander order or acquiesce in criminal acts the commander concerned may have no alternative but to resign his command.'[3]

A person in immediate fear of his own life, such as when he is threatened with a gun, cannot be charged with this law of criminal responsibility. Such a circumstance, says the *Manual*, will be 'comparatively rare'.[4]

One of the most graphic definitions of an unlawful order was

[1] Ibid.
[2] Ibid.
[3] Op. cit., para. 630
[4] Op. cit., para. 629.

offered at the trial in Jerusalem by the State of Israel of Adolf Eichmann, the Nazi administrator of the Jewish holocaust. The judgment stated: 'The distinguishing mark of a "manifestly unlawful order" should fly like a black flag above the order given, as a warning saying, "Prohibited". Not formal unlawfulness, hidden or half-hidden, nor unlawfulness discernible only by the eyes of legal experts, is important here, but a flagrant and manifest breach of the law, definite and unnecessary unlawfulness appearing on the face of the order itself, the clearly criminal character of the acts ordered to be done, unlawfulness piercing the eye not blind nor the heart stony and corrupt – that is the measure of manifest unlawfulness required to release the soldier from the duty of obedience upon him and make him criminally responsible for his acts.'[1]

The law of Israel is close to that of England and this colourful definition goes to the heart of the matter. The modern soldier is not expected to be a barrack-room lawyer but simply a human being conscious of his responsibility to humanity.

By such elementary yet vital standards, what soldier can justify participation in the annihilation of whole populations? The *Manual* confirms that even the highest in the land cannot escape responsibility: 'Heads of State and their Ministers enjoy no immunity from prosecution and punishment for war crimes. Their liability is governed by the same principles as those governing the responsibility of State officials except that the defence of superior orders is never open to Heads of State and is rarely open to ministers.'[2]

This is confirmed by a leading English law authority: 'The Minister or servant of the Crown who takes part in giving expression to the Royal will is legally responsible for the act in which he is concerned and he cannot get rid of his liability by pleading that he acted in obedience to royal orders. Now supposing that the act done is illegal, the Minister concerned in it becomes at once liable to criminal or civil proceedings in a court of law.'[3] Soldiers can take some comfort from the fact that those at the top are, or are supposed to be, fully exposed to the law.

The *Manual* goes on to examine yet another concept, that of

---

[1] L. Green, *Superior Orders in National and International Law*, Netherlands 1976.
[2] Op. cit., para. 632.
[3] Dicey, *Law of the Constitution*, 8th ed., London 1923.

'military necessity', which has been used many times in the past to camouflage unlawful military action. But, the *Manual* declares: 'Unless in any convention or customary rule express allowance is made for military necessity, officers and other members of the armed forces are not entitled to violate specific prohibitions of the law of war on the plea of military necessity.'[1]

This definition stems directly from the Hague Conventions and is further explained by the *Manual*: 'The rules of the law of war have evolved by custom or have been established by treaty after the full requirements of military operations and needs have been taken into account.' The *Manual* refers to the Hague Convention's desire to diminish the evils of war and provide a 'general rule of conduct', and to Article 1 of the 1949 Geneva Convention, which requires 'respect for the present Conventions in all circumstances.'[2]

How can violations of the law be prosecuted? 'Charges of war crimes,' says the *Manual*, 'are subject to the jurisdiction of military courts, whether national or international, or of such other courts as the belligerent concerned may determine.'[3] The courts of neutral States may also exercise jurisdiction, civil or military, in respect of war crimes. According to the *Manual*: 'War crimes are crimes *ex jure gentium* and are thus triable by the courts of all States. It is fundamental that there must be a trial before punishment. British military courts have jurisdiction outside the United Kingdom over war crimes committed not only by members of the enemy armed forces but also by enemy civilians and other persons of any nationality, including those of British nationality or the nationals of allied or neutral States. It is not necessary that the victim of the war crime should be a British subject. Persons accused of war crimes are properly charged not with an offence against the municipal (national) law of the belligerent but with an offence or offences against the laws and customs of war, although the constitution and procedure of the particular national court trying the case may be determined by the municipal law.'[4]

This reflects the experience of the post-war crimes trials, conducted by both international and municipal military tribunals. The *Manual* cites the Nuremberg Charter, Article 6: 'That Article

[1] Op. cit., para. 633.
[2] Ibid.
[3] Op. cit., para. 637.
[4] Ibid.

conferred upon the Tribunal, in addition to jurisdiction over so-called crimes against peace and crimes against humanity, jurisdiction with regard to war crimes.' It is clear that the laws of war are a genuinely international branch of the law which may be enforced by a variety of means. The *Manual* describes the wide international scope of recent law enforcement: 'Tribunals established by the national authorities of the various Allied States adjudicated upon large numbers of charges of war crimes by former members of the enemy armed forces and by civilians. The United States and Great Britain, in particular, established military courts for that purpose in their zones of occupied Germany and Italy. In Belgium, France, Holland, Norway, Czechoslovakia, Poland, Yugoslavia and some other countries, national tribunals pronounced sentences upon war criminals surrendered by virtue of arrangements made by the United Nations War Crimes Commission.' This Commission was set up in 1943.

'Members of the British armed forces who commit war crimes,' says the *Manual*, 'are tried under appropriate provisions of the Army Act, 1955, or the Air Force Act, 1955 or the Naval Discipline Act.'[1] So a British soldier charged with committing a war crime may be tried by a British military court, or by a foreign court, or by an international tribunal. If that crime also transgresses British criminal law, as it may well do, he may also be tried in a criminal court.

As for punishment for such offences: 'All war crimes are punishable by death, but a more lenient penalty may be pronounced. Corporal punishment is excluded, and cruelty in any form is prohibited.'[2] The Royal Warrant of 1945 is cited, which says that a death sentence may be carried out 'by hanging or by shooting'. The Manual adds that all parties to the Geneva Conventions of 1949 undertake to 'search for persons alleged to have committed, or ordered, "grave breaches", and, regardless of their nationality, to bring them to trial in their own courts.'[3]

Next comes the sticky issue of 'reprisals'. It is a popular fiction that 'anything you can do I can do better' is an unwritten law of war, providing a gloss of legitimacy for the escalation of violence neatly described in F. R. Scott's poem 'Degeneration':

[1] Ibid.
[2] Op. cit., para. 638.
[3] Op. cit., para. 639.

The first to go are the niceties,
The little minor conformities
That suddenly seem absurdities.

Soon kindling animosities
Surmount the old civilities
And start the first brutalities.

Then come the bold extremities,
The justified enormities,
The unrestrained ferocities.[1]

Reprisals may be used to 'induce the enemy to desist from his unlawful conduct', says the *Manual*. But 'reprisals against prisoners of war, against sick and wounded and against ship-wrecked members of the enemy armed forces, against buildings, vessels and equipment protected by the Wounded and Maritime Conventions, as well as against civilian protected persons and their property in occupied territory and in the belligerent's own territory, are now prohibited'.[2] It is clear that the law forbids reprisals which involve indiscriminate attacks on protected persons.

The *Manual* is specific on this point: 'Not only do all reprisals against wounded and sick, prisoners of war, and civilians protected under the Civilian Convention, constitute war crimes ... but acts of reprisal that are grossly excessive against non-protected persons also constitute a war crime.'[3] Nuclear retaliation cannot be contained within legitimate reprisal.

The British *Manual of Military Law*, even without the incorporation of the important Additional Protocol 1, 1977, gives us an insight into the soldier's relation to the law restricting military violence. It is a relationship of binding complexity and the penalties for violation are severe. It imposes a professional standard of conduct which would be immediately recognizable to military heroes such as Nelson and Wellington. The law permits the soldier to kill, but only within strict limits. A soldier must not murder. 'We call them murderers,' writes one commentator, 'only when they take aim at non-combatants, innocent bystanders (civilians) wounded or disarmed soldiers'.[4]

[1] F. R. Scott, *Selected Poems*, London 1966.
[2] Op. cit., para. 644.
[3] Op. cit., para. 648.
[4] Michael Walzer, *Just and Unjust Wars*, London 1980.

To complete this summary of British military law and war it is necessary to see how the armed forces have begun to digest the laws defined in the Additional Protocol 1, 1977. This comprises 102 Articles covering fifty pages, and updates and strengthens protection for non-combatants in time of war. The British soldier is already affected by its provisions, in spite of the British Government's delay in ratifying it. Lack of a ratifying Act of Parliament is not, however, of great significance. As the Ministry of Defence in London has confirmed: 'It will be appreciated that the Protocols are largely declaratory of existing international law already binding on states independently of ratification.'[1]

This is confirmed by the 'Law of Armed Conflict' lecture notes used at the British military academy, Sandhurst. Some of the Protocol's laws are 'declaratory of customary law', regardless of ratification. 'International Law,' says this document, 'of which the law of war forms part, has been developed through custom, practice and treaties, to govern relations between States. The peculiarity of the law of war is that it also imposes duties on individuals.

'To understand the law of war,' the young officers are told, 'it is necessary to grasp certain basic principles as follows:

a. A distinction must be drawn between combatants and non-combatants. The former are permitted to take part in hostilities, whereas the latter are not. The former may be attacked, while the latter are protected from attack.

'Why is it necessary to comply?' asks the paper. 'First and most important, because the law of war requires all States and individuals to do so. It is the policy of the UK Government to comply.'

Apart from the legal reasons, it says, 'there are a number of moral and practical reasons for compliance.' Among these it lists 'the need for the support of the population both in the combat area and at home; reciprocity; human instinct tends to lead to response in kind; the pressure of world opinion is not an insignificant factor.'

Protocol 1 is used, without qualification, to justify the following definition of legal protection of civilians: 'Only military objectives can be attacked. Direct attacks on civilians are prohibited. So are attacks on undefended towns, villages or buildings. Civilians and

[1] Letter to the author from the Directorate of Army Legal Services, Ministry of Defence, 4 November 1982.

civilian property must be spared as far as possible from incidental damage, especially schools, hospitals, churches and historical monuments and works of art. This means that an effort has to be made to identify a target as a legitimate military objective and that it must be engaged in such a way that incidental damage is minimized. There has been a tendency to forget these rules in the confusion of guerrilla warfare or the concept of total war.'

This is the closest these 'Law Notes' come to confronting the legal implications of nuclear war, rather as if bubonic plague were to be analyzed without reference to rats. But the document marches on, regardless: 'War crimes can be prevented if: soldiers know the basic rules of the law of war; officers set a good example themselves and maintain firm discipline; and those concerned with policy and plans take legal advice wherever necessary ... It is clearly essential,' says the document, 'that an officer should not place his subordinates in an invidious position and undermine discipline by ordering them to do something he knows to be unlawful.'

British officers are required by law to act only within strictly prescribed limits, which include a prohibition against any attack on non-combatants. The basis of British defence strategy, the nuclear deterrent, is not mentioned, suggesting that the British armed forces do not know how to reconcile 'population extermination' (Conservative MP Julian Critchley's definition of British deterrent policy[1]) with professional rules of conduct. They have every reason to be embarrassed.

So much for the letter of the law concerning the soldier's profession. But we know how vast and shadowy is the chasm between law and behaviour in our death-cell civilization. No single aspect of British military behaviour better illustrates this official lapse into crime than the steps by which the RAF moved over the years from the romantic gallantry of World War One air aces to the infernal cauldron of Dresden, a process accelerated by Polaris submarines and their city-busting missiles.

'Some time ago, I'm not sure when,' wrote an RAF veteran of World War Two bombing missions over Germany, 'sickened by what seemed now the waste of the lives of my comrades in the RAF ... and the knowledge of my part in the death of innocent civilians

[1] *Guardian*, 5 March 1984.

in German towns, I took the two war medals I had earned, together with my log book that recorded details of the thirty-three operational flights I had flown, items of which I was once so proud, and dropped them in our household waste bin.'

He had been brought up to believe in the 'rules and ethics of fair play. If a pilot baled out of his shot down aircraft, one did not attempt to machine gun the pilot as he parachuted earthwards. I was soon to discover that someone had forgotten to make rules about it being wrong to drop bombs on civilian women, children and old people, out of the darkness of the night sky ... This was the ethics of modern warfare. It wasn't possible to see ten thousand families incinerated in a matter of minutes from 15,000 feet up in the night sky ... When flying on operations I certainly had no idea we were engaged upon the calculated destruction of German towns and their civilian populations. I do, however, remember being disturbed by the fact that at our briefings we were always given information that went like this: "and don't forget, chaps, if you have to abort your mission and turn back over enemy territory, don't bring your bombs back. If you see a light, bomb it!" '[1]

He was wrong about the rules but right about the policy to destroy cities and 'enemy morale', official euphemism for people. This nineteen-year-old airman was told nothing about the law. Yet barely thirty years earlier, above the bloody fields of north-west France, a different code of conduct ruled: 'Never since the Middle Ages and the invention of the longbow had the battlefields of Europe seen this kind of single combat. When the champions of either side met to fight spectacular duels in and out of the clouds, the rest of the war seemed forgotten, even the men in the trenches paused to watch, as the hosts of Greece and Troy stood by when Hector and Achilles fought.

'On one occasion, a German pilot dropped one of his expensive fur gloves during a raid over a French airfield. The next day he returned to drop the other; with a note begging the finder to keep it, as he had no use for only one glove. With medieval courtesy, the recipient dropped a thank-you note over the donor's base .... When Boelke himself was killed (in a collision with his best friend) planes from every British airfield within range dropped wreaths on his base, regardless of the risk involved.'[2]

[1] Letter to author, April 1982.
[2] Alistair Horne, *The Price of Glory*, London 1962.

That spirit of respect was never to reappear, except partially in the more ruthless Battle of Britain, and in the tank battles in the Western desert of North Africa during World War Two. It was fading even before the First World War ground to a halt. In 1916, German aircraft caused outrage when they dropped poisoned sweets and confetti. More ominously, Major-General Trenchard, commander of the British air force, said: 'The moral effect of bombing stands undoubtedly to the material effect in a proportion of 20 to 1.'[1]

The seeds of city bombing had been sown. When, in 1918, the King of Spain suggested, prompted by the German Government, that open towns should not be bombed, the British response was negative. 'At any rate the hint, for it was nothing more,' say the RAF's official historians, 'was regarded by the British Government as a sign that the Germans would suffer more damage by strategic bombing than they could inflict and it was consequently rejected.'[2] This was the kind of rationalization doomed to drag down every disarmament initiative for generations to come, seeing only weakness in a willingness to negotiate.

The law lagged behind the rapid growth of air power. An attempt was made at the turn of the century to ban projectiles dropped from balloons, 'or by other new methods of a similar nature'. This limited agreement at The Hague in 1899 was confirmed in 1907, and remains in force, unloved and disowned. Britain and the United States were signatories, with thirty others, including Austria-Hungary but not Germany or Russia. More important, the Washington Conference of 1922 on the Limitation of Armaments established a Commission of Jurists at The Hague (1923/4) to prepare 'Rules of Air Warfare'. These rules were never adopted in legally binding form but according to a leading law authority are important 'as an authoritative attempt to clarify and formulate rules of law governing the use of aircraft in war'.[3] Their continuing relevance is due to the fact 'that they correspond to the customary rules and general principles underlying the conventions on the law of war on land and sea'.[4] Britain and the United States formed part of this Commission.

[1] Webster & Frankland, *The Strategic Air Offensive Against Germany 1939–45* (3 vols.), London 1961.
[2] Ibid.
[3] Schindler and Toman, *Law of Armed Conflict*, The Hague 1981.
[4] Ibid.

Killing defenceless people was still a crime. The rules of air bombardment made this clear: 'Aerial bombardment for the purpose of terrorising the civilian population ... or of injuring non-combatants is prohibited.'[1] 'Aerial bombardment is legitimate only when directed at a military objective . . . . The bombardment of cities, towns, villages, dwellings or buildings not in the immediate neighbourhood of the operations of land forces is prohibited.'[2] If a military target could not be attacked 'without the indiscriminate bombardment of the civilian population' there must be no attack.[3] The commander of an aircraft must take 'all necessary steps [to] spare as far as possible buildings dedicated to public worship, art, science, or charitable purposes, historical monuments, hospital ships, hospitals and other places where the sick and wounded are collected.'[4] These are seeds of the Nuremberg Charter and its branding of 'wanton destruction' as war crimes.

Such careful attention to the detail of war seems as quaint in our nuclear age as Greek architecture would have appeared to tribesmen of the dark ages. War was a gentle wind in the minds of those jurists, not the nuclear hurricane which threatens to sweep away all in its path. Soon the cynical quip would become current: 'hitting Cologne cathedral may be a war crime, but missing the railway station is war'. The two buildings are adjacent, like the forces of care and crime in the human mind. But as an indication of how customary law concerning air warfare developed, it is worth recalling a British contribution. In 1938, responding to growing public anxiety about the horrors of air bombardment, a British Conservative Prime Minister, Neville Chamberlain, won the support of the House of Commons for a declaration that all bombing of cities and civilians is a violation of international law. His legal advisers, unlike those of today's Prime Minister, were in no doubt of the law, years before it was strengthened by Nuremberg, the Geneva Conventions, the Genocide Convention and the Additional Protocol 1.

In September 1938 the League of Nations adopted without dissent a resolution proposed by the British Government, thus applying the weight of world opinion to this interpretation of law.

[1] Loc. cit., Article 22.
[2] Loc. cit., Article 24.
[3] Ibid.
[4] Loc. cit., Article 25.

1. The intentional bombing of civilian populations is illegal.

2. Objectives aimed at from the air must be legitimate military objectives and must be identifiable.

3. Any attack on legitimate military objectives must be carried out in such a way that civilian populations in the neighbourhood are not bombed through negligence.

So rapid was the unravelling of these minimum laws of restraint in the heat of World War Two that the general descent to crime would inspire a modern Dante.

During 1939 and much of 1940, the antagonists circled each other suspiciously, without much action. Just before the outbreak of war, on 14 August 1939, there was an Anglo-French Staff Conversation. The British representative said: 'Whatever course we adopt, we should take all possible steps to make clear, not only to neutral countries but also to the German people, that our air action is directed only against those objectives whose destruction is calculated to shorten the course of the war, and that we have no intention of attacking the civil population as such.'[1]

On 1 September President Roosevelt made an appeal for belligerents to refrain from unrestricted air warfare. Britain agreed on the same day, followed quickly by the Germans and French.

Hardly had assent been given when German bombing of Poland caused second thoughts within the RAF. But Air Commodore Slessor noted in a Department of Planning Memorandum: 'Indiscriminate attack on civilian populations as such will never form part of our policy.'[2] Hitler told his generals on 9 October 1939: 'The ruthless employment of the *Luftwaffe* against the heart of the British will-to-resist can and will follow at the given moment.'[3] In May 1940 the German bombing of Rotterdam, which caused much less damage than at first reported, indicated that the gloves were off. 'Mr Churchill,' according to the official historians, 'like many other people in the country, was now anxious that the Germans should get as good as they were giving, and he suggested to Sir Charles Portal that Bomber Command should henceforth spread its bombs as widely as possible over the cities of Germany.'[4]

[1] *Strategic Air Offensive Vol. I.*
[2] Ibid. Dated 7 September 1939.
[3] Ibid.
[4] Ibid.

It was becoming obvious that strategic bombing would violate the accepted rules of war: 'The Air Staff . . . believed that what was inevitable was also desirable only in so far as it remained a by-product of the primary intention to hit a military target . . . Bomber Command, as represented by its Commander-in-Chief, Sir Charles Portal, now believed that this by-product should become an end-product. He believed that the time had come to launch a direct attack on the German people themselves.'[1]

Not only were the gloves off, but the referee was about to be thrown out of the ring, to be replaced by savagery.

In terms of the laws of war the RAF now entered a period of politically sanctioned gangsterism from which it has never fully emerged. A high-level directive confirmed this drift: 'Successive sorties should . . . focus their attacks to a large extent on the fires with a view to preventing the fire services from dealing with them and giving the fires every opportunity to spread.'[2] As the Chiefs of Staff said in a minute to Churchill on 7 June 1941, 'the most vulnerable point in the German nation at war is the morale of the civilian population under air attack'.

RAF Bomber Command produced a plan for Churchill which 'envisaged the complete destruction of forty-three selected German towns which included the majority with a population of more than 100,000 and which had a total population of some fifteen million.'[3] The plan was modified but its intentions approved. 'Area bombing' had arrived, the process by which the centre of a city was marked by a pathfinding plane with flares, guiding in bombers to the bull's eye.

As so often, technical rationalization paved the way for evasion of the law. The RAF could only bomb at night, because of vulnerability to air defences. Its capacity to find and hit specific military targets at night was so limited that bomb-spreads covered a huge area, much of it open countryside. There was more point in bombing cities than fields, ran the prevailing logic. 'Bomber' Harris, who became the next and famous head of Bomber Command, described the options graphically to Churchill: 'while it takes approximately 7,000 hours of flying to destroy one submarine at sea, that was approximately the amount of flying necessary to

[1] Ibid.
[2] Ibid. Air Chief Marshal Douglas to Sir Richard Peirse, dated 30 October 1940.
[3] Ibid. Bomber Operations memorandum of 22 September 1941.

destroy one third of Cologne, the third largest city in Germany, in one night'.[1]

While Hitler was trying to 'wipe Leningrad off the face of the map', Churchill was applying the same treatment to Germany's major cities. The signs pointed to Hiroshima and beyond. Air Marshal Harris fathered the thousand-bomber raid, a massive organizational challenge: 'He reckoned that from two to four consecutive thousand-attacks on a city the size of Cologne "would have the effect of virtually destroying the objective to the extent of putting it out of action for any foreseeable duration of the war".'[2]

His appetite grew with what it fed on. 'We can wreck Berlin from end to end,' Air Marshal Harris said on 3 November 1943, 'if the USAF will come in on it. It will cost us 400–500 aircraft. It will cost Germany the war.' He was confident: 'It is not possible to dogmatize on the degree of destruction necessary to cause the enemy to capitulate but there can be little doubt that the necessary conditions would be brought about by the destruction of between 40% and 50% of the principal German towns.'[3]

We have now arrived at the ultimate conclusion of this murderous logic, when victory involves the total destruction of all concerned. The RAF's official historians put it this way: 'It might appear, and it has often been suggested, that a great moral issue was involved in this situation, but the moral issue was not really an operative factor. The choice between precision and area bombing was not conditioned by abstract theories of right and wrong, nor by interpretation of international law. It was ruled by operational possibilities and strategic intentions.'[4]

Or, in short, the end justifies the means. Neither morality nor the law was operative. A vengeful robot within the human brain had taken over, indifferent to suffering and humanitarian law. Meanwhile, cities became gigantic graveyards. The bombing of Coventry by the *Luftwaffe* destroyed one hundred out of a possible 1,922 acres. In Hamburg the figures were 6,200 out of 8,382, and in Essen 1,030 out of 2,630. The historians describe

[1] Ibid. Note of 28 June 1942.
[2] Ibid. Letter from Harris to Air Chief Marshal Portal of 20 June 1940.
[3] *Strategic Air Offensive Vol. II*, op. cit. Letter to Air Ministry of 7 December 1943.
[4] Ibid.

the final 740-bomber assault on Hamburg as a 'macabre climax' to earlier raids.

These historians admit that 'general area bombing works almost on the principle that in order to destroy anything it is necessary to destroy everything'.[1] Hitler had something similar in mind. So have our nuclear strategists. The gruesome story of RAF bombing policy, like that of modern armaments, defies human comprehension because it denies human feeling. The torn flesh and the screams die away, leaving only a cold whisper of facts, statistics and rationalizations.

Just a glimpse is offered of the nightmare created with such energy, sacrifice and devotion to duty: 'The fire storm caused by the simultaneous outbreak of a large number of fires in a densely populated city was unique and rendered useless the ordinary methods of defence. Thousands of people were trapped in the shelters in what had become a furnace and were burnt or, in most cases, more mercifully asphyxiated. The rush of air produced by the intense heat carried burning timber and other inflammable material far through the air and spread similar fires in other unburnt areas ... the shock to the humanity gathered in the big city was as great, if not so enduring, as that caused by the most destructive earthquakes of the past.'[2]

Last in this particular line of dragon's teeth came the destruction of Dresden in the last weeks of the war in Europe: 'It was the crowning achievement in the long, arduous and relentless development of a principle of bombing which the Royal Air Force had initially adopted, as a retaliatory measure, in the attack on Mannheim of December 1940. A crowning achievement which was both tragic and unnecessary, according to Air Marshal Sir Robert Saundby, RAF: "that the bombing of Dresden was a great tragedy none can deny. That it was really a military necessity few ... will believe".'[3]

The bomb-aimer of a Lancaster bomber on that raid was clear about his feelings: 'it was the only time I ever felt sorry for the Germans. But my sorrow lasted only a few seconds; the job was to hit the enemy and to hit him hard.' Another bomb-aimer was more descriptive: 'I confess to taking a glance downward as the bombs

---

[1] Op. cit., *Vol. III*.
[2] Op. cit., *Vol. II*.
[3] David Irving, *The Destruction of Dresden*, London 1974.

fell and I witnessed the shocking sight of a city on fire from end to end. Dense smoke could be seen drifting away from Dresden, leaving a brilliantly illuminated plan view of the town. My immediate reaction was a stunned reflection on the comparison between the holocaust below and the warnings of the evangelists in Gospel meetings before the war.'

Despite these feelings, the bombers were divorced from those on the ground. A Dresden pensioner, writing five days after the raids, described the scene: 'One shape I will never forget was the remains of what had apparently been a mother and child. They had shrivelled and charred into one piece, and had been stuck rigidly to the asphalt. They had just been prised up. The child must have been underneath the mother, because you could still clearly see its shape, with its mother's arms clasped around it.'

'Never,' said the director of rescue operations,' would I have thought that death would come to so many people in so many different ways. Never had I expected to see people interred in that state: burnt, cremated, torn and crushed to death; sometimes the victims looked like ordinary people apparently sleeping peacefully; the faces of others were wracked with pain, the bodies stripped almost naked by the tornado; there were wretched refugees from the East clad only in rags, and people from the Opera in all their finery; here the victim was a shapeless slab, there a layer of ashes shovelled into a zinc tub. Across the city, along the streets wafted the unmistakable stench of decaying flesh.'

The fire storm stripped many of the victims naked: 'In the middle of the square lay an old man, with two dead horses .... A few yards further on lay two young boys aged about eight and ten clinging tightly to each other; their faces were buried in the ground. They too were stark naked. Their legs were stiff and twisted into the air.'[1]

How can the mind encompass such an orgy of violence? The scale of it cuts off feeling because to feel the suffering is to be drowned by it. The RAF bomb-aimer stifled his feelings of pity, obeyed his orders and hit the enemy hard. A mother and child were the enemy, and two boys who clung together. According to the law, soon to be used to convict Nazi war criminals, mothers and children are not legitimate targets. But by then the law was itself a

[1] Ibid.

victim of the fire-storms raging across Germany, twisted out of recognition by mad revenge.

What better picture of this barbarism than that caught by the camera of the RAF target plane in Dresden? Its job was to identify and hit the centre of the target zone, as a marker for the incoming bombers far above: 'from two thousand feet the Mosquito dived to less than eight hundred feet, opening its bomb doors as it entered upon the straight run-in to the aiming-point. The first flash cartridge fired as the camera was pointing at the Dresden-Friedrichstadt Krankenhaus, the biggest hospital complex in Central Germany. In its lens the camera trapped the picture of the 1,000 lb target indicator bomb slipping out of the bomb-bay, the finned canister silhouetted menacingly on top of a small oblong building in the hospital grounds.'[1]

Had the Germans won the war, there is no doubt that this photograph alone would have been enough to convict RAF airmen of war crimes. Despite the silence of the lawyers and the lies of the government, the British people became increasingly uneasy as the destruction increased. According to the official historians: 'The conduct of the strategic air offensive had long been regarded with suspicion by sections of public opinion in Britain. It was generally regarded as morally legitimate to bomb strategic objectives such as factories, oil plants, dockyards and railway centres, even if this did incidentally cause severe destruction of residential areas and of civilian life and limb. On the other hand, the view that it was morally legitimate to bomb residential areas, even if the object was to reduce military or industrial activity, was frequently challenged, and the more apparent it became that in the majority of its major area attacks, Bomber Command was, in fact, aiming at the centres of residential areas, the more pronounced the protests became.'[2]

The truth of this bombing campaign was not only masked from the RAF crews but the public at large. The Minister of Air, Sir Archibald Sinclair, 'did not concede that one of the objects of area bombing was the reduction of civilian and especially industrial morale by the bombing of housing and public utilities and so, of course, of the populations themselves. He usually, and on public occasions invariably, suggested that Bomber Command was aiming at military or industrial installations, as, of course, it

[1] Ibid.
[2] *Strategic Air Offensive Vol. III.*

sometimes was. He did not conceal that severe and sometimes vast damage was done to residential areas, but he either implied, or on some occasions said, that all this was incidental and even regrettable. Only in this way, he explained to Sir Charles Portal in October, 1943, could he satisfy the enquiries of the Archbishop of Canterbury and the Moderator of the Church of Scotland.'[1]

Almost exactly one year before the destruction of Dresden, the Bishop of Chichester, Dr Bell, spoke in the House of Lords against city bombing, quoting the Commission of Jurists' 'Air Rules' of 1923. His was a lonely voice. Richard Crossman, Minister of a post-war Labour Government, described the deteriorating values involved: 'In 1940, we thought it absolutely inhuman and a violation of every human right to bomb the centre of an unprotected city. Then we started preparing to do it ourselves. We started systematic plans for what we called de-housing, which meant deliberately not bombing military targets but systematically destroying working class areas in German towns. That was the policy of Bomber Command. It was absolutely inhuman.'[2]

It was also illegal, but by then the nuclear era was established, obliterating in the minds of politicians and lawyers alike all sense of legal boundaries to warfare.

Those, and they are many, who defend 'Bomber' Harris and area bombing, point to the Casablanca Directive of 21 January 1943, approved by President Roosevelt and Churchill. It laid down Bomber Command's war aims: 'Your primary objective will be the progressive destruction and dislocation of the German military, industrial and economic system and the undermining of the morale of the German people to a point where their capacity for armed resistance is fatally weakened.' This indicates full approval at the highest level for the bombing campaign which followed it. It also, as an admirer of Harris points out, took us into the arms of nuclear weaponry: 'Critics have claimed the offensive was a failure because it did not turn out to be decisive on its own. It took the invention of the atomic bomb to provide the scale of devastation that Harris was seeking and which now effectively deters aggression.'[3]

The official historians' view of Harris is illuminating: 'In legend, Sir Arthur Harris was seen by his men as a forceful, ruthless,

[1] Ibid.
[2] *Hansard*, 4 March 1954.
[3] Air Commodore Cooper in the *Daily Telegraph*, 7 April 1984.

single-minded and great leader .... To the Commander-in-Chief was given, in all but miraculously few cases, an absolute obedience.' Their own assessment points to other qualities: 'Sir Arthur Harris made a habit of seeing only one side of a question and then of exaggerating it. He had a tendency to confuse advice with interference, criticism with sabotage and evidence with propaganda. He resisted innovation and he was seldom open to persuasion.'[1]

But the most perceptive insight into his character came from himself: 'The feeling such as there is over Dresden could be easily explained by any psychiatrist. It is connected with German bands and Dresden shepherdesses. Actually, Dresden was a mass of munition works, an intact government centre and a key transportation point to the East.'[2] Feeling, in his eyes, was sentimentality. It had certainly proved as fragile as Dresden china.

But politicians have to pay more attention to public feeling than air marshals. Alarmed by signs of public revulsion at the growing carnage, Churchill drafted a Minute to his Chiefs of Staff: 'It seems to me that the moment has come when the question of bombing German cities simply for the sake of increasing the terror, though under other pretexts, should be reviewed. Otherwise we shall come into the control of an utterly ruined land .... The destruction of Dresden remains a serious query against the conduct of Allied bombing. I am of the opinion that military objectives must henceforward be more strictly studied in our own interests rather than that of the enemy. The Foreign Secretary has spoken to me on this subject, and I feel the need for more precise concentration upon military objectives ... rather than on mere acts of terror and wanton destruction, however impressive.'[3]

There was immediate protest from the RAF chiefs. The prospect of a damaging public row made Churchill try to bridge the gap. On 1 April he re-wrote the Minute: 'It seems to me that the moment has come when the question of the so-called 'area bombing' of German cities should be reviewed from the point of view of our own interests. If we come into control of an entirely ruined land, there will be a great shortage of accommodation for ourselves and our Allies: and we shall be unable to get housing

---

[1] *Strategic Air Offensive Vol. III.*
[2] Letter of 29 March 1945.
[3] Minute to Chiefs of Staff of 28 March 1945. Harris's letter of 29 March was in reply to this.

materials out of Germany for our own needs . . . . We must see to it that our attacks do not do more harm to ourselves in the long run than they do to the enemy's immediate war effort. Pray let me have your views.'

Such factors as terror, blame, guilt, wanton destruction – the stuff of morality and law – were ushered out of sight as quickly as they had appeared. All that remained was concern about housing materials. The Nazi virus had spread, paralyzing feeling at every level of military and political life. 'Bomber' Harris clearly did not give a fig for the laws of war. He had no more sense of humane restraint than a meat-grinder. The taint of corpses in the rubble of Hamburg, Cologne and Dresden hung about him until his death. But he was no more than a big cog in a murderous machine, and was right to say in 1960: 'The strategy of the bomber force which Earl Attlee criticizes was decided by HM Government, of which he was for most of the war a leading member. The decision to bomb industrial cities for morale effect was made, and in force, before I became Commander in Chief of Bomber Command.'[1]

Nuclear weapons were soon to make Harris's efforts as out-of-date as Hitler's. The change of gear from conventional to nuclear weaponry was smooth and painless. Lawyers, politicians and soldiers looked on, applauding or silent. On New Year's Day 1946, three British Chiefs of Staff sent their report on atomic development to the Prime Minister, recommending deterrence: 'We must be prepared for aggressors who have widely dispersed industries and populations. This means that in order to be effective as a deterrent we must have a considerable number of bombs at our disposal.'[2]

Once disguised and a source of shame, mass destruction had come of age as a guardian of peace. Soon there would be silver cups awarded to air crews capable of destroying entire cities: 'RAF Vulcan and Valiant bombers and four American bombers are taking part in a navigation and nuclear bombing contest over Britain. London, Glasgow, Birmingham, Manchester, and other large cities will be the targets. A cup will be awarded to the winners.'[3]

But they in turn would soon be superseded, by nuclear submarines and multi-targeted missiles. At the very moment when

[1] David Irving, op. cit.
[2] Margaret Gowing, *Independence and Deterrence Vol. I: Policy Making*, London 1974.
[3] *Daily Telegraph*, 19 May 1958.

British Polaris submarines were being updated, secretly and at huge cost, a British Labour Government was busy negotiating in Geneva comprehensive laws protecting non-combatants in time of war (the Additional Protocol 1). The Foreign Secretary who signed those laws on behalf of Britain was David Owen, later to become leader of the Social Democratic Party. When I asked him some years later, in 1984, why he did not uphold these laws, he told me they are 'unenforceable'.

We can understand now, perhaps, why the RAF group-captain in Bedford told me that he had never before been asked what laws restrict RAF operations. It was in 1940, after all, before the group-captain was born, that the RAF parted company with the law, to learn the art of mass destruction. If and when the nuclear nightmare is banished and the law upheld, the RAF may want to erect a monument to that mother and child burnt into the pavement of Dresden, and to the two small boys who clung to each other when hit hard.

According to the Incitement to Disaffection Act, 1934: 'If any person maliciously and advisedly endeavours to seduce any member of His Majesty's forces from his duty and allegiance to His Majesty, he shall be guilty of an offence under this Act.' 'His Majesty' is the State and the State is nothing without the law. The law has been perverted by successive British Governments, maliciously and advisedly, so that today's British soldier has been made the unwitting accomplice of a strategy based on threats of mass murder. It is not the first time that a State has stepped outside the law of nations, degrading the military oath of allegiance. The Nuremberg Tribunal imposed the law on selected criminals. It is our task to renew that law and enforce it again.

It is evident that the British soldier, no less than the lawyer and the judge, and the rest of us, is both victim and agent of the nuclear nightmare. By their own regulations and law, the British armed forces are bound by the judgment of Nuremberg and the minimum standards of international law. Yet in relation to nuclear policy they are mute, leaderless and lawless. The British soldier is loyal pawn and mindless outlaw.

If he is ever to rediscover his professional integrity, the British soldier may wish to find inspiration in an earlier oath of allegiance. The fifteenth-century knights of Aragon knew their worth in relation to their king and made sure he knew it: 'We who are as good as you swear to you, who are not better than we, to accept you as our king and sovereign lord, provided that you observe all our liberties and laws; but if not, then not.'[1]

[1] Dorothy Carrington, *Granite Island*, London 1984.

Chapter Seven

The German Soldier's Tale

'. . . there is at the centre of the miracle of Germany's material
resurrection such a profound deadness of spirit, such an
inescapable sense of triviality and dissimulation'
– George Steiner

'Why do you permit these tyrants to rob you, step by step,
openly or secretly, of your rights, till one day nothing will be
left but a mechanized State operated by criminals and
alcoholics?'
– 'White Rose' leaflet, Munich, 1943

It was not just Goethe who invented fiction to 'get the past off my
neck'. We all do it. But whereas Goethe was able to write great
novels, most of us tend to write fiction in our heads, using a fantasy
lens to colour reality. No modern soldier carries on his neck a
heavier burden of the past than the German (this chapter is
addressed to West Germans but most of it applies equally to East
Germans). How does he stand today in relation to warfare, nuclear
weapons and the law?

For most of the twentieth century Germany has been a focal
point of European power, violence, ideas, wealth and chaos. The
violence is now locked within Cold War confrontation, a million
times more devastating than before. As a punishment for Nazi
crimes, today's German soldier must serve rather than control the
main forces of military violence. There is no German finger on the
nuclear trigger. Germany is the trigger. Germany is programmed
by East and West as a nuclear detonator. *Götterdämmerung* still
rules okay, under wraps and ready to go. The nuclear nightmare
engulfs East and West Germany with equal malevolence.

Recent wealth has shone a bright light on this dark scene,
illuminating a circle of frenetic activity while blinding eyes from
everything around. I was driving late at night recently between
Munich and the border with Czechoslovakia, along a main road.

Suddenly blue and orange lights flashed ahead. Police sirens wailed, heralding a thunderous roar and rumble. Police cars waved us aside imperiously as behind them loomed a convoy of tanks, their tracks rattling the windows as they sped by. The speed and tension of that German convoy matched the latent hysteria of the country they protected. German experience of the twentieth century is horrific beyond description.

By contrast, the German soldier of the eighties offers a placid face to the world. No longer the strutting bully in jackboots of the Hitler days, he is more civilian than soldier. Yet this exterior is deceptive, and disturbing when examined. The laws within which he operates are liberal and, by British standards, lax. But they are not laws of his choice. They were imposed on a shattered post-war Germany by the Allied powers. Fascist militarism had to be exorcised, by means of laws which stressed individual accountability. The awful lessons of Nuremberg must be taught without reservation. By guaranteeing the right to question authority, the citizen soldier would compel the military machine to respond to his will, and that of society. That was the intention.

So the 'Soldier's Law', the basic internal code of the *Bundeswehr*, embodies many democratic principles. Section II states: 'The soldier must obey his superiors ... it shall not be deemed disobedience to ignore an order which violates human dignity or is not given for service purposes. . . . An order must not be complied with if a crime or gross misdemeanour would be committed thereby.'

Through the 'military complaints order', every serviceman is guaranteed the right to submit complaints of wrongful action to higher officers, with a right of appeal to civilian courts. Every unit has a *Vertrauensmann* (confidential representative) elected to speak for conscripts, who form the bulk of the armed forces. He cannot be removed or punished by a commander.

I shudder at the thought of such rules during my own service with a 94% conscript regiment of the British army in post-war Germany. Our dislike of army life would have taken wing, with unimaginable consequences. It is ironic when the victors of a war to defend democracy trust their soldiers less with democratic principles than those of the former enemy. Perhaps with good reason. The modern German soldier has made no use yet of this latitude to challenge the legal status of the NATO defence posture of nuclear retaliation. A concerted demand for a full-scale government inquiry would yield interesting results.

The rights of the citizen soldier are confirmed in the context of international law by Article 25 of the Basic Law of the Federal Republic: 'The general rules of public international law are an integral part of federal law. They shall take precedence over the law and shall directly create rights and duties for the inhabitants of the federal territory.'

If, as we have seen, the law offers the British soldier scope to reject a criminal militarism, this is even more true for his German colleague and ally.

When the door of a cage is open and the occupant remains inside, the evidence points to an inner compulsion. If traumatic shock is the deadening legacy of disaster, then Germany has every reason to be traumatized to the point of inertia. While external evidence of life in Germany is everywhere and startling, there is an eerie stillness at the core which reflects another reality. Representative of the most dynamic economy in Europe, the German citizen soldier has a languid spirit more in keeping with a tropical banana republic.

Does this matter? Better a sheep than a wolf, some would say. But both animals are unfit for human emulation. Our look at the law in Britain should be sufficient warning of the disasters which flow from a failure to express a full range of human qualities. The nuclear terror is not just an external poison but a creeping paralysis of mind and spirit, drugging feeling and creative imagination. It is a wasting disease which attacks laws of restraint which depend on a lively sense of world-wide responsibility. The self-righteous ignorance of the British soldier is no less damaging to civilized law than the docile indifference of the German.

Revitalization of law requires revitalized people, able to saw through the fraudulent bars of their cage and free enough in spirit to step outside. This means understanding what has happened and why the burden of the past is so heavy. The first step for the German soldier must be to realize that the weight of his past is the weight of ours too, and that it is we who have conspired to heap our own load of shame onto his neck. The story of twentieth-century Europe is the story of wasps in a jam jar, each one deluded that it is uniquely right, and willing to kill to prove it. Yet the closer we look at these wasps the harder it is to tell them apart.

Not since the time of Beethoven, Blake and Goethe has European civilization had even a semblance of integrity. Even then there were rifts and cracks in the surface, stretch marks of a growing industrial and military imperialism. As the empires swelled, so did their armaments, pride and paranoia. A human scale of thought, feeling and action, so characteristic of the three mentioned, was swept aside by compulsive gigantism. Vitality drained out of the villages and towns, into cities which spread like a cancer. As pretentions grew, bolstered by pomp and power, the individual psyche shrank. Soon the city-dweller, isolated and afraid in ant-heap anonymity, was left with only one source of security and confidence, the power of class and State. Such conglomerations offer no real support, only material gain and illusions of power. Defeating an enemy, or finding some way of asserting national superiority, became the European way of life, a way which led, at first slowly and now with giant strides, to death.

As far as nuclear weapons are concerned, it is as if the law has been buried beneath the rubble of two world wars, given up for dead but commemorated by ornamental replicas. The German soldier's indifference to this fact is due to his own entombment in the past. We helped to pile on the rubble and we must help to dig him out.

It is Europe and its polarized extensions, the Soviet Union and the United States, which generated two world wars, not just Germany. Huge internal tensions built up inside a volcanic industrialization. The European mind fragmented under the stress. One segment clung to the myth of individual destiny, using the rags of a religion of love to cover obsessive material greed and power. The other promoted an ideology of equality and brotherhood to disguise a terror of creative exploration, its hot Marxist lava cooling into rigid bureaucracy. The fascist upheaval of the thirties and forties stemmed more from the first than the second myth. Germany, for many reasons, was a latecomer to the imperial game played for so long by Britain and France. No established gang likes a rival. British and French imperialism were already a hollow force, with home cultures torn by economic civil war. Germany was a convenient and willing scapegoat, acting out the regressive passions barely suppressed elsewhere.

Two world wars, a collapse of civilization of volcanic proportions, were rationalized but never understood. Like aristocrats reduced to the state of tramps, we preferred to live in the past, blaming Germany for our reduced state and wretched guilt. Nothing better illustrates this schizoid culture than the Nuremberg trial. It was the judicial act of a Cyclops, a one-eyed version of law and justice. Only one criminal was in the dock, the Nazi, yet the principles of law expounded were universal in range and meaning. 'Who would be the physician, should be the patient.' We know enough of these wars, if we dare face truth at last. But can we disentangle our minds from the lies we have woven on our own behalf? The law itself has been cynically perverted by this hypocrisy, made a shadow of itself and a pawn of our pretensions.

The German soldier is a creature of this charade. He, and the German people, have a surface vitality but underneath the veneer is a black hole filled with the murdered dead of these wars. He has been made to swallow our guilt as well as his own. As long as this fiction remains imposed and our guilt denied, the laws of humanitarian restraint will remain ornamental. Only a shared recognition of shared crime can free us to become real people living in the present. Far from being the price of our freedom, as the dreamers claim, the nuclear nightmare is the high cost of fantasy in a real world.

The German soldier may begin by looking with us at the nature of warfare today. 'One had to go to species as far removed from man as certain kinds of ants to find anything comparable to human warfare,' says a psychiatric study on nuclear war. The authors of this study 'wonder whether the word "denial" adequately describes the failure of emotional comprehension of an event that not only has never been experienced, but is unimaginable by virtue of its extraordinary magnitude'. These American psychiatrists note the elaborate precautions taken to ensure that only sane operatives have access to these mad weapons, but warn: 'A skilful paranoid individual can conceal his delusions from the examiners, and a soldier may become psychotic between examinations.'[1]

The German soldier will remember, hopefully, how similar vetting ensured that only the best recruits entered the SS. He will not be impressed. He will recall how Adolf Eichmann, the administrator of the Jewish holocaust, was examined by five psychiatrists at his trial in Jerusalem, and pronounced sane by all. We all know

[1] 'Psychiatric Aspects of the Prevention of Nuclear War', reported in *The Times*, 30 January 1965.

from personal experience how well paranoid individuals can conceal their delusions, even from themselves. We know because we do it. It seems evident that we have a notion of sanity as accurate as that to be gained from inmates of an asylum. In a nuclear world sanity must be pieced together from a million shattered fragments, with the care of an archaeologist. It is not to be bought whole, off the shelf.

It will be useful for the citizen soldier to look closely at some of the examples set by soldiers and citizens of the Nazi era, not merely because they illustrate German courage and German crime but because they are human beings under stress, like him and the rest of us. It is of no use to review the many thousands of German soldiers, perhaps most of them, who did nothing but fight within the normal discipline of warfare. That line of behaviour continues today, in every armed force, and it has failed to halt or divert the nuclear machinery of mass destruction. It is not normal military behaviour, bound by the laws of war, which spawned nuclear terrorism, but its opposite, an abnormal, wanton criminality.

Fritz Stangl contributed something to our madness. Finally arrested in Brazil and tried in Germany for contributing to a million murders, while commandant of two extermination camps in Poland, Treblinka and Sobihor, he was sentenced to life imprisonment in 1970 and died six months later of a heart attack. He was always a devout Catholic and went to Mass every day while on leave from Treblinka.[1] He had no interest in ideology and thought the Jews were being killed for their money.

Far from being as monstrous as his deeds, Stangl has been described as 'utterly commonplace and boring. He was not a sadist or fanatic or criminal, but a dreary, mindless blinkered official, obedient and conventional. He was personally harmless and never hurt anyone directly. He was friendly with Jews and found the Chairman of the Jewish Council, with whom he travelled to Austria, "a very nice fellow".'[2]

Like his superior Eichmann, Stangl did what he was told and imagined that his orders were legitimate. The laws of war developed around the notion of individual responsibility, the basis of sane behaviour, but modern weapons and methods of war have placed a huge distance between killer and killed. Just as the

[1] Gitta Sereny, *Into that Darkness: from Mercy Killing to Mass Murder*, London 1974.
[2] Hugh Trevor-Roper, in the *Sunday Times*, 8 September 1974.

bomb-aimer saw nothing but the outline of a city, so Nazi killers seldom looked into the face of their victim. As Eichmann's interrogator at Jerusalem put it: 'Since neither the *Führer* nor the *Reichsführer* wanted to bloody their hands, they needed tools; in other words an apparatus of commanders and followers, organizers and thugs, murderers and white-washers. Most of these were provided by the SS; they were the most disciplined and the most unscrupulous. They regarded themselves as the élite of the National Socialists.'[1]

Once the fragile link between military discipline and the laws of personal restraint are broken, the individual loses his identity. Only orders can offer reassurance. Eichmann was a weak character whose only strength came through absolute allegiance to SS discipline and orders from his *Führer*. On a rare visit to a concentration camp he felt sick: 'I was horrified. My nerves aren't strong enough. . . . Even today, if I see someone with a deep cut, I have to look away.'[2] But safely back at his desk, he was ready and willing to administer the machinery of death. A desk-murderer.

Hoess, the commandant of Auschwitz extermination camp, was also sensitive to the problem of face to face brutality and said that gassing was the only practical way of disposing of large numbers: 'shooting was absolutely impossible and also too hard on the SS men involved, having to shoot women and children'.[3] Today's German citizen soldier may note that it is a function of irresponsibility to mask brutality with self-pity. Shooting women and children becomes hard on the executioner rather than the victims. To obey at all costs is, after all, the function of a young child rather than an adult. For a child, self-pity is a natural defence.

Eichmann was asked whether he believed that the German nation could survive 'only if all the Jews in Europe were exterminated'. To which he replied: '*Herr Hauptmann*, if they had said to me: "Your father is a traitor", if they had told me that my own father was a traitor and I had to kill him, I'd have done it. At that time I obeyed my orders without thinking. I just did as I was told. That's where I found my – how shall I say? – my fulfilment. It made no difference what the orders were, *Herr Hauptmann*.'[4]

[1] *Eichmann Interrogated*, London 1983.
[2] Ibid.
[3] Ibid.
[4] Ibid.

Eichmann used as his defence the same plea of *Befehlnotstand* (compulsion to obey orders) as those on trial at Nuremberg. He was asked if he knew what German military law had to say about orders. He claimed he was not subject to the Hague Conventions but to 'SS and police jurisdiction. Our . . . our highest judicial . . . highest judicial authority was Himmler. Naturally, the highest was the *Führer* and Chancellor. Delegated to Himmler in matters concerning the SS and the police.' But what about illegal orders? Should they be obeyed or not? 'How shall I put it?' he replied, 'such distinctions were never even mentioned. Because it was taken for granted that a superior's order was an order and had to be carried out as specified in the oath.'

Regardless of the nature of the order? 'During the war,' he replied, 'you click your heels and say, "Yes, sir." That's all there is to it.' His interrogator persisted: 'How about military law? Did it have a clause dealing with illegal orders?' Eichmann: 'I don't believe so. We certainly had no such thing in the SS. A subordinate has no business interpreting a command.' But what about a 'glaringly illegal order?' Eichmann replied: 'A subordinate, *Herr Hauptmann*, can't carry out an illegal order, certainly not in war-time. He can do only one thing: obey his commander.'[1]

For Eichmann there could be no illegal order from a superior officer. There was no line to be drawn. He was convicted and hanged. He died but the Eichmann syndrome lives on, in the armed forces of the nuclear powers, where the writ of the law runs only to the edges of conventional warfare. The German soldier may be modest and claim that, as Germany has no nuclear weapons, he has no responsibility for their use. But he is an integral part of NATO, and NATO's military posture is based on nuclear weapons. Nuclear weapons, as we have seen, violate the laws of armed conflict in spirit and in detail.

Ignorance of the law can be no defence. If it was, it would be used by every criminal. Eichmann's ignorance, real or pretended, did not help him. Today's citizen soldier may be interested to know that even during Hitler's reign the German military penal code had something useful to say about illegal orders. According to the edition published on 10 October 1940:

[1] Ibid.

Article 47: In case of the penal code being infringed by an order, only a superior who has given the order is responsible. However, the subordinate who complies is liable to punishment as an accomplice:

1 – if he has gone beyond the terms of the order;
2 – if he knew that the order of his superior implied a criminal or injurious act, in a general or military sense;
3 – if the culpability of the subordinate is very little he may escape punishment.

Even in Nazi Germany there were laws which reflected humane values, almost lost among those drawn up to facilitate murder and oppression. German courts since the war have done their best to catch up with the most flagrant Nazi crimes. As late as 1983, a court in East Berlin echoed to the sobs of a former SS officer who confessed to 'lining up terrified French villagers and shooting them in one of the most notorious Nazi massacres of World War Two'.[1] He said he was only obeying orders but added: 'Politicians today should see to it that such things can never happen again.'[2] Soldiers are citizens too, and can demand that politicians obey and enforce the law.

If soldiers as well as citizens let go their responsibility for civilized laws, they let loose all hell. 'Emergency powers' are soon claimed by those in power, 'in the national interest'. Hitler's example stares us in the face. His rubber-stamp parliament, the *Reichstag*, granted him dictatorial power on 26 April 1941, following military setbacks:

In the present war, in which the German people are faced with a struggle for their existence or their annihilation, the Führer must have all the rights postulated by him which serve to further or achieve victory. Therefore – without being bound by existing legal regulations – in his capacity as Leader of the Nation, Supreme Commander of the Armed Forces, Head of Government and supreme executive chief, as Supreme Justice and Leader of the Party the Führer must be in a position to force with all means at his disposal every German, if necessary, whether he be common soldier or officer, low or high official or judge, leading or subordinate official of the party, worker or employer –

[1] *The Times*, 31 May 1983.
[2] *Daily Telegraph*, 31 May 1983.

to fulfil his duties. In case of violation of these duties, the Führer is entitled after conscientious examination, regardless of so-called well-deserved rights, to mete out due punishment and to remove the offender from his post, rank and position without introducing prescribed procedures.'[1]

There is something comic about this 'head cook and bottle-washer' grasp of absolute power, but it is a brutal process which has happened since in many parts of the world. Who can doubt that in the days leading to nuclear war there would be a similar concentration of authority? Dictatorship is built into the very heart of nuclear terror. Even Hitler could not obliterate rights and life with the impartial certainty of nuclear weapons. For the German soldier to swallow the lie that such weapons can defend civilized democratic values is to be as gullible as the new arrivals at Auschwitz, who believed the assurance that they would be de-loused in the building marked 'BATHS'. The 'mushroom-shaped' vents of the gas inlets above those provide us with uncomfortable symbolism. Instead of 'BATHS' we have 'DETERRENCE'.

The German soldier may wish to compare the characteristics of the leading Nazi Himmler with those required to manage and operate nuclear weapons. He 'was not a sadist. There was nothing terrible or volcanic in his character. His very coldness was a negative element, not glacial, but bloodless. He did not delight in cruelty, he was indifferent to it, and the scruples of others were to him not contemptible, but unintelligible.'

Himmler had the psychopathic qualities of a Grand Inquisitor, 'the man who is prepared to sacrifice humanity to an abstract ideal. The Grand Inquisitors of history were not cruel or self-indulgent men. They were often painfully conscientious and austere in their private lives. They were often scrupulously kind to animals.'[2]

Are not the high priests of nuclear deterrence similarly committed to the logic of sacrifice on a grand scale, when required? They are to be seen frequently on our television screens, arguing their case with the same trivial conviction as Himmler.

The latter leans over the shoulder of every nuclear operative: 'this dual character of Himmler, his impersonal efficiency as an executor, and his oceanic credulity as a thinker, is, I believe, the

[1] William L. Shirer, *The Rise and Fall of the Third Reich*, London 1964.
[2] Hugh Trevor-Roper, *The Last Days of Hitler*, London 1947.

key to his fantastic career.'[1] It would be hard to find another
Hitler, perhaps, but there are more Himmlers in our nuclear
civilization than can be counted. Outwardly normal and mild-
mannered, they are virtually enslaved by an absolute nuclear
Führer.

But even the original Himmler has lost some of his devilry, at
least for some. I recently overheard a woman in a Suffolk pub
explaining loudly how she had once attended a party in Berlin
where Himmler was present. 'He pinched my bottom,' she
announced, with evident pride.

The German soldier may compare the suicidal tendencies of
Hitler with our own. If a nuclear war breaks out it will be because,
so we are told, there is no other way of defending ourselves. It will
be our final solution. We will drag the temple of life down with us.
Hitler had similar aims:

'In his last days Hitler seems like some cannibal god, rejoicing in
the rule of his own temples. Almost his last orders were for
execution; prisoners were to be slaughtered, his old surgeon was to
be murdered, his brother-in-law was executed, all traitors, without
further specification, were to die. Like an ancient hero Hitler
wished to be sent with human sacrifices to his grave; and the
burning of his own body, which had never ceased to be the centre
and totem of the Nazi State, was the logical and symbolical
conclusion of the Revolution of Destruction.'[2]

Trevor-Roper does not make the embarrassing link between
Hitler and our own sacrificial State, but he does add a perceptive
comment: 'The prospect of universal destruction may be exhilarating to some aesthetic souls, especially to those who do not intend
to survive it and are therefore free to admire, as a spectacle, the
apocalyptic setting of their own funeral. But those who must live
on in the charred remainder of the world have less time for such
purely spiritual experiences.'[3]

One of Hitler's closest aides, Albert Speer, describes the Godfather of nuclear holocaust: 'He was deliberately attempting to let
the people perish with himself. He no longer knew any moral
boundaries; a man to whom the end of his own life meant the end

[1] Ibid.
[2] Ibid.
[3] Ibid.

of everything.' Hitler said it too, on our behalf: 'If the war is to be lost the nation will also perish.'[1] Next time he may well be right.

Nazi hatred of Jews has been replaced by something similar in principle and effect. The German soldier may care to reflect on the role of poison, then and now. In his last will and testament, Hitler referred to the Jewish people as the *'Weltvergifter aller Völker'*, the universal poisoner of mankind. As if to prove the point, he (probably), Eva Braun, Himmler, Goering, Goebbels and his wife and six children all died of poison. It was self-administered. Hitler even offered poison to his secretaries in the Berlin bunker where he died, apologizing for not giving them a better farewell gift. Even the word 'gift' means poison in German. We are told by scientists that a major nuclear war would poison the world for generations, perhaps for ever. Is the German soldier really willing to lend his energies to such criminality? Does he realise how like Hitler he and the rest of us have become?

The nuclear nightmare is Hitler's farewell gift to us and it has all but engulfed our civilization. 'All in all,' he told his friends, 'it is surely best for someone who has no heir for his house to be burned with all its contents, as though on a magnificent funeral pyre.'[2] The German *Götterdämmerung* myth, where evil finally triumphs, was attacked by Nietzsche when it appeared in the operas of Wagner. Hitler transformed this story of despair into international politics. The nuclear apologists are his heirs. Ultimately it is a myth of primitive fatalism. Nobody assumes responsibility for anything. The people bow down to the leader. The leader feels himself to be the instrument of fate. There is nothing in charge but a ferment of hatred, fear and servility. Responsible humane law is replaced by authoritarian whim. Leaders with their finger on the nuclear button are no less divorced from integrity of feeling and action.

But the German soldier can take heart from the immediate effect of Hitler's suicide. Despite the roar of approaching Soviet artillery there was a dance in the bunker, and light-hearted chatter. The evil spell had been broken. It can be broken again.

Having recognized his Hitler image in the mirror, alongside ours, the German soldier can seek inspiration to lift his mind and soul above this 'trumped-up doom'. He can find it in a thousand brave examples from the Hitlerian past, in the lives of men, women

[1] Ibid.
[2] J. P. Stern, op. cit.

and even children who stood up to the gangsters. He can start by asking the same questions as the former *Luftwaffe* sergeant who wrote to a newspaper in 1951, during the Eichmann trial:

> I just had to write this to you. I can't help it. I must say aloud what I felt and feel when I read your report on the Eichmann Trial ... I am ashamed because I am a German and was once compelled to wear this uniform. An incredible accident of fate saved me from joining the commandos that were ordered to commit such atrocities. Horrified, I ask myself again and again what I would have done, if I had been ordered to perpetrate such crimes. Would I have had enough character or humaneness to swing my weapon around and shoot those who dragged children from their mothers and simply gunned them down? Would I have shown the same bad character to fire on wounded women and children who, with great effort and pain, had worked their way out of a mountain of corpses? ... Of those who fired and those who obeyed such orders, there are surely some who are still alive. Were they really commanded to be so brutal? Can they honestly be called "soldiers"? ... And Eichmann? Lay it all before him, bit by bit, act for act, since he didn't dirty his hands, he just gave the orders. He gave the orders and we carried them out... [1]

Such questions are best asked before war breaks out, if the answers are to be positive. General Beck posed his own questions. Chief of the German Army General Staff between 1935 and 1938, General Beck was responsible for the preparation and conduct of land warfare under Hitler. On 30 May 1938 Hitler made known his 'unalterable decision' to attack Czechoslovakia within a short time. General Beck protested strongly at what he saw as a casual, risk-laden, unnecessary use of force. 'Not for nothing,' he said, 'do historians tell us of wars which were won or lost before they began; and in the last resort politics were nearly always to blame.' He opposed Ludendorff's belief in 'total war', a belief in total annihilation rooted in the carnage of the First World War. General Beck still clung to the traditional, professional belief that war without a 'moderate political objective' cannot lead to a 'satisfactory peace in the Bismarckian sense'. Even modern war, he thought, can be

---

[1] Letter in *Die Welt*.

limited and controlled, 'not by technical or military measures, but through a policy based on moral principles which should prevail in all circumstances, so that war should be a political instrument and subordinate to politics; and by a new sense of morality and idealism which would govern the State and its relations with other nations'. The political leader, he thought, 'should be a man of integrity who must in the last resort be subject to his personal moral law, his conscience'.[1]

General Beck tried to organize opposition to Hitler's policies by the combined Chiefs of Staff, who were to threaten mass resignation if the war plans were not abandoned. This proved impossible and on 18 August he resigned and was released from the Army three days later. Hitler kept the whole matter secret, no doubt because of its far-reaching implications. General Beck became a leading figure in the resistance to Hitler and was closely associated with the abortive assassination attempt and coup on 20 July 1944. On the same evening, when he knew the plot had failed, he committed suicide in Berlin.

The citizen soldier will recognise the flaws in General Beck's experience. Why had he been so naïve as to believe that Hitler could ever be subject to his conscience? But he may reflect on the fact that no NATO or Warsaw Pact general of such high rank has, so far, dared to oppose as criminal the policies of annihilation and total war which underlie their 'defensive' strategies. And far from being shot for opposition to a fanatical dictator, General Beck survived to organize further resistance.

General Gert Bastian, though of less military significance than General Beck, offers the citizen soldier a more recent example of principled opposition. A volunteer in Hitler's army at the age of sixteen, Gert Bastian fought on the Russian front and was twice wounded, before being sent to the Western front, where he was taken prisoner by the Americans. He joined the post-war *Bundeswehr*, convinced of the need to oppose communism, but as he rose quickly through the ranks to command the 12th Panzer Division, he began to doubt three major NATO articles of faith. He did not believe nuclear weapons could serve as instruments of defence. He was not convinced that Warsaw Pact forces were superior in weapons, and he did not believe that the Soviet Union wanted to

[1] Annedore Leber, op. cit.

promote world revolution. In January 1980 Gert Bastian sent a memorandum to the Defence Minister in Bonn, criticizing the proposed deployment of nuclear missiles, and he was forced to resign. He became a leading member of the Green Party and was elected to the *Bundestag*. He regards Soviet nuclear strategy as equally pernicious. He is a soldier who thinks for himself.

Few of those who opposed the Nazis knew how to use the law on their own behalf, but they had the courage to assert an inner law of personal integrity. The Auschwitz trial in Frankfurt in 1964 exposed the exaggerated nature of claims that resistance to Nazi orders was impossible. Ludwig Woehrl, a grocer in Munich and former Auschwitz inmate, told the court how he had been ordered by an SS medical orderly to give lethal injections to sick inmates. He had refused and nothing had happened to him. 'That,' he said, 'is a small contribution to the subject of acting under the compulsion of higher orders'.[1] A court in Brunswick, trying the so-called SS Cavalry case, in which SS officers were accused of murdering Jews, were told by an historian, Dr Seraphim, that 'not a single case was known of an SS man being punished because he had refused to take part in mass executions'.[2] A vain search for such instances had been made at the time of the Nuremberg trials. 'But there were countless examples of refusal to obey such orders receiving little or no attention.' Dr Seraphim mentioned the example of an SS commander who 'successfully applied to Himmler against the order to shoot Jews, and whose unit was then transferred to the Russian front'.[3]

This was confirmed by Dr Hans Bucheim, of the Munich Institute of Contemporary History, who told the court at Brunswick that 'the SS men had plenty of opportunities to dodge carrying out orders to shoot people. But most of them had lacked the courage not to obey.'[4] A Viennese doctor and former Auschwitz inmate had been saved by a camp doctor who had attended the same medical school before the war. Her estimate was that 'between 5 and 10 per cent of the SS men were sadists or war criminals in the clinical sense'.[5] The rest were 'perfectly able to distinguish between good and evil'.

[1] *The Times*, 7 April 1964.
[2] Ibid.
[3] Ibid.
[4] *Guardian*, 3 April 1964.
[5] *The Times*, 3 March 1964.

An Austrian-born Jew, Dr Wolken, told the Frankfurt court about a fourteen-year-old boy in Auschwitz, the leader of a group of children. Naked and about to be taken to the gas chambers, the boy said to Dr Wolken, 'I'm not afraid. It's not so terrible here. I'm sure it will be better in heaven.' The boy turned to his friends, who were crying: 'Don't cry. You've seen your parents and grand-parents die. Now it's our turn.' Then he said to the SS guards: 'Don't think you'll get off free. Your turn is coming.'[1] As the lorries drove off the boy was being beaten.

Then there was the unlikely case of the 'angel of Auschwitz', a German SS nurse and devout Catholic. 'Her name was Maria Stromberg,' an Austrian witness, Dr Langbein, told the Frankfurt court. 'As early as 1942 she helped the prisoners, knowing they were members of an underground. She also smuggled letters for me to Vienna.'[2]

Even simple villagers were sometimes capable of following humane principles, despite the polluted fog of Nazi power. An Englishwoman who had married a German lawyer in 1934, Chris-tabel Bielenberg, wrote later of Black Forest villagers who shel-tered her and who were 'so little affected by war propaganda that they treated a shot-down American airman as an "honoured guest".'[3]

Students, too, were capable of extraordinary courage, though most were docile. In 1943, at the height of the war, the citizens of Munich were astounded to read anti-Hitler slogans painted in large letters on the walls of the Ludwigstrasse: 'Down With Hitler', 'Long Live Freedom', and 'Freedom'. Leaflets denouncing the regime were scattered in the corridors and stairways of the univer-sity. This movement spread to other German cities and was eventually traced to a small group of Munich students. Five of them, and a professor of philosophy, were arrested by the Gestapo, tried before the infamous People's Court, and beheaded.

Two of them were brother and sister, Hans and Sophie Scholl. They had joined the Hitler Youth in 1933, but were gradually disillusioned. Their father was imprisoned in 1942 for speaking out against the government. He had described Hitler to a woman

---

[1] *The Times*, 28 February 1964.
[2] *The Times*, 7 March 1964.
[3] *Guardian*, 8 March 1984.

employee as a 'scourge of God upon the human race', and been denounced to the police.

The 'White Rose' leaflets produced by this student group warned Germans to uphold civilized values and law. In a criminal State this made them outlaws. 'If each of us waits for the others to begin', said one leaflet, 'the messengers of avenging Nemesis will draw closer and closer until the last victim has been thrown in vain into the jaws of the insatiable monster. . . . Nothing is less worthy of a civilized country than passively to allow itself to be "governed" by an irresponsible gang of bosses who have surrendered to their lower instincts.'

They quoted the Greek philosopher and law-giver, Solon: 'If the constitution of a State prevents man from developing all the powers which lie in him, if it hinders the growth of the mind, it is reprehensible and harmful. . . .'

Professor Huber, one of this group, told them: 'We must try to fan the spark of resistance that is in the hearts of a million honourable Germans. . . .' They packed their leaflets into suitcases and took them by train to such cities as Frankfurt, Stuttgart, Vienna, Freiburg, Saarbrücken, and Mannheim. Precursor of nuclear suicide, the newspaper headlines of those days blared such slogans as: 'We shall march on even if everything is smashed to fragments.'

Inevitably, the group was caught, sentenced and executed. Hans Scholl, about to leave his cell to appear in court, wrote on the wall a saying from Goethe: 'In face of all authority maintain thyself.' Hans, today's citizen soldier will be interested to know, was a soldier as well as a student. He had to face judges who had betrayed the very essence of civilized law. 'There is another justice besides this,' his father told him during their last meeting.

Professor Huber pointed to this other justice in his final statement:

As a German citizen . . . I regard it not only as a right, but as a moral duty, to help shape the destiny of my country, to uncover and to oppose manifest evils. . . . What I aimed to do was to rouse my students . . . to an ethical understanding of the grave evils of our present political life. A return to definite ethical principles, to the rule of law, to mutual trust between man and man – that is not illegal, rather it is the re-establishment of legality. . . .

Everyone [he continued] with any sense of moral responsibility should raise his voice with us against the menacing tyranny
of naked power over law, of naked despotism over the will to do
what is morally right. . . . There is an ultimate limit beyond
which all outward law becomes untrue and immoral. It is
reached when laws become a cloak for cowardice, for the fear to
oppose manifest infringements of justice. A state which forbids
all free expression of opinion, all justifiable criticism, and visits
the most fearful punishments on every proposal for betterment,
calling it 'Preparation for High Treason', breaks an unwritten
law which still has its place in 'healthy popular sentiment' and
must still retain it. . . .

I demand that freedom be restored to the German people. We
will not spend our short lives as fettered slaves, even though they
be the golden fetters of material abundance. . . . I have acted in
accordance with an inner compulsion. I accept the consequences
in the fine words of Johann Gottlieb Fichte:

> And thus you are to act,
> As though the destiny of German life
> Hung solely from your deeds and you,
> And you alone were accountable.[1]

Today's citizen soldier and all of Europe owes this brave man a
debt. What always happens when a problem remains unresolved is
that it becomes steadily more complex. The rubbish of the Nazi
regime has been swept away and its major criminals punished, but
the poisoned roots remain. Speech in the West is free enough, but
speech is little use to the paralyzed. Creative renewal is tightly
fettered by judges and politicians who idolise 'national security'
and the other euphemisms of brute power, but the most oppressive
gaolers of all are ourselves.

The first White Rose leaflet deserves to be reprinted by the
German Ministry of Defence, because it needles apathy:

If the German nation is so corrupted and decayed in its inner-
most core that it gives up, without lifting a finger . . . the highest
good that man has, the thing that raises him above the beasts, the
freedom of the will. . . . If the Germans are so completely lacking

---

[1] Inge Scholl, *Six Against Tyranny*, London 1955.

in individuality; if they have become no more than a cowardly and mindless herd, then – oh, then, they deserve extinction.

Goethe speaks of the Germans as a tragic people, like the Jews and the Greeks, but today the German people seems to be a shallow, will-less mob of yes-men, who have no marrow in their bones, no pith in their souls, and are willing to let themselves be driven to destruction. It seems so, but it is not so; rather each individual has been confined in a mental prison by a process of slow, insidious systematic encroachment, without becoming aware of his fate until he was lying there in chains. Few recognized the disaster when it threatened, and the reward of their brave warnings was death.

It quoted the warning contained in Schiller's account of Greek law:

The Spartan law-book itself preached the dangerous principle that men were to be regarded as a means rather than an end – thus the foundations of the natural law and morality were overturned by the law itself. . . . How much finer the spectacle provided by the rough warrior Caius Marcius in his camp before Rome, when he gave up his triumph and vengeance because he could not look upon a mother's tears.[1]

Does anyone encourage the citizen soldier to adopt such a mature vision of manhood, or is he left to find his own way out of the labyrinth of nuclear yes-men? The second White Rose leaflet continues the warning. It quotes Hitler's own comment in *Mein Kampf* ('My Fight'): 'You cannot believe how much you have to deceive a nation to govern it.' German intellectuals, it said, had gone into hiding, 'in cellars, where they gradually suffocated, mere nocturnal shadows, cut off from light and the sun'.[2] Today's intellectuals, by contrast, are more often than not seduced rather than attacked, egos massaged while feet are gently tied. Goethe has a message for them, too. Nobody, he said, is more a slave than someone who thinks he is free and is not.

Just as today, when most people, including most Germans, munch on dully in the golden trough of prosperity, outwardly unmoved by the nuclear threat, so even at the height of the war the

1 Ibid.
2 Ibid.

German people responded as apathetically to mass murder as the British. 'Why does the German nation show such apathy towards all these frightful and inhuman crimes?' asks the leaflet. 'Hardly anyone seems to trouble about them. They are accepted as facts and put aside, and the German people falls again into its dull, obtuse sleep, giving these fascist criminals the courage and the opportunity to continue their havoc. We are all guilty, guilty, guilty!'

The third White Rose leaflet spoke directly to the citizen who has heard it all before; '"We have known that for a long while," I hear you object, "and we do not need to be lectured again about it."' Why then, the leaflet asks, 'do you permit these tyrants to rob you, step by step, openly or secretly, of your rights, till one day nothing will be left but a mechanised State operated by criminals and alcoholics?.... Do not conceal your cowardice under a cloak of wisdom. Every day that you hesitate and fail to resist this hell-begotten system, piles up your guilt higher and higher like a parabolic curve.'[1] The group promoted sabotage in every part of German society.

Their final leaflet sought a 'renewal of the gravely injured spirit'. No punishment could do justice to Nazi crimes, but 'do not forget the minor scoundrels. Note down their names so that none escape. After these horrors they must not be allowed to change sides at the last moment and behave as though nothing had happened.... We shall not be silent; we are your bad conscience.'[2]

These few young Germans are still our bad conscience. They grew up in the city which gave birth to Nazi power, and they upheld the highest values of our civilization. That should hearten today's citizen soldier. But their warnings remain unheeded. Only the ranting Hitler has been replaced by a more subtle, smiling dictator, master of the 'soft sell.' Mass murder has become the 'lawful' weapon of democracy, the guardian of peace.

The excesses of German soldiers were sometimes challenged fiercely by leading Nazi officials. A document used as evidence at the Nuremberg Trial details one such incident in occupied Greece, when villagers were victimized to atone for partisan attacks:

[1] Ibid.
[2] Ibid.

Consider ... the massacre of Greek villagers, at Klissura. ...
When this incident became known to the German civilian
authorities in Greece, whose principal interest was in pacification of the occupied country, there was prompt and fiery
protest to the German Commander-in-Chief, Field-Marshal
Maximilian von Weichs. The message came from Hermann
Neubacher, the Foreign Office Plenipotentiary in SE Europe:

'... It is utter insanity to murder babies, children, women and
old men because heavily armed Red bandits billeted themselves
overnight, by force, in their houses, and because they killed two
German soldiers near the village. The political effect of this
senseless bloodbath doubtless by far exceeds the effect of all
propaganda efforts in our fight against communism.

'No matter what the final result of the investigation may be,
the operation against Klissura represents a severe transgression
of existing orders. The wonderful result of this heroic deed is
that babies are dead. But the partisans continue to live and they
will again find quarters by use of machine-guns in completely
defenceless villages. It is a further fact that it is much more
comfortable to shoot to death entirely harmless women, children
and old men than to pursue an armed band with a manly desire
for vengeance and to kill them to the last man. The use of such
methods must necessarily lead to the demoralization of genuine
combat morale.'[1]

The citizen soldier may justly complain that there is today a
resounding silence at comparable levels of German authority,
about the babies and defenceless people in NATO's sights. But he
can learn from the defiance of many Germans towards Hitler. To
enforce civilized law before war, as a preventive measure, is much
easier than after it starts. There is one man whose story bears this
out in gruesome detail. His name is Klaus Hornig, and his story
appeared in a French newspaper, *Le Monde Dimanche*, on 8 May
1983.

Hornig, a lawyer and Catholic, was unusual among opponents of
Hitler in that he made full use of the law on his own behalf,
particularly Article 47 of the German Military Penal Code which
tells subordinates to refuse criminal orders. Now living in the
Austrian Tyrol, he bears the scars of his remarkable life. Born in

[1] *Trials of War Criminals Vol. IX*: Nuremberg document NOKW–469.

Silesia in 1907, Klaus Hornig became a member of the Prussian police shortly before Goering became its chief. He was tall, blond, and athletic, apparently the ideal Nazi male.

With the Nazis in power, the first of Hornig's clashes with authority took place. Sitting in a cafe in Breslau, after attending a performance of *Tannhäuser*, he saw the chief of police enter, a leading member of the notorious SA, together with a group of subordinates. One of these, the chief's brother, approached Klaus Hornig and asked whether he would like to become the chief's personal aide-de-camp. 'Give your brother my respects,' Hornig replied, 'and tell him I will gladly do without a career which demands less of my head than the opposite end of my body.' This reference to the notorious homosexuality of many leading SA figures was followed next morning by a visit from the Gestapo, who warned him that his insolence had been noted. But eight days later, on 30 June 1934, Hitler led a massacre of SA leaders, accusing them of treachery and homosexual perversion. A note appeared in Hornig's personal dossier: 'expresses publicly his contempt for leading Party members'.

Hornig completed his law studies in Munich and found himself transferred to Himmler's SS at the start of the war, experiencing in Poland some of the brutality of this militarized police force. He was sent to occupied Luxembourg, where his frequent visits to Mass aroused comment. When a woman acquaintance's husband, a Jew, was arrested, she asked for Hornig's help. He told the Gestapo to release him as 'indispensable'. Hornig then became a law instructor at a police academy near Munich. He told his students, from the police and army, never to do anything against their conscience. When asked by the director of the academy why he did not contribute his physical attributes to the cause of the German race by fathering children in large numbers, Hornig told him that he was committed to family life.

He was sent back to Poland in 1941, at the start of Hitler's Russian campaign. The task of the SS was to fight 'bandits', execute Jews and Soviet political commissars, requisition food from farmers and evacuate people from large areas of occupied Russia. None of this had been taught at the academy. Hornig told his men that they must fight against armed partisans but not unarmed civilians. He told them about Article 47. Subordinates who survived the war confirm that they were forbidden to take part in SS massacres. *Oberleutnant* Hornig complained about the killing to his superior. The latter laughed and told him he must harden himself.

When he received an order in June 1941 to take his troop to a forest area between Zamosc and Krasnobrod, where he was to execute by a shot in the back of the neck 780 Soviet prisoners, Hornig refused. He said that such an order could only have come from Himmler and that as an army officer he could not be expected to obey it. He was shown an order signed by the commander-in-chief of the German Army, von Brauchitsch, which concluded: 'the liquidation of political commissars must take place after they have been taken away from the battle zone, in order not to attract attention, and under the command of an officer'.

Hornig told his superior that such an order violated the most elementary humanitarian laws and the Geneva Convention on the treatment of prisoners of war. As a lawyer and a Catholic, he would not obey the order, and invoked Article 47. He was accused of being a 'pedantic lawyer' and a coward, and told to protect the area surrounding the place of execution. As the execution of the naked prisoners proceeded, under the command of an SS lieutenant Meiert, Hornig shouted at him and his men to stop, accusing Meiert of failing to act like a professional soldier. Just then he was taken by the arm and a warning voice whispered in his ear. It was that of another officer, Schubert, a former student of Hornig's, who led him away from the execution site. The former, as if to explain his allegiance to institutional murder, told Hornig he was no longer a Christian. 'My religion is Germany,' he told him.

Hornig demanded to be sent to the front but was told by his commanding officer that if he would not take part in executions he would have to carry out some other aspect of the 'pacification' policy. He was sent to work as a law officer in Lublin and once delivered a special message to Himmler. He recollected Himmler's limp handshake, 'like a timid young girl's'. But fate, or at least its Nazi shadow, was catching up with Hornig. As a result of his 'open hostility to the SS and the police' he was sent to Frankfurt to await further instructions. There he was presented with a thirty-five-page denunciation, addressed to an SS tribunal.

This listed his public objection to the 'commissar' order, his numerous interventions on behalf of Polish people, his criticism of Himmler's orders and the SS. He had complained of the latter's anti-Christian values and assumed 'humanitarian pretensions' in Poland. He and his subordinates had celebrated Christmas rather than the official SS holiday. While teaching at the law academy he had insulted the SS, and he and his men had frequently attended Mass. He had even played the organ.

Hornig was thrown into prison. Once, under cover of an air raid, he tried to hang himself. After more than a year in prison he appeared before an SS and police tribunal in Düsseldorf. At no time was he reproached for invoking in his defence Article 47, but he was convicted under Article 2 for helping to 'demoralize' the army. Himmler confirmed the sentence and Hornig was sent to Buchenwald concentration camp. He repeatedly asked Himmler for a review of his case. On 15 March 1945, with the American army barely fifty miles away, he was sentenced to a five years and seven months prison term.

At this point in his life, Klaus Hornig appears like the hero of a morality tale. As the camp was about to be taken over by the advancing Americans, two communist inmates, believing Hornig to be an informer who kept in touch with Himmler, took him to a cellar, beat him until many of his teeth were broken and told him they would kill him if he did not hang himself. He pleaded with them and at last they were convinced, but his troubles were not over. An American interrogator was not convinced by his story. Why had Hornig been so bothered about the fate of the Soviet commissars? Was he perhaps a 'bit communist round the edges'? At that time, Soviet prisoners of war who had worked for the Nazis were sent back to Russia, where their fate was usually immediate death. Hornig was ordered to go by train to the Soviet Union, only for the order to be cancelled at the last moment. But he spent the next two years moving from one camp for suspected war criminals to another, as a 'prisoner-witness'.

It was this period, Hornig said, almost forty years later, which still brought back nightmares. The Nazi inmates considered him to be a traitor and he was repeatedly attacked. This nightmarish twist to his long sojourn in the hell of Hitler's military machine only came to an end when he was eventually made an official interpreter for the Americans at Dachau. On 21 August 1947, Klaus Hornig became a free man. After a spell as a taxi-driver he was granted the pension of a lieutenant-colonel by a Federal court. He added a doctorate in economics to his law doctorate and retired to his chalet in Austria. 'In exile', as he put it.

By an odd chance, Hornig recognized Meiert, the SS executioner of Zamosc, on a platform of Wiesbaden railway station in October 1947. The latter, who was with his wife and sister-in-law, fled, but the two women revealed to Hornig that Meiert lived there under a false name and had a good job with a large firm. Hornig did not learn until many years later that Meiert was arrested in 1948, during black market investigations, and was identified. The judge at Wiesbaden, after denouncing his evasion of justice, freed him.

Only by sharing a little of the torment of Klaus Hornig and the others who defied Nazi criminality can the citizen soldier of today appreciate the priceless value of their courage. He can then begin to extract himself from the false myth of modern German life. Nazi crime was not unique to Germany. It was a war on the human race, and on life itself, and it stemmed from the core of European industrial civilization, East and West. By punishing Nazi crime alone we denied our own, blinding ourselves to the nuclear criminality which now pervades an entire civilization. By substituting a 'Soviet menace' in place of the Nazi version we have perverted truth and law. Rejecting Soviet ideology or any other ideology is legitimate. Tying the fate of the world to such a dispute is madness.

The German citizen soldier may wake up to this fraud and expose it. He would do well to read again what was said of the German Army at a war crimes trial:

Somewhere there is unmitigated responsibility for these atrocities. Is it to be borne by the troops? Is it to be borne primarily by the hundreds of subordinates who played a minor role in the pattern of crime? We think it is clear that is not where the deepest responsibility lies. Men in the mass, particularly when organized and disciplined in armies, must be expected to yield to prestige, authority, the power of example, and soldiers are bound to be powerfully influenced by the examples set by their commanders. That is why ... the only way in which the behaviour of the German troops in the recent war can be made comprehensible as the behaviour of human beings is by full exposure of the criminal doctrines and orders which were pressed on them from above by these defendants and others. Who could the German Army look to, other than von Leeb and the senior field-marshals, to safeguard its standards of conduct and prevent their disintegration? If a decision is to be rendered here which may perhaps help to prevent the repetition of such events, it is important above all else that responsibility be fixed where it truly belongs. Mitigation should be reserved for those upon whom superior orders are pressed down and who lack the means to influence general standards of behaviour. It is not, we submit, available to the commander who participates in bringing the criminal pressures to bear, and whose responsibility is to ensure the preservation of honorable military traditions.[1]

The women and children, old and sick of Moscow and Leningrad are no more a legitimate target of the German soldier today than of the German soldier of Hitler's Army.

[1] *Trials of War Criminals Vol. XI:* US v. von Leeb.

Chapter Eight

The American Soldier's Tale

'This country, with its institutions, belongs to the people who
inhabit it. Whenever they shall grow weary of the existing
government, they can exercise their constitutional right of
amending it, or their revolutionary right to dismember, or
overthrow it'
– President Abraham Lincoln in his first inaugural address

'Before I got into flying I thought about it, and since I've never
been in doubt. If I could avoid the situation I would rather do
that. But in the event it ever happened, I'm prepared for that
fact'
– USAF, F-III pilot, Lakenheath, England.

'I gave them a good boy and they made him a murderer'
– mother of US Vietnam veteran

'All students are administratively certified and watched for
any tendencies towards irrational behaviour'
– Col. James Wohner, USAF, Head of Cruise Missile Training,
Arizona, USA

Where does the American soldier stand in relation to this nightmare age of total war? 'Peace is our Profession,' boasts the US Air
Force. The self-image of the US fighting man is one of guardian of
freedom and democracy. But what does he look like when the
touchstone of minimum world sanity, international law, is applied
to his thinking and behaviour? What does he have in common with
his British and German counterparts? What is his record? Which
way is he heading?

Ironically, the concept of legitimate violence is more deeply
engrained in the American mind than most. It is barely two
hundred years since the American nation was born in violent
overthrow of established power. The right to reject tyranny with
force is an article of American faith whose by-products are the
Western myth, widespread private ownership of guns, a huge

murder rate and the largest arsenal of military weapons ever assembled on earth. Perhaps the most remarkable of all American achievements during this short period of history is the phenomenal growth of its military power. Other countries are as rich, or richer. Other countries have evolved democratic procedures, some with more obvious success. But none, not even the Soviet Union, approximates to the worldwide military grasp of Uncle Sam.

The relation of such enormous destructive power to the laws of military restraint is bound to be difficult. What may restrain the dogs of war is unlikely to hold a tiger. An offshoot of European civilization, despite its distinctive character, the United States acknowledges a law whose roots are in Europe. The humanitarian thought of the Dutchman, Hugo Grotius, nurtures this law as it does that of all laws of armed conflict: 'The danger of disobedience ... ought not to be objected ... if the war be unjust it is no disobedience to decline it. Disobedience in such cases is in its own nature a less evil than homicide, especially when taking away the lives of many innocent people.'[1]

There were other, non-European tributaries of thought, flowing into the American legal process, evidence of universal revulsion against wanton destruction. According to one American researcher, 'early Muslim *jihad* (holy war) armies were instructed to avoid unnecessary harm to fruit trees, beehives, wells, camels, non-combatants, and religious persons and places; and they were prohibited from using poisoned arrows or from impaling the heads of their victims on their spears. Inca warriors were ordered to treat conquered peoples fairly; they were not to abuse them or steal from them.'[2] This was not idealism but common sense self-interest.

It was the American Civil War whose ferocity inspired the world's first systematic formulation of laws of warfare. The celebrated General Robert E. Lee made known his concern for the 'yet unsullied reputation of the army'. He warned his soldiers:

the duties exacted of us by civilization and Christianity are not less obligatory in the country of the enemy than in our own. The commanding general considers that no greater disgrace could befall the army, and through it our whole people, than the perpetration of the barbarous outrages upon the innocent and

[1] Grotius, op, cit.
[2] Peter Karsten, *Law, Soldiers and Combat*, Westport, Conn. 1978.

defenceless and the wanton destruction of private property that have marked the course of the enemy in our country. Such proceedings not only disgrace the perpetrators and all connected with them, but are subversive of the discipline and efficiency of the army and destructive of the ends of our present movements. It must be remembered that we make war only on armed men, and that we cannot take vengeance for the wrongs our people have suffered without lowering ourselves in the eyes of all whose abhorrence has been excited by the atrocities of our enemy, and offending against Him to whom vengeance belongs, without whose favour and support all our effort must all prove in vain.

The commanding general, therefore, earnestly exhorts his troops to abstain with most scrupulous care from unnecessary or wanton injury to private property, and he enjoins upon all officers to arrest and bring to summary punishment all who shall in any way offend against the orders on this subject![1]

These sentiments reflect professional self-respect and discipline, Christian beliefs, a concern for suffering and a very American regard for private property. What would the US soldier of today make of those commands from a military hero? They were not an isolated statement of principle. Francis Lieber, German veteran of the Napoleonic wars and then Professor of Columbia College, New York, was asked by President Lincoln to codify the laws of war. These 'Instructions for the Government of Armies of the United States in the Field', known as the Lieber Rules, were promulgated by President Lincoln as General Orders No. 100, on 24 April 1863.

Consisting of 157 Articles, these rules remained in force until 1914, when they were replaced by an army field manual, the basis of today's manual. 'It is set forth therein that the laws of war are part of the law of the United States, and that they may be enforced against both soldiers and civilians.'[2]

The Lieber Rules strongly influenced the formulation of the Hague Conventions of 1899 and 1907. They were a creative, unilateral initiative in the development of the law. Article 15 emphasizes the moral basis of law: 'Men who take up arms against one another in public war do not cease on this account to be moral beings.' Article 24 defines the relation of civilized law to barba-

---

[1] Karsten, op. cit.
[2] Telford Taylor, *Nuremberg and Vietnam*, USA 1970.

rism: 'The almost universal rule in remote times was, and continues to be with barbarous armies, that the private individual of the hostile country is destined to suffer every privation of liberty and protection, and every disruption of family ties. Protection was, and still is with civilized people, the exception.'

Retaliation is carefully assessed. Article 28 states: 'Unjust or inconsiderate retaliation removes the belligerents farther and farther from the mitigating rules of regular war, and by rapid steps leads them nearer to the internecine war of savages.' Poison is forbidden, continuing a long tradition in many areas of the world. Article 70 states: 'The use of poison in any manner, be it to poison wells, or food, or arms, is wholly excluded from modern warfare. He that uses it puts himself out of the pale of the law and usages of war.' Radiation poisoning, the American soldier will note, now threatens the entire world.

'Prisoners of war,' says Article 76, 'shall be fed upon plain and wholesome food, whenever practicable, and treated with humanity.' Political assassination is regarded with revulsion. Article 148 declares that: 'Civilised nations look with horror upon offers of rewards for the assassination of enemies as relapses into barbarism.'

Once again, it is the bottom line of civilization which is being underwritten by these rules, not utopianism. As Henry Thoreau, that sturdy American radical, said a few years before these rules were promulgated, there is nothing wrong with building castles in the air, if you put foundations under them. The Lieber Rules were just such an effort to build foundations under the laws of armed conflict. Their influence flowed on through the Nuremberg Trial and into the nuclear era. It remains to be seen whether they have also run into the sands of time, to vanish in a silt of murderous euphemism.

The American soldier today is bound by the *US Army Field Manual* of 1956, a close cousin of the British and German manuals. In the judgment of leading American experts in the laws of war: 'The provisions of the US Army Field Manual indicate the extent to which American soldiers are held criminally accountable for compliance with the laws of war. Such provisions are highly relevant to the indictment of men who engage in battlefield atrocities. These provisions do not, however, concern the status of crimes of higher officials who make the decision to initiate warfare

and to pursue battlefield tactics. The provisions of the Field
Manual, if applied to low-level perpetrators of war crimes, might
serve the larger purpose of providing scapegoats for policies whose
real architects are allowed to live among us as esteemed citizens,
and even leaders.'[1]

The *Manual* declares that the purpose of the laws of war is to
'diminish the evils of war'. Fighting must be conducted 'with
regard for the principles of humanity and chivalry'. 'The law of war
is binding not only upon States as such but also upon individuals
and, in particular, the members of their armed forces'. Laws are
incorporated by statute and by 'the custom of nations'. Regarding
responsibility, the *Manual* states that 'when troops commit massacres and atrocities ... the responsibility may rest not only with
the actual perpetrators but also with the commander'.

If the American soldier is inclined to regard the laws of war as
Mickey Mouse-law he will be disappointed. Explaining the 'Force
of the Law of War' the *Manual* states firmly: 'Under the Constitution of the United States, treaties constitute part of the "supreme
Law of the Land" (Art. VI, clause 2). In consequence, treaties
relating to the law of war have a force equal to that of laws enacted
by the Congress. Their provisions must be observed by both
military and civilian personnel with the same strict regard for both
the letter and spirit of the law which is required with respect to the
Constitution.'

Conspiracy is a crime, as it was at Nuremberg: 'Conspiracy,
direct incitement, and attempts to commit, as well as complicity in
the commission of, crimes against peace, crimes against humanity,
and war crimes are punishable .... War crimes,' declares the
Manual, 'are within the jurisdiction of general courts-martial,
military commissions, provost courts, and other military tribunals
of the United States, as well as of international tribunals'.

The *Manual* cites various treaty laws, including the Geneva
Conventions of 1949. As for punishment for war crimes, the
Manual says that: 'The punishment imposed for a violation of the
law of war must be proportionate to the gravity of the offence. The
death penalty may be imposed.'

As in the majority of the world's States, the defence of superior
orders is not admitted, except in mitigation. And in line with the

[1] Richard Falk et al. (ed.), *Crimes of War*, New York 1971.

Nuremberg Principles, the *Manual* states, in relation to government officials: 'The fact that a person who committed an act which constitutes a war crime acted as the head of a State or as a responsible government official does not relieve him from responsibility for his act.' Arising from the indictment of Nazi 'law' there is a warning: 'The fact that domestic law does not impose a penalty for an act which constitutes a crime under international law does not relieve the person who committed the act from responsibility under the law.'[1]

The American soldier is left in no doubt that the modern laws of war apply to him directly. Unlike its German and British counterparts, the US *Manual* refers to nuclear weapons: 'The use of explosive atomic weapons, whether by air, sea, or land forces, cannot as such be regarded as violation of international law in the absence of any customary rule of international law or international convention restricting their employment.'[2]

The US Law of Naval Warfare expresses a similar opinion. It is here that the law is manipulated to suit the prevailing power system. The absence of an international convention prohibiting nuclear weapons does not negate the weight and meaning of customary law. The latter, as we have seen and will see, clearly condemns any form of warfare which is indiscriminate and unlimted in effect. The many side-effects of nuclear weapons, a poisoned environment and violated neutral rights, add to the evidence that nuclear weapons are outlawed. As General Robert E. Lee would certainly agree, the American soldier of today has been duped by a twisted legality. Law, counter law, no law, are the hallmark of the nuclear outlaw.

Law with a civilized face and murderous heart is not a relic in the museum of Nazi history, nor is it peculiar to American military law. It reflects our fragmented civilization. It reflects us. We have somehow to wake ourselves from this self-induced nightmare. The American soldier is not alone in this double-bind, but he is bound by all that is still vital and humane in him to reject perverted law.

He will do well to follow the direction indicated by Robert E. Lee, upholding the truth of humane principle and discarding the rubbish of convenience law. He may listen to another national hero, General Douglas MacArthur, when confirming the death

[1] *US Army Field Manual*, 1956.
[2] Ibid.

sentence imposed by a United States military commission on the Japanese General Tomayuki Yamashita: 'The soldier, be he friend or foe, is charged with the protection of the weak and unarmed. It is the very essence and reason for his being. When he violates this sacred trust, he not only profanes his entire cult but threatens the entire fabric of international society. The traditions of fighting men are long and honorable. They are based on the noblest of traits – sacrifice!'[1]

The fact that General MacArthur did nothing to counter nuclear weapons need not inhibit the American soldier from making good use of his principles.

We have already seen something of the American energy applied to post-war prosecution of Nazi and Japanese war crimes. In the zone of Germany administered by American authority, the US Army Judge Advocate General was made responsible for enforcing the law of war. Some 1,600 Germans, as compared with 200 at Nuremberg, were tried before military commissions and military government courts. Over 250 death sentences were carried out. About an equal number were tried by British, French and other military courts established by the countries that had been occupied by Germany.

A member of the US prosecuting team at Nuremberg, General Telford Taylor, offers the modern American soldier sound advice on the law. It has grown, he says, 'in somewhat the same manner that the common law of England grew in pre-Parliamentary times, and during the several centuries when very little of the basic civil and criminal law of England was to be found in Parliamentary statutes'. He regards it as 'highly important' that 'nations are regarded as bound by the laws of war whether or not they are parties to the Hague and Geneva Conventions'.[2] A nation, in other words, can no more opt out of the mainstream of the law than a citizen.

Telford Taylor offers the American soldier a direct warning: 'Unless troops are trained and required to draw the distinction between military and non-military killings, and to retain such respect for life that unnecessary death and destruction will continue to repel them, they may lose the sense of that distinction for

[1] Telford Taylor, op. cit.
[2] Ibid.

the rest of their lives. The consequence would be that many returning soldiers would be potential murderers.'[1]

The story of Vietnam amply confirms this warning. Telford Taylor acknowledges that the laws of war are far from perfect, 'very fuzzy round the edges', but he is convinced that they have a 'substantial core of recognised practice'.

He is well aware of the shortcomings of the post-war trials at Nuremberg and Tokyo: 'they were unilateral; they were constituted by the victor nations and had jurisdiction only over the vanquished, but they were intended to bring the weight of law and criminal sanctions to bear in support of the peaceful and humanitarian principles that the United Nations was to promote by consultation and collective action'.

The Charter of the United Nations assumed the force of international law, prohibiting 'the use or threat of force' and requiring that even self-defence must be referred to the Security Council.

Telford Taylor tells the American soldier that post-war war crimes trials had a world-wide ripple effect: 'outside the legal dimension ... the Nuremberg trials had perhaps an even more significant impact on the governments and peoples of the world, in spreading a sense of the moral and political importance of the issues with which the trials were concerned. Before Nuremberg, the laws of war were embodied in professional military tradition, field manuals, international law treaties and occasionally in little-noticed court-martial proceedings. Nuremberg made them the preoccupation of great statesmen and generals, and the stuff of newspaper headlines.'

Even more significant for today's soldier is Telford Taylor's conclusion: 'however history may assess the wisdom or unwisdom of the war crimes trials, one thing is indisputable. At their conclusion, the United States Government stood legally, politically and morally committed to the principles enunciated in the charters and judgments of the tribunals.'[2]

The American soldier has a mass of sound, authoritative advice and interpretation to choose from. He can be proud of the fact that it was the American delegation at the United Nations which presented the resolution by which the UN General Assembly endorsed the Nuremberg Principles.

[1] Ibid.
[2] Ibid.

The American soldier can learn from Telford Taylor that the bombing of cities, culminating in the atomic destruction of Hiroshima and Nagasaki, destroyed much more than the target: 'Since both sides had played the terrible game of urban destruction – the Allies far more successfully – there was no basis for criminal charges against Germans or Japanese, and in fact, no such charges were brought.'[1] It is appropriately ironic, then, that only Japanese courts have considered the legality of aerial bombing.

On the first occasion, following General James Doolittle's famous carrier-based air attack on Japan of April, 1942, laws were passed by the Japanese Government designed to punish airmen for attacking illegal targets. Some of Doolittle's pilots and crew were captured, tried and punished. After the war several Japanese officers were sentenced for commiting war crimes, on the grounds that the US airmen had been executed without a fair trial.

Later, in 1955, the Shimoda case brought the issue of nuclear attack into court for the first time, in a Tokyo district court. Five Japanese citizens, four survivors of Hiroshima and one of Nagasaki, were prevented by a peace treaty from suing the United States Government, so they did the next best thing. They sued their own government. They sued for personal injury, and for a declaration that the atom-bombing was illegal under international law. The plaintiffs, three men and two women, were scarred and in poor health. Shimoda, whose name was given to this case, was suffering from tumours and could not work. Suji Hamabe was an office-worker from Nagasaki whose entire family, a wife and three daughters, were killed in the blast.

Their lawyers depicted the horrific impact of the attack: 'People in rags of hanging skin wandered about and lamented aloud among dead bodies. It was an extremely sad sight beyond the description of a burning hell, and beyond all imagination of anything known before in human history.'[2]

They cited various international laws, including the Hague Conventions, the Geneva Gas Protocol, 1925, and the Draft Rules of Air Warfare, 1923, to prove that attacks on undefended cities and civilians were prohibited. The Government, defending, used the same arguments as those used today by the nuclear powers: that there is no treaty specifically banning nuclear weapons; and that

[1] Ibid.
[2] Institute for World Order, *War Criminals, War Crimes*, New York 1974.

the Hague Conventions pre-date nuclear weapons. Paradoxically, the newly democratized Japanese Government mimicked Hitler's 'total war' logic: 'War is originally the condition in which a country is allowed to exercise all means deemed necessary to cause the enemy to surrender ... the first consideration is to crush the military forces of the enemy.'[1] Hitler, post-war Japan and the United States converged in an unholy and illegal alliance of logic.

A further twist in this story is the fact that the post-war Japanese Government contradicted the official protest of the wartime government, following the bombing of Hiroshima. The latter had complained through the neutral Swiss Government that the attack was a violation of international law. The country which had been brought to its knees by the atomic bomb now claimed that the bombing was legal.

The Tokyo court judged the bombings illegal. It cited four main reasons: indiscriminate bombing of undefended cities is forbidden by international law; it could not be proved that bombing the cities was due to 'military necessity'; the cities were not 'military targets' with important munitions factories or army bases; and the atomic bomb caused even more suffering than those weapons already outlawed for producing unnecessary and cruel forms of suffering. This principle applies to all weapons, whether already developed or not.

The court decided that it had no power to award the plaintiffs financial compensation, but its condemnation of the atomic bombing, on the basis of existing international law, is a judgment of great importance. There is no doubt that if nuclear war were to break out, and there were survivors able to sue the agents of that war, the Shimoda case would provide a precedent. What is of more relevance to the American soldier of today, and ourselves, is the value of this case in helping prevent a nuclear war by branding as criminal the weaponry and strategy involved.

Another famous American soldier, General Patton, made his own contribution to the laws of war, on the other side of the world, in Europe, and with conventional warfare. On 27 June 1943, he spoke to officers and men of the US 45th Infantry Division, on the eve of the invasion of Sicily. It was a typically fiery speech, in which he said: 'The fact we are operating in enemy country does not

[1] Ibid.

permit us to forget our American tradition of respect for private property, non-combatants and women .... Attack rapidly, ruthlessly, viciously and without rest, and kill even civilians who have the stupidity to fight us.'[1]

Several days after the invasion, which resulted in fierce fighting, a Captain Compton lined up forty-three captured Germans, some of whom were wearing civilian clothes, and had them executed by machine-gun. Captain Compton had earlier lost several of his men, killed in the fighting. At about the same time, in the same general location, a Sergeant West, from another company, shot and killed thirty-six Germans he was escorting to a prisoner-of-war camp. When he heard of these outrages, General Patton ordered both men court-martialled on charges of pre-meditated murder. At their trials the two men cited in their defence General Patton's pre-invasion speech. The latter was exonerated, but not until he had appeared before a board of investigating officers and given them the text and an oral rendering of the speech. The two accused were convicted as charged.

In the years leading up to the military and political quagmire of Vietnam, there was another case which concerned the killing of a prisoner of war. The judgment asserted primary principles of behaviour: 'human life being regarded as sacred, moral, religious and civil law proscriptions against its taking existing throughout our society, we view the order as commanding an act so obviously beyond the scope of authority of the superior officer and so palpably illegal on its face as to admit of no doubt of its unlawfulness to a man of ordinary sense and understanding .... In our view no rational being of the accused's age (20), formal education (grade 11) and military experience (2 years), could have considered the order lawful.'[2]

It was in Vietnam that the modern American soldier's relation to the law was most cruelly exposed. More than a national disaster, it was a revelation of the universality of crime and the need of firm universal law to combat it. Not the pedantic law of a legal profession steeped in narcissism, but law rooted in the moral imagination of Hugo Grotius and the small group, including Americans, who have kept alive a sense of humanitarian justice.

Like every nation, the United States is committed by law to

[1] Green, op. cit.
[2] US v. Kinder, 1954.

make known the laws of armed conflict to its military personnel. The many thousands of conscripts and professional soldiers sent to Vietnam in the sixties were supposedly informed of the laws restricting military violence. There is no doubt that legal training did take place, and no doubt that it was inadequate. The American soldier should be aware of what went right, and wrong. He is heir to the results, including devastating criminality.

The Judge Advocate General's School of Law warns that soldiers must distinguish between soldiers and non-combatants: 'The killing of resisting or fleeing enemy forces is generally recognised as a justifiable act of war, and you may consider any such killings justified in this case. The law attempts to protect those persons not actually engaged in warfare.'[1]

It was the helicopter, more than any other single weapon, which exposed the criminal aspect of warfare in Vietnam. During World War Two, distance lent a cloak to crime, the physical distance of the bomber pilot from his victim, or the psychological and emotional distance between the Auschwitz guard and his prey. On the ground, between fighting forces, the laws of armed conflict remained surprisingly intact. The helicopter bridged the gap between the unseen and the seen; far enough to reduce sensitivity, close enough to permit all manner of devilry.

The legal training of the US Army helicopter pilot in Vietnam was improved as a result of bitter experience. One such training programme was named 'Cobra Strike':

You are the flight commander of a Cobra fire team providing support to the armed forces of a developing country. He directs you to attack a target which he identifies as an enemy concentration at specific co-ordinates. You approach the target and determine that it is in a village occupied by men, women and children. You observe no weapons and receive no fire. Based on your understanding of the rules of engagement and the rules of land warfare, you determine that you should not attack the target.

You inform the advisor of your decision. He, in turn, passes your message to the ground unit commander . . . to the unit. In about two minutes the advisor, senior in rank to you, returns to the radio. He says, 'The unit commander has the final authority

---

[1] Green, op. cit.

to clear fire missions in this area and he wants the target hit. It's his responsibility. You are ordered to hit it.'

Since you have no doubt that it is not an appropriate target you refuse to change your decision not to attack the target. However, in order to avoid a confrontation with the advisor, you simply declare a malfunction and low-fuel state, inform the advisor and return to your base.

The next day, reading the INSUM [intelligence summary], you discover that the target you had been given was attacked by artillery ten minutes after you left the area. Forty-five enemy was reported KIA [killed in action]. Since the co-ordinates describe exactly the area you reconnoitred, you suspect that a war crime may have been committed.

1. What is your action now with regard to the report carried in the INSUM?
2. Have you contributed to a possible war crime?
3. Can you analyse the pressures on the advisor who said, 'You are ordered to hit it'?[1]

As I discovered during my own military service, training is one thing, its execution another. The life-and-death pressure of warfare in Vietnam affected Cobra pilots as much as anyone: 'Their [Cobra pilots] response was straightforward: one never allowed oneself to get close enough at a slow enough speed to a target to tell whether the target was legitimate or not in terms of the formal rules of engagement. "You pick an access and an escape route, go in, hit it, and get out. You never know who's there."'

A former US sergeant in Vietnam, Peter Martinsen commented on his comrades-in-arms: 'If you encounter a man who likes to shoot water buffaloes you may ask him, "Why do you like to shoot water buffaloes?" and he says, "Because I like to shoot water buffaloes." It's so absurd. I remember a man who was a helicopter door gunner and he liked to kill people on the ground, but only playing with them like a cat with a mouse with his machine-gun, chasing them around, etc.'[2]

Gratuitous violence of this kind was not uncommon. A Vietnam veteran recalled how helicopter gunships were often called in to watch in case enemy troops were flushed out of a village. Once,

[1] Karsten, op. cit.
[2] Ibid.

nothing happened, and soon 'the gunships got bored. So they made a gun run on a hootch with mini-guns and rockets. When they left the area we found one dead baby, which was a young child, very young, in its mother's arms, and we found a baby girl about three years old, also dead. Because these people were bored; they were just sick flying around doing nothing. When it was reported to the battalion, the only reprimand was to put the two bodies on the body count board and just add them up with the rest of the dead people. There was no reprimand, there was nothing .... We tried to call the gunship off, but there was nothing you could do. He just made his run, dropped his ordnance, and left.'[1]

In Vietnam the 'enemy' was not in a defined space, like an opposing football team, to be attacked and overrun. He was everywhere, all around, even below, and often disguised. The American soldier was a watchdog in the midst of a swarm of bees, a born winner who could only lose. He compensated for a collapsing self-image by reducing his opponents to the level of an insect pest.

'Pretty soon you get to hate all these people,' said one US veteran. 'You get to fear them, too. They're all out for your ass one way or another, out to take you for everything you've got. You don't know which ones are your enemies and which ones are your friends. So you begin to think that they are all your enemies. And that all of them are not quite human, some kind of lower order of creature. You give them names to de-personalize them, to categorize them as you've become convinced they ought to be categorized. They become dinks and slopes and slants and gooks, and you begin to say, and believe, "the only good dink is a dead dink". You echo the comments of your buddies that "one million of them ain't worth one of us. We should show up all those slant-eyed bastards.'[2]

The gooks even got into the law. A young US law officer in Vietnam explained the 'Mere Gook Rule' to one observer: 'He explained that the expression had been adopted facetiously by some army legal officers who believed that military courts were lenient to Americans who killed Vietnamese civilians, because the

[1] Bill Adler (ed.), *Letters from Vietnam*, New York 1967.
[2] Telford Taylor, op. cit.

Vietnamese were regarded as somehow second-class human beings, or "mere gooks".[1]

Conscripts with a negative or deprived background found Vietnam a 'free fire zone' for their pent-up aggression. One returned to New York and murdered his girl-friend. He described his experience in Vietnam to an interviewing psychiatrist: ' "I didn't have to just sit back and take abuse from people and all that bullshit. In 'Nam there was no law, I mean there was laws, but you didn't pay attention to them. 'Cause you knew when it came right down to it, you were on equal terms with everyone. There was nobody that had odds against you. 'Cause everybody had a gun, and everybody had a right to kill. . . .

' "When I first started using a gun out there it was like someone saying to me, "We're here. This is your right to fucking do whatever you want, whatever you think is right." 'Cause all my life I was on the receiving end of abuse and everything. And here I was given a chance to fucking make up my own mind" . . . '[2]

A former sergeant in Vietnam, James Henry, commented on the sudden switch from helpless anonymity in the States to life-and-death power in Vietnam: 'they have never had this power before, they have never had *any* power before.'[3] Today's American soldier may reflect on the fact that many Vietnam veterans describe their more brutal comrades as 'dregs', 'drop-outs', 'real fuck-ups', and 'clearly associated their more humane comrades with college, and "middle class" and "good homes".'[4] When the more privileged have a higher stake in the law than the poor, the law itself is perverted.

An American Vietnam veteran expressed his concern in poetry:

> *Thap Ba*
> The old Cham temple of Thap Ba,
>   the locals say it's a thousand years
> old,
>   older than this stilted Anglo-
> Saxon language I use
>
> Older they say than the use

[1] Telford Taylor, op. cit.
[2] Karsten, op. cit.
[3] Mark Lane, *Conversations with Americans*, New York 1970.
[4] Murray Polner, *No More Victory Parades*, New York 1971.

of bullets, ballots and the printing
press
older than the airplane and the bomb
older than napalm

Was hit yesterday by a twenty-year-old
helicopter pilot
fresh from the States
who found it more ecstatic than
the firing range
for testing his guns.[1]

The stress imposed by war on minimum laws of restraint is well illustrated by the story of one Vietnamese peasant's brush with death. A college graduate, Private First Class Rocky Bleier was out on patrol in Vietnam:

Three of us went off to find water and suddenly came across a little man, less than five feet tall. He seemed to come out of nowhere . . . . It was a man of about thirty. My two colleagues grabbed him by his black pyjamas.

'You VC, You NVA?'

He said nothing.

'Papa-*san*, you VC? You VC?'

We didn't know what to do with him.

The point man said, 'Hell, let's kill him. I should have killed him right away. Then we wouldn't have to worry.'

The other guy said, 'Maybe we should tell him to *di di* (get out of here). Then we can shoot him as he's running away.'

The point man replied, 'Let's just tie him to a tree and shoot him right here.'

It was a few incredulous moments before I realized what they were saying. 'What are you guys talking about?' I said. 'We can't shoot this guy. Let's take him back to the lieutenant.'

'No,' the point man said. 'The lieutenant said he didn't want any prisoners. What's he gonna do with him? We'd just have to watch the gook and take him with us on the march. The lieutenant doesn't want to be bothered with him. We can't take him back.'

---

[1] Poem by Jan Berry in L. Rottmann (ed.), *Winning Hearts and Minds*, New York 1972.

I said, 'Let's take him back and let the lieutenant decide. If he wants to kill him that's his business.'

'Well, I don't know. The lieutenant might be sore because we brought him back. He said he didn't want any prisoners. He's gonna be sore.'

'Well, let him be sore,' I said. 'We can't shoot him. He doesn't have a weapon. He hasn't tried anything. Just showed up.'

Finally we took him to the lieutenant, who checked him out and freed him.[1]

War blurs senses while sharpening reflexes. A punch-drunk boxer finds it as hard to remember and obey the rules of the game as a soldier who has watched death in a thousand forms. One Vietnam veteran put it this way: 'People wonder when a guy comes back from a place like Vietnam and acts like an animal. Well, I myself have changed just in the last three days. I'm hard on the inside, and as far as I am concerned, if anyone stands between me and my job, I'd just as soon kill 'em. Life isn't worth much anyway, besides some of those people are better off dead . . . . Sometimes I just don't know whether I give a damn if I die or not. A lot of guys here feel as I do.'[2]

Atrocities pervaded the war in Vietnam, on both sides. Many participated, many stayed silent, a tiny minority spoke out. One who stayed silent after hearing atrocity stories explained why:

'If they were true, it meant my company had murdered people; it meant I had helped by making sure the weapons worked . . . . If I decided not to do my job any more I would be sent to gaol and court-martialed. It meant a lot of people would think I was a traitor to my country because I didn't believe in the war any more: it meant that some of the people in the company and outside the Army would hate me because they wouldn't understand why I had changed my mind; it meant I would get a dishonourable discharge; it meant I would find it hard to get a job; it meant losing the privileges of the GI Bill for schools and hospital care; it meant hardship on my parents. It meant a lot of bad things I didn't want to think about, based on stories I didn't know were true. So I decided to forget about it.'[3]

[1] Karsten, op. cit.
[2] Charles Levy, *Spoils of War*, Boston 1974.
[3] Karsten, op. cit.

When obeying the law becomes hard for an ordinary soldier, the military system stands condemned. In such conditions of criminal conformity it is a wonder that any rebelled. Yet, as in Nazi Germany, there were young American soldiers in Vietnam who risked their lives to expose war crimes. What became known as the 'incident on Hill 192' revealed one such remarkable man. His name was Eriksson. His story has some of the features of Klaus Hornig's during World War Two.

Eriksson was part of a small US foot patrol in Vietnam. Before the patrol set off the sergeant in charge told his men that he would take along a Vietnamese peasant girl for their entertainment. He was an experienced soldier who had been selected to march in President Johnson's inauguration parade in Washington, an honour limited to 200 men with unblemished records. The girl was duly abducted from a neighbouring village and later raped by every member of the patrol except Eriksson. She was then murdered, and her body hidden on Hill 192.

The patrol members, said Eriksson later, 'appeared to assume a self-protective air of disbelief' following this murder.[1] He was deeply shocked by the experience and tried to raise it with his commanding officer, without success. Such events reflect badly on the unit and it was best to forget about it, he was told. Eventually, some while later, Eriksson was transferred to another regiment and decided to tell the chaplain about the murder.

This time the response was immediate and urgent. The chaplain called in the Criminal Investigation Division. Eriksson had never even heard of it. Within a few days he was closely questioned by pathologists, CID agents, lawyers, and ballistics and fire-arms experts. They were secretly flown by helicopter to Hill 192, where the body was hidden. Their findings established conclusively that Mao (the dead girl) had been stabbed three times, in the rib cage and the neck, and that her skull 'presented a "crushed" appearance, showing the shattering effects of two high-velocity missile wounds.'[2]

The rest of the patrol were immediately arrested and charged with her murder and rape. It was a gruelling but revealing experience for Eriksson. He had learned by bitter experience how elusive is responsibility in the army. 'That was the thing about the chain of

[1] Daniel Lang, *Incident on Hill 192*, London 1970.
[2] Ibid.

command,' he said later, 'you couldn't tell who was to blame for what. It had nothing to do with a man's being responsible for his own behaviour. Just as long as he stayed in line, just as long as he kept the set-up going, he could do whatever he wanted.' Eriksson described army life as 'living in an over-organized jungle – full of names, ranks and serial numbers, but not much else'.

This trial reflects the overlap between military and domestic law. Murder and rape are the same crime under each jurisdiction. Eriksson told the court: 'I realize we are over here fighting a war, but to go out and kill an innocent person has nothing to do with the war.' He knew nothing about the laws of war in detail, but understood them very well in principle. The defendants, on the other hand, had lost almost all sense of morality and law. They were amazed to be tried at all, giving the impression that 'only the sheerest, most improbable sort of accident could explain their being hauled before a tribunal. Their testimony indicates that they were so inured to the epidemic, occupational violence of war that they found it hard to recognise their judicial plight as a type of retribution.' When one of them was asked why he had joined in the rape, he replied that it helped to 'keep the thing running smooth. It makes for an easier mission and no problems.'

All were convicted, receiving sentences ranging from 8 to 15 years, but were freed within a few years. Eriksson learned a lesson from that experience which points to the heart of the laws of war: 'I decided that whatever jobs I'd get, they weren't going to be as important to me as the way I lived. That had to have some purpose. If it didn't, then coming back from that patrol meant nothing.'[1]

The US Army, and its patrol, were in Vietnam, according to the American President, for the grandest purpose of all, defending freedom and democracy. Yet they were in reality bereft of both ideals, their only substantial allegiance being to the immediate group, right or wrong, lawful or criminal. As Eriksson said, it was an 'upside-down mentality . . . . We had to answer to something, to someone – maybe just to ourselves.'[2] He obeyed the law, not because of the army but in spite of it.

In the end the US Army tried to redeem itself. Eriksson received the following citation from his divisional commanding officer:

[1] Ibid.
[2] Ibid.

1. You are to be commended for the important part you played in seeing that justice was done in the recent court-martial cases involving four soldiers charged with the rape and murder of a young Vietnamese woman. Your prompt reporting of this serious incident to your superiors and subsequent testimony in court were essential elements in the apprehension and trials of the men responsible for this brutal crime.

2. The great pressures you were subject to during those critical months are appreciated. Yours was not an easy task, but you did your duty as an American soldier. You should know that the courage and steadfastness you demonstrated make me proud to have you as a member of this division.

> John J. Tolson
> Major General, USA,
> Commanding 1st Cavalry (Airmobile)
> Division.[1]

Today's American soldier should beware. The US Army behaves like a whimsical father with his children, often indifferent and suddenly punitive. The US Army in Vietnam created the conditions for the incident on Hill 192, but once alerted to a specific crime the response was immediate, positive, decisive. The law is there to be used. Eriksson showed how.

Even more instructive of the schizoid quality of American military response to the laws of humanitarian restraint was the case of Lieutenant William Calley and the My Lai massacre. Crime and courage were both evident, in extreme form.

On 16 March 1968, 'Charlie' Company, 1st Battalion, 20th Infantry Regiment, 11th Brigade of the 23rd US 'American' Division, 'swept through several hamlets attached to the Vietnam village of Son My in Quang Ngai province. In the hamlet, My Lai 4, members of "Charlie" Company's 1st platoon systematically rounded up and executed in a ditch some 400 to 500 unresisting men, women and children. The brigade commander reported the killing of 128 "combatants", thus masking what had really happened. Soldiers who expressed distress at what had happened were warned to keep their feelings to themselves.'[2]

There was nothing secretive or hidden about this assault: 'Above

---

[1] Ibid.
[2] Karsten, op. cit.

them, at various altitudes were gunships, observation and command helicopters. There was constant radio communication between the various units and their superiors, and these were monitored at brigade headquarters. A photographer and a reporter from an Army Public Information Detachment went in with the troops and witnessed and recorded the course of events virtually from start to finish.'[1]

Warrant Officer Hugh Thompson was one of the helicopter pilots at the scene of this massacre. Appalled by what he could see on the ground below, he 'immediately reported to brigade head-quarters several indiscriminate killings he had seen, landed his aircraft beside Calley and his victims, ordered his door gunner to fire at anyone who shot any more detainees, hastened to place himself between Calley and his victims, located nine survivors among those who had been cut down by Calley's fire, and shep-herded them back to safety.'[2]

On the following day, 17 March, the *New York Times* reported this sweep as a victory: 'The operation is another American offensive to clear enemy pockets still threatening the cities. While the two companies of United States soldiers moved in on the enemy force from opposite sides, heavy artillery barrages and army helicopters were called in to pound the North Vietnamese soldiers.'

The newspaper noted the 128 soldiers reported dead. Two Americans had died and ten had been wounded.

A young helicopter pilot, Ronald L. Ridenhour, from Phoenix, Arizona, was flying over the area some days later when he saw the body of a Vietnamese woman lying in a rice paddy. He had heard rumours of a massacre from soldiers who said they were told to go in and kill anything that moved. The story of a fierce battle with Vietcong soldiers, he was told, had been 'invented to make "Charlie" Company look good'.[3] If this was true, he realized, war crimes would have been committed. That same year, 1968, the US Command in Saigon had issued the following directive: 'It is the responsibility of all military personnel having knowledge or receiv-ing a report of an incident or of an act thought to be a war crime to

[1] Telford Taylor, op. cit.
[2] Karsten, op. cit.
[3] Institute for World Order, op. cit.

make such an incident known to his commanding officer as soon as possible.'

Ridenhour asked further questions but was too alarmed about his own security to do more until he returned home in December, nine months later. He sent copies of a detailed report on My Lai to President Nixon, leading Senators and congressmen, and to officials at the Pentagon, the State Department and the Joint Chiefs of Staff. 'After hearing this account,' he said in his report, 'I couldn't quite accept it. Somehow I just couldn't believe that not only had so many young American men participated in such an act of barbarism, but that their officers had ordered it.'

He concluded his report with the following words: 'I remain irrevocably persuaded that if you and I do truly believe in the principles of justice and the equality of every man, however humble, before the law, that forms the very backbone that this country is founded on, then we must press forward a widespread and public investigation of this matter with all our combined efforts.'[1]

It is ironic, looked at from our vantage point many years later, that this appeal to uphold the law was addressed by a young helicopter gunner to a President later shown to be criminal. Not for the first time in modern history, the law depended more on the humble than the great.

An investigation was conducted, in the strictest secrecy, during 1969. On 5 September 1969 Army press officers announced at Fort Benning, Georgia, that First Lieutenant William L. Calley had been charged with 'violation of Article 118 [of the Uniform Code of Military Justice], murder, for offences allegedly committed against civilians while serving in Vietnam in March, 1968'.

It is more than likely that Calley's trial would have proceeded with minimal attention had not a well known American journalist, Seymour Hersch, been tipped off by a friend in Washington who told him: 'The Army's trying to court-martial some guy in secret at Fort Benning for killing Vietnamese civilians.'[2] Overnight, in the classic American manner, the story of the Calley trial became front page news across the United States. Photographs taken at the time of the massacre suddenly appeared in all their gruesome detail.

[1] Ibid.
[2] Ibid.

One man's concern had eventually triggered a massive inquiry involving 400 witnesses and 20,000 pages of testimony.

But the trial itself had some of the mundane, anti-climactic quality of the Eichmann trial in Jerusalem. Calley was no monster, but a small, inoffensive, rather dim-witted soldier who inspired more pity and contempt than fear or anger.

Calley's pathetic ignorance serves as warning to the American soldier of today. He was acting on orders from a Captain Medina. 'Were you motivated by other things,' he was asked in court, 'besides the fact that those were enemy?' 'Well,' he answered, 'I was ordered to go in there and destroy the enemy. That was my job on that day. That was the mission I was given. I did not sit down and think in terms of men, women and children. They were all classified the same and that was the classification we dealt with, just as enemy soldiers.' Captain Medina, said Calley, had said that 'everything in that area would be the enemy and everyone there would be destroyed. All enemies would be destroyed.'

He was asked at one point: 'Now, at any time did you stop and consider the legality or illegality of those orders?' He replied 'No, sir.' While awaiting the verdict, Calley told a reporter. 'Many people say war is hell who have never experienced it, but it is more than hell for those people tied up in it.'[1]

When convicted, on 29 March 1971, Calley made a statement which still echoes in US military and political circles: 'When my troops were getting massacred and mauled by an enemy I couldn't see, I couldn't feel and I couldn't touch . . . nobody in the military system ever described them as anything other than Communism.'[2]

In fact Calley was lying. He could see very clearly, at a distance of a few yards, the living bodies of the women and children he shot. He could hear their screams and watch the blood flow as bullets raked through them. But he was telling the truth, too, about the all-pervading presence of his country's enemy. He was poorly educated and poorly trained, like many thousands of the US armed forces in Vietnam. Worse still, he was put into the firing line by politicans and generals whose vision of the modern world was fundamentally distorted.

The former US prosecutor at Nuremberg, Telford Taylor, exposes the criminal implications of village assaults in Vietnam: 'it

[1] Ibid.
[2] Ibid.

is clear that such reprisal attacks are a flagrant violation of the Geneva Convention on Civilian Protection, which prohibits "collective penalties" and "reprisal against protected persons", and equally in violation of the Rules of Land Warfare. Son My, after all, was suspected of harboring the Vietcong, and if (as has been seen) it was nonetheless a war crime to round up the inhabitants and shoot them without trial, it would be equally criminal to have killed them by a surprise air attack.'[1]

During the Second World War many US soldiers were court-martialed and severely punished for killing or assaulting civilians in violation of local laws and the laws of war, but news of those events was drowned in the flood of war reporting. The Calley case attracted attention in many countries but there was a tendency in the United States to limit its effect by regarding it as a freak crime. The US Congress Hebert Sub-Committee on the case declared in 1970 that what happened at Son My 'was so wrong and so foreign to the normal character and action of our military forces as to immediately raise a question as to the legal sanity at the time of those men involved.' Chairman Hebert also said angrily that his committee was 'hampered by the Army in every conceivable way.'[2]

Behind the glossy press handouts in Vietnam lay ugly evasion. Despite the careful wording of the orders, says Telford Taylor, 'and the optimistic releases from the Pentagon about "pacification", virtually all observers report death, destruction and troop attitudes that indicate that the restraint called for by the orders is not exercised.'

He quotes the comment of four US Army sergeants, shortly after the Calley massacre: ' "You know this is a VC (Vietcong) village, they are the enemy, they are a part of the enemy's war apparatus. Our job is to destroy the enemy, so kill them ... I want to come home alive, if I must kill old men, women and children to make myself a little safer, I'll do it without hesitation." '

If that is what happens, says Telford Taylor, 'then all our talk of "pacification", to say nothing of the Hague Conventions, is the sheerest hypocrisy, and we had better acknowledge at once that we are prepared to do what we hanged and imprisoned Japanese and German generals for doing'. The Vietnam war should warn today's US soldier that the Nazi virus is alive and well, infecting modern

---

[1] Telford Taylor, op. cit.
[2] Ibid.

militarism in every country and at every level. As one US Army private put it: '"The trouble is, no one sees the Vietnamese as people. They're not people. Therefore it doesn't matter what you do to them."'[1]

All the ingredients of a nuclear war were present in Vietnam, a micro-demonstration of a macro-threat. As when the reasoning powers of a madman go haywire, so the laws of minimum restraint were shredded and mocked by a war which confused the aggressive and the helpless, the well and the sick, babies and assassins. Without coherent aim or method war becomes criminal violence, feeding on itself. 'My feeling is,' said the Commander of the US Marine Corps, General Wallace M. Greene, 'that you could kill every Vietcong and North Vietnamese in South Vietnam and still lose the war.'[2]

The most powerful nation in history had applied its military might to Vietnam because, in President Kennedy's words, it was 'prepared to go anywhere, pay any price', to defend freedom. Instead, it became 'completely submerged' under 'an avalanche of death and destruction'. That was a high price, but the result was not freedom. The judgment of the American leadership was disastrously wrong. Yet only about fifty Americans were prosecuted for criminal military activity in Vietnam, minor agents like Calley. The legal diet was the same as usual. Gnats were strained at and camels swallowed.

The US soldier should link the crime of Vietnam with the assessment by his own countrymen of Nazi responsibilities, some years earlier: 'the only way in which the behaviour of the German troops in the recent war can be made comprehensible as the behaviour of human beings is by a full exposure of the criminal doctrines and orders which were pressed on them from above by these defendants and others'.[3] William Calley may reflect on the irony of that judgment.

Action in Vietnam was often criminal, but the law remained intact. The military Appeal Court which re-assessed the Calley verdict had no doubts: 'Whether Lieutenant Calley was the most ignorant person in the United States Army in Vietnam, or the most intelligent, he must be presumed to know that he could not kill the

---

[1] Ibid.
[2] Ibid.
[3] *Trials of War Criminals Vol. XI*: US v. von Leeb.

people involved here . . . . An order to kill infants and unarmed civilians who were so demonstrably incapable of resistance to the armed might of a military force as were those killed by Lieutenant Calley is . . . palpably illegal . . . .'[1]

Following the Calley case, in 1970, the US Department of the Army issued a document to guide instructors whose task is 'to familiarize military personnel with their rights, duties and obligations under the Hague Conventions of 1907, the Geneva Conventions of 1949, and the customary law of war regarding . . . obedience to superior orders.' The document warned soldiers: 'an order to clear an area of the enemy is not one to kill everyone and destroy everything you see. Rather it means to find the enemy soldier and destroy his ability and will to resist. Such an order obviously does not include looting a store, burning a farmer's house or murdering the women and children . . .'

Should a soldier receive an illegal order, he is warned: 'you must disregard such an illegal order. This takes courage, but if you fail to do so you can be tried and punished . . . . The Code of Conduct states, "I am an American fighting man, responsible for my actions, and dedicated to the principles which made my country free". The American soldier who follows that code should have no problem with illegal orders.'

The soldier is advised to discuss a suspected illegal order with a judge advocate or military lawyer, although 'many soldiers prefer to discuss problems with the Chaplain.' As Eriksson did following the 'incident on Hill 192'.

If it was hard to enforce the law in Vietnam on the ground, it was doubly difficult high up in the air where the jet bombers flew. In the words of one legal commentator: 'The impersonality and blind character of such a modern weapons delivery system as the jet bomber makes it a ready vehicle for war crimes, both when the bomber is commanded by an irresponsible pilot and when it is assigned to an improper mission by an irresponsible leader. Such a leader may be guilty of violating the laws of war . . . for one or more of a number of reasons.' The latter 'may be captive of his own "Pentagonesque" world (a world with nice-sounding but danger-ously defective phraseology such as "surgical strike" and "search

[1] US v. Calley, 1973, in the Military Appeal Court.

and clear"), a captive of his physical and mental distance from the
battle field.'[1]

A US Navy law officer confirms this warning and strengthens
it: 'An unintentional error in judgment can still amount to a
dereliction of a criminal nature in certain circumstances. Furthermore, a "disproportionate" use of firepower does not result in an
"incidental" or non-criminal injury to civilians, but a war
crime.'[2]

John Floyd was a Marine 'Intruder' pilot operating out of Chu
Lai air base, Vietnam. He described the war from the pilot's
standpoint as 'very impersonal': 'You fly. You see flak at night.
That's about as close to war as we get; you don't see any of the
explosions. You can look back and see 'em, but you don't see any
of the blood or any of the flesh. It's a very clean and impersonal
war. You go out, fly your mission, you come back to your
air-conditioned hootch and drink beer or whatever. You're not in
contact with it. You don't realise at the time, I don't think, what
you're doing.'[3]

A senior U.S. Air Force officer was aware of the uncomfortable
implications of strictly enforced law. ' "I'll put it to you frankly,"
he said. "If they come out with a book on the laws of air warfare
and then go by it, we're all going to be out of jobs." '[4] In fact the
laws of war already restrict air operations, by means of the same
basic principles which apply to all conflict.

As we have seen, the law was being applied in Vietnam less by
initiative from the top than by the personal courage of individual
servicemen. Before America withdrew from Vietnam there were
growing signs of military revolt, based on principles of ordinary,
civilized behaviour: 'In a development unparalleled in the history
of the Air Force, two combat pilots refused to fly bombing
missions, in opposition to US policy. On December 18 1972, at
the very outset of the renewed attack, 26-year-old Dwight Evans,
pilot of an F4 Phantom in the 34th Tactical Fighter Squadron,
balked when ordered to strike North Vietnam and stated he could
no longer participate in the war. Nine days later, Captain Michael
Heck, a B-52 bomber pilot, stationed at U Tapao, decided, as he

[1] Karsten, op. cit.
[2] Captain J. Paust, *Naval War College Review*, January to February 1973.
[3] Karsten, op. cit.
[4] Ibid.

said later, that "a man has to answer to himself first", and also refused to fly.'[1] The latter was a veteran of 200 combat missions.

Captain Heck invoked the Nuremberg principles and claimed that ' "no man has the right to surrender his conscience to any authority, military or civilian. A man has not only a right but an obligation to disobey an order that is conscientiously objectionable." ' A year later, four US pilots based on the island of Guam challenged the constitutionality of bombing Cambodia. One of them, Captain Donald E. Dawson, a B-52 bomber pilot, refused to fly and said he had begun 'to think of what had happened on the ground after a mission'.[2]

The US Navy was not immune to this simmering revolt. A group of ten sailors on the USS *Oriskany* refused to serve in Vietnam, declaring that 'the only way to end the genocide being perpetrated now in S.E. Asia is for us, the actual pawns in the political game, to quit playing'. So many US ships were affected by such feelings that the US Congress Armed Services Committee reported a major crisis of discipline. 'The US Navy,' it said, 'is now confronted with pressures which, if not controlled, will surely destroy its enviable tradition of discipline. Recent instances of sabotage, riot, wilful disobedience of orders, and contempt for authority, instances which have occurred with increasing frequency, are clear-cut symptoms of a dangerous deterioration of discipline.'[3]

Telford Taylor, who viewed Vietnam through personal experience gained at Nuremberg, summed up US intervention in Vietnam as 'the most costly and tragic blunder in American history'.[4] He commented bitterly on the cynical invocation of the spirit of Nuremberg and the UN Charter to 'justify our venture in Vietnam, where we have smashed the country to bits, and will not even take the trouble to clean up the blood and rubble. None there will ever thank us; few elsewhere that do not now see our America as a sort of Steinbeckian "Lennie", gigantic and powerful, but prone to shatter what we try to save. Somehow we failed ourselves to learn the lessons we undertook to teach at Nuremberg, and that failure is today's American tragedy.'[5]

The men who devised and promoted US policy in Vietnam were

[1] David Cortright, *Soldiers in Revolt*, New York 1975.
[2] Ibid.
[3] Ibid.
[4] Telford Taylor, op. cit.   [5] Ibid.

highly educated academics and administrators, people like Secretary of State Dean Rusk, Defense Secretary McNamara, McGeorge Bundy and Rostow. They had learned the lessons of history, or so they claimed. But it was the wrong lesson. Aggression must not pay, they told the world. But they failed to examine the complex reality of 'aggression' in Vietnam, and the methods used to combat it became inhuman and criminal as they strove to cover the initial error of judgment.

I visited the United States several times during the war, and argued with many educated, law-abiding citizens who believed that the United States was in Vietnam for good reasons. They had a genuine belief in principle but did not know how to apply it. Justice Jackson had warned at Nuremberg that the poisoned tree of Nazi example must be torn up by the roots if it was to die, adding that war crimes 'are crimes whether the United States does them or whether Germany does them, and we are not prepared to lay down a rule of criminal conduct against others which we would not be willing to have invoked against us'.[1] It was the ordinary people of America who finally could stand the killing and failure no longer, not their blinkered leaders. In 1968, President Johnson did not dare to attend his own Democrat Party convention in Chicago, where I watched regiments of blue-helmeted police charge into a yelling and non-violent crowd of anti-war protesters. The chickens had come home to roost.

The modern US soldier may learn something from Vietnam. It may help him to avoid further disaster in Central America and elsewhere. His country has been recently, and can be again, disastrously wrong in its policies and methods. There is no such thing as an American monopoly of virtue. Vicious crimes have been committed by Americans of all ranks, as they have by other nations of every political shade. Outstanding courage in defence of basic principles of humane behaviour is a feature of mankind rather than one nation. In such a world it is folly to pretend otherwise. And in case he thinks his lowly rank is a protection he should remember the fate of Lieutenant Calley, brutalized, criminalized and humiliated.

He may like to remember, too, how unreliable is public opinion as a guide. It can be supremely vicious. Barely two years after the

[1] Falk et al., op. cit.

leading Nazis were condemned for waging criminal war on whole populations, the Berlin crisis of 1948 aroused fears of another world war. The US Secretary of Defence, Forrestal, wondered how the American public would react to the possible use of atomic bombs. He consulted with various media experts, and was assured that 'in the event of war the American people would not only have no question as to the propriety of the use of the atomic bomb but they would expect it to be used'.[1] By 1951, according to the editor of the Forrestal Diaries, the American public 'would probably have had little hesitation in incinerating any number of Communist troops, or Communist women and babies, in the nuclear fires.'

The US soldier may reflect on the racist tendencies of military opinion. A study based on a survey of US soldiers during World War Two revealed that 'six times as many said that they would "really like to kill" Japanese as Germans'. Over half wanted to destroy Japan entirely. Only 13% felt the same way about Germany.[2] Yet Japan, too, had its quota of law-abiding soldiers.

Colonel Imai, a Japanese hero of the Bataan campaign during the Second World War, received orders near the end of the war to 'kill all prisoners and those offering to surrender'. He demanded a written order and meanwhile told his staff to release all the prisoners after advising them of the best means of escape from the area. His staff stared at him in disbelief, but more than 1,000 American prisoners were released. 'The Colonel told himself that no Japanese General would issue such an inhumane order, but if he had, he would have to pretend that the prisoners had escaped.'

But none of what we have discovered is much comfort to an American soldier expected to act out the role of guardian of our nuclear peace. General Robert E. Lee, preoccupied with the tangible problems of the American Civil War, would hardly recognize as a soldier a man trained to spend his military life in an underground bunker, ready to throw switches which would kill whole city populations across the world. He would not comprehend the logic or moral perception of this man, proud and glad of the 'job satisfaction' of a task which has 'more responsibility that I would obtain in a civilian world'.[3]

Abraham Lincoln, who promulgated the world's first systematic

[1] Millis (ed.), *Forrestal Diaries*, New York 1951.
[2] Karsten, op. cit.
[3] *The Times*, 16 June 1981.

laws of warfare, would be puzzled by the responsibilites of the US
Air Force officer at the Headquarters Base, Omaha, Nebraska.
'We have two tasks,' the latter told a reporter. 'The first is not to let
people go off their rockers. That's the negative side. The positive
one is to ensure that people act without moral compunction.'[1]
Lincoln believed that man is a moral being, with adult responsibilities. What would he say to the young nuclear missile operator who
prefers to enjoy ignorance and irresponsibility, and says, 'I don't
have a need to know to start with. Secondly, I'd feel kind of
emotional about what kind of people I'd be destroying'?[2]

Abraham Lincoln would no doubt find it hard to adjust to
modern notions of sanity-vetting. In those simple days, sane
behaviour was a matter of behaving like an honest, God-fearing
citizen. But at the Cruise missile training base in Arizona, sanity is
wrapped in official cellophane, to be examined minutely. The
attitudes of the young missile teams are monitored under a 'Personnel Reliability Program'. Colonel James Wohner, head of the training school, says that 'all students are administratively certified and
watched for any tendencies towards irrational behaviour ....
Their commander at Greenham Common, England, will give them
final certification.'[3] Would President Lincoln be reassured to know
that life on earth, not to mention countless millions of Soviet
citizens, could only be destroyed by a man certified sane?

The President who believed that a soldier must identify his
target and attack only soldiers, would find the operating procedures of a Cruise missile team curious, to say the least. 'We
would launch within a time window directed by the nuclear release
authorities,' said Major William Phillips, chief training instructor.
'They would tell us that they would want our weapons to be at a
particular place at a particular time. We would receive a battle plan
number from the nuclear release authorities telling us which war to
fight. The battle plans are already on tapes in the computer.'

Lincoln might be too polite, or dumbfounded, to ask what might
happen if the wrong war was programmed, or whether the missile
team might like to know which towns they were obliterating and in
which country. If he did ask, what would he make of the answer?

[1] *Guardian*, 9 October 1975.
[2] *The Times*, 16 June 1981.
[3] *Observer*, 3 July 1983.

'We don't know what the targets are. We just shoot in the dark.'[1] He would be glad to escape from this nightmare sanity to the common sense of the dead.

The American soldier will realize that compared to the nuclear operative of today, the bomber pilots of Vietnam were in close touch with their victims. The nuclear dimension of war is of less obvious emotional value to the operator than playing through a 'video nasty'. It has taken the human race barely one hundred years to move from direct confrontation with an enemy to computerized anonymity.

When destructive power is married to absence of responsible feelings, the result is a psychopathic, robotic human being capable of any kind of crime. Nuclear weaponry has sucked the extermination camp guard and bomber pilot on to a plane of ultimate suicidal destruction. Our American soldier is trapped. Ordered to obey the laws of war, he is given only the semblance of its possibility. He is trained in the arts of conventional weaponry, where some element of responsible, lawful control seems possible. But this is a sham, as far as Cold War confrontation is concerned. As much a sham as the flowerbeds and 'BATH' signs outside the gas chambers of Auschwitz. Behind the façade of legitimate war stands the lunatic spectre of nuclear oblivion. Nuclear weaponry, method and logic poison the law as surely as Zyklon-B poisoned millions of Jews.

Can the American soldier wake from this induced trance? Will he realize in time how degrading and absurd his role has become? There are one or two signs of life. It was an American admiral, Leahy, who declared of the bombing of Hiroshima that Americans had 'adopted an ethical standard common to the barbarians of the Dark Ages. I was not taught to make war in that fashion, and wars cannot be won by destroying women and children.'[2] Another admiral, and former deputy director of operations of the US forces in Europe, said 'there is not a single military man in any service in NATO who will justify these weapons in military terms'.[3] That is all very well. There was no shortage of generals in Nazi Germany who muttered disapprovingly behind Hitler's back. Yet despite the murmurings, 'there are over 700 American and 150 NATO

[1] Ibid.
[2] William D. Leahy, *I Was There*, New York 1950.
[3] *The Times*, 1 November 1983.

units certified to use nuclear weapons', according to the Washington Institute for Policy Studies.[1] Total world tonnage, according to the same source, is around 10,000 megatonnes. Dresden, Hiroshima and all other World War Two targets together consumed three megatonnes.

The American soldier, as he struggles with this nightmare, will be pleased to know that NATO, according to its Secretary-General, Lord Carrington, is determined to 'safeguard the freedom, common heritage and civilization of their peoples, founded on the principles of democracy, individual liberty and the rule of law.'[2] He will be glad of this reassurance that all is for the best in the best of all possible free worlds. But if he is alive to the evidence of American experience and his own senses, he will ask what kind of law is it which permits life on Earth to be lawfully ended if the worst comes to the worst. He has only to look up his own manual of military law to find out that it permits no such thing. Final solutions are criminal, whatever the official wrapping paper may say.

[1] *Guardian*, 10 January 1984.
[2] *The Times*, 29 May 1984.

Chapter Nine

The British Politician's Tale

> 'We but teach
> Bloody instructions, which, being taught, return
> To plague the inventor: this even-handed justice
> Commends the ingredients of our poisoned chalice
> To our own lips'
> – *Macbeth*, William Shakespeare

> 'In one way or another, we are living in a wave of violence
> throughout the world, which I can only ascribe to a
> widespread weakening of the respect for moral values and
> political and social authority, without which ordered society is
> impossible'
> – Lord Hailsham, Lord Chancellor

> 'Executive incompetence, economic folly and above all moral
> obtuseness on the part of England or any of the Allies can
> utterly overwhelm any good which Nuremberg may have
> germinated.'
> – *Nuremberg*, Peter Calvocoressi

When intelligent people say and do stupid things there is reason to suppose that they are hiding uncomfortable truth. Most politicians, even those of the more radical variety, whether they admit it or not, are sensitive to the law. Not because they always agree with it but because they know very well that no society can function without it. And most politicians have a lively intelligence. They would be proud to be described as people of 'great intelligence, nimble wit, wide grasp and immense energy'. But they might be less pleased to know that Hitler's partner in crime, Goering, is described in this way by a British analyst.[1] Intelligence alone is clearly no guard against crime, in Nazi Germany or today. Experience confirms, time and again, that real opposition to crime stems from exceptional personal integrity, with little regard for rank or status.

[1] A. Tusa and J. Tusa, *The Nuremberg Trial*, London 1983.

The modern politician, and we are interested here mainly in the politician of a nuclear State, is close to the core of our investigation into law and war, because the power to enforce the law or blow up civilization is ultimately a political power. Academic lawyers, as we have seen, have extensive knowledge but cannot act on it. They have spun cobwebs of detail around the brutal reality of mass murder and its machinery, hiding plain truth from common sense. Like spiders, they are quick to scuttle into hiding, when power shows its face.

Lawyers have demonstrated a scarcely greater integrity. Pampered and protected, their skills and service are bought and sold in the manner of the oldest profession on earth. During a dark half-century of city-bombing anarchy, conventional and nuclear, lawyers have been the parasites of power, not its monitors. They will defend or prosecute the cause of mass murder as readily as any other cause.

Judges claim and are awarded very special status, power and privilege. They are, we are told, independent and incorruptible guardians of law and dispensers of justice. But when it comes to nuclear mass destruction, where are these judges? Like military midwives attending nuclear tests, they turn their eyes from the 'destroyer of worlds', in case they should be blinded. The prospect of universal chaos is too much for them, so they cobble together a judicial screen between civilization and its inner desert. Inside this limit is an unmapped land governed by a divine monarch, national security. Far from regarding this judicial no-man's-land as the very antithesis of law, the judges bow down before it. Bewigged and robed in scarlet, they are not too proud to worship at the altar of naked power. The judges, in short, are corruptible, dependent, mediocre mortals, like the rest of us. They are traitors to the legal principles upheld at Nuremberg.

As for the soldiers, well, we have seen that they are simple agents of power. When their orders are good they too can be good, and when their orders are bad they tend to carry them out. Soldier ants seldom turn on their queen, even when she is a bad one, because most of them obey first and think last. Their training is very thorough and the teaching very poor. It is not surprising that soldiers who obey the law at a time of authorized anarchy are few and far between, as rare as Admiral Nelson and General Robert E. Lee. Our nuclear confusion has infiltrated the military profession, the mad logic of mass murder seducing it from its allegiance to the helpless.

The politician has a very special place and responsibility in this situation of confusing normality. The professional roles which we have investigated have been limited in scope, however privileged. Even the judges dare not cross the border of national security. But the politician is contained within no borders. Subject to the law he may be, yet when the bright wrapping is taken off the constitution of the nuclear State, we see that it is the politician who appoints and pays the judges, and is the intimate confidant of and spokesman on national security.

So we should not be surprised if we find that the politician, his image magnified at the core of the State, reveals in every fractured detail of his being the true face of our plight. But as with all the other witnesses at our open court, we examine the politician's tale, not for satisfaction at its flaws but insight into a sane post-nuclear legality. Will we find such insight, or merely the depressing knowledge that in nuclear matters the nuclear politician is a 'decent man according to his own standards, whose standards are those of a murderer and liar'?[1]

In an age like ours, of ultimate crisis, it is not normal expectations which must be levelled at the politician. A desert is not responsive to a weekend gardener, but requires creative intervention of the highest order if it is to bloom. The Nuremberg Trial was just such an initiative, imperfect though it was. But its effect was short-lived. Our minimum demand of the politician today is of an order as different in magnitude to Nuremberg as nuclear missiles are to the Lancaster bomber. There is no sense in preparing for a post-nuclear-war Nuremberg. Those left behind will tear apart surviving leaders, limb from limb. What is needed is a pre-nuclear-war Nuremberg. Not an old-fashioned grand trial, with pedantic procedures and a hangman's rope, but a citizens' inquest into misuse of power. Not a self-righteous inquiry which caricatures right and wrong, but one which recognizes the all-pervading poison of total war. What kind of politician is capable of that?

My experience of British politicians and the laws of armed conflict, based on personal interviews, questionnaires and observation, confirms the fact that almost none of them has any substantial

[1] Reference made to Field-Marshal Kesselring in Tusa and Tusa, op. cit.

understanding or knowledge of these laws. A small number of those on the left want to know more. Most, including the many lawyers among them, are evasive as well as ignorant. One Foreign Secretary of the Labour Government which negotiated and signed the most extensive international laws protecting non-combatants ever agreed, (the Additional Protocol 1, 1977), told me that these laws are 'unenforceable' and hence of little account. This comes from the leader of a new and supposedly radical political party,[1] whose country made good use of substantially weaker laws at Nuremberg to prosecute war criminals. A politician seriously concerned to enforce humanitarian law would advocate concrete plans for doing so, as did the politicians who initiated the International Military Tribunal at Nuremberg. No such plans, no such demands, are in evidence, from any quarter of the British political horizon.

Perhaps the politician needs refreshing about the law, particularly that part which relates to the threat or use of weapons of mass destruction. The law on the matter is no more remote, morally or in fact, than the law against simple murder. Only the psychopathic gangsters of history have considered it legitimate to kill women and children, the elderly, wounded and sick, in the name of 'defence'. Every modern army, including those of the nuclear powers, forbids its soldiers to attack non-combatants, in the name of the law. The British *Manual of Military Law*, as we have seen, confirms the point, as do the 'Law Notes' used to train British Army officers.

Our politician should take note of paragraph 632 of this Manual op. cit.: 'Heads of State and their Ministers enjoy no immunity from prosecution and punishment for war crimes. Their liability is governed by the same principles as those governing the responsibility of State officials except that the defence of superior orders is never open to Heads of State and is rarely open to ministers.'

Like the defenders of a mediaeval fortres, the politician usually falls back under the pressure to an inner fortification. Using such weapons may be illegal, but the threat is so awful that they will never have to be used. This evasion has no substance in logic, law or morality. If terror is legitimate then the implications are as limitless and degrading as nuclear weapons themselves. Boiling oil could be a handy aid to school discipline, and someone has

---

[1] Letter from David Owen to author of 28 May 1984.

suggested that strapping live babies to car bumpers would reduce collisions. Chopping hands off shop-lifters, stoning adulterers and crucifying embarrassing prophets have all been tried. For a society to defend principles of respect for the individual with threats to annihilate millions indiscriminately is self-evident lunacy, except to those blinded by fear. For politicians to rely on such weaponry while claiming to uphold the law compounds the witches' brew of deception.

Our politician knows very well that the law of the land does not permit threats of violence. To walk around with a loaded machine-gun is a crime, because the act implies a threat to commit a crime. It is the politician who has perverted law and logic by making nuclear weapons 'legitimate' and the flick-knife criminal. The politician does not draw an artificial frontier of responsibility around any area of activity except defence.

Our politician cannot hide behind domestic law, in the hope that international law can be turned back at the national frontier. As the US prosecutor at Nuremberg, Telford Taylor, said: 'They [the trials] brought about a great expansion of the principle that individuals may be held criminally liable under international law, even though their conduct was valid under, or even required by, domestic law. Intrinsically this was not a new concept, for the laws of war had always been regarded as binding on both governments and individuals, and beyond abrogation by local law.'[1]

The politician who tries to distance himself from the law would do well to remember what Telford Taylor said during the Nuremberg Trial itself: 'We must not forget that to kill a defenceless prisoner of war is not only a violation of the rules of war. It is murder. . . . We have heard so much of mass extermination that we are likely to forget that simple murder is a capital offence. The laws of all civilized nations require that a man go to some lengths to avoid associating himself with murder, whether as an accomplice or accessory or co-conspirator.'[2]

At Nuremberg, the politician may need to be reminded, the law was not treated as a feeble and distant relative, to be disowned when inconvenient, but a war-tested guard of civilization. As our politician contemplates his threat to kill the children of Moscow, among others, he may also consider his personal responsibility for

[1] Telford Taylor, op. cit.
[2] Quoted in Peter Calvocoressi, *Nuremberg*, London, 1947.

such crime. It was the chief British prosecutor at Nuremberg, Sir Hartley Shawcross, who said: 'There is no rule of international law which provides immunity for those who obey orders which – whether legal or not in the country where they are issued – are manifestly contrary to the very law of nature from which International Law has grown. If International Law is to be applied at all, it must be superior to State law in this respect, that it must consider the legality of what is done by International and not State law tests. By every test of International Law, of common conscience, of elementary humanity, these orders – if indeed it was in obedience to orders that these men acted – were illegal. Are they then to be excused?'[1]

The British politician can learn from a British authority on international law: 'The traditional rule is that customary (international) law automatically forms part of English law; this is known as the doctrine of incorporation. Lord Chancellor Talbot said in Barbuit's case in 1735 that "the law of nations in its fullest extent is and forms part of the law of England".'[2]

And in case our politician imagines that such law is best left to the judiciary, he can learn something else from the same source:

> Most English judges and barristers know very little about international law, and therefore tend to overlook much of the evidence of customary international law. They usually seek evidence of customary international law only in the sources which are most familiar to them – in judicial decisions of English courts or of the courts of other common law countries. . . . It is the heavy reliance on judicial decisions which is dangerous, because the most recent judicial decision may have been decided a long time ago, and customary international law may have changed since then. There is thus a danger that English courts may apply obsolete rules of international law instead of modern international law, and may invent a new rule which conflicts with customary international law.[3]

Or there is yet another way in which an English court can misapply the law, as in the appeal case at Oxford in 1983,[4] when

---

[1] *International Military Tribunal Vol. XIX.*
[2] Michael Akehurst, *A Modern Introduction to International Law*, London 1984.
[3] Ibid.
[4] R. V. Needham, etc.

Judge Mynett heard arguments to the effect that international law prohibited nuclear weapons and their deployment, concluding that the latter were within the prerogative and exclusive discretion of the Crown and could not be challenged in a court of law. Judge Mynett ate his law and had it, in the sense that he said the court had 'no power whatsoever' to question Crown prerogative, and went on to say that if it did have such power he would have 'decisively rejected' the submission and arguments of the appellants. This will-o'-the-wisp use of the law, now you see it now you don't, marks the boundary between law and brute power in modern Britain.

It is a common trick of the politician, in the House of Commons or at Nuremberg, to claim responsibility when convenient and fade into the mob when not. The French prosecutor at Nuremberg put it well: 'Genocide, murder or any other crime becomes anonymous when it is committed by the State. Nobody bears the chief responsibility. Everybody shares it; those who by their presence maintain and support the administration, those who conceived the crime and those who ordained it, as well as he who issued the order. As for the executioner, he says to himself, "Befehl ist Befehl": an order is an order, and carries out his hangman's task.'[1]

When I spoke to a British Conservative MP, a lawyer, about this problem, he claimed that 'if the Russians bomb London and kill a couple of million people then we have a right to do the same to them'.[2] The most astonishing thing about such a comment is not its intrinsic criminality and suicidal disregard for minimum civilized law, but the fact that it is a view shared by most politicians in the nuclear States. Responsibility for taking part in the destruction of life on Earth would be, in his view, shared among all right-thinking patriotic British people.

When told that it was the declared policy of the British Government to comply with international law, this MP became evasive. The nuclear issue, it is clear, is for him locked in a law-tight container. But when it comes to the arena of conventional warfare, as can be seen when we look at the Falklands conflict, international law is acceptable currency.

The politician's attitude to the law, aggressively firm on one level, ephemeral as whipped cream on another, recalls what a defence

[1] *International Military Tribunal Vol. XX.*
[2] Trevor Skeet, MP.

lawyer of the Nazi Reich Cabinet had said at Nuremberg: 'One of the worse oppressions we in Germany suffered under the Nazi regime was the feeling of legal insecurity. We, who had to deal professionally with these matters, experienced daily what it meant for a legal-minded person to know that there was no legal system based on fundamentals and codes to give the individual that protection which alone makes him a free person.'[1]

The campaign which I and others recently promoted to enforce international law against all forms of mass destruction – INLAW – has encountered exactly that problem in Britain and abroad. The Nuremberg principles are candy-floss in the mouth of the nuclear politician.

Goering, arch-gangster of the Nazis and devil's advocate at Nuremberg, had a sharp nose for cant, especially of the Allied variety. He pointed out some of the poisoned undergrowth which now threatens to overwhelm us. The Allies denounced German need for *Lebensraum* (room for expansion), he said, but what about their own boast that 'three quarters of the world' is 'their own'? And was it not Churchill, he asked, who had said that 'in the struggle for life and death there is in the end no legality'?[2]

Such barbs were brushed aside at Nuremberg, but they remain to haunt us. Current contempt for the law owes more than a little to Winston Churchill and others before him. The cynical evasion of today's politician has grown in fertile soil, as prolific as it is contaminated.

If our politician doubts the present relevance of the Nuremberg Trial he may care to examine the link between a Nazi political leader and convicted war criminal, von Ribbentrop, and his own thinking: 'there remains the primary problem for Europe and the world; will Asia dominate Europe, or will the Western powers be able to stem or even push back the influence of the Soviets at the Elbe, the Adriatic Coast and at the Dardanelles? In other words, Great Britain and the United States today face the same dilemma as Germany faced at the time when I was carrying out negotiations with Russia.'[3]

Even as the famous trial continued, this Nazi attitude was becoming the basis of Allied policy. When news of Winston

---

[1] *International Military Tribunal Vol. XXII.*
[2] Tusa and Tusa, op. cit.
[3] *International Military Tribunal Vol. XXII.*

Churchill's 'Cold War' speech in the States reached the Nuremberg prisoners they were elated. They imagined, wrongly, that their own anti-Soviet views would be rewarded. Germany was indeed to become a born-again member of an alliance against the Soviet Union, but with a fresh batch of politicians and a custom-built constitution. Never were two countries so quickly transformed. There was no lack of quick-change artists in the ruined theatre of European civilization, but the management was unchanged. As nuclear heirs of this tragi-comedy there is ample proof that we have learned nothing yet.

Politicians have instinctively tried to distance themselves from international laws which, if enforced with energy and conviction, would require radical reformation of military and foreign policies. They prefer a no-man's-land separating domestic and international law. The wish has become father to the deed, stifling the law. The Nuremberg judgment offers the politician a clear assessment: 'The relation of leader and follower does not preclude responsibility here any more than it does in the comparable tyranny of domestic crime.'[1] International law is a continuation and development of domestic law, their common life-blood reflecting a common humanity.

The nuclear politician has failed to heed the warning of one British commentator that 'executive incompetence, economic folly and above all moral obtuseness on the part of England or any of the Allies can utterly overwhelm any good which Nuremberg may have germinated.'[2] No British politician can understand the nature of this failure without examining the roots of British illegality. The First World War was a collision of national fantasies to which millions were sacrificed. A tattered, bloody remnant of law was laid over the putrefying corpse. Post-war politicians were tormented by guilt but had fed too long on cheap patriotism to lift their eyes above this vista of death. They felt compelled to justify, adapt, rationalize, but not to face the truth. Legalism and murder had started a deadly romance.

A German, Hermann Hesse, felt this profound betrayal of civilized Europe. In August 1917 he wrote an open letter 'To a Cabinet Minister', in which he expresses his feelings. If only the Minister would listen to an inner voice, he would hear 'nothing

[1] *International Military Tribunal Vol. XXII.*
[2] Calvocoressi, op. cit.

more about the labour shortage and the price of coal, nothing more about tonnages and alliances, loans, troop levies, and all the rest of what you have hitherto regarded as the sole reality. Instead, you would see the earth, our patient old earth, so littered with the dead and dying, so ravaged and shattered, so charred and desecrated. You would see soldiers lying for days in no-man's-land, unable with their mutilated hands to shoo the flies from their mortal wounds. You would hear the voices of the wounded, the screams of the mad, the accusing plaints of mothers and fathers, sweethearts and sisters, the people's cry of hunger.'[1]

If only the Minister could hear 'the voice of mankind . . . you would shut yourself up in your room and weep'.

In those far-off days, when crime and effect were fresh in the poetic imagination, there was a lively sense of actual and impending madness, a premonition of nuclear extermination and its official undertakers. Of the many British poets, Wilfred Owen mediates hell most directly:

> Therefore still their eyeballs shrink tormented
> Back into their brains, because on their sense
> Sunlight seems a blood-smear; night comes blood-black;
> Dawn breaks open like a wound that bleeds afresh.
> – Thus their heads wear this hilarious, hideous,
> Awful falseness of set-smiling corpses.
> – Thus their hands are plucking at each other;
> Snatching after us who smote them, brother,
> Pawing us who dealt them war and madness.

Since then the killing has multiplied and feeling has drained away, leaving a cold, concentration-camp mentality to guide us. The politicians and their nuclear agents, twist and turn as they do, cannot escape the awful falseness of set-smiling corpses. They wear this image because it fits. The First World War is still with us. We cower in its trenches, pawed at by its ghosts.

In the modern jargon, we are 'serial murderers' led on inexorably from one slaughter to the next. Today, in the opinion of a conservative military historian, the dogs of war are wagged by their tails. 'Western strategists,' he tells us, 'plan for the destruction of Soviet cities, and vice versa, not because their political masters

[1] Hesse, op. cit.

have any serious political motive for extirpating the societies of their adversaries, but because in a grotesque inversion of logic the means now dictate the ends.'[1] Politicians are now addicts of destruction, compulsively translating the slaughter of Passchendaele into nuclear absolutism.

Could politicians have arrested this malignant process? What is certain is that they did not. One moment of failure to exert positive leadership on behalf of humanitarian law was the birth of city-bombing. In reply to questions about the indiscriminate potential of bombing, the 'father of the RAF', Lord Trenchard, sent a statement to the Chiefs of Staff in 1928, to pressure them: 'The fact that air attack may have that result is no reason for regarding the bombing as illegitimate provided all reasonable care is taken to confine the scope of the bombing to the military objective. . . . What is illegitimate . . . is the indiscriminate bombing of a city for the sole purpose of terrorizing the civilian population. It is an entirely different matter to terrorize munition workers (men and women) into absenting themselves from work.'[2]

This spurious logic was quickly exposed by the British Army and Navy, who had no love for an upstart RAF. Respondent memoranda from the Admiralty and War Office declared: 'though the objective might be a given boot factory, the actual target would be the town in which the factory happened to be located. . . . It is ridiculous to contend that the dropping of bombs would hit only so-called military targets . . . the impression produced by the acceptance and publication of such a doctrine will indubitably be that we are advocating what might be termed the indiscriminate bombing of undefended towns and of their unarmed inhabitants. . . . It is for His Majesty's Government to accept or refuse a doctrine which, in plain English, amounts to one which advocates unrestricted warfare against the civilian population of the enemy.'[3]

Armed with this conflicting advice, His Majesty's Government made no decision to nip crime in the bud. Instead, it allowed the lie to persist that bombing factories is permissible and bombing civilians is not. A white lie, because the lawful intention could not be translated into lawful fact, as the Army and Navy knew well and

---

[1] Michael Howard (ed.), *Restraints of War*, Oxford 1979.
[2] Geoffrey Best, *Humanity in Warfare*, London 1980.
[3] Ibid.

was soon proved in World War Two. The set-smiling face of
official crime became a permanent feature of government. On 14
August 1939 the British representative at an Anglo-French staff
meeting assured his audience that the RAF would attack only
'purely military targets. . . . We have no intention of attacking the
civilian population as such.'[1] In the eyes of political leadership the
killing of civilians was from now on lawful because 'accidental'.

But the RAF's official historians make it clear that in reality the
killing of civilians soon ceased being a 'by-product of the primary
intention to hit a military target'. They tell us that: 'Bomber
Command, as represented by its Commander-in-Chief, Sir Charles
Portal, now believed that this by-product should become an
end-product. He believed that the time had come to launch a direct
attack on the German people themselves.'[2]

Far from being challenged by the Prime Minister, Churchill, this
new policy was endorsed and encouraged by him: 'he . . . suggested
that Bomber Command should henceforth spread its bombs as
widely as possible over the cities of Germany'.[3] 'Promiscuous
bombing', as it has been called, became the order of the day. If our
politician suggests that such a policy merely matched that of the
Nazis, he should be asked what place is there for the law when crime
may compete with crime. The Nuremberg Trial was designed to
uphold and enforce the law, not to write its death certificate.

Law, and its companion, morality, were seeping into the sand of
this volcanic desert: 'The choice between precision and area
bombing was not conditioned by abstract theories of right and
wrong, nor by interpretation of international law. It was ruled by
operational possibilities and strategic intentions.'[4]

What could be done would be done. What should be done did
not count. The law had been effectively withdrawn from this
inferno, with the express permission of the political leadership,
and has not yet been restored. Moscow and Leningrad, and each of
their citizens, live today under suspended sentence of death at the
hands of our nuclear missiles, thanks to this long-term, insidious
political corruption.

The RAF historians are addressing us when they say: 'General

[1] *Strategic Air Offensive Vol. II*
[2] Ibid.
[3] Ibid.
[4] Ibid.

area bombing worked almost on the principle that in order to destroy anything it is necessary to destroy everything.'[1] Hitler could not have put it better. Crime was feeding on itself and waxing fat. After Dresden there was a momentary shame, when Churchill complained that the 'question of bombing German cities simply for the sake of increasing the terror though under other pretexts', should be reviewed. Was it not time, he wondered, to his Chiefs of Staff, that 'mere acts of terror and wanton destruction, however impressive', should cease? The RAF chiefs were outraged by this death-bed conversion and Churchill's minute was rewritten in more normal terms. The twinge of conscience came and went.

Politicians, unlike elephants, soon forget. When the war ended, 'the Prime Minister and others in authority seemed to turn away from the subject as though it were distasteful to them and as though they had forgotten their own recent efforts to initiate and maintain the offensive'.[2] But holding one's nose does not eliminate a bad smell. The Lancaster bomber was already a museum piece. So was the thousand-bomber raid. One plane and one bomb could now do the job better. The nuclear era was under way.

Was there no opposition among politicians to this indiscriminate bombing? Certainly none that was effective. But one MP, Richard Stokes, was dubbed the 'MP for Hamburg' because of his private campaign against the indiscriminate bombing of German cities and towns. He considered it a war crime serving no military purpose.

The transition from Dresden to Hiroshima and beyond was smooth, Britain becoming ever more closely bound to America. Winston Churchill did not lack words to bless this evolution: 'To avert a vast butchery . . . to give peace to the world, to lay healing hands upon its tortured peoples by a manifestation of over-whelming power at the cost of a few explosions, seemed, after all our toils and perils, a miracle of deliverance. . . . The historic fact remains . . . that the decision whether or not to use the atomic bomb to compel the surrender of Japan was never even an issue.'[3]

Appropriately enough, after the first atomic explosion in the New Mexico desert, Churchill received the news in a telegram from the US Government. It said, simply, 'Babies satisfactorily

[1] Op. cit., *Vol. III*.
[2] Ibid.
[3] Winston Churchill, *Triumph and Tragedy*, London 1953.

born'.[1] Whether or not the babies themselves were satisfactory was another matter, undiscussed, though Churchill is reported to have referred later to the atomic bomb as 'the second coming in wrath'.[2] Modern industrial civilization had 'called forth spirits from the vasty deep' and they had come when they were called. The nuclear wind was sown and we are reaping the whirlwind.

Conceived in fear and born in hatred, the new baby had naïve god-parents. Clement Attlee, who had replaced Churchill as Prime Minister, confessed that 'at the time we knew nothing . . . about the consequences of dropping the bomb, except that it was larger than an ordinary bomb and had a much greater explosive force. . . . We knew nothing whatever at that time about the genetic effect of an atomic explosion. I knew nothing about fallout and all the rest of what emerged after Hiroshima. As far as I know, President Truman and Winston Churchill knew nothing about these things either. . . .'[3]

'We have got to realize we are living in a new world,' Churchill had told the House of Commons in August 1946, but nobody knew what kind of world.

The nuclear baby grew up in an atmosphere of obsessive secrecy and misinformation. The no-go area of national security spread outwards from the core of society, the damage protected rather than exposed by lawyers and politicians alike. But like thieves fingering a charm, our political leaders have often invoked the law. 'It is now for Japan to realize,' said a statement on the atomic bomb, prepared by Churchill and announced by Attlee, 'in the glare of the first atomic bomb which has smitten her, what the consequences will be of an indefinite continuance of this terrible means of maintaining the rule of law in the world.' The weapon which had cooked mothers and children alive was now equated with a policeman's baton. When suspicion began to close in on the bomb, 'Mr Attlee and his closest colleagues wanted the public to know as little as possible lest an enemy learn even more. The minimum of information was given to Parliament and press, who for the most part accepted the situation with great, indeed excessive, docility.'[4]

[1] Ibid.
[2] Article by Harvey H. Bundy, *Atlantic Monthly*, March 1957.
[3] Francis Williams, *A Prime Minister Remembers*, London 1961.
[4] Gowing, op. cit.

One MP dared to comment on atomic development in the House of Commons: 'When an Hon. Member asks the Prime Minister about the atomic bomb he looks as if he asked about something indecent.' American journalists found British officials 'circumspect to the point of neurosis'. It was as if the radical implications of this weapon were sensed but not admitted. According to one commentator, this response was governed by 'awe and fear'. Britain was not alone in its deceit and confusion. The Washington Declaration of 15 November 1945, signed by the United States, Britain and Canada, said that, '"faced with the terrible realities of the application of science to destruction, every nation will realize more urgently than before the overwhelming need to maintain the rule of law among nations and to banish the scourge of war from the earth."'[1]

These countries offered and demanded wholehearted support for the new United Nations.

The humbug concealed within these fine words was quickly apparent. No serious initiative was made to develop and enforce laws banning all forms of mass destruction. The rule of law was left to a Security Council paralyzed by the veto. Within nine months of the Declaration, the United States had made most forms of atomic collaboration with other countries, including Canada and Britain, illegal. The set-smiling face of statesmanship was still beaming at its public, but the underlying reality was each nation for itself and the devil take the hindmost.

In this cut-throat atmosphere British politicians wanted their own bomb. The decision to make one, like everything else surrounding the new saviour, crept up on the nation like a sea fog: 'It emerged from a body of general assumptions. It had not been a response to an immediate military threat but rather something fundamentalist and almost instinctive – a feeling that Britain must possess so climactic a weapon in order to deter an atomically armed enemy, a feeling that Britain as a great power must acquire all major new weapons, a feeling that atomic weapons were a manifestation of the scientific and technological superiority on which Britain's strength . . . must depend. . . .

'Ministers had approved special arrangements with the object of concealing not only the technical details of the weapon and the

[1] Ibid.

organisation and methods by which it was to be produced but also the fact that work was being done on it at all.'[1]

The whole basis of British security for the post-war period, involving values and means which might annihilate millions, was decided in the manner of bank robbers planning a break-in.

Far from vetting this process, every inch of it, with the care it deserved, our politicians now described the new idol, once destroyer of worlds, as keeper of the peace. At last, on 12 May 1948, the British public were let into the secret of their safety, 'the only information vouchsafed to the public in four years that Britain was on her way to becoming a nuclear military power.'[2] In reply to a question about weapons development, the Labour Minister of Defence, A. V. Alexander, said: 'Yes, sir . . . research and development continue to receive the highest priority in the defence field, and all types of weapons, including atomic weapons, are being developed.'

Could he give any further information on the development of atomic weapons? 'No,' said the minister, 'I do not think it would be in the public interest to do that.' The interest of the public, it seemed, had little to do with the public interest. 700 years after the Magna Carta, the citizens of Britain could not be trusted with more than a teaspoonful of truth. The inmates of Auschwitz were hardly more in the dark about their fate. The biblical claim that the 'truth shall set you free' was replaced, not only at the entrance to Auschwitz but all over the modern world, with the creed of greed: 'Arbeit Macht Frei!' ('Work will set you free!')

It was left to the British Foreign Secretary, Ernest Bevin, to apply the political art-work to this socialist fraud. 'It has really become a matter of the defence of Western civilization,' he told the British Cabinet in March, 1948, 'or everyone will be swamped by this Soviet method of infiltration. Unless positive and vigorous steps are taken it may well be that within the next few months, or even weeks, the Soviet Union will gain political and strategic advantages which will set the great Communist machine in action, leading to the establishment of World Dictatorship or to the collapse of organised society over great stretches of the globe.'[3]

An apocalyptic weapon requires an apocalyptic rationale. It

---

[1] Ibid.
[2] Ibid.
[3] Ibid.

certainly would not do to describe the Soviet Union of that time as an exhausted, violated ramshackle empire in desperate need of recuperation and renewal. Such a view would do nothing to cool the fever of fear, guilt and weariness which afflicted the Western mind. There was neither will nor heart for a creative change of direction. The military impetus must be maintained, at all costs. A Soviet menace must justify it.

Governments have changed, but not their methods. According to Cabinet minutes, reported in *The Times* of 21 July 1980, Clement Attlee's Government decided to go ahead with nuclear development on the basis of a five-man inner Cabinet. Margaret Thatcher used a similar inner Cabinet to control the Falklands conflict and decide on Trident submarine development. James Callaghan's Labour Government came to power with the unambiguous election manifesto pledge of October 1974 not to proceed to a third-generation British nuclear weapon after Polaris. When he decided not only to upgrade and develop Polaris missiles but plan further ahead for nuclear modernization, he 'confided in only three colleagues, who met at No. 10 in conditions of strictest secrecy'.[1] They were Denis Healey, Chancellor of the Exchequer, Frederick Mulley, Secretary of State for Defence, and David Owen, Foreign and Commonwealth Secretary. It is worth reminding today's politician that one of these, David Owen, was engaged at that time in complex negotiations at Geneva to formulate updated laws protecting non-combatants in war, the Additional Protocol 1, 1977, – laws which he would later dismiss as 'unenforceable'. Polaris, as defined by Conservative defence expert and MP Julian Critchley, is a means of 'population extermination'.[2]

Today's politician, in Britain at least, tends to be like a judge in his reliance on precedent, which is why law-breaking as an article of political faith and action needs close monitoring down the years. Churchill's heroic image conceals a consistent and cold-blooded contempt for the law when inconvenient to his military plans. He was ready to meet the German rocket threat to Britain by drenching Germany with poison gas. A minute to his Chiefs of Staff dated 6 July 1944, instructs them to make a 'cold-blooded calculation . . . as to how it would pay to use poison gas, by which I mean principally mustard. I want the matter studied in cold blood by

[1] Ibid.
[2] Loc. cit.

sensible people and not by that particular set of psalm-singing, uniformed defeatists which one runs across now here and there.'[1]

He argued that it was absurd to consider the moral dimension of poison gas as everybody had used it in the First World War, although the bombing of cities, 'a commonplace in the Second World War, was then regarded as forbidden. . . . It is simply a question of fashion changing, as she does between long and short skirts for women.' He asked for the support of the Chiefs of Staff: 'We could drench the cities of the Ruhr and many other cities in Germany in such a way that most of the population would be requiring constant medical attention . . . I do not see why we should always have the disadvantages of being the gentleman while they have all the advantages of being a cad.'[2]

The logic, even the words, are almost interchangeable with Hitler's. Churchill was neither a gentleman nor a cad, but a ruthless outlaw served by yes-men and armed with devastating weapons. His philosophy lived after him in the corridors of power. In July 1946, after his replacement by Attlee as Prime Minister, a report on 'Future Developments in Weapons and Methods of War' was handed to the British Chiefs of Staff. It included a list of Soviet target cities with a population of more than 100,000, and said: 'The tremendous destructive power of the atomic bomb and the devastating effects against live targets expected from biological weapons, which can be produced with relatively small effort in terms of manpower on the part of the attacker, lead us to infer that the most profitable objects of attack by the new weapons will normally be concentrations of population, centres of distribution and communication.'[3]

The list included fifty-eight target cities, making up 77.5 per cent of the Soviet Union's urban population.

Contempt for the most basic laws of military restraint was politically institutionalized, beyond the reach of normal enquiry. A central area of the body politic had gone dead. Modern nuclear society had drifted, step by step, into a psychopathic state. Not a ranting madness but the cold kind where the mind calculates with ant-like energy, unhindered by feeling. Many observers of this process, and even some of its protagonists, are quick to denounce

[1] *The Times*, 1 May 1981.
[2] Ibid.
[3] *The Times*, 15 June 1981.

this madness for what it is. The Secretary-General of the United Nations recently appealed to the superpowers to end their 'madness' and stop their nuclear confrontation. The Commonwealth Secretary-General, Mr Shridath Ramphal, said that 'the rules of international law are being made subservient to superpower paranoia and national machismo'.[1]

But denunciation is no cure for such a deep-rooted complaint. As idealistic observers our political leaders brand nuclear terrorism as mad. But as decision-makers they claim it is necessary. The nuclear politician is like a child who has stolen a car. He knows it is a crime but will go on driving until he is caught. But the politician is not a child, and it is the world which is being driven, not towards a police cell but oblivion.

One aspect of this crisis of perception is the temptation of the politician to cling to a nursery tale version of war experience. The terrorized corpses are safely buried, leaving behind a nostalgic myth of comradeship and unity of purpose. There is no myth without some element of truth, and war has usually generated a spirit of unity in the face of a common enemy. A Scottish professor of sociology lamented to me that he had not experienced a sense of social unity and purpose since the fight against Hitler. An English duke reminisced about his days as an RAF squadron-leader in the Western desert of North Africa. The animation in his face told me that it was perhaps the only period of his life which had real meaning for him. But the reality of war, even the mini-war of the Falklands, marks a sharp descent from childish euphoria to hysterical brutality. It is a poisonous drug, raising spirits in order to dash them down. A British Conservative, Lord Alport, gave the readers of *The Times* newspaper a thumb-nail sketch of this dangerous myth: '[We] experienced the exhilaration which came from belonging to a united nation under great leadership, determined to fight off a mortal challenge to its physical, political and spiritual survival.'[2]

Myths of this kind pop up like mushrooms in the damp fog of our nuclear confusion. They insulate us from ghastly surroundings, requiring neither hard thought nor action. The British politician inhabits a fairy-tale castle of mythology, the House of Commons. It is a place where 'law and order' is much discussed,

[1] *Guardian*, 22 November 1983.
[2] *The Times*, 13 November 1983.

and where the whole ground and basis of the law has been eroded by rationalized violence.

A *Times* parliamentary correspondent analyzed the House of Commons with a merciless eye:

> The sense of inferiority felt by the Commons is no complex: they really are inferior.... A leading politician told his fellow members what has long been known but seldom acknowledged: they had lived in a sort of archaic fairy-land, stripped of real power and useful only as a passive forum for the warring party machine.... Today the Executive reigns supreme. Only the procedures and institutions of a once-proud Commons remain; standing now like rotting piles in a breakwater smashed by the tide of history. They can be gawked at as a tourist attraction. They can provide a backcloth for the best circus in town. What they cannot do is stand as monuments to a dynamic power house which is watching over the public interest, because the public know better....
>
> The decisions which affect the voter – the man who elects the Commons in the blind hope that he can influence his own future – are now taken in secret. In the secrecy of the Cabinet room; in the secrecy of the private party meeting; in secret consultations with 'interested parties' before legislation; above all, perhaps, in the Stygian secrecy of Whitehall. And on all of them the Commons can have no more influence than a puppet on the hand that guides it.'[1]

As soon as the press gained access to the Commons, continues this observer bitterly, the real power moved elsewhere: 'the press was left holding the cloak while the villain stole away and employed his dagger elsewhere – and out of sight.' The Commons is hardly better than a 'diversionary exercise to keep the press and public happy'. One of the 'few signposts along the downhill path', says the writer, is the Official Secrets Act of 1911: 'It has led ... to the assumption that anything official is secret.'[2] Edmund Burke is quoted approvingly: 'Where mystery begins, justice ends.'

A generation later the situation is worse. Modern centralized government has become an elaborate vanishing act, a mirage of democracy which recedes as it is approached. What the *Times*

[1] *The Times*, 13 January 1967.
[2] Ibid.

correspondent did not realize was that even in the inner Cabinet, where a handful of people control weapons of mass annihilation, there is still no core of responsibility to be found. Confronted with the survivors, if any, of a nuclear war, these modern warlords would invoke the myth that they were safeguarding freedom and the value of the individual, not killing and scorching strangers by the million. The Commandant of Auschwitz, Hoess, would recognize the problem.

So moribund is the law in the mind of the British politician, in relation to nuclear mass destruction, that defence debates proceed without a single reference to laws essential to justice at Nuremberg. A powerful force when applied to the mugger and the robber, the law is a shrinking violet when mass murder is abroad in the guise of defence. Set on his fantastic course by Churchill, Attlee and others, it is not surprising when John Stanley, the Minister of State for the Armed Forces, opens a debate with words devoid of feeling and restraint. Verbal toy soldiers are paraded in a standard uniform of hollow rhetoric: 'I suggest that there can be only one logical and responsible starting point for the debate – a cool and dispassionate assessment of the potentially hostile military capabilities ranged against us. We cannot afford to take rhetoric, emotion or wishful thinking as our starting point . . . we must start from a position of realism, hard experience and clear-headedness towards what is ultimately the most important responsibility of Government. The realities and the past experience are uncomfortable, but to ignore them is to take refuge in illusion.'[1]

So numbed are his colleagues by generations of such double-speak that there is no outburst of derisive laughter from the members present, no angry challenge. Just a few nods and yawns. It has all been said before, a thousand times, and will continue to be said until the pantomime closes down. Outside, the public is indifferent. Apart from a handful of mild complainants there is no discernible response to the 'most important responsibility of Government'. The tree of State is hollow, so life clings to the rim. There is more substance to a football match or bingo hall than this pygmy farce and the programmed droning of the nearly dead goes on, with or without an audience: 'There is no doubt that the most cost-effective way of meeting our requirement for an invulnerable

---

[1] House of Commons Official Report, 19 June 1984.

strategic nuclear system which would have an absolute deterrent value is through a submarine-launched ballistic missile.'[1] No medieval impostor selling wonder-cures for the plague could improve on such patter. All that is required of the open-mouthed audience is a little superstition and the 'absolute deterrent' is sold. There is no link between this quackery and the squirming victims of Hiroshima and Dresden, because there is no connection in the speaker's mind between vicious, compulsive rationality and the feelings which prompt him to kiss his daughter goodnight. In the real world of nuclear mass murder this politician, with his 'hard experience', makes himself out to be a hardened, if not an experienced criminal. Smooth-talking and well-educated, no doubt, but a criminal nonetheless.

There is an official opposition in parliament to this doomsday sales talk, but it too is part of the pantomime, the back legs of the donkey. A major opposition speech in this defence debate contained the phrase, 'I do not complain about the good will behind people's views'. Weapons of 'population extermination' being promoted with good will? The notion would be preposterous anywhere but the House of Commons. When law loses its potency, anything seems reasonable, or at least arguable. There is no bottom line to policy, only social decorum. A member of the House of Commons may be barred from the House for days or weeks for using terms of abuse such as 'liar' or 'madman'. But an absolute refusal to take part in an institution committed to the absolute deterrent, on grounds of criminal conspiracy, is unthinkable. Politicians trained to obey arcane rules seem incapable of such direct action.

Centuries after Magna Carta our nuclear politician speaks the language of democracy, but in relation to issues of life and death he is as tough as a fly in Al Capone's soup. It is only as we get closer to political leaders that we can discern how politics and law are used to protect the idol of nuclear deterrence. The paths of authority are ambiguously marked, a maze to exclude the common and curious. The law is especially well shrouded behind Gilbertian pageantry. The Attorney-General is the Government legal front man, a politician-lawyer who prosecutes on behalf of the Crown. In other words, he enforces the law on behalf of the Government, in matters

[1] Ibid.

concerning the national interest. He is not a member of the Cabinet but has the ear of the Prime Minister.

The Lord Chancellor is the other major law authority, suspended precisely above the dividing line between the judiciary and Government. He is a member of the Cabinet but tends to keep a low profile, politically, in order to promote judicial independence. He appoints judges and speaks publicly on their behalf. He sits in the House of Lords, the ultimate court of appeal which includes eleven Law Lords. It is the Lord Chancellor more than anyone who determines the behaviour of the judiciary. It is he, in collusion with the Prime Minister, who tries to keep the absolute deterrent inviolate in terms of the law, hidden inside the no-go area of national security. If nuclear war occurs, and the most criminal act in history is committed, the British contribution will be due in large part to the success of the Lord Chancellor in keeping the law at bay. In Gilbert's words, 'a most ingenious paradox'.

The nuclear politician probably knows little about the Lord Chancellor and his views on law and politics. The views of one recent incumbent may help enlighten us. In a public lecture he makes his thoughts evident on a range of issues:

> Society must be based on 'abiding standards of value' and must stand firm against the threats of modern military technology, the bombs which deal death indiscriminately, the murder weapons of sub-machine guns, and the instruments of mass destruction of which the nuclear range is only one and not necessarily the most lethal. . . . [my] appeal to the common people is based on my belief in the sanctity of the individual human soul, the sanctity of the human family, and the natural propensity we all have to love our fellow man.[1]

These qualities are the foundation of the law.

It would appear from these sentiments that the Lord Chancellor would seek every means to enforce the law against any and all forms of mass destruction. Not a bit of it. These humane insights are for domestic use only. They are not universal principles, as true for the Chinese peasant as the Old Etonian, but national virtues, to be protected by whatever works best. He remarks what is 'inherently aggressive' about the Kaiser, Hitler and Krushchev, and the

---

[1] 1983 Hamlyn Lecture, 'The British Legal System Today'.

'present progressive increase in Soviet armaments'. The impartial majesty of the law must keep out of this danger area. 'Relations between the fire and the fire brigade are not a proper field for judicial impartiality.'

It is plain from this last image that he sees Britain as the solution and the Soviet Union as the problem. Hitler would say amen to that, with Germany taking Britain's role. Oddly, he then goes on to pinpoint 'the existence of sovereignty and rivalry at the top level' as the most likely cause of war. Presumably our sovereignty is good, theirs bad.

The Lord Chancellor takes back with the right hand what he offers with the left. He supports traditional institutions and values yet complains of a 'growing sense of despair and exasperation at the appalling conservatism of the legal profession'.[1] British judges are independent and impartial, yet 'by far the bitterest and most frequent complaints I receive from the public relate to the professional judiciary'.[2] He refers to the 'perfectly proper distrust of the public, and therefore of jurors, of persons in authority, including police, judges, counsel, public officials and experts. . . .'

British freedom, he has no doubt, 'depends as much on the independence, impartiality and integrity of the judiciary as upon parliamentary government'. Judges, most from the same privileged background, should not be described therefore as right-wing. '"Be you never so high but the law is above you" is a rule for judges no less than Ministers.' The Lord Chancellor does not like judges who lay down the law on everything that may come into their heads: 'if they generalize on matters not properly before them, they bring the profession of a judge into deserved criticism'.

Regarding precedent, the judicial stick upon which judges most often lean, the Lord Chancellor warns: 'If he sticks pedantically to precedent he may easily fall into the trap of producing logical or jurisprudential absurdity, countenancing oppression and fraud, or leaving the injured party without a remedy at law.'

In the context of his active support for a nuclear defence strategy, the British politician should note the Lord Chancellor's views on violence within Britain:

[1] Loc. cit.
[2] 'The British Legal System Today', loc. cit.

I am profoundly dismayed by the extent to which violence has increased, and in particular, by the extent to which even otherwise civilized persons seem to tolerate it as a means of drawing attention to political or social grievances. I do not myself believe that murder, maiming, or torture is any less horrific because it is inspired by political motivation. On the contrary, I regard political motivation in general as an aggravating, and not a mitigating, facet. . . . Law and order I regard as a seamless robe. You cannot tear one part of the fabric without damage to the whole. . . .

In one way or another we are living in a wave of violence throughout the world, which I can only ascribe to a widespread weakening of the respect for moral values, and political and social authority, without which ordered society is impossible.

The Lord Chancellor's views, apart from their judicial references, are echoed in every corner of British society. What is significant about them is that they relate directly to judicial practice, the use of the law. We have already seen evidence to prove that the law in relation to international violence has been systematically degraded and manipulated by Britain and every nuclear State. It is the politician, above all, the person who seeks power with obsessive zeal, who must answer first for this corruption. It is not the law which is the seamless robe, except in its thwarted intention, but the evasive and pervasive conservatism which denies its universal scope.

The Lord Chancellor pleads in conclusion for a 'revived recognition of objective moral principle and respect for authority'. This is the same man who has given his wholehearted support for many years to the concept of absolute destruction as an integral part of the absolute deterrent. It is the ultimate irony of such perversion of law that the use or not of nuclear extermination depends officially not on the Lord Chancellor's or any other British citizen's sense of moral responsibility, but on Soviet behaviour. It is a basic element of our nuclear law-breaking that the leading British political guardian of the law subverts the very thing he claims to protect. There is black humour in a situation where disrespect for legal authority is the precondition of upholding the law.

The Lord Chancellor and British politicians are united in their failure, so far, to recognise the significance of what a leading

Conservative MP has said about the nuclear deterrent: 'One would like to believe that it has begun to dawn on the strategists of both sides that weapons of mass destruction are, as I am inclined to believe, unusable. . . . It requires something of a revolution for British Ministers and defence officials to resign themselves to abandon the objectives of population extermination. For the traditional objective of the British "nuclear deterrent" . . . has all along been Moscow, as the evidence given to the defence committee of the House of Commons makes clear.'[1]

The fact that Julian Critchley manages to combine this logic with a need to have Trident nuclear submarines cannot disguise the reference to 'population extermination'. At last the black cat of mass murder, concealed with so much difficulty by Churchill and others, has been let out of the bag. It is a measure of the moral and legal sedation which drugs the British MP that there was no hint of outrage at this confession. It seems that population extermination is just another form of insecticide to the modern politician, and his constituents. When a chairman of the Conservative Party declares that 'in a democratic country it is part of the conscience to obey the law',[2] we can be sure he does not mean the embarrassing law which says that a threat to commit mass murder of enemy citizens is a crime. We are told that hitting an old lady over the head for her money is a foul crime, but exterminating the population of Moscow in defence of liberty may be necessary and lawful.

The Prime Minister confirms such nonsense. She pleads the sanctity of the national interest and national security, while affirming total allegiance to the law: 'Every Minister, every Prime Minister is within the law and must be seen to be within the law and must of course be subject to the law.'[3]

'We shall vigorously uphold the rule of law and fight crime,' she says. The 'rule of law must prevail over the rule of the mob,' she warns.[4] Her Home Secretary tells us: 'When violence is threatened it is for us all to search our conscience and ask whether or not we can make a contribution to prevent violence by speaking up against it.'[5]

[1] Julian Critchley MP in the *Guardian*, 5 March 1984.
[2] John Gummer MP in the *Guardian*, 6 August 1984.
[3] House of Commons 17 July 1984.
[4] *Daily Telegraph*, 9 March 1984.
[5] *Guardian*, 31 May 1984.

Officially approved double standards are revealed time after time by leading political figures. The Attorney-General is one. 'There is absolutely no justification,' he warns, 'in present-day English society for the law to be broken for political or self-interested ends.'[1] He is aware of a crisis of law enforcement, but it is the awareness of a rabbit which has lit a forest fire and complains of smoke in its burrow.

'In almost every generation,' he says, 'there comes a time when a grave challenge is made to the accepted standards of society'[2] It is not the unlimited destruction of the absolute deterrent which he has in mind. His comments are charged with unintended irony. 'A tyranny may have a legal code which appears impeccable,' he says.[3] He means the criminal 'legality' of a Hitler, while all around him is the shadow of unrestrained nuclear power, the most tyrannical force ever experienced.

The Attorney-General touches on the theme beloved of politicians who like to think that international law is all very well but, regrettably, unenforceable. Again, his thoughts are narrowly focused. 'We must,' he tells us, '. . . do all we can to reduce the areas in which the law is unenforced. If a law is persistently ignored, then either it or the means of enforcement should be reconsidered.' The Government 'could not safely allow a situation to develop where the law was brought into disrepute by an inability to enforce it'. Any 'self-interested attack' on the law by a particular group must be met by a Government determined to 'stand firm and to take all the steps in its power to facilitate the enforcement of the law under attack'.[4] But what happens when it is the Government which is the self-interested group undermining its own law?

A Lord Chancellor wonders whether we are living in 'a dying civilization': 'From that terrible August 4, 1914,' he laments, 'the world has been going down whereas up to that point it had been going up. The standards of behaviour which are now rife throughout the world, civilized and less civilized, are so much worse that what was expected in 1914, that one does begin to think that it must be the City of Destruction.'[5]

[1] *Daily Telegraph*, 1 December 1983.
[2] *Daily Telegraph*, 9 April 1984.
[3] *Guardian*, 9 April 1984.
[4] *Daily Telegraph*, 9 April 1984.
[5] Guardian, 25 May 1984.

He is right, more right than he imagines, because the Government are active agents in the dissolution of civilized life. He makes no reference to the Hague Conventions which preceded the First World War and imposed laws of military restraint which successive British Governments have signed, flouted, enforced and evaded. 'In the end,' he admits, 'law is a confidence trick', and 'if enough people start flouting authority'[1] it will collapse.

The law has spoken, and it speaks crime. Crime dressed up in the ideals of a once vital, long dead past. It is a counterfeit law and the confidence trick must be exposed if we are ever to dissolve our nightmare. Consistent violation of laws signed by British Governments has created a legal vacuum at the heart of British society, a vacuum filled by arbitrary political and military power. Every nuclear weapons power is worm-eaten with this idolatry of State violence. A man who was head of a British Prime Minister's 'Think Tank', the Central Policy Review Staff, has first-hand knowledge of this concentrating power at the centre: 'Of one thing I am sure. We do need strength at the centre, if, as a nation, we are to find a way out of our troubles. The role of a Prime Minister at the centre has increased, is still increasing, and will not be diminished.'[2]

A similar logic was used not long ago to justify the elective dictatorship of Hitler. He taught, and we have yet to learn, that law and personalized power are incompatible, except in a fantasy world where benevolent rulers perform fairy-tale roles of unalloyed virtue.

The modern British politician plays a servile and disgraceful role at the court of dictatorial power. Only wilful ignorance can lead otherwise intelligent people to tolerate a political and judicial conspiracy to protect the vast domain of national security from the reach of the law. Politicians, as well as judges, have betrayed trust by accepting the edict of a Lord Chief Justice that this area covers 'any action taken under royal prerogative which can truly be said to have been taken in the interests of national security to protect this country from its enemies or potential enemies'.[3]

Even the normally sedate *Times* choked on such stodge. By what right did judges impose such a 'total exclusion zone over so large

---

[1] Ibid.
[2] Sir Kenneth Berrill in the *Observer*, 7 November 1982.
[3] *The Times*, 7 August 1984.

and dark and expanding an area of official activity'?[1] The implications, and it is the business of the politician to be alive to them,
are crucially important, as *The Times* recognizes: 'For the courts to
say they have no point of entry into the whole area of prerogative
power in relation to national security, or that they are not permitted to enter (permitted by whom?) is to withdraw the protection
afforded by the law in relation to a sensitive and uncomfortably
large area of official business.'

The Times quotes Lord Denning's assurance that no British
Government would misuse such powers, but 'if the judges will not
look into these matters, how do they know any such thing? If they
will not inspect even the form and procedure surrounding prerogative decision affecting the liberties of the subject taken in the name
of national security, what value have their assurances that all is
well?'

The three checks on the abuse of State power, it says, are a
'diligent parliament, a free press, and a correct and courageous
judiciary.'[2] It is clear that politicians and judges are neither diligent
nor courageous when it comes to confronting national security.

Blinded as he seems to be by the glare of nuclear weapons, the
British politician is capable of paying close attention to the more
peripheral details of international law. When a military dictator in
the South Atlantic invaded small islands inhabited by a couple of
thousand sheep farmers of British origin, the resultant conflict
provoked an outburst of commitment to the law. 'It's Britain who
stands up for the international rules of law,' said the British Prime
Minister,' and it's Britain that says, "Enough is enough, this must
be made to stop".'[3]

The Foreign Secretary told the House of Commons: 'What we
are seeking is not the military humiliation of Argentina but a
victory for the rule of law in international affairs.'[4] As if by magic,
the United Nations, left to stew impotently in vetoes since its
inception, suddenly appeared in a pure light. The Security Council
resolution urging Argentinian withdrawal from the islands was
held aloft by the British like holy writ. 'There is a mandatory
resolution of the Security Council which has the force of inter-

[1] Ibid.
[2] Ibid.
[3] *The Times* report on Jimmy Young Show, 20 May 1982.
[4] *The Times*, 5 May 1982.

national law, and no statement can overcome something that has the force of international law and also under that United Nations Charter.'[1] Forgotten were the numerous occasions when Britain had used its Security Council veto to stifle and obstruct action. And forgotten was the example of the Nazi SS and its macabre determination to impose the rule of law on corrupt concentration camp officials.

British politicians, the same who affect ignorance of the essential nature and purpose of international laws prohibiting mass destruction, gladly wallowed in righteousness. The newspapers and television screens blossomed with legal experts and politicians touting the law. A few brave souls opposed the cant. E. P. Thompson was one of these: 'It is because we have ceased to take the United Nations seriously as a peace-enforcing agency ... that we have turned away from the legitimate and obvious recourse. In scouting its injunctions we have made the world an even more dangerous place.'[2]

If British politicians had sought to uphold and enforce international law with real conviction, Britain would have set the world an example of civilized maturity. Instead, it had done the opposite, showing the world how a sophisticated nation can dispense a cheap magic, using essential laws of human survival to disguise a seedy militarism. The law had been made a prostitute and Britain was its pimp.

The cant reached its climax, appropriately, when the Prime Minister spoke on the day of the Soviet leader's funeral: 'We shall be looking for signs of a greater respect for human rights and international law than we have seen in recent years.'[3]

The mutual delusions of a schizoid civilization were alive and well, the common diet of politicians and public alike. The devil was at home, behind the eyes inside the skull.

At least some of the less demanding rules of war were obeyed. The Convention protecting prisoners of war was respected during the Falklands conflict. But the cost of failure to uphold and enforce the main principles of international law is a weak response to fresh violations. A Mafia godfather is not the most convincing adviser for a delinquent adolescent. Suspected use by Iraq of poison gas in its

[1] Editorial in *The Times*, 27 April 1982.
[2] *The Times*, 29 April 1982.
[3] *The Times*, 16 November 1982.

war with Iran provoked a flurry of condemnation. Britain was accused by Iran of supplying the gas. The British Government denied the charge angrily and demanded a full investigation by the International Red Cross or the United Nations. Britain was correct, having destroyed all chemical weapons in 1957, but what is the world to believe of a nation which manufactures nuclear weapons for its security?

When the United States invaded the tiny West Indian island of Grenada, in 1983, in order, so it said, to protect its own citizens from a Marxist government, there was an international outcry against use of military force. The British Government was caught between Uncle Sam and the deep blue Caribbean Sea. It clearly disapproved of arbitrary use of force against a Commonwealth State, but dared not offend its nuclear ally. Like a priest at a medieval torture, it wrung its hands in silent agony. As usual in such circumstances the official Labour opposition bubbled with righteous anger. The Government was 'lacking in grit, lacking in fibre and lacking in resolution', it said. But the British Foreign Secretary was not to be knocked off his knees. 'I do not believe,' he said, 'that it would have served the common interests of Britain and the United States to have amplified and magnified opposition to the invasion.'[1] As with nuclear weapons, discretion was the better part of law.

There is nothing new about the abject failure of political leaders to uphold and enforce minimum laws of civilized life. But never has the price of failure been so high, and never have the rationalizations of crime been so sophisticated and backed by so much power. The rough and tough Middle Ages can teach us something. 'In medieval political thought a king,' writes one commentator, 'though absolute as against his subjects, was yet under God and under the law. The ordinances which he promulgated were aspects of the eternal law of God by which he was bound, and any king who promulgated an ordinance which was not in accordance with the eternal law thereby *ipso facto* became not a king but a tyrant against whom his subjects might rise and lawfully make war.'[2]

The no-go area of absolute power was put in its proper place on the human map by Thomas Paine, the Anglo-American political thinker: 'When it is laid down as a maxim,' he wrote, 'that a king

[1] *Guardian*, 27 October 1983.
[2] Calvocoressi, op. cit.

can do no wrong, it places him in a state of similar security with that of idiots and persons insane, and responsibility is out of the question with respect to himself.'[1]

The widening circle of absolute centralized discretion over national security issues gives the nuclear ruler more power than any tyrant in history. The size of that circle is an exact measure, not only of the ruler's idiot status but our own.

As main agents of this spreading lawlessness, the judges and the politicians bear a major responsibility. They are traitors to the long tradition of British social justice for which thousands have suffered and died. But worms have a habit of turning, as Thomas Paine warned: 'I do not believe that the people of England have ever been fairly and candidly dealt by. They have been imposed on by parties and by men assuming the character of leaders. It is time that the Nation should rise above those trifles.'[2]

It is not utopia which is required of the British politician, but recognition that the law condemns mass murder of any kind. If that is too much to ask of the British politician then he is too much for the British people to endure.

[1] Thomas Paine, *The Rights of Man*, London 1958.
[2] Ibid.

Chapter Ten

The American Politician's Tale

'The concept of assured destruction, and its derivatives . . .
appear to be directly opposed to international law and hence
contrary to both domestic law and to Department of Defense
directives governing individual action affecting the
acquisition, procurement and use of weapons'
– Rand Corporation Report, 1982

'The Law of Armed Conflict is essentially inspired by the
humanitarian desire of civilized nations to diminish the effects
of conflict. . . . It has been said to represent, in some measure,
minimum standards of civilization'
– USAF pamphlet, 1976

Criminal rationalization of mass destruction and its weaponry has
evolved from the primitive simplicity of Hiroshima to the sophisticated carapace of current jargon. Any cancer, unchecked, follows a
similar pattern. There was a technological and quantitative acceler-
ation of violence between Dresden and Hiroshima, but the deadly
indifference to pain and law remained constant. We have proved to
ourselves and to the universe, if it is interested, that we can and will
kill and poison limitless quantities of people in whatever cause we
consider sufficiently important. We claim that this mass murder is
necessary and lawful.

We have a giant's strength and the creativity of a dwarf. As a
dominant nuclear power, what is the role of the United States in
this saga? How does the American political system relate the
machinery and logic of unlimited destruction to laws of humanitarian restraint? More specifically, what does the American politician
say to our criminal investigation?

It is a measure of the advanced state of criminalized policy that a
modern American President can say without a hint of irony, 'The
years of the pseudo-intellectual apologies for crime are over . . . I
once played a sheriff on TV who thought he could do the job
without a gun. I was dead in the first twenty-seven minutes of the

film'. And then go on to quote a psychologist: ' "Choosing a career in crime is not the result of poverty or of an unhappy childhood or of a misunderstood adolescence: it's the result of a conscious, wilful, selfish choice made by some who consider themselves above the law, who seek to exploit the hard work, and sometimes the very lives, of their fellow citizens." '[1]

This man who assumes that preserving peace by threatening to kill millions of people is entirely legitimate, uses fiction to justify official violence. Had the film told a story where the unarmed sheriff won the day, would the President have thrown his weapons away? Of course not. He would have looked for another story. The actor uses fiction to justify policy, and the American people have shown that of all their citizens they prefer as leader the former actor. The leader of the 'free world' has the fate of the world at his finger-tips, inspired by fiction. He has power beyond law, yet denounces those who choose a 'career in crime', and 'consider themselves above the law'. Threats of nuclear mass murder are rationalized by superficial prejudice.

But the President is no freak. The thread of his reasoning leads back a long way. He interprets a conventional wisdom. Nuclear weaponry is part of a continuing development of military power, but represents an immense surge of destructive power. We have taken off on a nuclear broomstick, high into the stratosphere. At the start of this upsurge there was still room for natural feelings of awe. 'This is the greatest thing in history,' President Truman is reputed to have said about the atomic bomb,[2] but this crude excitement hid a more sensitive response. During the weeks before the attack on Hiroshima, Truman wrote: 'We have discovered the most terrible bomb in the history of the world. It may be the fire destruction prophesied in the Euphrates Valley era, after Noah and his fabulous ark. This weapon is to be used against Japan between now and August 10. I have told the Secretary of War, Mr Stimson, to use it so that military objectives and soldiers and sailors are the target and not women and children. Even if the Japs are savages, ruthless, merciless and fanatic, we as the leader of the world for the common welfare cannot drop this terrible

---

[1] Speech by President Reagan at Hartford, Connecticut, reported in the *Daily Telegraph*, 21 June 1984.
[2] Leahy, op. cit.

bomb on the old capital or the new' [a reference to Kyoto and Tokyo].[1]

This handwritten journal, written in July 1945 and rediscovered among Truman's papers thirty-five years later, continued: 'The target will be a purely military one and we will issue a warning statement asking the Japs to surrender and save lives. I am sure that they will not do that, but we will have given them a chance. It is certainly a good thing for the world that Hitler's crowd or Stalin's did not discover the atomic bomb. It seems to be the most terrible thing ever invented, but it can be made the most useful.'[2]

These comments may be made with an eye to history, but they mark one of the last moments of contact, faint as it is, between nuclear super-power and the laws of armed conflict. Women and children, the notes imply, are not a lawful target. The cultural city of Kyoto must not be attacked. A warning must be issued. These are direct echoes of the Hague Conventions. How different from current assumptions in Washington and Moscow that targets are to be assessed in terms of their missile/damage ratio, not blood flow. As we know, the first atomic bomb fell on a city of minimal military value. Plenty of women and children died. The US politician will note that President Truman wrote these comments some months before the Nuremberg Trial began.

There was never real doubt in Washington about the use of the bomb, at least among the politicians. Some of the scientists who had made it were less certain. While Truman was writing his notes, two of them, Frank and Szilard, wrote a report which included this warning: 'If the United States were to be the first to release this new means of indiscriminate destruction upon mankind, we would sacrifice public support throughout the world, precipitate the race for armaments, and prejudice the possibility of reaching an international agreement on the future control of such weapons. Much more favourable conditions for such an agreement could be created if nuclear bombs were first to be revealed to the world by a demonstration in an appropriately selected and uninhabited area.'[3]

Scientists and politicians were on the same broomstick, whatever their private fears. Some years later, in 1961, I met Leo Szilard in Washington. He was there to lobby the new administration of

[1] *The Times*, 3 June, 1980.
[2] Ibid.
[3] Report of 11 July 1945 quoted in M. Yass, *Hiroshima*, New York 1971.

President Kennedy, against nuclear testing and development. He was a nuclear sorcerer's apprentice, come with his moral bucket to stem the flood he had helped to start. He was a man in a hurry, obsessed with nuclear disaster and dying of cancer. Some days later I met the Dean of Washington Cathedral, a nephew of President Woodrow Wilson and friend of President Kennedy. He too was anxious about the nuclear devilry pervading the capital and described US defence policy as 'amoral'. He had refused to give his blessing at the annual graduation of a nearby naval academy, breaking a long tradition. At a time when television programmes discussed the pros and cons of 'shooting your neighbour' in the event of a squeeze on fall-out shelters, the most hopeful person I met there was an English artist. She was a leading member of Women Strike for Peace. None of us had the slightest impact on the proliferating cells of nuclear violence.

The feeling tone of nuclear rationalization was quickly apparent and has remained constant. Colonel Tibbet, the commander of the attack on Hiroshima, received the Distinguished Service Cross and a citation which referred to ' . . . the culmination of many months of tireless effort, training and organization unique in American Air Force history, during which he constantly coped with new problems of precision bombing and engineering.'[1]

Like the Lancaster bomber pilot over Dresden, one of the problems he did not try to cope with was the effect of his tireless effort on those below. How would Colonel Tibbet have responded to the 'hundreds of injured people who were trying to escape to the hills. . . . Their faces and hands were burned and swollen; and great sheets of skin had peeled away from their tissues to hang down like rags on a scarecrow'?[2]

The official mind of modern industrial man would protect him from such pain, glazing over rapidly. A natural defence, perhaps, to nightmare suffering.

No military or political mind comprehended this tidal wave of disaster, but poets tried:

> When the bomb fell on America it fell on people.
> It didn't dissolve them as it dissolved people in
>   Hiroshima

---

[1] Ibid.
[2] Michihiko Hachiya, 'Journal of a Japanese Physician': entry of 14 August 1945.

It did not dissolve their bodies.
But it dissolved something vitally important
   To the greatest of them and the least.
What it dissolved were their links with the past and
   with the future. . . .
It made the earth that seemed so solid, Main Street,
   that seemed so well paved,
A kind of vast jelly, quivering and dividing
   underfoot. . . .
What have we done, my country, what have we
   done?[1]

But poets were not in charge. The politicians had no room for doubt. 'At no time,' said the Secretary for War, Stimson, ' . . . did I ever hear it suggested by the President or by any other responsible member of the Government that atomic energy should not be used in the war. . . . We were at war, and the work must be done. . . . The possible atomic weapon was considered to be a new and tremendously powerful explosive, as legitimate as any other of the deadly explosive weapons of modern war. If victory could be speeded up by using the bomb, it should be used.'[2]

The Second World War confirmed Hitler's belief that might is right, in all but secondary issues. The atomic bomb was the mightiest of all. No law and no feeling could oppose it. A US general relayed his sense of this power to a politician: 'Thirty seconds after the explosion came first the air blast pressing hard against the people, to be followed almost immediately by the strong, sustained, awesome roar which warned of doomsday. The tension in the room let up and all started congratulating each other. Everyone sensed, "This is it! No matter what might happen now, all knew that the impossible scientific job had been done. Atomic fission would no longer be hidden in the cloisters of the theoretical physicist's dreams".'[3]

Across the Atlantic, preparations were beginning for the Nuremberg Trial, where the American judge, Biddle, would say: 'the very essence of the Charter is that individuals have international duties which transcend the national obligations of obedi-

[1] Hermann Hagedorn, 'The Bomb that Fell on America', quoted in Yass, op. cit.
[2] *Harper's*, February 1947.
[3] General Farrell in a memorandum to Secretary of War Stimson, 18 July 1945.

ence imposed by the national State. He who violates the laws of war cannot obtain immunity while acting in pursuance of the authority of the State if the State in authorising action moves outside its competence under international law.'[1]

But the nuclear outlaw of absolute destruction rode into town and took over the whole show. Every day, now, was doomsday. The world was under sentence of death, suspended for a while at the whim of the high priests of power. The United States and its politicians had come a long way since 1918, when Secretary of War Newton D. Baker promised that the United States would never participate in an air attack 'that has as its objective the promiscuous bombing upon industry, commerce or population in enemy countries.'[2] Such reasoning is as foreign to the ear of the nuclear politician as Plato to a feudal peasant.

As we have seen, it was not the Nuremberg Trial judgment which was heeded but the logic of its defendants. The infant nuclear 'balance of terror' was based on the notion that a vile enemy responds only to extreme fear, echoing the order of the Nazi Field-Marshal Keitel, quoted by the US judge, Parker: 'The order stated that "It should be remembered that a human life in unsettled countries frequently counts for nothing and a deterrent effect can be obtained only by unusual severity".'[3] Keitel was hanged and the nuclear deterrent is his monument.

The world, or rather the outlaws who had taken it over, was set on a nuclear path. The Soviet Union exploded its first test bomb in 1949. Britain followed suit in 1952. Then came France in 1960 and China in 1964. India followed on, in 1974. According to a report prepared by the Secretary-General of the United Nations in 1980, 'The largest weapon ever tested released an energy approximately four thousand times that of the atomic bomb that levelled Hiroshima.' At that time the world arsenal consisted of about one million Hiroshima bombs. It is still growing in quantity and design.

The American politician, apparently, cannot stem this malignant process. He floats downstream, feeding where he may and congratulating the river on its wise course. Expert in public prejudice, he neither knows nor cares about the legal principles underpinning

---

[1] *International Military Tribunal Vol. XXII.*
[2] Karsten, op. cit.
[3] *International Military Tribunal Vol. XXII.*

civilization. When he buys his own stale fantasies and blunders into Vietnam, it is not he who pays with his life or sanity. The common soldier is subjected to tighter law than he is.

The American politician would not wish to be on the receiving end of this Vietnam war judgment: 'A member of the United States Army is not and may not be considered, short of insanity, an automaton, but may be inferred to be a reasoning agent who is under a duty to exercise moral judgment if it directs the commission of a crime under United States law or under the law of war. . . . An order to attack and kill armed enemy personnel in battle is lawful. But it is unlawful to order the killing of enemy troops who have laid down their arms, or belligerents who are unarmed. . . . '[1]

Many young military personnel have been prosecuted and convicted under such legal principles, while the politician who placed them in the firing line walks free. 'The alternatives to murder are limited only by our imagination,' said the US Army 'Lesson Plan', following the My Lai massacre. The American political imagination sees no such limits.

Occasionally the sheer insanity of the nuclear stand-off percolates through to the core of the political machine. A former Chief Scientific Adviser to the British Government, Sir Solly Zuckerman, relates that 'soon after McNamara took over as US Secretary of Defense, one of his more cynical Assistant Secretaries "explained" the position to me in this way. "Don't you see?" he asked. "First we need enough Minutemen to be sure that we destroy all those Russian cities. Then we need Polaris missiles to follow to tear up the foundations to a depth of ten feet, maybe helped by Skybolt. . . . Then, when all Russia is silent, and when no air defences are left, we want waves of aircraft to drop enough bombs to tear the whole place up down to a depth of forty feet to prevent the Martians recolonizing the country. And to hell with the fall-out".'[2]

Busy strategists have tried to paint a veneer of reason onto this asylum logic. Nuclear weapons have become more accurate and flexible. Military targets can be identified and hit, just as in the good old days when the rules of war held sway. Theatre nuclear weapons make the drama of war seem as safe as *Julius Caesar* at the

[1] US v. Hutto, 1970/1, quoted in 'Instructions' at US Judge Advocate General's School of Law.
[2] Sir Solly Zuckerman, *Nuclear Illusion and Reality*, London 1982.

Globe. Such illusions, however comforting, cannot disguise the truth.

' "Taking out an interdiction target in a theatre of war" ' would mean, says Sir Solly Zuckerman, 'the total destruction, with a nuclear weapon, of a town with, say, a population of 100,000, 200 miles behind the lines, for no reason other than it happened to be a railway centre.'

More theatre weapons might mean that more targets would be hit, he agrees, 'but it would be ridiculous to suppose that those which are the most important, and these include the capitals of NATO countries, are not already targeted, in the same way as those in Warsaw Pact territory.'[1]

US and British politicians have tried to give the Trident submarine a gloss of rationality by exalting its supposed military accuracy. But this fanciful evasion of reality has been exposed: 'We Americans know from the repeated declarations of our senior military leaders that our own strategic plans have always been focused mainly on military targets, but we also know from a recent unclassified report that a retaliatory strategic strike on just such targets would put some sixty warheads on Moscow. There may be room for argument about this "military" target or that one, but niceties of targeting doctrine do not make the weapons themselves discriminating.'[2]

A former US Assistant Secretary of Defense for Systems Analysis has described the unlimited implications of so-called limited nuclear weapons: 'Tactical nuclear weapons cannot defend Europe; they can only destroy it. . . . Twenty years of effort by many military experts have failed to produce a believable doctrine for tactical nuclear warfare.'[3]

And a former US Secretary of State, Henry Kissinger, has exposed some of the irrational flaws of current NATO policy. He has warned America's European allies not to keep asking the United States 'to multiply strategic assurances that we cannot possibly mean or if we do mean, we should not want to execute, because if we execute we risk the destruction of civilisation.'[4]

[1] Ibid.
[2] McGeorge Bundy (former member of the Kennedy administration) at the 1979 annual conference of the Institute of Strategic Studies.
[3] Alain Enthoven, *Foreign Affairs Journal* 53 (3), 1975.
[4] *International Herald Tribune*, 27 October 1979.

Even the NATO Commander in Europe has his doubts about the absolute deterrent. NATO's defences are 'mortgaged to the nuclear response,' he says, '... which strains the credibility of that deterrent.'[1] The US politician, as well as the NATO Commander and those he protects, may remember that an original meaning of mortgage, according to the Oxford Dictionary, is a 'dead pledge'.

In place of minimum laws of restraint based on simple universal principles, a motley confusion of religious prejudice and military 'credibility' dance attendance on the nuclear idol. President Reagan's description of the 'evil empire' of Soviet communism, coupled with an appeal for a 'great spiritual awakening', was hailed by a distinguished American historian as 'the worst presidential speech in American history', and 'a gross appeal to religious prejudice'.[2] Once the law is discarded as a restraint on nuclear power, the vacuum is filled by an unholy marriage of superstition and robotese. At the core of American politics, as in every nuclear state, there lies the same no-go area of national security, the heart of darkness where mass murder is laundered and made respectable in the name of defence. It is an area of clinical madness, where personal responsibility is as rare as a butterfly in space.

The US politician does not expose this disaster but stands guard over it, using side-issues to distract attention from the swollen carcase of a militarism which rewards loyalty richly. Extolling the law out of one side of his mouth, he perverts it from the other. From time to time, when truth threatens to catch up, a sacrifice is thrown to pursuing wolves. A Lieutenant Calley is punished to prove that the law still holds. The corpse blinks.

But as many murderers have discovered, the dead are not easily disposed of. *Macbeth* is a play which fits nuclear anarchy as snugly as a Polaris missile its tube. Alive on the back of fifty million war dead, we can share Macbeth's complaint:

> The time has been
> That when the brains were out the man would die
> And there an end; but now they rise again,

[1] *Guardian*, 22 November 1982.
[2] Prof. Henry Commager, *Guardian*, 20 April 1983.

With twenty mortal murders on their crowns,
And push us from our stools. This is more strange
Than such a murder is.[1]

Uncomfortable reminders of the law pop up, like the dead, in unlikely places. Nothing seems less likely than admission by a wealthy, conventional American research institution, recipient of Government contracts, that current nuclear policies violate the law. Yet this has happened. The conservative Rand Corporation sponsored a research project by two American lawyers. They were to investigate the nuclear concept of assured destruction in the light of international law. In January, 1982, they published their report. It is a sharp warning to nuclear freedom fighters: 'Some of the basic concepts underlying US policies for the acquisition and control of strategic nuclear arms appear to be inconsistent with international law. Most notably, the deliberate destruction of societies, as contemplated in the concepts of Assured Destruction and Mutual Assured Destruction, is unlawful under the international law of armed conflict.'[2]

The authors state that their focus is more narrow than the far-reaching implications of international law and armed conflict, such as individual criminal responsibility and the 'uneven application' of the law by war victors. They speak directly to 'those lawmakers who commit the nation to observe international law'. 'Take care', they are told, 'that you do not resort to theories of weapon use that are contrary to international law. . . . '[3]

The customary gloss of American defence politics is rudely exposed as illegal and contradictory: 'those in the Department of Defense who are responsible for the development and acquisition of nuclear arms find themselves in a double bind: They are obliged by DoD directive and by domestic law to adhere to the international law of armed conflict, but may find themselves prevented by elected government officials . . . from acquiring more discriminating weapons for their only lawful purpose – attacks on military objectives.'[4]

The American politician is reminded that the law of armed

---

[1] Act III, sc. iv.
[2] Builder and Graubard, op. cit.
[3] Ibid.
[4] Ibid.

conflict 'is most consistent about one important idea; that the parties to a conflict are obliged to distinguish between civilians and combatants'. The report points out the absurd fact that an illegal policy of mutual assured destruction implies that arms control policy-makers are seeking agreement under the law while simultaneously breaking it. MAD, they assert, is 'a shoddy foundation for US efforts, under international law, to control the burdens and risks of nuclear arms.' They also point out the ironic fact that, far from the law inhibiting traditional military values it enhances them, by containing military discipline within a positive framework of law.

The politician is challenged directly: 'Does the Congress want the Department of Defense to pursue weapons acquisition and procurement programs consistent with international law or not?'[1] The question remains unanswered.

The report confirms what we have found. The history of American military illegality is 'long and complex': 'It represents the compounding effect of many ideas, events, and people. It can be found in the early theories about strategic bombing and in the policy of Massive Retaliation proposed in the 1950s. It departed from international law in many small steps, some in the perceptions of conflict and some in the evolution of law, until we are now confronted with an enormous gulf. The awareness of that widening gulf between the law and the concept of Assured Destruction has probably been masked by the esoteric nature of international law and of strategic warfare. Experts on both sides of the chasm have probably suspected that all was not well, but they may have been put off by the intricacies of the other profession and assumed that each side was more aware than it was.'

The authors are kind. Neither Admiral Nelson nor General Robert E. Lee would have been baffled by the 'intricacies' of military restraint. It is we who have erected a hedge of thorns around the most simple principles of common humanity. Clear spring water has become a dying lake, thanks to generations of deceit. The Rand report draws attention to this aspect of the problem: 'If the basic thrust of our policies and the intent of international law are obviously opposed in their plain language interpretation something is wrong which cannot be made right by

[1] Ibid.

theories of possible exceptions. The detailed aspects of our policies or the law ought not to contradict what they strongly and repeatedly imply on their face.'

The authors state that a closer look by policy-makers and lawyers at this problem is needed: 'If the policies and law are not consistent, they should indicate the changes necessary in either to make them so. If they are consistent, the actual policies and basis in the law should be made explicit. If deterrence requires that we threaten something we do not really intend to do, then we must be sure that we do not deceive ourselves in the process. Otherwise we may find ourselves with no choice other than the execution of our threats.'[1]

Defence intellectuals, the authors warn, 'have an obligation to ensure that the policies they advocate are consistent with the law'. We have already seen how the former tend to subordinate their thinking to the dictates of established power. American intellectuals have shown little sign of recognizing the profound implications of nuclear illegality. Perhaps because such a radical reappraisal might amount to sawing off the branch they are sitting on. But if they can bring themselves to such a point, they might, says the report, 'be able to close the chasm that now yawns between the international law and US strategic nuclear policies'.

The US politician cannot wriggle free of responsibility to uphold the law in all its dimensions. The Rand report reminds him that nuclear mass destruction 'is more the creature of civilian than military minds'. Nuclear weapons were supposed to be cost-effective, to give 'more bang for the buck'. Far from enhancing military prestige and power, nuclear weapons have sucked the military profession into a black hole of criminality. With wry humour, the politician is reminded that 'so many in civilian leadership are trained in the law' that perhaps they may care to work out 'a useful set of new arguments' about nuclear policy. The fact that America's many lawyer politicians have connived so cosily and so long with nuclear illegality makes this suggestion seem optimistic.

The Rand report quotes with approval a statement by the chairman of the Joint Chiefs of Staff, General Brown, and printed in an official USAF pamphlet: 'We recognize that wanton destruc-

[1] Ibid.

tion and unnecessary suffering are both violations of these military developed legal principles and counter-productive to the political military goals of the Nation.' The same USAF pamphlet, published in 1976, says: 'Every legal system is based on rights and responsibilities. One of the best ways to protect rights is the diligent fulfilment of responsibilities.'[1]

The US politician is made aware of the extent to which the US armed forces are bound by law, at least on paper. A Department of Defense directive of 5 November 1974, declares that 'The Armed Forces of the United States will comply with the laws of war in the conduct of military operations and related activities in armed conflict however such conflicts are characterized.'[2] Training in the law is promised.

The Rand report makes full use of the Additional Protocol 1, 1977, which updates and strengthens laws protecting non-combatants. It makes no mention of the fact that the US Government, like the British, signed the Protocol while adding a reservation specifically seeking to exclude nuclear weapons from its scope. This reservation not only spits in the face of the law, by supporting and undermining it at the same time, but is of dubious legal status. The Protocol states, among many such principles, that 'indiscriminate attacks are prohibited' (Article 51). To sign this law while asserting that such attacks are lawful if conducted with nuclear weapons is bare-faced fraud.

I wrote to the International Committee of the Red Cross in Geneva, the sponsors of this Protocol, to seek legal opinion on this reservation. The reply is specific: 'It is not intended, of course, that the protection of civilians be suspended during a nuclear conflict. In this kind of conflict, should it ever occur, the instruments of international humanitarian law remain entirely in force and do produce their full legal effects. As they are designed to protect victims of all armed conflicts, the reservations, excluding from their scope of application, any type of conflict, would be clearly incompatible with their paramount objective and, hence, inadmissible.'[3]

The US and British reservations, swallowed dully by politicians and people, are in law as fraudulent and worthless as they seem. A

[1] Ibid.
[2] Ibid.
[3] Letter to the author, 10 December 1982

nightmare which swallows reason and hope has silenced politicians whose job it is to monitor the law.

The Rand report reminds the politician that UN General Assembly resolutions, while not having the force of law, are indicative of customary law because they reflect prevailing values. Resolution 2444(XXIII) of January 1969 is quoted: 'the right of the parties to a conflict to adopt means of injuring the enemy is not unlimited'. The authors add that: 'The US later expressly declared that it regards this resolution as an accurate declaration of existing customary law.'[1]

Robert McNamara was later to serve humanity through the World Bank for Development. He had good reason to, having spent some time as US Defense Secretary, when he described US nuclear policy in the following terms: 'I would judge that a capability on our part to destroy, say one-fifth to one-fourth of [the USSRs] population and one-half of her industrial capacity would serve as an effective deterrent. Such a level of destruction would certainly represent intolerable punishment to any 20th century industrial nation'.[2]

Cold-blooded mass murder, presented statistically in this manner, contradicts official military efforts to uphold minimum humanitarian law. It was a statement of Government policy, accepted by the overwhelming majority of American politicians as such. It was not rejected as evidence of criminality and loss of normal feeling.

The days of easy nuclear crime may soon be over, for politician and public alike. As nuclear fraud is exposed in detail, by reports such as this, the politician will begin to feel exposed. Once a bemused public rubs the sleep from its eyes there may be a switch of political allegiance, from law-foul to law-fair. As if by magic, the politician will discover the law and lift it on high, a born-again sheriff of the nuclear frontier.

The authors of this valuable report reflect on the roots of nuclear disgrace. They find a 'marvellous microcosm' of this modern rake's progress in the experience of an Englishman, Freeman Dyson, who worked at RAF Bomber Command during the Second World War:

---

[1] Op. cit.
[2] 1969 Department of Defense Annual Report, in Builder and Graubard, op. cit.

The last spring of the war was the most desolate. Even after Dresden . . . the bombing of cities continued . . . I began to look backward and to ask myself how it had happened that I let myself become involved in this crazy game of murder. Since the beginning of the war, I had been retreating step by step from one moral position to another, until at the end I had no moral position at all. At the beginning of the war I believed fiercely in the brotherhood of man, and was morally opposed to all violence. After a year of war, I retreated, and said, unfortunately, non-violent resistance against Hitler is impracticable, but I am still morally opposed to bombing. A couple of years later, I said, unfortunately, it seems that bombing is necessary in order to win the war, but I am still morally opposed to bombing cities indiscriminately. After I arrived at Bomber Command, I said, unfortunately, it turns out that we are, after all, bombing cities indiscriminately, but this is morally justified, as it is helping to win the war. A year later, I said, unfortunately, it seems that our bombing is not really helping to win the war, but at least I am morally justified in working to save the lives of the bomber crews. In the last spring of the war, I could no longer find any excuses . . . I had surrendered one moral principle after another, and in the end it was all for nothing. . . .

The root of the evil was the doctrine of strategic bombing, which had guided the evolution of Bomber Command from its beginning. . . . The doctrine of strategic bombing declared that the only way to win wars or to prevent wars was to rain down death and destruction upon enemy countries from the sky.[1]

The Rand report wonders how the laws of armed conflict could have eluded political control: 'They probably were not completely missed. They have been more clearly accounted for in our tactical warfare policies. And many, inside and outside the defense community, have probably suspected that all was not correct in our strategic policies; but they may have been put off by the esoteric philosophy of deterrence theory and by reassurances that public statements do not necessarily reflect actual war plans. On the other side, the strategic planners probably have suspected that their policies were not strictly lawful; but they may have been put off by the esoteric nature and uncertain stature of international law and

[1] Freeman Dyson, *Disturbing the Universe*, New York 1979.

by the acceptance that war is hell and that the losers are often punished under some theory of law.

'Perhaps,' the report goes on, 'the lawyers and the strategic planners have each left the other to pursue his own concerns and the issues raised here have been simply dropped through the cracks. It would not be the first time that something important has been overlooked because of the isolation of esoteric bodies of knowledge. But the international law and strategic nuclear policies are complex enough to suppose that the two are resolvable in the "fine print" – in the exceptions and ambiguities that obviously exist in both. But the questions raised here flow from what our strategic nuclear policies and the international law say on their face. . . . The ambiguities in our policies or the exceptions in the law ought not contradict what they strongly and repeatedly imply on their face.'[1]

The authors are a little indulgent of the reasons why vital areas of knowledge become 'esoteric' and exclusive. When clean water and fresh air are rare it is because human beings corrupt the environment by breaking principles of good husbandry. When minimum laws of military restraint are violated it is because human beings are wounded in their inner being. The murderer is dead inside before he kills. The crime is no more natural or excusable than drug or alcohol addiction. The remedy lies not in blame or indulgence but the most thorough investigation of root causes. Evidence points to the fact that the policies and machinery of mass destruction are no more rational than the everyday life of a mass murderer who manages to hold down a normal job during daylight. The fact that a sophisticated mask of rationality has been imposed on ugly reality complicates our task. We and the authors of this report are a part of the problem which we are examining.

The Rand report deserves our gratitude for insisting that the law and the problem of mass murder must be judged first and foremost by plain language interpretation of what is visible on their face, not in the 'fine print' area of ambiguity and exception. Whatever the law does or does not say, there is no doubt that it says, over and over again, that the killing of helpless people is a crime. Indiscriminate mass destruction is crime inflated to its limit.

The American politician has so far hidden from this radical

[1] Builder and Graubard, op. cit.

challenge, preferring to make hay while the sun shines. But there are some in the US armed forces who care whether we will blind the sun tomorrow. The Rand report quotes approvingly the thoughts of a former Secretary of the US Air Force, John McLucas: 'while it is easy to perceive the shortcomings of law that frequently relies on the coercive power of individual states or groups of states for its execution, we also need to recognize the inestimable value of international law, which introduces norms of behaviour and establishes identifiable parameters of acceptable actions; and we must continue to strive to substitute the rule of law for the rule of force in international relations. As Thomas Baty, a well known publicist, noted in 1954. . . . "International law is the last stronghold of true law" since its permanence is "based on a general consciousness of stringent and permanent obligation". This is, indeed, a major consideration. International law is not promulgated by decree, but, rather, by reasoned consent and co-operation. "This", he says, "is its outstanding merit". We in the Air Force constantly benefit from the existence of international law, are sensitive to its changes, and contribute to its formulation in many functional areas. Above all, we actively support it in the hope that it will lead mankind to a peaceful world.'[1]

The USAF does not live up to this commitment, but statements of this kind can and must be used as a basis for new and strict enforcement of the law. The Rand report concludes by asking whether there is 'something we can do'. It suggests that there is a clear call for a 'closer look by policy-makers and lawyers at the questions raised here,' particularly at the highest levels of Government. Second, 'defense intellectuals' should take a fresh look at their work in the light of the law, and beware of 'research activities that might support policies opposed to the basic principles of international law'.[2]

These suggestions are unreasonably reasonable, assuming as they do a level of reason in government and college which is plainly absent, as far as nuclear weaponry is concerned. The thief caught with his hand in the till is not the best person to advise on finance. It is precisely reason itself which has been seduced into allegiance to the mad idol of nuclear security. To rely heavily on this pale, defeatist creature for radical law enforcement is as idiotic as

[1] Ibid.
[2] Ibid.

electing the biggest crook in town as sheriff. The two lawyers who
wrote the Rand report have dared to expose a massive breach of the
law. We, and the US politician, must make the best use of their
evidence to get to the heart of the problem. Law must be restored
to people. Rejection of mass murder is a natural responsibility of
citizens, not research matter for intellectuals.

If the US politician stands condemned for gross violation of the
law concerning national and human survival, there are at least a few
signs of hope at a lesser level. Hope rests on our ability to upgrade
this limited response. Since Vietnam, the United States has continued to blunder across frontiers in a futile attempt to impose its
will. Cambodia, Lebanon and Central America all bear the scars.
The image of an American battleship pumping sixteen-inch high-
explosive shells into Lebanese villages, as happened in 1983,
reflects a foreign policy whose regard for law is marginal. The USS
New Jersey 'damaged civilian property while hitting nothing of
military value, according to defense sources in Washington.'[1]

American intervention in the chaotic affairs of a tiny West
Indian Island, Grenada, was further evidence of an alienated
superpower in action. American public opinion thrilled to this
trivial adventure, as the British had done to their Falklands
conflict. A huge pall of patriotic fantasy descended on a small patch
of sordid reality. There was no communist devil to be handcuffed
by the brave sheriff, only poor people trying to make sense out of
poverty.

But the law was not totally submerged. Tip O'Neill, the
influential Speaker of the US House of Representatives, admitted
that the American people supported the invasion. He did not. 'Is it
the right thing to do?' he asked. 'No, it isn't. It's the wrong thing.
We have to abide by international law. What he [Reagan] did the
other day, that's gunboat diplomacy, and that's wrong'.[2] Eight
well known American academic lawyers described the Grenada
invasion as a 'gross violation of the most fundamental principles of
international law', and particularly of the UN and OAS charters.[3]

Selective law, rightly condemned in everyday life, has become
the hallmark of US behaviour abroad. A recent US ambassador to
the United Nations confirmed this when she said that international

---

[1] *Daily Telegraph*, 17 February 1984.
[2] *Guardian*, 29 October 1983.
[3] *Guardian*, 29 November 1983.

law 'is not a suicide pact. . . . Unilateral compliance with the UN Charter's principles of non-intervention and non-use of force may make sense in some specific and isolated instances, but are hardly a sound basis for . . . US policy.'[1] Such offhand cynicism echoes what was heard so often at Nuremberg. Might is right. Law is optional. She and the modern American politician should take a look at Article VI, Section 2 of the US Constitution, which provides that international treaties, the US Constitution and the laws of the US shall be 'the supreme law of the land'.

The law received a blow on the head, and a shot in the arm, when the US Central Intelligence Agency mined the approaches to three Nicaraguan ports in 1984. There was an immediate outcry against this violation of international shipping rights. The Government of Nicaragua took the matter to the International Court of Justice at The Hague. The US Government said it would disregard the decisions of the court concerning any dispute in Central America for two years. The court then issued an interim unanimous decision on 10 May 1984, that the United States must cease 'immediately and refrain from any action restricting access to or from Nicaragua's ports and, in particular, the laying of mines'.[2]

This unique decision by a US Government to defy the world court was denounced throughout the United States as contempt of the law, by individuals and institutions of many political beliefs. For the first time in its seventy-eight-year history, the American Society for International Law voted overwhelmingly at its annual conference on 12 April 1984, to urge reversal of the Government's decision. More important, Congressmen were assailed by angry citizens demanding an end to illegal military intervention. The House of Representatives and the Senate voted by large majorities to condemn Government action. Funding for the mining operation was cut off by Congress. The Government was clearly shocked by this unexpected public law enforcement. It stated that the world court's decision would not affect it, then said that it 'respects the court and the rule of law.'[3] A leading Republican Senator, Mark Hatfield of Oregon, warned the President not to

[1] Jeanne Kirkpatrick, speech to the American Society for International Law, 12 April 1984.
[2] *Daily Telegraph*, 11 May 1984.
[3] Ibid.

continue the legal and political battle, but if he 'wants to put his head in the buzz-saw again, that's up to him'.[1]

Senator Edward Kennedy was scathing. 'This policy defies all logic,' he said, 'it defies all reason. And it defies all law.'[2] The Senate minority leader referred to the mining as 'an act of terrorism'.[3] This episode indicates how international law can be enforced, however hesitantly, by the court of public opinion, national and international. The worm had turned. What it could do once it can do again, better.

Chemical weapons have also prompted signs of revolt among American politicians. The 1925 Geneva Gas Protocol was ratified by the United States after fifty years, but US policy has followed close to the nuclear track, requiring chemical weapons for retaliation while advocating a complete international ban. This is a mirror image of Soviet policy. There are reports that 10,000 tons of US poison gas are stored in West Germany, enough to 'kill all life on earth'.[4] But the US House of Representatives has become reluctant to grant funds for planned expansion of these weapons, voting in 1984 by 247–179 to deprive the Government of funds for this purpose.[5]

The American politician has allowed chemical weapons to develop under his nose with minimum critical attention. The Protocol says that use is forbidden but not possession, in case of unlawful attack. This weakness is cherished by the chemical weapons States, such as the US and the USSR. But it ignores the more fundamental prohibition of customary international law which prohibits indiscriminate attacks and attacks on protected persons, as well as the use of poison at any time.

Chemical weapons are related not only to nuclear radiation but to conventional weapons such as napalm and the poisonous defoliants used by US forces in Vietnam. Similarities in these criminal poisons are ignored by the politician anxious to appease his military guard-dog. Superficial differences are polished up for the shop-window of counterfeit law.

The experience of Nicaragua and the mining of its ports suggests

[1] *Guardian*, 27 June 1984.
[2] *Daily Telegraph*, 11 April 1984.
[3] *Guardian*, 10 April 1984.
[4] *Guardian*, 20 August 1982.
[5] *The Times*, 19 May 1984.

strongly that the American politician cannot be trusted to enforce the law against mass destruction without the determined insistence of ordinary people. The core of American politics is rotten with generations of connivance with criminal levels of military violence. The laws are there, flawed but adequate. They remain unused while the self-appointed sheriff pursues his Mickey Mouse myth of omnipotence.

For the American politician who objects that the law is only worth obeying if everyone, including the Soviet Union, obeys it, there are several answers. The United States contains more than its fair share of domestic law-breakers, yet the law is not discarded on that account. As Abraham Lincoln, General Robert E. Lee and many Americans have known and acknowledged, there are clear limits to human action, imposed by human nature and the universal principles of civilized society. Threatening the annihilation of foreign nations is not only outside the law but beyond belief and sanity.

To base US security on such a foundation is to expose every cherished American value as a fraud. The founders of the American Constitution believed that 'all men were created equal' in the eyes of God and man. That includes Soviet citizens. There are many legitimate ways of approaching the Soviet Union and its political system. Threatening to exterminate it in the manner of Hitler is not one of them.

Before he can reach the hard floor of legality the American politician must recognize the nightmare fantasy in which he is adrift, where ordinary words are treacherous. 'This man really understands us,' said an American arms control negotiator in Geneva of his Soviet counterpart, 'and he knows how to twist words ... it's like Alice in Wonderland. Words mean whatever they want them to mean.'[1] But it is not only Soviet negotiators who are lost in the fog. American Senators are somewhere in it too: listen to Senator Glenn: 'I get lost in what is credible and not credible. The whole thing gets so incredible when you consider wiping out whole nations. It is difficult to establish credibility.' And Senator Brown: 'That is why we sound a little crazy when we talk about it'.[2]

Or, as Alice said in Wonderland, when confronted by official nonsense. 'Who cares for you? You're nothing but a pack of cards!'

[1] *Daily Telegraph*, 30 December 1982.
[2] US Senate, 16 September 1980.

Chapter 11

The Enemy's Tale

'No punishment shall be imposed on a subordinate if he commits a criminal offence pursuant to an order of a superior given in the line of official duty, unless the order has been directed towards committing a war crime'
— Soviet military lawyer

'Those who occupy the top layer of our society have a sort of separate thinking'
— Dr Andrei Shakharov

'Young people are tired of having to tell themselves that a weapon in the hands of the workers serves the cause of peace, but in the hands of the imperialists serves the cause of war'
— President of the Lutheran Church, East Germany, 1981.

What of 'the enemy at the gates', a foe so vile that we must become a destroyer of worlds to keep him out? An absolute deterrent requires an absolute enemy. What nightmare meaning lies in this dependence on unlimited violence? It is not the fine print of the law which we are investigating, but its plain meaning in relation to the most extreme form of military violence, mass destruction. What we are looking for is a shaft of light in our man-made fog. To grasp the simple but profound meaning of laws against mass murder in relation to our chosen enemy will be to glimpse a path ahead.

There are many facts about the nuclear cold war but none so obvious as the ignorance which afflicts each side about the other. Not one of us in the West knows more than a tiny fraction of Soviet and Eastern bloc reality. They may know even less, if that is possible, about us. This ignorance is indicative of neurotic aversion. A reasonable society would be desperately interested to study and get to know its main rival. Instead, for every traveller to the Soviet Union or its allies there are tens of thousands who prefer to sun-bathe among 'friends'.

I have met many Russians, mostly officials or peace activists.

Because such meetings are rare I pay them close attention. One such encounter will stay in my mind. I was in Prague to discuss the law and nuclear weapons, as part of the World Peace Congress of 1983. One sunny evening I was on the roof garden of the huge conference hall, overlooking the city and its winding river, when I caught sight of a Soviet lawyer whom I had met some months earlier in West Germany, at Nuremberg. He came over to talk to me and for the next hour or so we discussed various legal and political issues. I knew no Russian and he spoke no English, so we used imperfect German. It was an appropriate language. At one moment he gazed thoughtfully out over the sunlit city and asked me if I knew the significance of the date, 21 June. When I said no, he reminded me that it was on that day of 1941 that Hitler's armies had invaded the Soviet Union. He had been a young officer of the Soviet Army and the war was clearly a bitter experience. I was very conscious of a basic difference of background. I came from a country which had not been invaded for almost a thousand years.

It is easy to argue about Soviet intentions, but harder to deny the facts of history. Russia has been invaded, with catastrophic results, many times. This quiet, courteous former colonel expressed genuine apprehension about the West and its aims, which he considered aggressive. When I suggested that the current American President had no personal experience of war, and that his politics were 'Hollywood politics', he repeated this description to himself with a faint smile. As a young man, I reflected, he had been our ally. Now he was our enemy, the same man, only older. One polite Soviet colonel does not make world peace but I was looking for a common humanity, not perfection.

Detailing the humanity of the enemy, all of whom live each minute under suspended sentence of death from our missiles, gets us nowhere when human feeling is at a discount. Apostles of nuclear deterrence and the Soviet 'evil empire' will usually agree that the 'Soviet people are quite normal, but it is their Government which is wicked and aggressive.' Soviet citizens say the same about us. But this logic undermines rather than supports the theory of deterrence. If it is the hallmark of a totalitarian regime that most of its citizens are helpless politically, then how can weapons be justified which would kill millions of them? If anyone is going to escape the devastation of a nuclear attack it will be

leaders and high officials. So our nuclear missiles threaten the least
'guilty' and worst protected, standing traditional military logic on
its head.

We, like the people of Eastern Europe, are willing to annihilate,
in the name of defence, millions of people we know to be much like
us. We, and our Governments, rationalize this criminal lunacy by
promoting the fiction of an evil clique which controls the enemy.
Both sides do it. We are no better than baboons attacking our
image in a mirror. We are worse, because a part of our brain is
rational and knows the other part is irrational, and because we are
prepared to destroy the world to prove our half-truths are whole.
Hollywood politics, life as neurotic fantasy, is a common element
of the East/West confrontation. Modern industrial civilization is
deadlocked within a nightmare civil war. Can it be that this
common nightmare, embracing as it does a sham contest of good
and evil, is rooted in the mass murder of this century, and the
cultural schizophrenia which inspired it? Murderers tend to cover
their tracks and assume a disguise to divert the law. Cornered, they
point at other suspects. We have already seen how we in the West
have consistently lied to ourselves and the world about our killing,
claiming that the enemy was wicked and we were upholding
civilized values. The sane part of us knows that the enemy was and
is overwhelmingly like us, and that we violated the most basic
principles of humanitarian law by murdering helpless people.

The Nuremberg Trial reflected this deep split. How did the
Soviet Union play its part in that trial, which succeeded in punishing one evil at the very moment when a new and even more virulent
strain of violence was growing within the judging nations? By the
time the trial ended, in the autumn of 1946, the Cold War was well
rooted. The 'gallant Russian ally' had become overnight a threat so
absolute and overwhelming as to require nuclear deterrence, the
threat of mass annihilation. The 'Western ally', likewise, was now
an imperialist capitalist, whose insatiable greed required exactly
the same brand of murderous opposition.

Yet the Nuremberg Trial had shown that when the two half-
truth cultures of Western civilization recognized a common
problem with common sense, unclouded by poisonous fantasy,
they were capable of co-operating. The Soviet judicial system
differed in many respects from the British, American and French,
as indeed the last three differed from each other. It took time,

patience and a shared purpose to hammer out a legal framework for the trial. There was much national pride and prejudice at stake, and much sensible compromise. When a heated exchange took place over the apparel to be worn by the judges, the Soviets complained that gowns look medieval and wigs absurd. In the end they wore military uniforms and the rest gowns.

The Soviets wanted the trial to be held in Berlin, a four-power city within their own zone of occupied Germany. Nuremberg was in the American zone but was one of the few suitable sites for such a large trial in a country with many public buildings in ruins. In the end a compromise was reached. Berlin would be the official permanent place of the trial while the real thing would take place in Nuremberg. Honour was satisfied. The Soviets accepted a British judge, Sir Geoffrey Lawrence, as president of the court.

In the context of nuclear weaponry, what does the Soviet role at Nuremberg have to tell us about their attitude to the law and its restraints on military violence? The Soviet lawyers came from a country which had suffered losses of twenty million men, women and children. Huge areas had been systematically burned and destroyed. Combined British and American losses were fewer than one million. The Soviets had no doubt that the Germans had violated the very essence of international law governing warfare. Stalin joked about shooting the Nazi leaders out of hand, but even he recognized the need for a properly conducted trial. Despite his ruthless policies within the Soviet Union, Stalin wanted the world to acknowledge Soviet allegiance to international principles of justice.

When General Rudenko put the Soviet case for the prosecution at Nuremberg he at once mocked German corruption of military legality: 'How can they [German General Staff] attempt to whitewash themselves by referring to the "duty of the soldier", "the honour of an officer", and the "obligation of fulfilling orders"? Since when has the "duty of a soldier" and the "honour of an officer" been compatible with the shooting, without trial, and the branding of prisoners, as well as with the extermination of women, children and old people?'[1]

He touched on the hope of all criminals that they will never be caught: 'These are the facts which are confirmed by the words of

[1] *International Military Tribunal Vol. XX.*

the defendants themselves, uttered at a time when they did not suppose that they ever would be defendants.'

He spoke with feeling in support of this unique international tribunal: 'For the first time in the history of mankind, criminals against humanity are being held responsible for their crimes before an International Criminal Tribunal; for the first time nations are trying those who have flooded immense areas of the earth with blood, who have annihilated millions of innocent people, destroyed cultural treasures, who have instituted a system of massacre and torture, of the extermination of old people, women and children. . . .'[1]

He echoed the words of the British prosecutor, Sir David Maxwell Fyfe: 'Cold-blooded mass-murder regarded as honour!' He heard the British lawyer identify Soviet with Allied generals, within a common identity of values: 'Will you try to imagine a British or an American or a Soviet or a French army commander telling his major-generals: "What happens to a Russian, to a Czech, does not interest me in the slightest". . . .'[2]

He heard the American prosecutor Telford Taylor describe some of the wanton horror experienced within the Soviet Union at German hands: 'On the Eastern Front, the callous indifference of the German warlords to violations of the laws of war and to mass suffering and death produced results equally criminal and, because on a grander scale, far more horrible. The atrocities committed by the Wehrmacht and other agencies of the Third Reich in the East were of such staggering enormity that they rather tax the power of comprehension. Why did all these things happen? Analysis will show, I believe, that this was not simply madness and blood-lust. On the contrary, there was both method and purpose. These atrocities occurred as the result of carefully calculated orders and directives, issued prior to or at the time of the attack on the Soviet Union. . . .'[3]

The enormous scale of brutality and murder on Soviet territory quickly overloaded feeling within the court. Horror floods imagination, cutting off pain. The Soviet recital of bloodshed went on for days. It began to seem commonplace, even boring: 'In the small town of Vyasma alone, by order of the chief of the Gestapo, several

[1] Ibid.
[2] Op. cit., *Vol. XXII*.
[3] Ibid.

thousands of peaceful citizens were killed or tortured to death. . . . In the village of Zaitchiki, in the Smolensk district, the men of the Gestapo drove into one house twenty-three old men, women and children, set the house on fire and burned alive all those inside. In the psychiatric hospitals of Riga the Gestapo exterminated all the inmates of these asylums. . . . In the town of Krasnodar, and in the Krasnodar region, the Gestapo . . . exterminated by carbon monoxide poisoning over 6,700 Soviet citizens. . . . In the outskirts of Krasnodar, in a big anti-tank ditch, were buried several thousand bodies of Soviet citizens who had been poisoned by gas and thrown there. . . .'[1] It went on and on.

General Rudenko told the court that the People's Commissar for Foreign Affairs, Molotov, had complained in 1941 and 1942 to the German Government and the whole world about this 'violation of the most elementary principles of international law and of human morality'.[2] The inventory of destruction in the Soviet Union included: '1,670 Orthodox churches, 337 Catholic churches, 69 chapels, 532 synagogues . . . 1,710 cities and over 70,000 villages, almost completely destroyed . . .'[3] together with hundreds of millions of domestic animals and poultry. Hospitals, schools, libraries were smashed beyond counting.

Soviet prisoners of war were branded, starved, tortured, forced to work and killed by the Germans, all in gross violation of the customary rules of war. At one camp alone, 130,000 were killed. If anything, the crimes against civilians were worse. 'The Russian prosecutors handed to the judges samples of tanned human skin and soap made from human bodies.'[4] A journalist in the court wrote of the tedium of horror: 'He was speaking about the murder of millions of men, women and children. The court yawned. . . . We were thankful when the court rose and we filed to the Tribunal cafeteria to sup tea and talk sweet nothings. Presently a little Russian captain entered. We saw him pay 1/6 for his snack and put down his tray. Suddenly he plunged his head into his hands and began to sob. "Oh mother, sweet mother, dear father, why did they kill you? . . ." Then, with understanding in our hearts we went back to court.'[5]

---

[1] Ibid.
[2] Ibid.
[3] Tusa and Tusa, op. cit.
[4] Ibid.
[5] *Daily Herald*, 4 March 1946.

The Soviet prosecutor showed a forty-five-minute film of Nazi atrocities. 'It showed the warehouse at Maidenek where 800,000 pairs of shoes had been neatly stacked, the piles of skulls, broken bodies, mutilated corpses. There were sequences where naked women were driven to mass graves; they lay down and were shot; the guards smiled for the camera.... The women bending over corpses stiffened by cold, trying to identify their husbands and children, patting the dead shoulders ...'[1] The court was stunned into silence during a further six days of horror.

Jacob Vernik, a Warsaw carpenter, spoke from the hell of his own experience: 'Awake or asleep I saw the terrible visions of thousands of people calling for help, begging for life and mercy. I have lost all my family, I have myself led them to death. I have myself built the death chambers in which they were murdered. I am afraid of everything. I fear that everything that I have seen is written on my face. An old and broken life is a very heavy burden, but I must carry on and live to tell the world what German crimes and barbarism I saw.'[2]

Those crimes were named and punished at Nuremberg, but they live on in our terror-stricken policies. We too are afraid of life, with absolute weapons as a mortgage to our fantasies. Our crime is written on our face, and heard in sanctimonious lies. So desperate are we to find an enemy awful enough to match our fantastic needs that we include in their number both the Russian captain and the Warsaw carpenter. They share our nightmare. We are deadly enemies today who were once allies, and we have 'built the death chambers'.

The Soviet judges at Nuremberg wanted the most severe penalties for those found guilty. Their leading judge, General Nikitchenko, was determined that international law must be enforced without quibbling: 'The rules of land warfare expressed in the (Hague) convention undoubtedly represented an advance over International Law at the time of their adoption. The convention expressly stated that it was an attempt "to revise the general laws and customs of war" which it thus recognized to be then existing, but by 1939 these rules laid down in the convention were recognised by all civilized nations, and were regarded as being declara-

---

[1] Tusa and Tusa, op. cit.
[2] Ibid.

tory of the laws and customs of war which are referred to in Article 6(b) of the Charter'[1]

Soviet behaviour at the Nuremberg trial proves, if nothing else, that they took international law as seriously as any of the nations involved in the prosecution. The common ground among the Tribunal's judges was far more extensive than the differences of interpretation which emerged. Cold War apologists will say that this merely indicates the depth of Soviet duplicity. While Stalin acted at home like a Mongol dictator, he was happy to act the law-maker abroad. If so, Soviet behaviour bore a marked similarity to that of the Allies. We have seen how the latter managed to gloss over the criminal implications of city-bombing, thanks to a pervasive lying about what was happening. Atomic bombs had been used in the cause of 'saving lives'. Anything was possible in the name of national security. Yet at Nuremberg the Allied powers, including the Soviet Union, enforced humanitarian law with care and determination.

It would be absurd to equate exactly Western and Soviet experience or behaviour. The differences are obvious, and often objectionable to people who consider their own life-style to be uniquely right. But what cannot be denied is the fact that the Soviet people were our allies in the Second World War, despite their communist system and its dictatorial leader, that they co-operated positively in the creation and conduct of the Nuremberg Tribunal, thus affirming a strong commitment to international law, that they are people much like us and have suffered far more in the bloody chaos of this century. It is evidence of the collective neurosis of both sides that such basic facts can be acknowledged and disregarded at the same time. A criminalized law, fair of face and foul of mind, is a common feature of our East/West deadlock.

Beneath all the ritual political snarling of the Cold War, the Soviet soldier is bound by laws similar to those which bind the soldiers of every modern State. Article 96 of the Military Code, 1946, says that Soviet soldiers have 'the right to make complaints about illegal actions and orders of commanders'. A leading Soviet military lawyer has written: 'A soldier carrying out the unlawful order of an officer incurs no responsibility for the crime, which is that of the officer, except where the soldier fulfils an order which is

[1] *International Military Tribunal Vol. XXII.*

clearly criminal, in which case the soldier is responsible together with the officer who gave the order.'[1]

Article 362 of the Military Code adds: 'No punishment shall be imposed on a subordinate if he commits a criminal offence pursuant to an order of a superior given in the line of official duty, unless the order has been directed toward committing a war crime or any other grave offence, or if the subordinate knew that by obeying such an order a criminal offence would be committed.'

So much for the law. News filtering out of Afghanistan suggests that Soviet soldiers there experience pressures and problems very similar to those young Americans in Vietnam. There are the rules and the orders, and there are the sudden fears and panic of guerilla warfare, which obliterate discipline. Deserters may or may not tell the truth, but Soviet deserters have described war crimes committed in Afghanistan. One twenty-six-year old soldier, Sergei Mescherliakov, is reported to have deserted because he 'did not want to kill women and children'.[2]

An English doctor, Simon Mardel, who spent four months in the war zone with a French medical team, is reported to have said of Soviet attacks by helicopter gunship: 'When they go in they are firing at anyone they can see. At first the Russians used only to attack the Mojahadin headquarters . . . in each village, but now they are shooting at mud huts.'[3] Two young Soviet soldiers who were captured by the guerillas and eventually reached London, described how war crimes were committed. One of them, Sergeant Igor Rykov, aged twenty-two, said: 'It happens in a very simple way. Soviet soldiers are passing a village and the officer demands to have the village searched to see if there are any Mojahadin in it. What usually happened is that we found a cartridge or a bullet and the officer said, "Okay, this is a bandit village. It must be destroyed." They bring the women into a separate room. The men and young boys are usually shot right where they are and they try to kill the women by throwing grenades.'[4]

Sergeant Rykov said that the majority of civilians were killed in air raids. Villages were left in ruins. Drug addiction among the Soviet soldiers was rife and their morale low. He added that 'to go

[1] *Soviet Military Criminal Code*, 1949.
[2] *Frankfurter Allgemeine Zeitung*, 18 February 1983.
[3] *Guardian*, 26 July 1984.
[4] *Daily Telegraph*, 28 June 1984.

back to the Soviet Union and hear from the Soviet authorities how Soviet soldiers are helping to cultivate Afghan gardens was just impossible'.[1] As in Vietnam, simple young men, armed to the teeth, were being expected to enforce an official fantasy reality. What they encountered were real people with a mixture of feelings and needs, speaking a foreign language in a strange environment. The enemy, as in Vietnam, was anyone and everywhere.

This does not mean that the Soviet Army is more criminal than any other. The British bombed Afghan villages in the 1930s. 'Policing the Empire,' it was called by Government spokesmen in London, if anyone cared to ask. The French Army committed numerous atrocities in Vietnam and later in Algeria, against 'freedom fighters'. I had a French friend in the 1950s who wept bitterly when she heard about the brutality of French soldiers in their futile effort to stifle Arab nationalism. We have already seen what happened to US conscripts and professional soldiers in Vietnam. Enforcement of the law in any language or army requires strict discipline, strong leadership and individuals who will oppose crime. Above all, it requires political leadership able to distinguish between fact and fantasy, the fact of common humanity and the fantasy of absolute right.

If Soviet enforcement of the laws of armed conflict is much like ours at the ground level of conventional warfare, decidedly patchy, what of their performance in the realm of nuclear weapons and mass destruction? Shocked by American development of atomic bombs at the end of the Second World War, the Soviet Union rejected the American 'Baruch Plan', based on the Lilienthal Report, which offered to place atomic development under international control. Proposed by a seventy-five-year-old politician, Bernard Baruch, in 1946, it is doubtful whether even the US Government had any serious belief in this plan. The temptation to keep a monopoly of nuclear weaponry was strong. The Soviet Union countered with its own proposal. According to one commentator: 'They wanted a convention under which governments would undertake not to use atomic weapons under any circumstances, to forbid the production of such weapons, and to destroy within three months all stocks of finished or semi-finished atomic weapons. They envisaged strict supervision and control to police the agreement.'[2]

[1] *Guardian*, 28 June 1984.
[2] Gowing, op. cit.

This too was rejected. The now familiar circle of power logic was complete. If you are weak you cannot get a worthwhile agreement. If you are strong you do not need one. If power is balanced, why bother? What neither side proposed, despite the example of the Nuremberg Tribunal, was that the machinery of war should be reduced and strictly controlled according to law. Nightmares and law are incompatible. Irrational fantasy fears reason. The morbid language of mega-death took over where the judges of Nuremberg left off.

But when it came to containing this nuclear monster during the coming years, the Soviet Union, whatever its motives, did more than the West to apply the constraints of international law. In 1961, twelve African and Asian states submitted a resolution to the UN General Assembly (1653,XVI). It sought a ban on nuclear weapons, 'recalling that the use of weapons of mass destruction, causing unnecessary human suffering, was in the past prohibited, as being contrary to the laws of humanity and to the principles of international law. . . .'

The use of such weapons, it said, was 'a crime under international law'. A nuclear war would be 'against mankind in general'. The vote was 55 in favour, 20 against, with 26 abstentions. The Soviet Union and its European allies supported the resolution; France, Britain, the USA and most West European nations voted against it. The West adopted a characteristic pose. Whatever the Soviet Union supported must be worth opposing because Soviet motives are always suspect. As there were more Soviet troops on the fringes of Western Europe than those available to oppose them, it was assumed that Soviet opposition to nuclear weapons must be designed to maximize this supposed conventional advantage. Like a goat, paranoia feeds on anything and everything, creating a desert.

The 'chasm' between law and policy, mentioned in the Rand report, was growing wider daily. In 1972 the Soviet Union proposed another and similar resolution to the UN General Assembly (2936,XXVII). It sought non-use of force in international relations, in conformity with the UN Charter, and a permanent prohibition of the use of nuclear weapons. It referred to the earlier resolution of 1961. It asked the Security Council to take 'appropriate measures' to implement the resolution. The other nuclear powers abstained.

When declarations of principle are not tested, bluff, if any, remains uncalled. The West did not meet this Soviet inititative by developing argument and law to their logical conclusion. It did not argue that banning use is not good enough, because possession implies threat of war, which in turn increases tension and violates the law. It did not propose a re-affirmation of the Nuremberg Principles, demanding a world-wide ban on all forms of mass destruction and a reformed code of military conduct for every soldier in every army. It did not link such a move to radical renewal of a world weighed down with weapons and starved of food and clean water.

Instead there was sophisticated suspicion and cynical inertia. The Test Ban agreement, 1964, was the agreement of two fat man-eating lions which had just lunched off a couple of missionaries. They would abstain for a while and enjoy a siesta. Underground tests were sufficient, in any case, to keep the arms race going.

By now the mirror-image projections of East and West had reached obsessive proportions. The world watched impotently as the super-powers and their agents preached like saints and behaved like villains. When Argentina tried to swallow the colonial relic of the Falkland Islands, the British reacted with outraged decorum. The law had been flouted. The UN Charter was invoked. In 'self-defence' the British kicked out the Argentinians, which prompted passionate Soviet denunciation. It accused the British of 'the grossest disregard' for international law and for the UN resolutions calling for de-colonization.[1] Law was a puppet of power, a weapon of prejudice, its vital roots cut.

Stung by American and Western criticism of its presence in Afghanistan, the Soviet Union was filled with righteous indignation over the US occupation of Grenada. The Communist Party newspaper *Pravda* said it showed the United States 'at its foulest, as a country which does not consider itself bound by international law and norms of morality, as a country for which the fist has become the principal argument and instrument of foreign policy. . . . The unprovoked intervention against the sovereign state tears away the last fig-leaf of "peaceableness' from the US Administration.'[2]

[1] *The Times*, 4 May 1982.
[2] *Guardian*, 1 November 1983.

But beneath the histrionics and self-righteousness of both sides there is a hard core of genuine concern about legality. Every nation must cling fast to its own version of the law in order to maintain any coherence. When a South Korean airliner was shot down over Soviet territory, in 1983, there was a storm of abuse and counter-abuse, but at the eye of the storm was the law. The Soviet Government issued a statement claiming to have acted according to the law: 'Such actions are in full correlation with the law. . . . Dozens of international air routes pass through the territory of the Soviet Union and foreign planes have been flying them for many years and nothing happened to them if they observed the present rules. . . . We will act in the future with the correlation of our laws to the full degree corresponding to international norms. . . . This is one of the commonly adopted norms of international law on which relations between states are built.'[1]

In turn, many Western nations accused the Soviet Union of violating the law by shooting down a passenger plane. As so often when such disputes are examined, right or wrong are not clearly marked. It is feasible that the airliner was used as a 'trigger' to switch on Soviet defence systems in a sensitive military area. If so, the law was used to serve rather than restrain military purposes.

We have seen how the British and the Americans have subverted the laws of armed conflict to suit their own reality, hiding criminal threats of mass destruction in a legal no-go area. Politicians, lawyers, judges, soldiers and public have colluded with this illegality. The blacker the Soviet devil the whiter appears their own murderous history. Much of the same process of evasion goes on in the other, left-hand side of a benighted civilization.

Soviet perception of international law, like ours, stems from a distinctive national experience. Like ours, it is shot through with flaws and contradictions, serviced by a legal profession which tends to obey its master's voice. A British legal observer has described the Soviet legal system in terms which make it feel quite close to home:

> The Soviet legal system on paper provides most of the safeguards for human rights which we would expect in the most tolerant and free society. . . . The Soviet Constitution itself promises to fulfil "obligations arising from the generally recognized principles

---

[1] *Guardian*, 7 September 1983.

and rules of international law, and from the international treaties signed by the USSR". According to these documents, Soviet citizens are guaranteed the right to leave their country, the right to freedom of expression ... freedom from arbitrary arrest ... and all the rights associated with a fair trial.... Three offences peculiar to Soviet law are "anti-Soviet agitation and propaganda"; "parasitism"; and "failure to comply with residence requirements". The first explicitly prohibits criticism of the system; the second arises from the official absence of unemployment in the Soviet Union ... the third reflects the rule that Soviet citizens are not allowed without permission to be outside of their approved residence for more than three consecutive days. All three laws are, however, enforced selectively against those whom the authorities wish to punish.[1]

The values implicit in such a system tend to overlap and complement our own. Communism stresses collective rights, virtues and duties. Full employment, however imperfectly administered, strengthens social unity as much as 'anti-State agitation' threatens it. Western values stress individual options and downgrade social unity, which leads to wide disparity of wealth and high levels of unemployment. Outspoken individuals tend to be tolerated, unless they begin to threaten the social balance. Judging by fact rather than principle, we have an institutionalized minority of poor, required to maintain the economic security of the majority. Britain and the United States have signed an international convention which declares that employment is a right.[2] Yet our laws do not permit the unemployed to sue the State for theft of economic rights. The poor in the West are no less victimized than Soviet intellectuals whose criticisms are officially silenced in their country.

Stemming as the Cold Warriors do from the same European civilization, we need all the bits of the East-West puzzle to complete the jigsaw. The Soviet system, like the elephant in the fable, fears the mouse of intellectual independence. Something which is huge, heavy, slow-moving, finds creativity as elusive as quicksilver. A Solzhenitsyn is soon lost in the uproar of Western bazaar chatter. In the Soviet Union his passionate voice will ring

[1] *Guardian*, 19 December 1983.
[2] The Covenant on Economic, Social and Cultural Rights, 1966.

across the quiet steppes like a siren. It is a measure of Cold War neurosis that his words, challenging in his own country, sound querulous and outdated in the United States. A strident exposer of Soviet flaws, fuelling Western prejudice, has nothing to say to the Western unemployed, who are free to say what they like, all day, in social limbo.

Every State has its catch-all laws for all reasons, legal putty useful for plugging holes. England has its pernicious 'breach of the peace' law, a relic of the Middle Ages. Every peace activist in England is aware of its sticky embrace. 'Peace' means the peace of mind of authority, not the peace of the world. If Auschwitz had been sited outside London, the first local citizens to protest would have been arrested for 'breach of the peace', or 'obstructing the highway'. Criminal nuclear bases have been protected by such means.

According to the legal observer already quoted:

> Soviet judges are elected and the People's Courts are meant to have a political and educational function, not simply to administer abstract justice. But the pretended adherence of the Soviet Union to international human rights law is sheerest hypocrisy. [But] many members of the legal profession here, including judges, are either apathetic towards human rights or they are more concerned to preserve the authority of the State. The degradation of the law in the USSR ... and other countries where arbitrary power has prevailed, is a terrible warning.[1]

In terms of the law and nuclear weapons, we have already seen how much-vaunted independent British judges kow-tow to authority, disclaiming judicial or personal responsibility. We have our 'terrible warning' and the Soviet people have theirs. We have a lot in common. We are enmeshed in fantasy.

Just as it is urgently necessary to revitalize our own vision of law and its purpose, the same is true in the Soviet Union. I feel comradeship with Dina Kaminskaya, a Soviet civil rights lawyer whose recent book describes her struggle to breathe more life into Soviet law.[2] She was finally debarred from practising after taking up the politically touchy case of the exiled Crimean Tartars. She

[1] Ibid.
[2] Dina Kaminskaya, *Final Judgment: My Life as a Soviet Defence Lawyer*, London 1983.

did it 'in defence of legality' and in the hope that it would develop 'a respect for the law among Soviet people'. She confirms that Soviet law 'works' but that its judges are dependent on the State. She also tells a success story, concerning her fight to gain justice for two boys falsely accused and sentenced for rape and murder. She exposed a corrupt judge and eventually won the case at the Soviet Supreme Court. She describes this as 'a triumph of Soviet justice'. No legal system, no nation, and no person is all bad.

As we poke around in the lumber of the Soviet judicial system and its values, we should stay close to Soviet behaviour in relation to the law and mass destruction. Like the West, the East has nuclear weapons and is prepared to use them in war. It is a paid-up member of the mutual suicide pact of European civilization. But its contempt for minimum humanitarian law is marginally less. It has pledged itself to 'no first use' of nuclear weapons, and has signed and sponsored United Nations resolutions condemning nuclear weapons as criminal if used. Such a pledge is not worth the paper it is written on, says the West, and resolutions are cheap propaganda. Perhaps. But why is it more virtuous to do what the West does, which is little except extol nuclear weapons for keeping the peace since the Second World War, while claiming an interest in getting rid of them? What credibility has a drug addict who claims that heroin has kept him in peace of mind since childhood, and adds that he wants to sign a comprehensive drug-ban treaty?

Neither side is worth trusting far, because both have flouted the law, lied to themselves and each other, meddled in the affairs of small States, and indulged in distorted experience and fact. Neither has the right to demand trustworthy deeds of the other until it demonstrates behaviour worth trusting. Each must enforce existing laws of restraint to which each pays lip-service. Inch by inch we can edge away from the chasm at our feet, not by paper agreement but common sense experience.

Before this vital process can begin it will help if we take a critical look at those who perpetuate and those who oppose nuclear antagonism. When hysteria is dispensed as responsible journalism, we should beware. A leading British commentator, conservatively inclined, greeted Solzhenitsyn's expulsion from the Soviet Union in 1974 with a revealing tirade: 'Rarely in all history has the moral bankruptcy of evil been better demonstrated than in this action . . . the hellhouse that is the Soviet Union for anyone who wishes to remain human . . . the million million daily lies in which the Soviet Union stands . . . a people who live in slavery . . . we who live in freedom. . . .'[1]

For such accusations to be justified, the writer would have to have detailed and extensive personal experience of the Soviet Union, together with a personal record of heavenly purity. Neither is the case. The Soviet Union is a society of almost 250 million people of varying nationalities, living in widely different environments. It is riddled with contradictions and imperfections, and victim of its own feverish fantasies and ours. It is no more 'hell on earth' than anywhere else on earth. This commentator is an influential part of a society whose Government is a past master of secrecy, double-talk and lies. Being an intellectual, he has sympathy for the plight of intellectuals, and rightly so, but he accepts without a hiccup the murderous nuclear rationalizations of his own society and ignores the plight of the British unemployed who prop up his standard of living.

It is more worthwhile to listen to what Russians say about themselves. Andrew Sinyavsky is a writer who left the Soviet Union in 1973, having been imprisoned there from 1966 to 1972. His comments derive from bitter personal experience: 'The Soviet Union is exclusively monological. The state delivers its monologue nonstop, while the citizen's duty is to join in like a chorus. We are the ones who speak, *you* are the ones who say yes. And if you start raising objections, it means you are against relaxing international tensions. It means you are anti-Soviet. In fact you belong in Siberia! . . . Is this sophistry? No, it's just monologue, heavy, pompous monologue, boring everyone to death including those who deliver it. . . .Dissidents are no more than common criminals or lunatics.'[2]

If dissidents ask awkward questions, says Sinyavsky, the State pretends not to hear and accuses the imperialists, but 'nothing can ensure salvation more than staying oneself and behaving naturally – thinking, asking and answering.' Why should we doubt these insights? They are part of a complex truth, one man's thoughtful response to experience. But such criticism merely adds fuel to fantasy if all it does is reinforce Western self-righteousness and hostility. I would like to read to Sinyavsky British Government

[1] Bernard Levin in *The Times*, 27 June 1976.
[2] *The Times*, 17 June 1977.

replies to questions about the legal status of nuclear weapons. The Prime Minister 'pretends not to hear', so does her Minister of Defence, and her Attorney-General and Lord Chancellor. Each answers questions which have not been asked while pretending not to see those asked. Our Prime Ministers, too, have the dreadful power of monologue, heavy, pompous, incapable of surprise or spontaneity.

What of the Soviet tendency to counter political criticism with medicine? We have seen how nuclear rationalization in East and West defies reason, betraying symptoms of insanity, an inability to respond to and assimilate reality. It is inevitable that the high priests of this lunatic cult should regard reason as madness. Law and lunacy are polarized. By sticking closely to the letter of the Soviet law, as most do, Soviet dissidents pose a difficult target for the authorities. Certifying them as mad becomes a 'quick fix', a means of instant disposal. The official mind, addicted to the nightmare of absolute enemies and absolute destruction, imposes drugs in order to confuse the free exercise of reason. So close to rigor mortis is the Soviet nuclear mind in its petrified rationalization of horror that it cannot even tell the truth about the health of the central actor in its play. A leader who is dying is said 'to have a slight cold'.

A British observer of the Soviet Union is harsh in his criticism of this interplay of law and lunacy. He regards the 'asylum procedure' as a 'microcosm of the whole'. Efforts to clarify Soviet policy in this sensitive area, he says, are met with 'constant obstruction of the most elementary kind, failure to answer letters, last-minute cancellations of arrangements ... lying, almost it seems for the sake of lying, unexplained rejection of points long before agreed upon, blank repetition of false statements already refuted and retracted.'[1]

This indicates not cold and confident authority but extreme insecurity, a terror of being found out, exposed, punished, defeated. This does not make official brutality easier to bear, but suggests remedial action which is the opposite of increased military or any other threat. East-West threats have inspired a downward spiral of fear and distrust. The lunatic dimension of nuclear man needs careful, critical understanding, based on humane prin-

[1] Edward Crankshaw in the *Observer*, 5 August 1984.

ciple, not mirror-image hostility. We can be volunteer guinea-pigs of our own treatment.

But we in the West do not make lunatics out of our dissidents, it may be objected. Does that not make us superior? We make monkeys of them instead. Our response tends to be more sophisticated, less crude, as befits a society trailing long, unbroken traditions. We are expert self-deceivers, happy to swallow quack medicine when it suits us, even when we know secretly that it can do no good. We tolerate peace movements, for example, which march and chant and talk and lobby. The authorities huff and puff, charge a few for trivial offences, lock up a few for a week or so. The media records symbolic peace drama on the streets. Books are written and television programmes produced. The Bomb may be hidden in the Soviet Union. Here it is besieged, chattered about.

But what happens? The scene-shifters shift madly but the theatre remains absurd and the play the same. The British body politic swallows its coloured water with ritual ease, like the man who 'shot his brains out on the bedroom floor, and then behaved exactly as before'. I have been part of the peace movement since 1957. It has not moved anywhere. It is tolerated because it is ineffective. Indeed, many if not most of its adherents take part precisely because it is ineffective. Success would involve seismic disturbance to suburban rhythms. Radical change is uncomfortable. A part of the British people, around 20%, are implacably opposed to nuclear weapons, just as they have been since the 1950s.

Pantomimes may be preferable to asylums, but neither is worth boasting about. What is certain, according to my own experience, is that when play-acting ends and effective opposition to nuclear crime begins, the situation becomes as fraught with pressure and suffering as in any other nuclear State. We have seen how deep are the roots of mass destruction in our recent past. They infiltrate every inch of our private and public being. To grapple with this all-pervading plague is hard. It means confronting madness at its source, in each of us. The Soviet Union occupies a wing of the asylum but uses different management techniques.

It was entirely appropriate when, in 1973, the Soviet Union's most celebrated dissident, the nuclear physicist Andrei Sakharov, opened a personal campaign against official use of drugs to control dissent at the time when a world conference on schizophrenia was about to take place in his country. Schizophrenia is one name for our nuclear nightmare, indicating partial loss of identity, crippling fears and fantasies, the hearing of voices, and inability to function successfully in the real world. East and West are as acutely aware of the lunacy as they are blind to the sanity of the other. Our controlling myths are hideously complementary.

Dr Sakharov, the 'father' of the Soviet hydrogen bomb and now its chief critic, endures the converging pressure of Soviet schizophrenia. There are many such 'repented sinners' in both East and West, at scientific, military and political levels. People like Leo Szilard in the United States, who toe the official line for years and suddenly denounce it. Dr Sakharov became a guardian of Soviet integrity, digging out basic principles buried under tons of bureaucratic rubble: 'I would like to believe that the perfectly loyal character of my activity would be understood. In the literal sense, loyalty to the law.... What I most preferred in the way of action you could hardly call a "democratic movement". It was help to certain people who fell victim to injustice, attempts to protest against unjust trials, unjust detention in insane asylums, and further help to families of such people.... In my opinion the authorities should not have any reason for disquiet, and especially none for reprisals. Any reason for disquiet is inside themselves.... Those who occupy the top layer of our society have a sort of separate thinking. They probably can't react differently to the situation than they do.'[1]

Like many Soviet dissidents, Dr Sakharov tends to romanticize the West and its freedoms. He hopes the West will not be fooled by policies of détente which favour the Soviet Union. He warns against the wolf's mind within Grandmother Russia, 'where everything that happens goes on unseen by foreign eyes behind a mask that hides its real face'. He has no experience of what can be and often is disguised by Western extroversion.

Panic-prone authority is afraid of the 'free-thinker', as Dr Sakharov thinks of himself, and when he received the Nobel Prize for peace he was publicly described in the USSR as 'an utterly ignorant person who grovelled before the capitalist order'.[2] Before we congratulate ourselves on our greater tolerance we should ask ourselves what effective Western dissident or peace activist ever won this prize, the legacy of an explosives millionaire. Perhaps

[1] *The Times*, 5 September 1973.
[2] *The Times*, 10 October 1975.

there are none of any account. Henry Kissinger was a prize-winner, a strange angel of peace who patched up temporary Middle East agreements while promoting nuclear deterrence with zeal.

Dr Sakharov, perhaps unconsciously, described the nuclear problem in universal terms: 'Every day I saw the huge material, intellectual and nervous resources of thousands of people being poured into the means of total destruction, something potentially capable of annihilating all human civilization. I noticed that control levers were in the hands of people who, though talented in their own way, were cynical.'[1]

He is indeed what the Nobel Prize citation called him, a 'spokesman for the conscience of mankind'. And so is anyone. Dr Sakharov knows little of the West and speaks little truth about it. Another Russian, Valentin Prussakov, emigrated to the United States and considers Sakharov's opinions of it 'an amazing blend of flippancy and naïveté'. Prussakov quickly shed his own illusions: 'It is useless to hope that the West . . . can cure ills which are alien, unknown and which it barely comprehends. We know that there exist in the USSR many healthy forces in the most varied strata of Soviet society.' It is to these positive forces, he says, that attention should be given, rather than naïve appeals to the West. Freedom and sanity, in other words, begin at home.

Prussakov stuck a sharp pin in the Achilles heel of Western complacency, distributing a leaflet which complained about the editorial policy of the *New York Times*: 'For ten years you have made proclamations about us, the creative intelligentsia, who are not free in the Soviet Union. We are now here before you in your own country. Why do you deny us the right to express our views in the pages of your allegedly free press?'[2]

The Charter 77 manifesto, issued in Czechoslovakia early in 1977, is yet another reflection in the distorting mirror of East-West fantasy. It too seeks to uphold and enforce the law. It refers to the International Covenant on Civil and Political Rights, and the International Covenant on Economic, Social and Cultural Rights, signed by the Czech Government in 1968 and ratified on October 13, 1976.

The Charter complains that many rights are infringed by Government directives which by-pass constitutional and legal

[1] Ibid.
[2] *The Times*, 9 August 1977.

safeguards, a problem of arbitrary power which we have already examined in terms of the British Government and its legal bolt-hole of national security. In Czechoslovakia, too, according to the Charter, 'defence of national security' is the pretext for imposing restrictions on basic rights. Such power 'is governed by no law and, being clandestine, affords the citizen no chance to defend himself.' In cases of political prosecution, the Charter says, 'the investigative and judicial organs violate the rights of those charged', as guaranteed by international covenant.

According to the London *Times*, 'the drafters of the Charter wanted to mobilize pressure on the existing Government to fulfil the legal, constitutional and international obligations to which it formally subscribes. . . . What it does is point out how Czech law is being violated by Czechoslovak authorities.'[1]

There are at least two points worth making about this brave attempt to make law enforcers enforce the law. It is the same problem faced by our own campaign to prohibit all threats and means of mass destruction. The Cold War is a single process of corrupt power, where law is locked in a dungeon, the key kept in a black box marked 'national security'.

Secondly, Charter 77 reflects the positive and negative side of Czech society. The right to strike, for example, is sought, but no mention is made of the right to work, which is part of the same provision of the Covenant on Economic, Social and Cultural Rights. Czechoslovakia honours this right to work with tolerable sincerity whereas the British Government, which ratified the same Covenant in 1976, tolerates a permanent caste of unemployed. It is a difference of experience and perspective which divides us in detail and unites us in principle. The Charter speaks for East and West when it says: 'everyone bears his share of responsibility for the conditions that prevail and accordingly also for the observance of legally enshrined agreements, binding upon all individuals as well as upon governments.'

Crime and punishment in East and West differ on the surface but are remarkably similar in essence, whether at the level of nuclear weapons or drunkenness. We project double-cream and condemn each other's poison, but the reality is skimmed milk. Official gloss may brighten this policy or that, but the people of

[1] *The Times*, 10 February 1977.

these feuding segments of mankind share much the same fears, hopes and needs. A Soviet expert on human rights, Valery Chalidze, deprived of Soviet citizenship because of his documentation of public abuse of authority, has written of the links between political and general crime in the USSR. The result of his studies indicates that criminals in different cultures have much in common. An American professor of law at Harvard University comments on Chalidze's documentation of a Russian underworld, 'whose rules and modus operandi resemble, in remarkable fashion, those of our own underworld'.[1]

In this look at the enemy who could be our ally, and once was, it is worth noting the unconscious energies which animate conflict. With the nineteenth-century advent of collective Marxism and its competing myth of individualism, European identity fragmented not just vertically but horizontally. The Cold War has made the psychological fault lines deeper and wider, to the point of ultimate disintegration.

This chaos has sexual tones. The West acts out, compulsively, an aggressive, unrestrained masculinity. It makes most noise, most things, and is quickest on the draw. Its capacity for invention and production is gargantuan, negated by over-consumption and pollution. It conveys the excitement and uncertainty of a teenager with enormous energy and no self-restraint. It dominates most of the globe yet complains of the slightest competition. It boasts of democratic individualism, yet its citizens are mostly conformist at heart, controlled by material and political fashion. Its military mind is that of the cowboy, with reality shrunk to fit the myth.

The East, by contrast, is equally fantastic, but feminine in character. Mother Russia embraces, geographically and psychologically. Far from charging off all over the globe, like Britain, France and the United States, the Soviet Union has suffered brutal invasion. Cautious, it boasts of collective family ties and privileges. Betrayal of family unity is treason. The curious, creative individual who transcends this family bond is a traitor, someone to be silenced or expelled. Secrecy and suspicion are a feature of unconscious feminine energy, a protection against what is conscious and new.

These masculine and feminine traits of the Cold War are not normal, but regressive, inflated, dangerous. They have flourished

[1] *Guardian*, 11 September 1977

on the countless murdered dead of two world wars. Instead of confronting the dreadful, chilling reality of our violence we have run away from it, seeking a new identity in the pantomime costumes of Good and Evil. The truth is that we share with our chosen enemy crimes of gruesome proportions, which await attention. Before we can uphold and enforce laws which protect civilization we must recognize the killer in our mirror. Only then can we look our enemy in the face, as fellow convict and ally.

In the last resort, to use the jargon of our leaders, the relation between law and enemy is very simple. The mothers, children, elderly, mad, sick and wounded of Moscow and throughout the East have been illegally sentenced to death by our nuclear missiles, the sentence suspended 'at Her Majesty's pleasure', for as long as our leaders decree. The bonfire on which they and the world may be sacrificed is laid, checked daily for faults, its minders vetted for signs of insanity. It can explode at the touch of a match.

The same is true the other way round. The Cold War and its criminality are like the Polish joke: 'What is the difference between communism and capitalism? Answer: under the first it is exploitation of man by man, but under the second it is the other way round.' We have no enemy worth a single missile, but must convince those frozen in nuclear winter. We have to penetrate the make-up of our nuclear clowns. In the West the disguise lies on the surface, in careless rhetoric, extravagant action and aggressive consumption. Behind this strident face lies a leaden sadness and sense of loss. The Soviet bloc, introverted by nature, with a wooden official face, uses cosmetic ideology. It too nurses a thousand wounds. While this suicidal masquerade persists there can be no law enforcement based on universal humanitarian principles. We must call their bluff, and ours, before it is too late. It was a black American who sang: 'you can't get to heaven in powder and paint, 'cos the Lord don't like you as you ain't!' This should hang above the desks of the Kremlin and White House. Superiority is a mug's game.

Chapter Twelve

The Citizen's Tale

'The human being, the natural person has never had so little
honour from life and from himself as today. He is imprisoned
in theories, in petrified religions, and above all, strangled in
his own lack of self-awareness'
– Laurens van der Post

'You are dealing with an evil streak in human nature – and evil
men are just as good at using the latest technology and placing
bombs at the most difficult times'
– Margaret Thatcher, Prime Minister, 1984

'What we're facing at the moment is not essentially a problem
of law – it's a problem of order – enforcing the law'
– Leon Brittan, British Home Secretary, 1984

We have looked at the professional life of the nuclear citizen, in key
roles, and we have seen how nuclear terror has inspired deceit. The
modern nuclear landscape is a shadowy place where phantoms
loom and fade, alarm and mock. The hard floor of civilized life,
law, is sunk in a marsh of pretence. Those whose special responsibility is to uphold the law do so with skill, except when basic issues
of survival are involved. Teachers of law, lawyers and judges are
guilty of criminal negligence where national security and mass
destruction are concerned. They distract attention from this
scandal by shining a harsh light of righteous morality and law
elsewhere, on the young, the poor, the brutal, the sexually deviant.

The citizen as soldier, according to the evidence, wields
immense destructive power with technical competence, yet lacks
even the most marginal grasp of the responsibilities imposed by
humanitarian law. The State robs him of identity, blinds him to the
law, and offers in return patriotic mob loyalty based on pride and
prejudice. The great soldiers of the past, whatever their defects,
were unique individuals capable of thought and responsibility.
The citizen soldier of the nuclear State is no more than a blank
agent of extermination.

The citizen as politician and leader has proved to be a high priest of nuclear idolatry. He has polluted the world with counterfeit logic, infecting its furthest corners. We have seen how this arrogance contorts experience, translating natural fact into nightmare horror. And all the while, the nuclear politician lulls us with sentimental invocations of high principle. One leader tells us of an 'evil empire', as if life is a child's fable. Another tells us: 'I am in politics because of the conflict between good and evil and believe that, in the end, good will triumph.'[1] Good and evil swim as twins in our bloodstream, yet this inane caricature is greeted, not with ribald laughter but dumb acceptance.

There can be no clear map of a nightmare, only fleeting glimpses of its nature and extent. We have seen through the deceptive clarity of nuclear logic, the rationalizations of NATO and Warsaw Pact leaders who promote their freedom-loving missiles while out-Pilating Pilate in washing hands of failure. They evade the law by dispensing fake morality, the notion that peace can be bought by extreme terror. This prettified gangster logic rules our lives in the name of democracy, individualism and the brotherhood of man.

To restore minimum law requires much more than rational analysis. Madness is not cured by description. Law and reason must enter hand in hand the haunted kingdom of national security, making use of what little is sane to counter what is mad. Madness, as we can see by looking at the present and likely effect of nuclear weapons, has evil consequences, but its origins are natural enough. It is as natural to hate as to love, but when hatred is embraced by millions, glutted with funds and weaponry, it becomes lunacy writ large.

We must learn to feel our way in the dark, testing each foot and finger-hold with care, never assuming that what we find is more than a grain of truth. What we are searching for is not the Holy Grail but something very simple, ordinary and basic, enforcement of the law against mass murder and its threat. For a drunkard to stand upright, every last ounce of co-ordination is needed. That is our challenge too. The first aim is not to love our neighbour or the world, but admit their right to live.

Before we can approach this problem we need to abandon the illusion that nuclear mythology is responsive to reason alone. To

[1] Margaret Thatcher in the *Daily Telegraph*, 18 September 1984.

evade the irrational, neurotic basis of nuclear logic is to indulge in frivolous soul-baring designed to gain the rewards of virtue without paying its cost. Adulterated medicine is more likely to kill than cure. Graham Greene's celebrated story of *The Third Man*, set in the ruins of post-war Vienna, describes the terrible effect of adulterated penicillin sold on the black market.

The Christian churches offer one such weak response. The overwhelming effect of the Christian churches on nuclear policy has been as collusive as the pilot fish with its shark. The church needs a tame devil to tut-tut over, as the medieval priest needed his baron. Each has a vested interest in the other. The Christian church likes to think it has the devil cornered, not loose at the heart of power and dancing on the altar.

Britain's most influential churchman is the Archbishop of Canterbury. I wrote to the then Archbishop, in the early sixties, asking why he did not do more to oppose nuclear weapons. Back came a long reply, courteous and convoluted. Yes, nuclear weapons are an abomination and all Christians should oppose them, but unfortunately, as things are, it could be folly to remove them from our part of the military balance of power, and so on. Two steps forward, two back. Stalemate. Was it the shadow of the devil, looming behind the Archbishop's rationalization of the status quo?

The tradition is maintained. Today's Archbishop, Dr Runcie, speaks out: 'I believe the Church has an absolute duty to point to the moral and spiritual dimension in political issues, to encourage thought and to provoke questions. There is need, pressing need, for a mature political debate. . . .'[1]

Fine. But when it came to the Falklands conflict in 1982, the Archbishop showed us that sophistry is alive and well. First the merciful gesture, then the smooth retraction. 'Cover your ass,' as the American soldier in Vietnam would put it. The Archbishop's performance is a classic of its kind: 'War is always an evil, even though it may be the lesser of two evils, and Wilfred Owen's sense of the "pity of war" must always be powerfully present. . . . The recent losses to both sides are sickening and they make it all the more important to remember that certain vital principles are at stake. In the House of Lords on April 14 I said, "the need to ensure that nations act within international law is the bulwark on which

---

[1] *Daily Telegraph*, 12 October 1984.

the future peace of the world depends. We would be gravely in breach of our moral duty if this country had not reacted as it did in this matter".'[1]

The Archbishop then quoted with approval the sixteenth-century Spanish theologian, Francisco de Vittoria: '"If some one city cannot be recaptured without greater evils befalling the state, such as the devastation of many cities, great slaughter of human beings, provocation of princes, occasion for new wars, it is indubitable that the prince is bound rather to give up his own rights and abstain from war".' ... 'Christians', went on the Archbishop, 'have the responsibility to urge that the force deployed must be subservient and proportionate to clearly defined and morally justifiable political objectives.... The purpose of using force is to achieve a just political settlement, not a military victory. When conflict breaks out, military logic tends to dictate the course of events.... We have already paid a high price, the greatest part of which may still have to come in a settlement in which we will not obtain all we want. That is very different from saying we should ignore the interests of the islanders or abandon the principles we set out to defend, that territorial claims should be settled by international law, not by armed force. We cannot accept the position that no principle is worth the shedding of blood. That theory would lead to a world with even greater injustice and with even less stability.'[2]

These comments apply to a limited conflict with conventional weapons, in which few civilians suffered directly. The surface plausibility of his words mask underlying contradictions. He says nothing with which the British Government would disagree. Governments love to play one 'evil' off against another because it gives them wide latitude: we regret the suffering we cause, but without it things would be much worse.

The reference to international law is misleading. According to the binding United Nations Charter, the use of force, even in self-defence, must be sanctioned by the Security Council. The latter made it clear to both sides in the conflict that each must withdraw and negotiate. Argentina refused. So did Britain. There are plenty of political excuses, most of which would point to the weakness of the United Nations and its peace-keeping machinery.

[1] *The Times*, 8 May 1982.
[2] Ibid.

This problem, as the Archbishop must know, owes much to British foot-dragging over the years. If the Archbishop genuinely believes that international law is the 'bulwark on which the future peace of the world depends', he would long ago have made it clear that nuclear deterrence is a conspiracy to commit mass murder. He has done no such thing.

Francisco de Vittoria's advice is wise and right, but its application to the Falklands is dubious. What 'clearly defined and morally justifiable objectives' had the British Government in mind? Military violence won back this maverick colony with its village population, at the human cost of around one life per four inhabitants. If this is suitably 'proportionate' it would imply that Britain would be right to go to war in its own defence at the cost of tens of millions of dead and far more wounded. The financial proportionality is equally fanciful, with the cost of subsidizing and defending the islanders at levels which would make millionaires of them all if the cash were to be put in their pockets instead of into airports and weapons.

The military victory was won, yet a 'just political settlement' is as far away as ever. A huge military investment in blood and money must be justified, tying the hands and closing the minds of negotiators. How will a British Government ever justify to the widows of the British dead a settlement involving UN trusteeship and an Argentinian presence? It shows no sign of even trying. Violence, in defiance of the law, has won a victory, not for universal principle but for outdated national conservatism.

This example of religious sophistry is relevant to our search because it reveals such a fundamentally weak grasp of principle. A principle is universal in meaning or it is nothing. A principle exalting the value of life cannot be upheld by killing people. But the latter can be justified by a principle of 'might is right'. Hitler believed in such a principle. The Archbishop believes that some principles are worth the 'shedding of blood' but he does not make clear what these are. He implies that we were right to attack the Argentinians in order to make them 'act within the law'. Bloodshed is thus invoked in the cause of law. The principle involved was therefore not the value of life. It was not the principle of self-determination, because the Falkland islanders have never had this right. They do not even have a member in the British parliament. So the only principle left intact is that of British sovereignty, a principle of nationalism which clashes inevitably with other nationalist principles.

The Church of England had nothing to say about this localized conflict of national interest except that British interests must prevail, even at the cost of bloodshed. The Falklands conflict, in other words, was an eccentric outpost of 'national security', violence in the cause of national prejudice. The law invoked by the Archbishop and his Prime Minister was distorted by selective interpretation. When the law coincided with national self-interest it was obeyed. When it did not it was disregarded.

This confused soup of religious precept, law and national interest is apparent in the Archbishop's response to war in its world dimension. He says of the Second World War: 'We fought not against a people – the Germans – but against what the Bible calls "spiritual wickedness in high places".'[1] Yet we have seen how millions of German people were killed, and how spiritual wickedness in high places is not a dragon to be struck dead but a virus affecting us all. Spiritual wickedness has gone forth and multiplied, cheeky enough to perch on even an Archbishop's shoulder. His rationale of war would justify a world war with nuclear weapons in which millions would die and the world itself lie stricken, on the grounds that extermination is 'not against the people' but against wickedness in the Kremlin.

The contradictions within the Archbishop's mind were exposed by a reader of *The Times* who asked: 'What has become of the Lambeth Conference resolution that "war as a method of settling international disputes is incompatible with the teaching and example of our Lord Jesus Christ", and its declaration that "the use of the modern technology of war is the most striking example of corporate sin and the prostitution of God's gifts"?'[2]

Fine examples are seldom what they seem. The Archbishop's view of violence and the law is further revealed in a House of Lords debate on violent crime. He, the Lord Chief Justice and the Lord Chancellor, among others, managed to debate this issue without a single mention of the nuclear issue and its enveloping violence. Let the Archbishop speak for himself: 'the level of violence in our cities has now reached quite terrifying proportions and sometimes takes extraordinarily cruel and perverted forms. . . . The threat of vio-

[1] *Guardian*, 4 June 1984.
[2] *The Times*, 29 May 1982.

lence is as corrosive of society as violence itself. . . . The prevention of violence is closely linked to family life. All too often in Britain there is not so much an absence of parental love as failure of parental nerve. . . . Many schools are the breeding ground for precisely the kind of mindless, tribal violence which it should be their task to outlaw.'[1]

Once again, fine principles end up as disconnected as chopped spaghetti. By failing to relate domestic national violence to the threat of nuclear extinction, a major part of the equation is excluded. If violence and its threat are corrosive of society when used by teenage thugs, why is not the same true of threats of mass destruction and their political and civic sponsors? Neither school nor family operate in a vacuum. Each is surrounded and pervaded by the paralyzing logic of the Archbishop and his like, which maintains that violence is entirely wrong, except when administered in the national interest.

The Archbishop is not cited because he is peculiarly irrational. His reasoning is typical of many Christian citizens of the nuclear State. The Church of England, as a whole, has failed to confront the personal and political menace of nuclear weapons. In 1983, the Church of England Synod refused to denounce nuclear weapons but supported by a wide margin a resolution banning any 'first use' of nuclear weapons. The Archbishop's influence was a vital factor in this decision. His line of reasoning, again, was almost entirely in line with that of the Government. The core of the problem, its neurotic essence, was ignored in favour of political rationalization: 'I do not believe that unilateral measures . . . will in fact have the effect of "getting multilateral reductions moving."'[2]

He questioned the morality of any renunciation of British nuclear weapons which might result in reliance on American nuclear protection. The church 'lead' turns out to be more of a slow handclap. 'No first use' is a dubious political tactic which has nothing to do with morality or law, except that it tends to confirm an Old Testament 'eye for an eye' attitude. Why is a second, or third, or fourth or any other use of mass murder morally worthy? The Archbishop and his flock know that the British Government promotes a policy of 'no first use of any weapon', meaning that it will never use weapons first. The Church of England, after all its

1 *The Times*, 16 November 1983.
2 *Guardian*, 11 February 1983.

anguished debate on the bomb, brings forth a mouse of a resolution, its 'native hue' very much 'sicklied o'er with the pale cast of thought'.

Such is the ruined character of religious thinking in the nuclear era that even this feeble gesture is opposed by many conservatives. The Bishop of London preserves the sanctimonious values of the Victorian headmaster fingering his cane above the prostrate evil-doer: 'In a fallen world there must be authority which is backed by the ultimate sanction of force if nations and people are to be dissuaded or prevented from acting in ways which are both morally wrong and injurious to their fellow human beings.'[1]

This assertion, too, when applied to real-life situations, crumbles. If and when a Government commits 'morally wrong' acts against some of its people, as for example, in Poland or Turkey, is the ultimate sanction of force to be applied? By whom, and how? What if a British Government compels a part of its people to live without work, at poverty level? Is that morally injurious? If so, who applies what sanction? The Bishop's logic is that of a blind guide whose directions lead over the cliff.

His line of reasoning is shared by a professor of Moral and Social Theology: 'There is a form of nuclear deterrence which is unacceptable – mutually assured destruction. But there is a form of nuclear deterrence which is acceptable, while being highly undesirable – limited, balanced deterrence.'[2]

If the latter form of deterrence breaks down, how is mutual assured destruction to be avoided? Does the professor imagine that nuclear weapons become magically selective and limited in effect because they are described in prudent language.

As if to confirm, numerically, schizophrenic church thinking on nuclear weapons, a television report found that twenty-four out of the Church Synod's fifty-two bishops opposed any use of nuclear weapons. Those who oppose all nuclear weapons tend to do so on the limited ground of reason, ignoring the sinister neurosis which spawns them. Such opposition is ineffective. This failure is often disguised by a dubious supposition that both parties to the agreement are 'equally horrified at the thought of killing millions of innocent people and irradiating the global environment'.[3] This is

[1] *Sunday Telegraph*, 9 October 1983.
[2] Ibid. Rev. K. Ward.
[3] Bishop of Salisbury in the *Observer*, 7 November 1982.

sentimental and false. If two people want to keep Soviet forces out of Britain, one by reason and the other by threat of mutual annihilation, how can it be said that both are 'equally horrified' at the thought of killing millions? It is such sentimentality which prevents the issue being seen in terms of legality and crime. Crime is not a valid option.

The convergence of church and government policy on nuclear weapons is made evident by no less a figure than a Minister of Defence, writing to a fellow MP, in which 'he adds that his own thinking comes out at about the same point as the Archbishop of Canterbury's rejecting unilateral disarmament as right or responsible.'[1] Far from dispersing the fear of annihilation the effect of such thinking promotes confusion and apathy in the name of Christianity.

The Roman Catholic Church clings no less ambiguously to the horns of this nuclear dilemma than its sisters. Centuries of mental dexterity are brought to bear on the problem. The Jesuit principal of a London college appears to damn nuclear deterrence. He cites the Second Vatican Council and its call for 'an entirely new attitude' to war; he writes of the 'grotesque terms' of mega-death, declaring that 'it makes sound moral sense to take steps now to ensure that what we should not wish to do we shall not be able to do'. He refers to 'the grim reality of an unconditional willingness to obey orders', adding the Biblical warning: 'Without vision the people perish.' Then comes the deprecating retreat: 'And yet . . . the collective moral choices open to any society are arguably different in character from individual personal decisions, and the clean prophetic stance of nuclear pacifism which may be admirable in an individual may be a social impossibility.'[2]

Certainties are transformed suddenly, at the point of choice, into crippling doubt. The dog which barks on a lead is often silent when free. British Catholic priests, according to one report, 'gave their "total commitment" to unilateral nuclear disarmament but failed narrowly to muster enough votes for their condemnation of nuclear arms to go to the Bishops' Conference in November'. American Catholic bishops want a 'nuclear freeze' but their French brothers 'have given worried and heavily qualified approval for nuclear deterrence'. They produced a statement that nuclear deterrence is

[1] *The Times*, 23 February 1981.
[2] J. Mahoney, S. J., in *The Times*, 21 February 1981.

'morally acceptable for the time being', but 'actual use' involves complex moral problems.

It is the leading British Catholic, Cardinal Hume, who reveals in all its embarrassing detail the convolutions of Catholic thought on this issue:

> Although nothing could ever justify the use of nuclear arms as weapons of massive and indiscriminate slaughter, yet to abandon them without adequate safeguards may help to de-stabilize the existing situation and dramatically increase the risk of nuclear blackmail.... In current conditions 'deterrence' based on balance, certainly not as an end in itself, but as a stage on the way towards a progressive disarmament, can still be judged morally acceptable.... This view recognizes that, because of the world situation, deterrence may be acceptable as the lesser of two evils, without in any way regarding it as good in itself. Furthermore, this view can be held even by those who reject the morality of nuclear deterrence. It constitutes an acknowledgment that even a morally flawed defence policy cannot simply be dismantled immediately and without reference to the response of potential enemies. To retain moral credibility, however, there must be a firm and effective intention to extricate ourselves from the present fearful situation as quickly as possible.[1]

The Cardinal reasons more like a fly in treacle than Jesus Christ. He admits that his 'may in some respects be an untidy view, risky and provisional'; hardly the inspirational conviction of Christ. Then the Cardinal offers comfort to servicemen who manage the deterrent: 'since the purpose and intention of deterrence is to avoid war and keep the peace service personnel can be rightly commended as custodians of the security and freedom of their fellow countrymen and as contributors to the maintenance of peace. None the less, they too face grave moral issues which they themselves do not ignore ... deterrence has to be seen clearly as a means of preventing war and not waging it. If it fails and the missiles are launched, then we shall have moved into a new situation. And those concerned will have to bear a heavy responsibility.'

The end justifies the means, in other words, unless it is a dead

[1] *The Times*, 17 November 1983.

end, in which case we will be with the Cardinal, in 'a new situation'. All that differentiates this rationalization of deterrence from that of governments is its tortuous solemnity, as if sheer weight of sorrow somehow adds up to religious insight. The Cardinal has a blessing for all concerned in the nuclear apocalypse, the priest who wrestles mightily, the government leader who does his best, and the missile operator who wants peace.

But he has nothing to say about the hard, simple fact that existing laws prohibit any form of mass destruction, blessed or unblessed, and that all who collude with violating these laws commit a crime. In fact the Cardinal turns the law on its head, when he declares about everybody's 'right to . . . conscientious beliefs': 'I would judge that this does not give us the right seriously to defy the law. . . . We must have due regard for democratic processes and for the institutions of a free society.'[1]

This leads to the conclusion that breaking laws of 'obstruction' or 'breach of the peace' is worse than breaking those which forbid mass murder and environmental destruction. The latter have already been defied.

The Jewish faith has done no more than the Christian, so far, to inspire effective opposition to nuclear lawlessness. The British Chief Rabbi is reported to have defended the deterrent with scathing loyalty: 'Unilateral nuclear disarmament was hypocritical, immoral and futile. . . . It was just as offensive to Jewish moral teachings to leave oneself defenceless as to take innocent life.'[2]

The nuclear deterrent is well served by its religious pall-bearers. Quick and sure when it comes to condemnation of sexual and financial crime, their rationalization of nuclear security shows that religion suffers the same sensory blight as afflicts the rest of nuclear society.

What is the ordinary citizen to make of all this? To follow church advice is to wander deeper into the labyrinth of suspended annihilation. A search through the cathedrals and synagogues for inspiration leaves us where we were, in the dark. It seems that none of the leading institutions of nuclear society is capable of penetrating to the core of this problem. Leadership has failed and is failing. In place of insight, vision and firm commitment to humanitarian

[1] Ibid.
[2] *The Times*, 15 December 1982.

principle, there is a worried patching of habit and prejudice. There is plenty of evidence of nuclear neurosis, but little sign of its cure.

At such a moment of institutional decay hope must rest with personal integrity, the capacity of each citizen to reach down into the well of private experience for truth. One by one, the pillars of established society have betrayed their trust. Even those who educate the young dispense 'objective' truth while colluding with corrupt power. Oxford and Cambridge are among the worst, claiming to represent the best. The not very well hidden curriculum of both is a butler's relation to Government, deferential to the mistress, superior to the maid.

'Yes,' said an Oxford professor of sociology to a journalist, 'there is a very close symbiosis between Oxford and the Establishment. I don't say that in a pejorative way either.'[1] Like all good butlers, Oxford and Cambridge seldom raise their voice or show emotion. At least, not in public. According to Oxford's professor of natural philosophy, Brooke Benjamin, there is a 'tremendous premium on control and poise'. A history lecturer said he could not possibly wear his Campaign for Nuclear Disarmament badge in the Common Room: 'the ridicule would be unbearable'. The same man, Christopher Haigh, said, 'There's an amazing reverence for authority, a reverence for the monarchy, a reverence for the Prime Minister, whoever's in power, and a feeling that, if the Cabinet have made a decision it's probably right.' An undergraduate at Oxford said he was being shown how to 'join the establishment'.[2]

Oxford and Cambridge are still at the apex of Britain's upstairs, downstairs culture. In relation to the nuclear threat and its profound implications they are no more use than the head waiter when the *Titanic* sank. Their skills are ornamental, carefully segregated from creative feeling, thought, insight. Expert at trivia, they incite trivial activity. What is serious is embarrassing. The heavenly twins of establishment education teach knowledge and betray learning.

These ancient, comforting institutions have divided reality into what can be admitted and what must be denied, destroying the universality of the university. Within their limited reality they are expert and well behaved. Ouside it, they inspire confusion. Their influence in the nuclear era is destructive by omission. They help to

[1] *Sunday Telegraph*, 4 March 1984.
[2] Ibid.

invent nuclear weapons but do nothing to stop their use. By idolizing the rational at the expense of the unconscious, they make an ornament of life, highly polished to reflect cleverness. Humour is for conversation and ridicule for action.

By their fruits we know them. Strong in science and satire during post-war years, their contribution to cultural and political life has been mediocre and predictable. They feed British Governments with the basic ingredients of Cold War tension, ministers who inflate our virtue and justify weapons of mass destruction. They educate the judges who hammer all except nuclear criminals, and train lawyers who serve them.

Where have we seen these characteristics before? Oxford and Cambridge, and the educational pyramid on which they rest, are sophisticated descendants of the Nazi concentration camp guard with his dual nature, part citizen, part criminal. How appropriate, then, that an Oxford don should describe this problem of dual personality and betrayal so well: 'in Hitler's court Albert Speer was morally and intellectually alone. He had the capacity to understand the forces of politics, and the courage to resist the master whom all others have declared irresistible. As an administrator he was undoubtedly a genius.... His ambitions were peaceful and constructive.... Nevertheless, in a political sense, Speer is the real criminal of Nazi Germany; for he, more than any other, represented that fatal philosophy which has made havoc of Germany and nearly shipwrecked the world.... He heard their outrageous orders and understood their fantastic ambitions, but he did nothing. Supposing politics to be irrelevant, he turned aside ... while the logical consequences of government by mad men emerged. Ultimately, when their emergence involved the ruin of all his work, Speer accepted the consequences and acted. Then it was too late; Germany had been destroyed.'[1]

This portrait, like the Nuremberg Trial itself, is too narrowly focused. Speer died but the problem lives on, grotesquely magnified. The author was not describing a stranger, but an Oxford *doppelgänger* who would re-emerge many years later, in 1983, when the same author pronounced fake 'Hitler diaries' to be genuine. The High Table mighty had bumped into a mirror. The leaders of British education have heard the 'outrageous orders' of nuclear

[1] Trevor-Roper, op. cit.

retaliation, our last resort. They understand from personal experience the 'fantastic ambitions' which motivate nuclear 'government by madmen'. Yet they do nothing to expose the counterfeit law and logic which fuel this final solution. Perhaps because they fear 'the ridicule would be unbearable'.

At the other end of the educational scale, the pressure to conform and bow down to established authority is much the same, if cruder. The imposition of discipline on 'difficult' school children often echoes the psychological manipulation at some Soviet hospitals. According to a British sociology lecturer, widespread use of drugs and therapy in the United States to manage hyper-active children has spread to Britain. By 1950, 587 full-time British pupils were classified as maladjusted. By 1970 the total was over 5,000, rising to almost 14,000 two years later. He notes that diagnosis has 'nothing to do with disease and everything to do with deviance'. Hyper-activity 'violates important school norms about paying attention to teacher, obeying teacher, and being responsive to teacher's wishes, instructions or commands . . . not answering teacher back or threatening or actually assaulting teacher . . . being orderly and disciplined.'[1]

It is in the classroom that the Nuremberg Principles are first broken. A child taught to obey rather than question authority will find it difficult later, if not impossible, to challenge criminal government policies. The nuclear dimension is either disregarded in schools and colleges or presented as a rational option. The first compounds the sinister mystery of annihilation and the second gives it a veneer of legitimacy. Both seek to hide from the child the lunatic reality of nuclear threats. Neither cannibalism nor child-sacrifice are suitable subjects for optional debate. It is time nuclear weapons went into the same trash can. Every child knows that nuclear weapons are a million times more dangerous than mugging or football hooliganism, yet many adults justify the former and denounce the latter.

The mass media compound this problem by a similar process of denial and distortion. As a veteran observer of Cold War dynamics, George Kennan, puts it: 'so extensively has public understanding and official habit been debauched'[2] by nuclear orthodoxy that discriminating thought has become almost impossible. Even the

[1] *The Times*, 1 December 1977.
[2] George Kennan, op. cit.

so-called quality press presents the nuclear issue through a lens of official legitimacy. Always it is the surface of the problem which is fought over, never the core.

The BBC is adept at this technique of avoiding a problem by pretending to confront it. After years of protecting its audience and itself from the gruesome implications of nuclear war, the BBC suffered a death-bed conversion and provided a three-part blitz on the issue in September 1984. A two-hour television portrayal of a nuclear attack on the city of Sheffield and its aftermath was followed next day by two consecutive programmes. The first described the possible effects of a 'nuclear winter', following a major war, and the second was a studio discusssion of these possibilities. The BBC followed the lead of American television, which had shown *The Day After* in 1983.

These programmes and the public response illustrate the distance between us and a post-nuclear security. They did well what they intended to do. An imaginative effort was made to approximate to the horrific impact of nuclear war and its long-term effects. A studio full of experts (all of them male) then discussed it all with polite concern. We were left in no doubt that nuclear war would be the end of civilized life and perhaps of all life.

The British citizen's response was either 'so what?', we all know nuclear war will be the end of everything, or gratitude that at last the BBC had dared to face reality. But the absence of two vital elements in these programmes went unremarked. Nuclear war was presented as the terrible breakdown of nuclear deterrence, but there was no focus of responsibility. It was like a visitation of the plague or a car accident multiplied a million-fold. In the words of the Nuremberg Trial, 'there was crime but no criminals'. There was not the faintest hint of recognition that weapons and policies designed to kill millions violate each day the most basic laws. Such recognition would identify a trail of guilt which leads to our political leaders, and to each one of us. It would identify crime in the hatching, in the mind of our nuclear Macbeth. Horror, especially nuclear horror, becomes morbid entertainment when deprived of responsibility. It becomes not painful recognition but artful disguise, the opposite of what is intended.

Compounding this problem was the total absence of advice about how to prevent such a catastrophe. What was the viewing citizen supposed to do after watching these dramatized disasters and discussions? The war began in the Middle East and, once the fuse was lit, the final bang became inevitable. The viewer, it was made obvious, was a voyeur at his own funeral pyre, not an agent of his own escape. Even the discussions reinforced helplessness, by providing a genteel cock-fight among experts. If knowing as much as they did failed to inspire remedial action, what hope can there be for the suburban citizen depressed in an armchair? Underlying this problem of remoteness is a deeper paralysis, the apathy of the weak confronted by crisis. The bigger the catastrophe, the more crippling the despair.

Perhaps the earlier anxiety of the BBC was no worse than this dramatised impotence. In 1981 the Director-General defended the ban then in force on the showing of *The War Game*, made in 1965, by invoking the frailty of elderly viewers and children: 'I do not believe that any broadcasting authority could take the responsibility for what the effect might be on these people, particularly those three million licence payers who we know live alone.'[1]

As usual, patronizing protection reveals more about the protector than the protected. There was no epidemic of suicides among pensioners after the 1984 showing. The nuclear citizen will conclude that the media prefer now to serve nuclear horror piping hot but stripped of the two essential vitamins, law and positive action. The media's nuclear concern is an integral part of the generalized addiction to unreality which we have examined in some detail. The fraud is often blatant but sometimes cleverly disguised, as when *The Times* newspaper lamented the Falklands 'crime' of the Argentinians. At first sight the paper's editorial seems impeccable:

Every crime has a motive and, therefore, an explanation. . . . An explanation for a crime should not become its excuse. We still hold individuals to be responsible for their actions and to have a sense of that responsibility. That is the basis of all morality in society. However, in the international community, a sense of morality is less demanding. The collective qualities of a society . . . put a premium on mediocrity. Man in the mass becomes anonymous and, therefore, irresponsible. That is what has happened today in regard to Argentina's responsibilities for the international crime of invading the Falklands. . . . No crime can be an isolated event. It begets indignation, guilt and hatred. The

[1] Sir Ian Trethowan in *The Times*, 13 March 1981.

wickedness of others becomes our own wickedness because it kindles something evil in ourselves. . . . It is not magnanimous to connive at an individual's act of self-deceit, so why should it be so at the international level? . . . It would be no service for Britain . . . to encourage the Junta and the Argentine people to behave as though breaking international law was something which could be dismissed lightly.[1]

As with a house groggy with dry-rot but still standing, the timbers look fine until poked. *The Times*'s sermon is soft-centred. Opposition to crime is indeed a service to the criminal, but opposition can take many forms, not all of them blood-stained. It was the bloody opposition of the British to Argentinian crime which begat further hatred and waste, kindling evil in all concerned, much of it wrapped in 'legality'. Equally if not more important, *The Times* does not apply its wisdom to the forbidden territory of the nuclear idol, where anonymous irresponsibility and deceit are the law and order of the day.

Our media are a daily reminder of our immature failure to digest our own evil. Their absurdity is a reflection of our own. They depend on us. The ultimate stage, perhaps, of this pantomime moralizing was expressed by a British daily paper, following a terrorist bomb in central London: 'Hell surely does exist, visibly created every day by the violence and pride and wilfulness of men . . . . We have become almost hardened to such outrages, but this one had seemed, because of the season at which it was committed, peculiarly horrible. It was, in Mrs Thatcher's words, "crime against Christmas". . . . We have all somehow understood that last Saturday's outrage was a crime not only against humanity but against God: it was a crime against the Christ Child.'[2]

Here again is the split morality of the concentration camp guard. Violence is wicked unless committed in the name of collective power. If war breaks out with the Soviet Union and Christmas Day became humanity's last day, is that a 'crime against the Christ Child', or just 'a new situation'? How can we escape such morbid sentimentality?

One by one we have examined the self-appointed guardians of society and each one has turned out to be in pawn to the nuclear

[1] *The Times*, 9 June 1982.
[2] *Daily Telegraph*, 23 December 1983.

outlaw. We can sympathize with Little Red Riding Hood. There is nothing so unnerving as stooping to kiss a sweet old grandmother and finding a wolf. (The British Prime Minister, Margaret Thatcher, once said during a Channel 4 interview, 'I would like to be the nation's grandmother.') It is we who have helped to hide the animal, in the exclusion zone of our minds. It is a daunting recognition. Once made, there can be no escape. But it offers us a hint of post-nuclear sanity. Knowing what the crime is, and where it is, we can begin to arrest its development. Somehow, we have to reclaim this lost ground in ourselves and our nuclear world. We have to find and administer the cure for our own profound, crippling neurosis.

Before we can organize a world-wide campaign to arrest the idol at the core of nuclear crime we must explore an inner madness, to discover how we collude with neurosis, and how it colludes with us. We know the false escape routes. There is no person or parental institution out there to carry the main responsibility. It is alarming but exciting to feel at the centre of life's stage, with a need for allies but not leaders. If there is to be a post-nuclear sanity, founded on a minimum humanitarian respect and law, this is where it will begin.

We are not alone in hell. It is crowded. Let us learn how our prison is constructed, so that we can take it apart. Why not start with Vietnam and its continuing contribution to personal madness and guilt? We have already seen some of it, at a distance, but an American, Emily Mann, has helped to bring the problem closer. She dramatized the post-Vietnam hell of one American veteran, culled from 100 hours of taped discussion with him, his wife and mistress. He is an alcoholic, violent and alienated from his own experience, which includes a war experience of wanton murder which he cannot explain. The wife is on drugs, lonely and frightened. The mistress stands aloof but comments on the close link between war and sex. War is a form of sexual rampage which destroys the capacity to relate because it is impersonal.[1]

These people have no key to their hell, but their torment is real, the reverse side of the counterfeit myth of freedom sold by a cynical leadership. American weapons are aimed at the Soviet Union but the real threat to that leadership lies in those who have been defrauded of identity and hope. Nuclear violence as national

[1] Emily Mann, *Still Life*.

security is not an abstract crime but as immediate as the air we breathe. Overthrow of the tyrant requires commitment to a whole life in a whole world.

It is not just the war veteran as citizen who feels the darkness. American violence infiltrates its double act into the lives of the most innocent-seeming citizen. Ken Bianchi became its victim, and he in turn victimized others, ten of them, all female and all murdered. Even the local police in a Los Angeles suburb found Bianchi handsome, helpful and charming. But he was only half what he seemed. After his arrest on a charge of murder, hypnosis exposed a dual nature. Calling himself Steve Walker, Ken Bianchi adopted a callous, macho pose: 'This broad I killed. Killing any fucking body doesn't matter to me.' Police do not believe in fairies and went searching for a real Steve Walker. They found him, a psychiatry graduate whose name and records had been stolen by Ken Bianchi. Fifteen text books on psychiatry were found in the latter's apartment.

Ken Bianchi was found to have taken part in a prostitution racket. A detective described him as 'what we call a snivelling little pooh butt. Say the girls were afraid of snakes, he put snakes on them to make sure they brought the money back'. Eventually it was judged that he had faked multiple personality and was sentenced to life imprisonment. He wept throughout the final court appearance but 'within three minutes of leaving the courtroom, he was feet on the table, smoking and laughing', according to the police.

Ken Bianchi's story began in Hollywood, where he moved for 'the sun, the girls, the beaches, the dream'. One night, cruising for victims in a car with his cousin, they stopped Kathy Lorre. Realising she was the daughter of the 'monster' actor, Peter Lorre, they let her go. Ken Bianchi could not distinguish acting from real life, and as he must have known that Peter Lorre had been dead for twenty years it seems that he could not tell the difference between life and death. Multiple or not, his life was a nightmare fantasy.[1] Not the officially authorized fantasy of the White House in Washington, with its freedom fighters and evil emperors, and its patriotic crime, but a personalized replica of the master copy.

It is a common psychological phenomenon that repressed life

[1] Report in the *Guardian*, 18 April 1984.

returns, often in symbolic form, to haunt the agent of repression. Ken Bianchi is one of a myriad reflections in the American distorting mirror. Another is Henry Lee Lucas, a one-eyed vagrant from Texas who is the leading mass murderer in US history. He boasts of 360 murders, from coast to coast, by stabbing, strangulation, shooting, mutilation and decapitation. So far, 144 of these 'serial slayings' have been verified. The Federal Bureau of Investigation estimates that serial murder is running at a rate of about 5,000 per year, whereas Interpol reports that not more than 50 such mass murderers have been identified in the rest of the world over the past 20 years. Another mass killer, James Huberty, who shot dead twenty-one men, women and children in a hamburger restaurant in 1984, was obsessed with guns and had once, by accident, blown up his own house with gunpowder.

These criminals are doing what the whole society is threatening to act out, random, indiscriminate killing of strangers in defence of a caricatured reality. The difference is between what is unofficial and isolated, and what is official and cleverly rationalized. Such schizophrenia is dramatic in the United States, but it has seeped quietly into quieter countries. Britain's own most recent example of the problem is Denis Nilsen, the killer of fifteen young men, most of them homosexuals. He is in the tradition of the well-behaved immaculate Nazi SS guard. He cannot understand the murderous side of his personality: 'It is a great enigma. These things were out of character.' He tried to describe himself: 'By nature I am not a violent man. You can look at my school report, army record and police service record and nine years in the Civil Service and you will find not one record of violence against me.'[1]

The Soviet Union is not immune. We have seen how it manipulates and is manipulated by nuclear neurosis, twisting reality and law to match its fantasies. The *Soviet Teacher's Gazette* of October 1984 quotes a young Soviet punk, whose T-shirt proclaims 'I am an idiot', as saying: '"We are the ones who despise the good life. The ones who despise lies and the rich people who are sprouting up everywhere. We believe in love." His schoolteacher is at a loss:

[1] *Guardian*, 20 June 1984.

"He smashed windows, he terrorized the teachers by questioning why this or that respected citizen said one thing and did
another. We then unanimously demanded that he stop asking
provocative questions"'

The *Teacher's Gazette* reflects on a problem which stretches from
Siberia to San Francisco:

'. . . as time goes by, many teachers are finding it increasingly
difficult to find a common language with growing youths. It seems
as if teenagers have become immune to methods of education
which only yesterday seemed so reliable.'

They seem to have forgotten the ancient tradition of the Holy
Idiot, whose 'madness' is a hint of sanity in a mad world.

It is the nature of neurosis to confuse reason. Adaptive neurosis
is in direct conflict with reason, understanding and the law. The
worse the pain the harder must work the engines of denial.
America is wracked with pain, guilt and shame, making the Soviet
Union a compensating monster of hideous proportions. Nothing
less could have 'caused' such pain. The more successful the
adaptation the more ruthlessly must truth and law be sacrificed to
the custom-built Red King Kong. Evidence that the Soviet people
are caught in a similar and complementary trap counts for nothing.
All is grist to the mill of unreality.

The Soviet punk points a way out. As each person struggles to
hold tight to personal truth, to recognize the shape and sound of a
lie, madness will move away and sanity come a little closer. We
have to shed the false skin of neurotic truth, scale by scale. It is
hard going. A young British journalist indicates just how hard.
Chris Birkett was on a crowded London underground train when
he found himself surrounded by a gang of thieves armed with
knives. Like us, he was caught in a crowd, helpless in the face of
silent, menacing violence. The victims on that train, so easily
robbed because so ill-prepared, did nothing to obstruct or arrest
the robbers. As Chris Birkett explained: 'Nothing quite prepares
you for this kind of experience. Like most people, I suppose, all my
training taught me to do was to stare ahead all the time, trying to
avoid eye contact, somehow hoping they would go away.'[1]

Despite its gloss of democratic individualism, nuclear society
maintains a neurotic balance because we are so well trained to avoid

[1] *Observer*, 2 September 1984.

eye contact with criminality, hoping it will go away. We are all dangerously adapted to this false myth, but none so snugly as the citizen as Polaris sailor. Life on a Polaris submarine reveals nuclear 'slave morality' at the level of fine art. Nietzsche would be open-mouthed to find his prediction of twentieth-century life so sharply confirmed.

I confess to a private fascination with the Polaris submarine. In 1965, when the latter was still an illegitimate twinkle in the eye of that master of political conjuring, Harold Wilson, I resigned my job (as Secretary of the National Peace Council) to fight a London by-election in opposition to this weapon of mass destruction. The new Labour Government had just reversed its election pledge not to build Polaris. Harold Wilson was now in power, and in the power of the nuclear myth. Like a Red Indian confronting advancing Whites, my feeble arrow bounced harmlessly off this hardened foe. But it did no harm to learn that political neurosis is not cured by indignation.

A defence correspondent went to sea in a Polaris submarine. He saw the heart of our darkness and made it fit the myth:

> . . . for all the grim reality of her task, the atmosphere on board *Repulse* is astonishingly relaxed . . . it is always shirt-sleeves order in the controlled environment of a submerged Polaris vessel . . . the all-encompassing quietness is one of the overriding impressions I took away with me. Sealed in that great steel capsule even the crew cannot always tell whether *Repulse* is surfaced or dived. . . . Polaris vessels would never transmit save in the direst emergency, but there is an unceasing vigil for incoming signals . . . there could be the specially-coded signal that means a 'Tactical Launch'. As might be expected of one of the world's most sophisticated and devastating weapons systems, *Repulse* is a microcosm of bewildering complexity. . . . Yet for all the intimidatingly incomprehensible equipment on every side – and the equally incomprehensible jargon on every lip – there are plentiful touches of humanity and little quirks of old-fashioned naval tradition.
>
> *Repulse* . . . is capable of unleashing more explosive power than was employed during both World Wars – even including the two A-bombs dropped on Hiroshima and Nagasaki. . . . When I looked over the shoulder of a young rating . . . it took me

a little time to realize that with no duties to perform he was actually immersed in a computer-game of *Star Wars*. . . . On the evening of my arrival there was a traditional film show . . . of vintage Hollywood slap-stick. . . . There is a small ship's library with thrillers, Agatha Christies and an intimidating number of technical manuals. . . . And the Captain, Robert Bradshaw, is a classical music enthusiast who is learning the clarinet.

In such a self-contained environment health is an obvious concern, and Polaris boats are the only submarines to carry a doctor. . . . 'Our approach is not to take anyone to sea with health problems'. . . . However, the one question that every thoughtful visitor must ask, on being taken round a missile submarine capable of wiping several million people off the face of the earth, must be: can the men, and the system they operate, be trusted not to pitchfork the world into nuclear Armageddon . . .?

The Polaris force is an élite within an élite . About half the complement are volunteers, and many tend to be educationally above average. . . . Standards are high, and selection exacting. Before a single missile can be launched a large number of people must go through every step of a highly complex procedure almost top-heavy with safeguards. . . . The process sounds exceedingly complicated, and it is . . . the safeguards extend to involve many of the crew. Under orders signed by the Commander-in-Chief they are obliged to stop any officer, by force if necessary, the moment he infringes the laid-down procedures – and they have truncheons issued to them with which to do it.

Petty Officer Booker . . . was categoric about it. 'I would have no hesitation in stopping any officer who appeared to be about to break the rules, and that goes for the Captain if need be'. . . . After being taken through the firing procedure, I came away satisfied that an unauthorized or accidental launch is not a realistic possibility. Two World Wars began, not because the aggressor feared British belligerence, but because he doubted British resolve.[1]

There could be no better description of our nuclear neurosis, in essence. Every line indicates a fake defence, fake legality, fake normality, fake sanity. Whatever is mad in us is laid out, neat and tidy. There may be no perfect lie, but this is a close approximation.

[1] *Sunday Telegraph*, 7 October 1984.

The Nazi SS did the spadework for this refined creation, just as the laborious Lancaster bombers pioneered the ten-minute nuclear missile. There is no rage, no hysteria, all is calm in this silent night of the imagination. The cultural ambience is self-sealing, deceptively quiet. The victim of severe neurosis, the unfeeling psychopath, often appears to cut off from the outside world, revealing no clue to his intentions. But there is often, as in the Polaris submarine, an acute intake of messages, unacknowledged though they are. Docile and relaxed, no different in tone above or below the surface, psychopathic Polaris gestates the end of this civilization. For months or years nothing may happen as it roams the oceans. It may never give birth to death. Or it may, if East-West nightmares collide, suddenly erupt and become what it already is, the destroyer of worlds.

The Middle Ages had the Black Mass and we have our nuclear submarine, Christ as Devil, sanity as madness, law as crime, defence as murder. So mad are we that only an 'élite within an élite', vetted each day for symptoms of lunacy, can be entrusted with absolute murder. Petty officers, like their captains and crews, have no comprehension of the minimum laws of conflict, but they would have no hesitation in stopping any officer who appeared to 'break the rules'. No doubt a pleasant fellow, good husband and father, such a sane-seeming, 'innocent' man incorporates a representation of each of us. It is we who have written his part. We have done it because we dare not look ourselves in the eye, fearing to look into hell itself.

Captain Robert Bradshaw will go on playing his clarinet to the end, as devoted to Mozart as Denis Nilsen was to the Civil Service. Neither is a violent man, so we are told, and we will find nothing in their records to indicate violence or unusual behaviour. We all live in a nuclear submarine, and if we want to get out we must put on a life-jacket. The men in Polaris think they are keeping war at bay, but they are already its victims. They have moved more than half-way to meet the murdered millions of world war, their imagination sterile and identity frozen. Behind their dutiful, earnest routines are the 'set-smiling corpses' which haunted Wilfred Owen, come to take their revenge.

The Polaris submarine is a reminder to the murderer in us that there is no escape without renewal, without rejection of mad 'rules'. Macbeth gives this gruesome problem its full meaning.

Macbeth walked into a swamp of murder, each step sucking him further down, as the Americans did in Vietnam, and as we are all doing in the mad territory of nuclear security.

Ross has something to tell the Polaris crew, if they will switch off Star Wars for a moment and listen:

> . . . cruel are the times, when we are traitors
> And do not know ourselves; when we hold rumour
> From what we fear, yet know not what we fear,
> But float upon a wild and violent sea
> Each way and none.[1]

For Macbeth, 'wither'd murder' makes daylight black as night, as like a ghost it moves towards its design. He tries to drive this nightmare away: 'Hence, horrible shadow! Unreal mock'ry, hence!' In the end he cries out to be relieved of his criminal neurosis and the unattended sadness which lies at its core:

> Canst thou not minister to a mind diseas'd,
> Pluck from the memory a rooted sorrow,
> Raze out the written troubles of the brain,
> And with some sweet oblivious antidote
> Cleanse the stuff'd bosom of that perilous stuff
> Which weighs upon the heart?[2]

Polaris murder lies not only in the future but in the past. The crew may not read *Macbeth* but they encounter murder in their Agatha Christie thrillers, where killers are caught, if seldom understood. Murder is light entertainment for minds trained to obey absolute rules. Perhaps only the Soviet punk can sense the force of Macbeth's final comment that our 'walking shadow' of a life 'is a tale told by an idiot, full of sound and fury, signifying nothing'. If the Captain of a Polaris submarine and the Soviet 'idiot' were to change places, that might signify something. The missiles, and perhaps the crew, would be tossed overboard.

The nuclear citizen can take heart from this look into the complex and criminal neurosis of HMS *Repulse* and its strange crew. They have absolute power but little else. Their dead end rules stress our responsibility to life. It is exhilarating to stand alone before a cold wind, to discard the accumulated lies of this

[1] Act IV, sc. ii.
[2] Act V, sc. ii.

brutal century and start from our self. We are lucky, much luckier than the French singer, Fania Fénelon, when she arrived at Auschwitz: 'I was no longer anything, not even a slave. For me there was no longer either code or law; I was alone, abandoned, consigned to the executioner. We had arrived at the journey's end: hell.'[1]

We are close to that state but are still free to turn back from the nuclear terminus. Soon after Hitler came to power, Laurens van der Post wrote: 'The windows of the individual mind are shattered long before stones are thrown in the street and the police put to flight by the mob. There is a riot in the human heart, and the forces of law and order in the spirit are first overthrown by a nightmare horde. Already, deep down in the human soul the individual is melting into the crowd.'[2]

Today the forces of law and order are controlled by people similarly split between two worlds. The Scottish poet Edwin Muir described this:

> A crack ran through our hearthstone long ago,
> And from the fissure we watched gently grow
> > The tame domesticated danger,
> > Yet lived in comfort in our haunted rooms ...
> We hear the lot of nations,
> Of times and races,
> Because we watched the wrong
> Last too long
> With non-committal faces.
> Until from Europe's sunset hill
> We saw our houses falling
> > Wall after wall behind us.
> > What could blind us
> > To such self-evident ill
> > And all the sorrows from their caverns
> > calling?[3]

He sensed the sadness and pain which encloses modern life, spawning neurotic fear: 'Sometimes we think of the nations lying asleep, Curled blindly in impenetrable sorrow'.[4] We each nurse a

---

[1] Fania Fénelon, *The Musicians of Auschwitz*, London 1977.
[2] Op. cit.
[3] 'Refugees' in Edwin Muir, *Collected Poems*, London 1960.
[4] 'The Horses', op. cit.

part of this sorrow, and in it is locked the creative energy which can banish the spectre of nuclear suicide. Disowning this deep sadness makes us suspicious, defensive, explosive, vengeful, hopeless.

As we retrace our steps into this forbidden area we may hear an echo of the unity and belonging which used to animate ancient tribes. Laurens van der Post writes of the integrity of the Kalahari bushmen, before their culture was shattered: 'The essence of this being, I believe, was his sense of belonging: belonging to nature, the universe, life and its humanity. . . . What is left of the natural world matters more to life now than it has ever done before. . . .'[1]

We have taken the world apart. How do we put it together again?

When a society imposes a collective neurosis on its citizens, as ours does, the individual must either seek illusory survival by joining the fraud, or recreate sanity and wholeness out of inner resources. Most take the easy way out. Many pretend not to. A few pass through their own unique part of the madness before moving up, like the released prisoners in Beethoven's *Fidelio*, into the daylight. My own version of this story is as painful as any other.

At first, I preferred to believe that my family was part of the solution, not the problem. We all rejected the nuclear illusion, or thought we did, by argument, writing, marching, thinking. But after many years I began to realise that the opposition was as counterfeit as the problem itself. The medicine did not work. The patient remained as sick as before, if not more so. I began to perceive, dimly, what was wrong. We had distorted the nature of the problem, as it had distorted us. The core of the problem lay not in government, or law, or outside on the surface somewhere, but deep inside nuclear normality, inside us, inside me.

It was a frightening admission, reached by examining closely the human beings in power who serve the nuclear idol, and by admitting the extent of my own no-go area. Both led to one conclusion. Nuclear normality and my family were one and the same thing, half mad, hiding truths driven crazy by isolation and rejection. To wake up in an asylum is not so bad, I suspect. There are doctors, drugs, nurses, comforting routines and no responsibility. But to wake up in a half-asylum is torture, as you may already know. Nothing is what it seems. Nobody helps because nobody is supposed to need help. What is said is not meant. What

[1] Laurens van der Post, *Testament to the Bushmen*, New York 1984.

is done is half-hearted. Everything is half-hearted and half-witted, but the opposite is believed. I had bitten the family apple and we were rotten at the core, yet entirely normal.

How did I respond? I tried to protect my two sons, by emotional vaccination. I tried to communicate to them the nature and extent of the problem, so they could begin to work out their own whole-hearted sanity. I explored below the surface of our normality. As I suspected, when I crossed the fortified frontier of our neurosis, all hell was let loose. Rejected family half-truths emerged, not as woebegone prisoners to be cared for, but avenging devils. The civilized façade was shattered. The balance of power was broken. Parents, brothers, sisters, aunts became a rabid gang of suspicious, angry, accusing people. I was horrified by this upsurge of honest devilry, in me and those I thought I knew, but I realized that the explosive energy also fuelled the nuclear nightmare. We were no longer complaining about nuclear weapons. We were a nuclear weapon and it had exploded in our faces. The fall-out was poisonous and part of us died.

We experienced the hell which so many wise people throughout history have known to be the barrier between regressive nightmare and the real world. It was a terrible experience, and essential. I now know that the tentacles of nuclear annihilation reach into the mind and heart of every person and family, and I believe that a minimum humanitarian law is the first step in securing world peace. Enforcement of this law takes us away from delusions of good and evil, us as God and them as Devil. I have solved nothing, but I have arrived at the beginning of a hard path. Recognition of our half-madness can be a priceless asset, proof of a whole life waiting.

The nuclear citizen has made little progress in exorcising policies of mass destruction because the two vital elements of neurosis and law have been ignored. Exaggerated rationality has played into the hands of governments who claim a monopoly of rationalist virtue. The citizen is quickly snared in a futile round of argument about facts, figures, weaponry, money and endless, useless detail. This arid sand swallows him up, leaving no trace. By ignoring law, the citizen ignores the one thing prized above all by governments. Nuclear neurosis whispers dark secrets into the ear of every nuclear leader and politician. The more insecure they become, the more desperately they cling to the veneer of legality; what is lawful must be right. What is truly lawful accuses the corrupt logic of nuclear

Humanizing Hell!

authority. Not law in the sky, abstract and remote, but law grounded in the unique experience of each one of us.

The huge mass of nuclear fog can be distilled into a few drops of humane principle. In the midst of the soggy rationalizations of absolute destruction is the clear, hard warning of Colonel Telford Taylor at Nuremberg in 1946: 'We must not forget that to kill a defenceless person "is not only a violation of the rules of war. It is murder. . . . We have heard so much of mass extermination that we are likely to forget that simple murder is a capital offence. The laws of all civilized nations require that a man go to some lengths to avoid associating himself with murder, whether as an accomplice or accessory or co-conspirator."'[1]

To know and accept that simple truth is not enough. We must find the energy to translate principle into fact. Half-hearted attempts have been made for generations. They deserved to fail. Each must awake the half of us which sleeps. Our neurosis takes many forms but we all share a common heritage of unatoned murder, the 'set-smiling corpses' of two world wars. It is the 'darkness' of that legacy which 'does the face of earth entomb', burying our vitality with it.

'What did you do in the war, daddy?' is a joke to disguise a deep wound. My father fought in both world wars. He survived and won, yet something in him lost. His heart was never whole again, or his sense of reality. He became adapted to a split, neurotic civilization, whose tormented normality has spawned the means of its own extermination. I inherited his neurosis, as you will have inherited someone else's. When Humpty Dumpty was blown off the wall and fell in fragments, 'all the King's horses and all the King's men, couldn't put Humpty together again'. They still can't. But we can do it ourselves. It is good to remember that it is not just our own split mind which we are healing but that of modern civilization itself.

Each tentative step we take into this haunted region of ourselves will be fraught with apprehension. We will glimpse ghosts behind every rock-ribbed prejudice. Our infant integrity will seem puny compared with the swaggering confidence we have left behind. But others have been this way, during every age. The process of inner renewal is described by an American psycho-analyst and writer, Dr

[1] Calvocoressi, op. cit.

John Perry: 'The more firmly structured a society becomes in its conventions and traditions, the more it tends to distrust innovation, deviance, change and intrusion by the unfamiliar, and the sharper grow its distinctions between inside and outside.... Deviance reflects a natural law of psychic process, as the psyche has an impulse to activate the potentials left out of the pattern of integration.'[1]

Rigidity and paranoia go together. The Cold War reflects this extreme defensive orthodoxy, personally and politically, where every thing beyond 'the pale of its little cosmos is seen as the enemy: innovations, oppositions and compensations are perceived in the image of demonic darkness and chaos.... Hence, it takes a truly heroic individual to break free of the binding collective consensus in such a society. The hero's journey dares this outsideness; it dips down into the darkness of that which is left out of conscious recognition or cultural acceptance, and fetches up from there the treasures of new insights and fresh experience.'[2]

These heroes include such people as Saint Francis, Joan of Arc, Beethoven and William Blake, all of whom were regarded by their contemporaries as eccentric, if not mad. But we have declined beyond the help of the lone hero. Today's dilemma requires the heroic response of thousands, if not millions.

There are traces of senile schizophrenia in nuclear society. The people who control nuclear threat systems are old in spirit. They contradict and corrupt the very ideals and principles which they advocate. They exalt the law and poison its roots. They describe the arms race as 'mad' and drive faster. They promote love and threaten half the world with death. We each do much the same. This half-mad idealism breeds mental confusion among those who are too sensitive and honest to join the conspiracy, children and reformers. Our children are told about 'gentle Jesus' and Uncle Lenin, asked to protect the weak and look after the earth, and expected to accept criminal defence systems to keep out a criminally mad enemy.

Dr Perry points to the political effect of this officially induced schizophrenia on those declared mentally ill. Many of them try to express the very ideals which society has faked, as if nature is pointing a way through their madness. They are the heroes and

[1] *Spring Journal* (journal of Jungian thought), New York 1971.
[2] Ibid.

heroines who fail, shot down at the perimeter fence like escaping prisoners of war in those interminable war films. Unable to sustain defiance they 'become trapped' in the process of renewal and 'become indeed psychotic when they realise their isolation, and then panic'.

Dr Perry suggests that the outer forms of democracy are of little real value without 'a form of psychological culture in which the regulative and integrative forces are found within the individual, in the image of king and code within the psyche.'[1] He cites the example of schizophrenic patients who have tried and failed to re-discover this inner and outer king and code. A woman has been given a special message by the Blessed Virgin for the world, that women should keep their marriage vows; a man is chosen to save the world from the atomic bomb, discovering a new David and Garden of Eden; a man has been given a special mission of restoring law and order to the world, ensuring racial equality; a woman is the fourth in a line of great religious leaders, Moses, Paul and Luther; a woman will give birth to a divine child; a man will become a heroic reformer who will change the world through communism; a woman will re-write the Bible with a new gospel of love and kindness; and so on, and so on.

There but for the grace of God go all of us. Their madness does not lie in grand, simple ideals. If it did we would have to declare all history mad. It lies in a sad inability to root those ideals in everyday life. These patients are equal and opposite reflections of our madness-inducing leadership, all victims of collective circulating neurosis, supporting Shakespeare's contention: 'lilies that fester smell far worse than weeds'.

We should beware an extension of this failure, the growing appeal of drugs. Schizophrenic patients may be lost in their private myths, yet the latter often bear uncanny resemblance to the imagery of love and brotherhood induced by some drugs. Confronted by the hardened political arteries of nuclear power, a drug sub-culture is growing which sells a still-born idealism.

We can accept a minimum truth to accompany minimum law, that the sinister neurosis of nuclear violence will swallow us unless

[1] Ibid.

we insist on the integrity of life. There can be opposition but no enemies, defence but no murder, and a minimum respect for life without which it is not worth living. If this is heroism in the nuclear age then the citizen's response must be heroic. Or useless.

Chapter Thirteen

Law Enforcement Campaign

'Faced with unprecedented problems, the instinct of the political establishment is to say, "I've found a difficulty. Now we can all go home." It's the mark of a failed culture . . . . The establishment fears change as the aristocracy fears revolution'
– Sir John Hoskyns, former Head of Policy Unit, Downing St

'Lord Gardiner was probably right when he said that people must make a stand at some time. There did come a point at which one had got to say, "I will rather die than do this . . . "'
– Justice Lawton, 1964.

'We cannot sharpen legality as our main weapon for the future and then scorn legality because it doesn't suit us at the present time'
– Neil Kinnock, Labour Party leader, 1984

To reach a remote destination, in the heart of darkness, the least that is needed is a map, reliable equipment and determination. That is just the starting price, and that is what we have tried to gain from our investigation, so far. Existing maps have proved inaccurate, with monsters in place of facts, like those of Africa in the old days.

Our nuclear map is emerging from a realization that beneath and beyond official reality lies another, larger, vastly more challenging and awesome prospect. The busy, complex foreground, cocooned in a nuclear capsule of limitless violence, is as much a sinister caricature of life as the railway station which greeted arrivals at Auschwitz.

Nuclear leaders who preach individual rights and comradeship have proved no more trustworthy than those who greeted the new arrivals at the station whose 'departure platform' was not for use. According to SS. Judge Morgen, cross-examined at the Nuremberg Trial, the welcoming speech at Auschwitz would go like this:

'Jews, you were brought here to be resettled, but before we organise this future Jewish State, you must of course learn how to work. You must learn a new occupation. You will be taught that here. Our routine here is, first, everyone must take off his clothes so that your clothing can be disinfected and you can have a bath so that no epidemics will be brought into the camp . . .'

After he had found such calming words for his victims, they started on the road to death. Men and women were separated. At the first place, one had to give his hat; at the next one, his coat, collar, shirt, down to his shoes and socks. These places were set up like check-rooms, and the person was given a check at each one so that the people believed they would get their things back. The other Jews had to receive the things and hurry up the new arrivals so that they would not have time to think. The whole thing was like an assembly line. At the last stop they reached a big room, and were told that this was the bath. When the last one was in, the doors were shut and the gas was let into the room . . . . When the air could be breathed again, the doors were opened and the Jewish workers removed the bodies.'[1]

Like an epidemic, that ugly microcosm of lies, murder and collusion has multiplied, infiltrating our lives at every level. But we still have a little time left in which to think, act, and use the departure platform.

We have seen that the problem of nuclear extermination is not rooted in ideology, or class, or this government or that. It is tempting to look for such objective causes, but they are all too limited. None of them implicates the individual observer in the crime. It was Lenin who said that there is no such thing as an innocent bystander, because a bystander is never innocent.

What confronts us is the nervous breakdown of a civilization, driven to distraction by fragmented pursuits yet immoblized in the sadness and guilt of mass killing. We are the agents of our breakdown, like a child in a playpen who has pulled life apart and is terrified to find the pattern is lost. We are less honest than a child and pretend that the fragment in our hand is the whole thing. This make-believe mushrooms to obscure truth. If our piece of the truth is the whole truth then other nations' fragments can neither be

[1] *International Military Tribunal Vol. XX.*

whole nor valuable. Each fraud requires a greater. Absolute truth requires an absolute threat.

In such a feverish environment the law is a cool touchstone of sanity, relating warring fragments to unifying principles. Counterfeit law, used to protect the nuclear idol, betrays itself by selective use. An effective campaign to reject the threat of annihilation must make full use of our surviving reason, to uphold and enforce world-wide law, offering every possible help to individuals.

Such a campaign is ambitious, perhaps the most ambitious project ever, because it seeks to change the course of a huge, established river of habit, prejudice and fear. It aims to rescue life from nuclear dungeons guarded by a panoply of modern centralized power. It aims to dissolve a nightmare and establish the basis of normal living.

Such a challenging goal cannot be reached by timid and partial commitments, any more than an encroaching desert can be stopped in its tracks by part-time gardening. The peace movements of this century are notable for their lack of movement. They have been walking up a downward-moving escalator, each forward step more apparent than real. Their tendency to self-pity betrays lack of maturity. They blame governments but it is their own half-hearted response which deserves failure. I have been part of this pantomime of failure since 1957, when I wrote my first leaflet condemning Britain's criminal new toy, the hydrogen bomb.

We can learn from mistakes. Some of the worst can be given priority treatment. There is the self-serving pretence that the problem of annihilation can be solved by rational debate alone. There is nothing the skeletal armies of official spokesmen, strategists and hangers-on like better than interminable, futile debate about the details of nuclear policy. Such debate, much loved by the media, gives a gloss of respectable reason to mad reality. Hitler followed the same path, considering it essential to be thought worthy of signing international treaties. Every gangster wants to be socially credit-worthy.

Intelligent people do silly things for a reason, and there is no stupidity committed by intelligent peace activists which does not stem from self-interest, however well-hidden. Inflating the rational content of the problem has such a purpose. It permits all concerned to keep daily life separate from the nuclear issue. This leads to all kinds of contradictions and absurdity. Not only is the most severe and pervasive problem of survival reduced to a minor walk-on role in everyday life, competing unsuccessfully with mortgages, jobs, holidays and a thousand family concerns, but the means of annihilation are paid for by the taxes of this peace-monger. The latter thus becomes as much a co-conspirator as the demoralized Jews at Auschwitz who helped to fool their own people.

Once this initial distortion occurs, everything else goes wrong. Having put the problem in a jar on the shelf, the neurotic implications of mass destruction safely neutralized, it only needs to be taken down and opened for special occasions. Unwilling to engage the real problem, the conventional peace activist converts it into safe symbolism. Like Christians substituting feast days for religious life, peace movements dot the calendar with symbolic events, regardless of effect. Enormous marches clog a major city with cheerful, excited crowds and banners, a festival scene which makes people feel good and usually coincides with a public holiday. I have taken part in many. What happens? The Government yawns, smugly congratulating itself on its democratic tolerance. The media are bored, after years of the same thing, but dutifully register a short report which comforts a public addicted to national rituals of any kind. A pebble drops into the pond. The ripples spread. A glassy calm returns. After a while the process is repeated.

Conscience-salving takes strange forms. A national peace movement demonstration in the North of England in 1984 was justified to me on the grounds that 'it is the turn of the South to go to the North', an all-encompassing equality.

There is an insulating foam of sentimentality which protects symbolic, part-time engagement in the problem. A person who crams peace-work into spare time is often exhausted by demands which cannot be met. Fatigue justifies the lie that everything possible is being done, encouraging false superiority towards those who do less. There is no time for accurate confrontation with the nuclear problem, so there can be no room for honest, comprehensive criticism, however positive. Criticism of that quality is only welcome when the work is of a similar standard, as with aircraft engineers or even nuclear physicists. But it is often considered unfair, even rude, to criticize the efforts of people who are 'giving up' their free time. Anyone who dares to challenge this complacent tactic will experience outraged hurt.

A soft-centred movement requires soft-centred leadership, which perpetuates failure. Rhetoric holds this static display of righteous indignation together. Coherent, consistent, radical action would tear it apart, like a jet engine replacing stone horses to pull Queen Boadicea's chariot in London.

The organization of the peace movement is appropriate. Supporters who spare only a few hours for the nuclear issue, compensate by wanting and paying for a centralized, professional staff. The latter, directed by elected central committees of volunteers, organize special events and pass down nationally recommended actions to local groups. Thus is weakness compounded. Action, despite the professional commitment of the staff, is geared to a spare-time membership. The latter want weekend events, preferably on a Saturday when it is easier to travel. So there are weekend demonstrations, often at military installations most of whose personnel are at home watching television. The cycle of futility is complete.

There is growing awareness of this problem. The Greenham Common women's peace camp set an example of consistency. Efforts are made to alert the public to Cruise missile convoys, whenever they are seen. But alerting a public sunk in gloom achieves little. Tigers moving in India are often heralded by a chorus of disturbed monkeys, high in the trees. Irritated, the tiger continues on its way. The Greenham women have followed the more tenacious example of the mongoose, teeth clenched tight on the cobra. But only a bite on the neck will kill the cobra, and the Greenham Common air base is not the neck of the nuclear cobra but its scaly, cold body.

Do I hear an angry chorus from the monkeys in the treetops? How can I give more time to the nuclear issue, without losing my job and destroying my family? What is the point of giving everything up and finding myself with nothing? And what do you do, anyway, that's so great? Three young lawyers asked me such questions. The answers are simple, if hard to swallow.

No problem is solved by pretending that it is half what it is. If a house is on fire, or a ship is sinking, someone with a teaspoon is not welcomed with cries of 'he's doing his best'. It is the overwhelming magnitude of the nuclear challenge which dictates our response, or should do. It is a teaspoon fantasy to imagine that such a complex, pervasive problem can be met by lesser energies than those devoted to a job in the Civil Service, factory or bank. The remedy must match the problem or it is frivolous.

There is an underlying pessimism in the peace movement which helps to explain its impotence. Challenging the value of an activity often exposes underlying despair. Activity can be distraction rather than cure, like knitting in Auschwitz. Sensitive people often see through the false optimism of the peace movement because they are acutely aware of their own. An artist and mother ascribed her own apathy to 'selfishness, a feeling of impotence, mixed with a strong suicidal tendency .... My head tells me that CND is wonderful but I have a gut reaction against it.' She went on to say that whenever she went to a meeting of the local peace group, 'I just can't feel part of it.' She feels that most peace group organizers seem to come from 'unhappy or broken relationships,' and thinks that compensation is 'not an honest way of tackling the problem'.

This response suggests that the failure of the peace movement, so far, to respond energetically and effectively to the irrational dimension of the nuclear issue, may owe much to its own problems. By demanding radical changes in Government policies while defensively hugging its own grief it gets caught in its own contradictions. A peace campaign can tackle this problem by bringing private and public suffering into focus, which requires a far higher level of mutual concern and communication.

Such a campaign will only deserve success if its members are committed to solving the problem rather than saving their jobs. There can be no single best method. Each of us must work out the means and method which make most sense. I decided several years ago that any job which failed to help me approach the nuclear problem was disposable. I was flooded with doubts and fears concerning children, income, and home. After some uncomfortable weeks I worked out a way of living and working, on the dole, which gave me more freedom and scope for research and action than any job I ever had. I learned how to be poor, knowing that I was richer than most of the people I knew in Africa and India. I knew that however inadequate my work might be, at least I was paying no direct tax to a criminal Government. I devoted much time to learning about the law and its nuclear implications. If this book is worth anything it is because I chose this course.

The nature of the threat which overhangs us is such that doing anything less seemed like fooling myself. Everything remains to be done. There is nothing to boast of. You may be far more effective than I am at this task. We may even help each other.

The issue of nuclear legality is directly affected by the level of personal commitment, not just within the peace movement in the way we have seen, but in the behaviour of the legal profession, especially those members of it who oppose nuclear weapons. By arguing the illegality of nuclear policies on a part-time basis, part of a busy professional programme in the courts, these lawyers cancel out their commitment. Their continuing allegiance to the established legal order implies a conception of the nuclear issue which can be accommodated within such a commitment. This flies in the face of what we now know about the legal profession and its long-standing collusion with criminal nuclear policies.

To organise public 'tribunals' which denounce nuclear illegality while supporting the profession which has done most to disguise official criminality, is an example of the bank robber putting coins in the offertory box. It is an irrational response to an irrational problem. One step forward, one step back.

One lawyer has brought job and problem into focus, demonstrating publicly against nuclear weapons, refusing to pay fines, going to prison. In response to a request for professional advice about an indictment against the Prime Minister he wrote: 'If it could be carried through to indictment, I am sure that it would be momentous. If I can help in any way in the planning, drafting, researching or presenting the application, it would be a privilege.' When members of the legal profession respond on such a level, we begin to glimpse daylight.

If the level of personal commitment rises to match the problem of law enforcement, there will have to be a radical change of campaign structure. Individual supporters will want to work out initiatives where they live, not delegate responsibility to an overworked group in the capital. National, symbolic events will give way to localised programmes designed to influence nuclear society in schools, courts, government, business offices and other work places. Nuclear irrationality seeps up through cracks in everyday life, and only when it is confronted can the foundations be laid of national and world-wide co-operation.

A group of committed activists can approach the whole local population through the media, by letters, articles and newsworthy action, and also through advertising. Money is needed. Half-hearted campaigns get the trickle of cash they deserve. Annual subscriptions of £5 or so, less for the unemployed, are a guarantee of failure. Much of this sum is swallowed up by membership administration. Worse, token subscriptions indicate a level of commitment which equates the issue of nuclear annihilation with ballroom dancing, yoga, pedigree dogs, Roman history and a thousand other distractions.

Serious concern will attract serious financing. I know from experience that even an unemployed person can give £1, or roughly 10% of income, per week, without starving or walking barefoot. Such a rate means an annual contribution of £52. The percentage contribution should rise with income. Someone earning £7,000 per year, for example, the average rate paid to British CND staff in 1984, could contribute 10% of income, or £700, about £14 per week. The size of the contribution is of course relative to the perceived nature of the nuclear problem. It could be much higher. Someone whose house is on fire does not save energy and time for the weekend. Only when the fire seems remote is the response leisurely and limited. A small activist group of thirty, one third of them unemployed, could generate an income of approximately £300 per week or £14,500 per year. This would be a starting point. Potential income, once a group is established, is large. There are many ways of raising funds to supplement this regular income. The total would be enough to pay for various activities, including regular advertising.

Our campaign will need increasing energy from its members. This means mutual help in disentangling the knots of nuclear paralysis which we have already recognized. As more of the psyche is reclaimed, more energy will flow. A realistic campaign will take shape.

The sad reality which lies behind our claim to individual autonomy is well exposed by Stanley Milgram, an American professor of psychology, whose research on obedience to authority is an invaluable guide.[1]

Stanley Milgram's experiments stemmed from the consequences of obedience in Nazi Germany. Two people were invited to a psychological laboratory to take part in a study of memory and learning. One is designated a 'teacher' and the other a 'learner'.

[1] Stanley Milgram, *Obedience to Authority*, London 1974.

The experimenter explains that the study is about the effect of punishment on learning. The learner is taken to a room, his arms strapped to a chair and an electrode attached to his wrist. He must learn a list of word pairs, mistakes resulting in electric shocks of increasing intensity. The aim of the experiment is to see how far the teacher will go in applying shocks, by using an impressive but simulated generator, with thirty switches, ranging from 15 volts to 450 volts. The teacher is a volunteer member of the public but the learner is an actor, who will protest with increasing emotion as the shocks increase. How far will the teacher obey orders before he refuses?

Each time the teacher-subject hesitates he is ordered to continue: 'To extricate himself from the situation, the subject must make a clear break with authority.' Pressure on the subject is considerably less than on a soldier in war. The experimenter lacks powers of coercion. Would you or I inflict pain? The evidence suggests we would: 'Despite the fact that many protest to the experimenter, a substantial proportion (over 60%) continue to the last shock on the generator.'

Stanley Milgram draws a number of conclusions from this series of experiments, none of them flattering to our sense of autonomy: 'Some subjects were totally convinced of the wrongness of what they were doing but could not bring themselves to make an open break with authority .... What they failed to realize is that subjective feelings are largely irrelevant to the moral issue at hand so long as they are not translated into action.'

He links what he learned to war experience: 'This may illustrate a dangerously typical situation in complex society; it is psychologically easy to ignore responsibility when one is only an intermediary in a chain of evil action. Even Eichmann was sickened when he toured the concentration camps, but to participate in mass murder he had only to sit at a desk and shuffle papers. At the same time the man in the camp who dropped Zyklon-B into the gas chambers was able to justify *his* behaviour on the grounds that he was only following orders from above. Thus there is a fragmentation of the total human act; no one man decides to carry out the evil act and is confronted with its consequences. The person who assumes full responsibility for the act has evaporated. Perhaps this is the most common characteristic of socially organized evil in modern society.'

He presents our campaign with a direct warning: 'As a strain reducing mechanism, dissent is a source of psychological consolation . . . . The subject publicly defines himself as opposed to shocking the victim and thus establishes a desirable self-image. At the same time, he maintains his submissive relationship to authority by continuing to obey . . . . The act of disobedience requires a mobilization of inner resources, and their transformation into a domain of action. But the psychic cost is considerable.'

Stanley Milgram relates this issue to the role of the large institution in modern society: 'Men do become angry; they do act hatefully and explode in rage against others. But not here. Something far more dangerous is revealed; the capacity of man to abandon his humanity, indeed, the inevitability that he does so, as he merges his unique personality into larger institutional structures.'

He considers that authority has a vested interest in the wasting away of individuality, despite pretensions to the contrary: 'Every sign of tension is evidence of the failure of authority to transform the person to an unalloyed state of agency . . . the state produced in the laboratory may be likened to a light doze, compared to the profound slumber induced by the authority system of a national government.'

This is even more evident in military training: 'A period of several weeks is spent in basic training. Although its ostensible purpose is to provide the recruit with military skills, its fundamental aim is to break down any individuality and selfhood.'

It is clear that the Eichmann syndrome, 'if it is authority it must be legitimate', is alive and well: 'the obedient subject asserts that he had no autonomy in shocking the victim and that his actions were completely out of his hands.' And 'whereas submission to authority is probably no less for an Ashanti than for an American factory worker, the range of persons who constitute authorities for the former are all personally known to him, while the modern industrial world forces individuals to submit to impersonal authorities, so that responses are made to abstract rank, indicated by an insignia, uniform or title!'

The implications for our nuclear dilemma are spelled out.

'Nothing is more dangerous to human survival than malevolent authority, combined with the dehumanizing effect of buffers . . . . On a purely quantitative basis, it is more wicked to kill ten thousand by hurling an artillery shell onto a town, than to kill one man by pummelling him with a stone, but the latter is by far the more psychologically difficult act . . . for the man who sits in front of a button that will release Armageddon, depressing it has about the same emotional force as calling for an elevator.'[1]

So much for the dark side. What about signs of hope? There are a few. Stanley Milgram varied the experiment, once deliberately confusing the source of authority by staging disagreement between two controllers. At once the level of rebellion rose: 'Once the signal emanating from the higher level was "contaminated", the coherence of the hierarchical system was destroyed, along with its efficiency in regulating behaviour.'

Human integrity is related to wholeness of experience and involvement: 'There was a time, perhaps, when men were able to give a fully human response to any situation because they were fully absorbed in it as human beings . . . .'

Then, when Stanley Milgram put the experimenter in the learner's chair there was a dramatic reversal of behaviour: 'At the first protest of the shocked experimenter, every subject broke off, refusing to administer even a single shock beyond this point . . . . Subjects often expressed sympathy for the experimenter, but appeared alienated from the comman man, as if he were a madman . . . . It is not what subjects do but for whom they are doing it that counts.'[2]

This harsh picture of human behaviour in response to authority confirms much of the evidence we have examined during this investigation of nuclear crime. Authority tends to erase individuality and the law which protects it. Stanley Milgram's research confirms that law will be a vital element in any worthwhile campaign to eliminate weapons of mass destruction. Reasoned argument must be used, but it should be clear by now that morality, reason and individuality are often easy prey to authority which has rationalized nuclear weapons. Our campaign must not only seek to influence people in authority who wield malevolent power, but also try to resolve our own temptation to use token dissent to mask underlying collusion.

Law is persuasive for basic, simple reasons. It is the language of authority and conservatism, more necessary to them than cosmetic

[1] Ibid.
[2] Ibid.

morality. It is a hallmark of radical impotence that 'law and order' has become the monopoly of orthodox power. The essential meaning and intention of the law, as we have seen, is to restrict power and violence and protect individual life. The law, shorn of legalistic dross, says that threats of mass destruction amount to a conspiracy to commit mass murder, the final solution of criminal authority. This must be stated and restated by our campaign, in all its simplicity, to every agent of nuclear terror and every citizen of nuclear society.

The law is on the side of sanity and a minimum integrity of life, not of Cold War rivals acting out dark fantasies of absolute good and evil. Nuclear authority must be confronted with this simple message, every day and everywhere it exists. We must rob it of the co-operation and collusion which gives it a veneer of respectability, cutting off 'slave morality' at its roots.

Another dimension of law, outside its plain meaning, is its emotional force. Crime attracts strong feeling. Its meaning penetrates the outer defences of neurosis. It can arrest irrational prejudice with the sudden, immobilizing shock of: STOP! POLICE!. People happy to defend policies of nuclear threat on grounds of strategy, patriotism, history, or necrophilia, are very uncomfortable when told that the law forbids it. Their self-image is threatened. They twist and turn, pretending that the law is obscure, cannot be enforced, does not apply to defence. Exactly the excuses they are quick to denounce when used by muggers, bank robbers and football hooligans.

The law and its relation to crime is the relation of mongoose to cobra. Determination to enforce the law against nuclear crime means sinking our teeth into the cobra at its most vulnerable point. To let go before the snake is dead is fatal. It is a fight for life.

On the outskirts of a town in India I once saw a large road sign which read: 'BEWARE OF ACCIDENTS!' We can beware of the ultimate 'accident' if we focus mind and courage sufficiently to call 'STOP! POLICE!' to those in power. During our investigation we have looked at the tactics of nuclear authority, the various means by which it rationalizes and perpetuates nuclear crime.

Our campaign must tackle each of these key areas. At present, colleges and schools collude with the problem. Teachers of law evade the nuclear issue. They are part of an educational system which preaches what it contradicts, open-minded learning. Even 'peace studies' can be self-defeating if nuclear threats of mass destruction are presented as a rational option. Murder is not a rational option. Nor is mass murder, however coyly wrapped.

Our campaign has already raised this issue in schools. The response is instructive and encouraging. Students and teachers with the usual defence arguments on the tip of their tongue are often silent and thoughtful when confronted with the law. The routines of prejudice are interrupted. Not only do teachers of all kinds have a duty to uphold laws of minimum respect for life, but they have a citizen's responsibility to help enforce them. Evasion of this fact is collusion with crime.

Our campaign must aim to shake lawyers awake on this issue. Paid handsomely to mediate the law, the legal profession has betrayed a long-standing and scandalous lack of integrity. The few lawyers who have let the scales of injustice fall from their eyes are beginning to make a vital contribution to the nuclear issue. But we must beware of those who effect a concern for nuclear illegality while maintaining their conventional life and work undisturbed. Such token dissent may be 'a source of psychological consolation', providing the lawyer with a 'desirable self-image', but it should not hide from us an underlying 'submissive relationship to authority'. This adulterated penicillin must be rejected. It is worse than useless, providing nuclear neurosis with yet another disguise.

If lawyers are expected to help this campaign to enforce the law, what of the judges and magistrates, the people who dispense justice from a lofty perch? We have seen something of their evasion of nuclear crime, by means of a logical conjuring trick which makes the law vanish into the fog of national security. They pervert justice by providing nuclear crime with a gilded alibi. British judges are deeply rooted in a conservative establishment of power and privilege, sharing a common background and common prejudices. They have grossly abused their privileged role, aiding and abetting official commitment to nuclear criminality.

We want an honest and direct answer from our judges to these charges. Initial approaches to the Lord Chancellor, who oversees the performance of the judiciary, have been met with patronizing indifference, as if no citizen has a right to question. Specific questions about the legality of policies of mass destruction are not answered. Such behaviour, appropriate to the King of Hearts in Wonderland, is offensive. Our campaign must break through this silence and insist on a full explanation of the failure of the judiciary to expose and suppress nuclear crime. Pressure can be applied through MPs, the media, by picketing of courts and offices, and by naming them publicly one by one, with details of their collusion. Judges constantly denounce those who act outside the law. It must be spelled out to them how they do likewise.

Judges and magistrates must be told that we will no longer accept courts which prosecute peace activists for minor offences of 'obstruction' and 'breach of the peace' while denying the criminal policies which incite these offences. The law insists that a citizen has a right and duty to report and prevent crime, particularly serious offences. This basic civic responsibility is being deliberately obstructed by courts which either declare themselves incompetent to enforce international law or listen wearily to such argument before ruling it irrelevant. Such evasion of the law is a wilful violation of the legal principles held to be binding at Nuremberg, and of the many international commitments made by British Governments. Regardless of international law, no politician or soldier is entitled to commit murder. Preparing to kill Soviet children, among others, in the event of war is not only conspiracy to commit mass murder, in violation of international law, it is simple conspiracy to commit murder.

British magistrates, most of whom are non-professional, are closer to the public than judges. They are more amenable to ordinary common sense and less able to hide behind a thicket of legalism. These men and women are often influential members of their local community. Each one of them must be approached by our campaign to stop nuclear preparations for annihilation. This is best done by those who live in the same area and may know them personally. Magistrates must be reminded that they owe the public a duty to uphold the law, including that part of it which has been hijacked by nuclear authority. Refusal to act on this issue should be greeted by direct protest action, including picketing of courts and places of residence. The monkeys of the jungle can do more than scream abuse from the treetops at the passing tiger. We can, to begin with, tie its tail to the nearest tree.

It is symptomatic of the peace movement's irrational fear of the law that it is so easily and so often ensnared by it. By imagining that law and morality are opposites, because of what they see of Government behaviour, peace activists often assert a moral standard by breaking a minor law, sitting on a road or cutting a fence. This has no practical effect on the problem itself and plays into the hands of an authority which contrasts such behaviour with its own commitment to law and order. Authority adds insult to injury by boasting of its tolerance in dealing so leniently with protest. This stage-managed legal pantomime succeeds too often in focusing attention on trivia and distracting it from the main problem.

Peace action of this kind is in effect more collusive than positive. A modern, centralized State has ample resources to keep half-hearted opposition at bay for ever. Two conclusions can be drawn. First, there are more direct ways of exposing and opposing official illegality, waiting to be explored. Second, if someone is in court on a minor charge which has no direct bearing on nuclear weapons, there should be no co-operation with the court unless it gives a full hearing to the international nuclear dimension of the alleged offence. Any fine imposed should be refused. Paying fines in such a case is a form of indirect taxation for criminal purposes, an official protection racket. Imprisonment is uncomfortable but paid for by the Government.

Our campaign must develop opposition to income tax which finances nuclear crime. Since Hiroshima, it is a sad fact that peace movements in nuclear States have contributed huge sums of money to the very weapons they oppose. Far larger sums, in fact, than have financed the peace movements themselves. This financial contradiction mirrors internal contradictions of commitment which have hobbled peace work.

Many brave individuals have resisted taxation for annihilation, so far without success. As in all other cases concerning nuclear mass destruction, the courts have plodded obediently in the wake of authority, refusing to admit that such taxation is no better than cash extorted by gangsters. One recent case illustrates the problem.

Canon Paul Oestreicher, a Quaker member of the Church of England Synod, decided to withhold a part of his tax payment, on the grounds that this sum would be used by the Government to pay for an illegal nuclear weapons programme. In his judgment, given at a London county court on 29 November 1983, Judge Edwards said that Paul Oestreicher had 'presented his defence with moderation, fairness and patent sincerity'. The prosecution based its case on two Finance Acts of Parliament and the case of Cheney v. Conn,

1967. Howard Cheney, a businessman and farmer, had refused to pay a part of his income tax, on similar grounds of Government illegality, citing in particular the Geneva Conventions Act, 1957.

According to Judge Edwards, 'The Act of 1957 created certain criminal offences in municipal law and the Convention as a whole was not part of the law of England.' This extraordinary statement ignores an important part of the process by which international law is assimilated into domestic law. Where an international law defines what is already recognized as customary law and the 'law of England', there is no need to repeat its provisions in an Act of Parliament. This is only necessary where entirely new law is agreed. Thus whatever there is of the 1949 Geneva Conventions which does not appear in the 1957 Geneva Convention Act is presumed to be already in force. No country can pick and choose which aspects of customary international law it wishes to obey. This principle was made abundantly clear at Nuremberg by, among others, British judges.

Judge Edwards then refers to the fact that Paul Oestreicher cited on his behalf the Genocide Act of 1969, which gave effect to the Genocide Convention of 1948, saying that the Act 'did not adopt the Convention into law but created criminal offences described in the Genocide Convention which were not previously criminal'. This interpretation is as contradictory as the first. By creating 'criminal offences' which 'were not previously criminal', the Act concerned did exactly what the judge says it did not do, bring the Convention into English law.

By this judicial sleight of mind, paralleled wherever law is a convenience of power, Judge Edwards arrives at the desired conclusion: 'I must say, I cannot distinguish between the legal effect of the Geneva Conventions Act and the Genocide Act for all present purposes . . . this means that the defence must fail.'

The judge decorated this decision by referring to 'serious arguments' involving such laws as the Hague Conventions and the 1925 Geneva Gas Protocol. This gesture in the direction of laws by which Nazi criminals were tried and hanged at Nuremberg, was a token pat on the head for the 'patently sincere' Canon. 'However,' said Judge Edwards, 'these are arguments which have been and ought to be addressed to the High Court of Parliament.' As for the Nuremberg example: 'That is an argument that by no means does not deserve serious consideration but it must be considered in the wider context of nations as a whole, not courts of law which have a duty to enforce . . . the revenue laws.'

This convoluted reasoning, part friendly, part evasive, is consistent with the performance of the judiciary as we have examined it. There is the familiar nod towards misguided sincerity, heavy reliance on precedent, arm's-length treatment of international law, as if it were a tropical disease, convenient neutralization of awkward meaning, and a final sigh of relief as the whole problem is thrown into the lap of parliament and the 'wider context of nations'. The law is thrown out with the legal bathwater, but the bath itself remains, as usual, immaculately intact, polished by a self-serving logic insulated from the simple horror of mass murder and its prevention.

As long as British judges persist in obstructive behaviour our campaign to enforce laws prohibiting mass destruction must supplement such personal initiatives as Paul Oestreicher's with other methods. The legal argument can be presented more concisely, focused on the simple fact that the British armed forces are committed by military, domestic and international law not to attack non-combatants. Any Government which adopts a defence policy implying such an attack, is therefore inciting its own forces to commit war crimes on a gigantic and suicidal scale. Any judge who dares to contradict this basic law should be publicly named and subjected to consistent pressure by every reasonable means. As we have seen, a leading British Conservative defence expert and MP has described current defence policy as based on 'population extermination'. If a judge fails to condemn such crime he must be opposed and exposed.

Withholding tax should be backed up by refusal to pay, even if this leads to sequestration of goods and property, or prison. An alternative approach is to ensure that income is low enough to escape tax altogether. Everyone must choose what makes most sense, but the campaign must make it clear that the law presents us with no option as to payment. To pay 'protection' money to a gangster for criminal activities is itself a crime, particularly when his arsenal consists of weapons of population extermination. To pay for Polaris, or Cruise, or SS20s, is to aid and abet a criminal conspiracy.

Our struggle is beginning to take the offensive against official perversion of the law. To prosecute governments, at a time when they control the courts in the vital area of national security, requires the highest level of personal commitment and an ability to focus on the simple essence of the law. Two British women, Cherry Quinn, a farmer, and Angela Hunt, a gardener, decided to take this campaign to the European Commission of Human Rights at Strasbourg. The Commission examines complaints and either rejects them or passes them on to the European Court of Human Rights in the same city, for legal judgment. British Governments have proved the worst violators of human rights in Western Europe, with eleven guilty verdicts against them: 'In the past decade we have established ourselves as the worst protectors of human rights in Western Europe. (Belgium is runner-up with eight guilty verdicts)'[1]

The two women were convicted at Banbury, Oxfordshire, on 10 August 1983, of obstructing the highway during a blockade of an American nuclear air base at Upper Heyford in the same county, on 2 June 1983. They pleaded 'not guilty' on the grounds that they had lawful excuse for their action, citing the Criminal Law Act (Section 3), 1967, which provides that a person may use such force as is reasonable in the circumstances to prevent a crime. They told the court that it was their 'conviction that nuclear threats of mass destruction violate the very essence of international laws restricting warfare'.

The magistrate refused to allow evidence concerning 'the defence of the country' and found them both guilty. Their appeal against this judgment was heard at Oxford Crown Court on 8 November 1983, before Judge Mynett. We have already seen how he dismissed their appeal, despite extensive and detailed evidence that both international and domestic law prohibit any form of indiscriminate mass destruction.[2] Judge Mynett likewise protected the Government from legal scrutiny, in violation of the most basic legal principles, confirmed at Nuremberg, that no aspect of human activity is above the law.

Cherry Quinn and Angela Hunt felt that this judicial response denied them justice because their defence case was not given equal legal weight with that of the prosecution. Judge Mynett had also added the gratuitous comment that 'the real purpose of the appeal

[1] *Observer*, 5 August 1984.
[2] See Chapter 5.

was to obtain publicity', a further indication of his inability to respond to the gravity of the nuclear issue.

The two women have decided to take their case to the European Commission 'to obtain a ruling which confirms the right of a citizen to challenge in a court of law the legal status of the Government's military policies. (Denial of this right places the security of the individual and the State outside the law).'

They ask the Commission to rule on their complaint that British justice has violated Section 1, Article 6(d) of the Human Rights Charter which declares 'the right to examine or have examined witnesses against him and to obtain the attendance and examination of witnesses on his behalf under the same conditions as witnesses against him.'

They further consider that Section 1, Article 7 was also contravened: 'No one shall be held guilty of any criminal offence on account of any act or omission which did not constitute a criminal offence under national or international law at the time when it was committed.'

Cherry Quinn and Angela Hunt were not asking for a ruling from the Commission on the legality of nuclear weapons, but simply for a ruling that the legal status of nuclear weapons is as much a subject for judicial investigation as any other aspect of life. They were, and are, challenging the no-go area of nuclear illegality.

Their case is of the utmost importance for our campaign. It shows how two determined people, with no legal qualifications or special status, can attack the cobra of poisoned authority. It is an approach which can be followed by dozens, hundreds, thousands, until there is a broad alliance of protest at the door of the European Court. 'No' must not be accepted as an answer to such appeals. Evidence of the British Government's vulnerability to this approach can be seen in the Strasbourg ruling, in response to the complaint of a Scottish mother, that corporal punishment in schools is illegal if conducted in defiance of parental wishes. Educational violence is collapsing under the weight of this judgment. Cracks are appearing in the dam walls of power-abuse. A trickle of principled defiance can grow into a flood.

A more elaborate and expensive approach to nuclear illegality is the lawsuit in New York against the US Government, brought by the Greenham Common women's peace camp in Britain in November 1983. The case was brought by twelve British women and their children and one American associated with the peace camp, together with two members of the US House of Representatives. They alleged that deployment of Cruise missiles at Greenham was illegal, contravening international law, and that deployment also violated US constitutional amendments protecting individuals under US protection from injury. The two congressmen alleged that Cruise deployment violated their congressional right to declare war, because nuclear weapons can be activated on a Presidential order alone.

Defendants in this case were the US President, Secretary of Defense, Secretary of the Air Force, and the Secretary of the Army. The case was heard in a New York Federal Court by Judge Edelstein. The plaintiffs' case was supported by many organizations in Europe and the United States, who sent amicus briefs (supporting argument). These included my own campaign, INLAW (International Law Against War). After many months of solitary consideration, Judge Edelstein dismissed the suit on 31 July 1984. An appeal against this decision was filed on 20 September 1984.

There are several useful lessons to be learned from this case. By stressing deployment of Cruise missiles, rather than the illegality of nuclear weapons as such, the plaintiffs gave the judge a line of escape which he followed gratefully. Their additional assertion that all nuclear weapons are illegal was pushed aside, as he elaborated his belief that the 'delicate' issues of foreign policy are best left to those elected to manage them.

Judge Edelstein countered the 'first strike' argument, and the risks which flow from it, with the US Government's assertion that the missiles are not 'first strike' but an integral part of a defensive strategy. The law is soon lost in such fruitless argument over military strategy. Neither assertion can be proved. Earlier cases were cited in evidence that foreign policy is beyond the competence of the courts and is a 'non-justiceable political question'. This reasoning asserts that there are 'no discoverable and manageable standards' within the complexities of foreign policy for the court to make use of. This is true, if the surface is examined rather than the underlying principle.

Judge Edelstein focused on the political implications of this line of reasoning: 'the court would have to determine whether the United States by deploying Cruise missiles is acting aggressively

rather than defensively, increasing significantly the risk of incalculable death and destruction rather than decreasing such risk, and
making war rather than promoting peace and stability'.

The nuclear fog rolled in once more, shrouding the Greenham
argument in a cloak of political speculation. It is a function of legal
irrationality to divert attention from the obvious and immediate
towards fantasy: 'The courts are simply incapable of determining
the effect of the missile deployment on world peace ... it is
precisely because the ultimate effects are not altogether knowable
that conjecture and predictions about them are best left to the
political branches of government.'

Judge Edelstein was home free, ading that the whole matter was
as abstruse as 'how many angels can dance on the head of a pin'.

American judges, like judges everywhere, adopt a me-too
approach to any fundamental issues which call into question the
prevailing values and conduct of society. They hide behind each
other. Judge Edelstein did what his British and other counterparts
have often done in such a situation, quote precedent. He chose a
cast-iron crutch to lean on, none other than US Chief Justice
Warren E. Burger, who had said in a case involving nuclear testing
(Pauling v. McNamara, 1963), when he was a Circuit Judge:

'That appellants now resort to the courts on a vague and
disorientated theory that judicial power can supply a quick and
pervasive remedy for one of mankind's great problems is no reason
why we as judges should regard ourselves as some kind of Guardian
Elders ordained to review the political judgments of elected representatives of the people. In framing policies relating to the great
issues of national defense and security, the people are and must be,
in a sense at the mercy of their elected representatives.'

The later Chief Justice went on to say that the people can get rid
of politicians, which made it all the more necessary for judges to
show that: 'We are neither gods nor godlike, but judicial officers
with narrow and limited authority. Our entire system of Government would suffer incalculable mischief should judges attempt to
interpose the judicial will above that of the Congress and President,
even were we so bold as to assume that we can make a better
decision on such issues.'

This statement is not only echoed in the opinion of British and
no doubt Soviet judges, but also echoes what most of the judges of
Nazi Germany had to say, and would not have been out of place on

the lips of King John's lawyers before Magna Carta clipped his wings. It was a common complaint of the judges at Nuremberg that the Nazi defendants claimed great authority when it suited them, yet pretended helplessness when it did not. The grain of truth in the Edelstein/Burger argument lies in the indisputable fact that courts have no right to meddle in the complexities of legitimate foreign and defence policy, just as they have no right to meddle in the legitimate affairs of a citizen.

What is entirely refutable is the notion that the universal principles of law do not bind this vital area of Government policy. If President and Congress are not subject to law they are by definition outlaws, in a nightmare world governed by superior force. It was the whole purpose of the Nuremberg Trial to deny such criminal logic. The superficial, corrupt nature of the Edelstein/Burger logic is exemplified by the US mine-laying of Nicaraguan ports in 1984, which flouted international law. The US Government attempted to prevent judicial examination of this action by withdrawing support temporarily from the International Court at The Hague. But the widespread outcry of denunciation stirred up by these events internationally and within the United States, compelled a change of policy. As we have seen earlier, much of this opposition was based on legal argument.

Our campaign can learn from the Greenham case that opposition to nuclear illegality must be based on the core of the problem, not its manifold extensions. The law specifically forbids an individual, soldier or statesman to commit murder or conspire to commit murder. Legitimate military action becomes murder when directed at non-combatants. Weapons and policies of mass destruction are intrinsically murderous and criminal. Cruise or any other nuclear missiles violate basic law. The Greenham case was too elaborate and discursive, allowing Judge Edelstein to treat the deployment issue as a matter of foreign policy rather than law. The additional complaint that Cruise deployment caused personal 'injury' was an irrelevance smacking of self-pity. It is the injury to be caused to people in the target area of these missiles which must concern us first, not our own inconvenience and distress. But as Carrie Pester, one of the Greenham plaintiffs, said: 'This is only the first step.'

This argument applies as much if not more to the armed forces of a nuclear State. As we have seen, the training of a soldier tells him to obey the law while compelling him to obey orders blindly. The result is that only a rare and exceptional soldier has the integrity to challenge criminal action in war. The often vast spatial distance between killer and killed in modern warfare compounds this problem of loss of identity. The crew of a Polaris submarine epitomize the pathological insulation of the nuclear mass murderer within a technological cocoon, a state-of-the-art Eichmann, the coronation of irresponsible man.

A campaign to enforce minimum law in this miasma of denial must seek to restore individual integrity, by focusing attention on each member of the armed forces, from highest to lowest. Leaflets have been circulated to British and US servicemen, warning them of their individual responsibility in law to oppose military crime. Each military person must be asked to face this issue, privately and publicly. It is not in the protected military base but at home and in public that this can be done. Renewal of commitment to the law at this level implies radical reform of defence policy. Strict enforcement of laws restraining violence will reach far beyond the nuclear sphere, into so-called conventional weapons. Reform of this kind will eventually transform the military into police, a service in the lawful suppression of crime able to operate without guns and bombs. Campaign groups can work out how to bring this issue to local military recruiting agencies.

An initial aim is to make our nuclear armed forces as committed to minimum law as an Israeli commander: 'The battalion CO got on the field telephone to my company and said, "Don't touch the civilians . . . don't fire until you're fired at and don't touch the civilians. Look, you've been warned. Their blood will be on your head." '[1]

Such a simple, humanitarian commitment would leave our weapon systems of mass murder without operators, because the latter would prefer to remain human. There are welcome signs of a revulsion against nuclear deterrence among some Western military leaders.

It is when we come to the political figures that our campaign confronts the densest confusion. It is they who have led the way in fouling the vulnerable springs of mutual respect and reason, the basic components of law, substituting a fantasy of reality. They

---

[1] Walzer, op. cit.: Israeli soldiers discussing the Six Day War.

mediate the hostility of the Cold War as pimps mediate sexuality. By setting themselves up as guardians of law and order they are more pretentious than pimps. Armed with nuclear weapons they are self-appointed executioners of life on earth, in the name of law and civilized values. They compel agreement with King Lear: ' 'Tis time's plague when madmen lead the blind.' A Conservative British politician confessed how sham ideals mask terrorism: 'Those who use terror to gain their political ends are the heirs of Hitler's Revolution of Destruction, however much they may claim to represent opposing doctrines.'[1]

It is ironic that this insight was not directed at the author's guiding doctrines. He not only supported the nuclear 'balance of terror', the ultimate in State terrorism, but was blown up by a terrorist bomb at the House of Commons many years later, the victim of British political failure to resolve political violence.

Attempts to relate politicians to the law and nuclear weapons have met with predictable resistance. The British House of Commons contains more lawyers than any other professional group, almost 20% of the total in 1984, yet few of these lawyers have any knowledge of international law, despite its relevance to British defence and foreign policy. Fewer still recognize the disastrous chasm which has opened up between the law and nuclear weapons. Even politicians of the left who want to ban nuclear weapons from Britain are reluctant to enforce the laws against them, despite the obvious advantage to be gained from applying laws which bind every nation, including the United States and the Soviet Union. A powerful and sustained political focus on nuclear illegality would put considerable pressure on every nation to conform.

Why is this so? We have looked at the hidden, irrational factor which diverts law and reason from the free-fire zone of national security, but this unconscious censor is not the whole problem. Politicians value room for manoeuvre above almost everything. They fear law because it imposes constraints on political action. This is not guesswork. Our campaign sent questionnaires to every British MP in the spring of 1984, asking to what extent they support international laws prohibiting all forms of mass destruction.

[1] Neave, op. cit.

Just over one hundred replied. The approximate percentage was: Conservative, 5%; Labour, 18%; Liberal, 25%; SDP, 28%; Plaid Cymru, 100%; Scottish National Party, 50%. The Conservative party of 'law and order' showed least concern and the smaller parties most, reversing stereotype behaviour and indicating awareness that the law poses a threat to prevailing Conservative policy, while offering some advantage to opposition parties which are more or less hostile to nuclear weapons.

Of the Conservative respondents, several were lawyers, none of whom consider nuclear weapons to be in breach of the law. What is interesting is not the negative response of politicians whose party embraces nuclear weapons, but the fact that all of them justified their position by political rather than legal argument; nuclear deterrence is defensive and has kept the peace, therefore it must be lawful. It is a line of argument which they would dismiss out of hand if used by a burglar who used his bank balance as a yardstick of legality.

Labour party members opposed to nuclear weapons accept the prohibitions of international law but know little about them, preferring to rely on political argument. They look at the law in relation to State policy rather than individual responsibility.

Follow-up meetings with individual MPs suggest that these are a fruitful initiative for our campaign. Ignorance of the law can be exposed in a face to face interview, politely but firmly. The more conservative MPs are uncomfortable when confronted with laws which make criminal nonsense of nuclear policies. There is no need for special expertise. It is enough to ask why laws which forbid attacks on non-combatants are not enforced, despite official statements that it is the policy of the British Government to obey the laws of armed conflict.

Depressing was the evasive response of leading Labour Party spokesmen who appear to have neither knowledge of nor real interest in the law. The Labour leader Neil Kinnock failed to reply to questions put to him. Even the Labour spokesman on defence was unwilling to commit himself on the legal implications of nuclear weapons. The irony of this reticence lies in the fact that the law offers the Labour Party a means of giving its opposition to nuclear weapons more credibility. By making a firm public commitment to uphold minimum international legal restraints on military violence, it would show its commitment to law while putting pressure on other nuclear States to follow suit.

No reply is more revealing than that of the leader of the Social Democrats, David Owen. He simply states that laws prohibiting nuclear mass destruction are 'unenforceable', only negotiation can work.[1] As British Foreign Secretary at the signing of the important Additional Protocol 1, 1977, he helped to commit the British people to a set of binding laws (102 Articles) whose main purpose is to protect the civilian population in war: 'Women shall be the object of special respect' (Art. 76); 'Children shall be the object of special respect' (Art. 77); 'In order to ensure respect for and protection of the civilian population . . . the Parties to the conflict shall at all times distinguish between the civilian population and combatants' (Art. 48). The preamble to the Protocol asserts that its provisions 'must be fully applied in all circumstances to all persons who are protected by these instruments, without any adverse distinction based on the nature of origin of the armed conflict . . . .'

David Owen not only approved these laws, which were agreed after years of negotiation, but promptly added a reservation on behalf of the British Government which sought to exclude nuclear weapons from their scope. The British and United States Governments were alone in adding such a reservation, which amounts to a declaration that these basic principles must be 'fully applied in all circumstances,' except when we consider nuclear mass murder to be in the national interest. To formulate and sign such laws, add a mocking reservation, and then declare them 'unenforceable' is the hallmark of corrupt politics. David Owen is not a solitary scape-goat. The nuclear landscape is overrun with them.

To enforce laws restraining the most criminal, irrational arms race in history is not easy. Law enforcement requires an unprecedented effort of determination. To give up with a cynical shrug, having compounded the problem, is a tactic of despair which our campaign must expose and oppose wherever it appears. Every relevant department of nuclear government must be approached and challenged. Individual politicians must be smoked out of hiding and cross-examined.

Some departments of the British Government have been approached. These include the Prime Minister, Defence Minister, Foreign Secretary, Attorney-General and Lord Chancellor. Their replies have been evasive, with questions left unanswered and

[1] Loc. cit.

answers given to questions which have not been asked. The British Prime Minister was asked how laws which forbid attacks on non-combatants can be reconciled with a retaliatory strategy of indiscriminate mass destruction. A reply from 10 Downing Street, dated 21 February 1984, does not answer this question but declares flatly: 'There is no aspect of current defence policy which is inconsistent with the Government's obligations under international law, including the laws of war. Claims that the possession of nuclear weapons contravenes international law are unfounded.'

The letter goes on to justify this by pointing to the Non-Proliferation Treaty of 1968, which 'specifically recognizes the possession by some states of such weapons'. It concludes by asserting that NATO policy is defensive. Not only is the basic issue of protection for non-combatants ignored in this letter, but there is no legal argument put forward of any kind, only flat assertions of legality. The treaty referred to was intended to be what it has proved to be, a confirmation of the nuclear status quo, despite a pious curtsey to disarmament. It does not in any sense alter the basis of the laws of war, which restrict violence, particularly violence directed at the helpless.

If the Prime Minister cannot come to terms with the law, who can? The Ministry of Defence does little better. It declares: 'The use of nuclear weapons is governed not by specific treaty but by customary law . . . any use of nuclear weapons would have to be judged as lawful or not in the light of the circumstances at the time.'[1]

Customary law leaves no doubt whatever that non-combatants must not be attacked, and indiscriminate 'total war' is forbidden. This makes nonsense of the second claim that any use of nuclear weapons must be assessed in terms of law at the moment when the finger of death reaches for the button. Nuclear weapons are already part of an official and international conspiracy to commit mass murder.

A Minister of State for the British armed forces argues: 'The use of nuclear weapons is . . . governed by the general principles of international law. Since the use of nuclear weapons may be lawful, the deterrent threat of their legitimate use is also lawful.'[2]

It requires an effort of imagination, such is our conditioning to

[1] Letter from Lord Trefgarne to Tom Arnold, MP, 27 March 1984.
[2] Letter from Peter Blaker, MP to M. Jopling, MP, 15 February 1983.

violence, to realize that what he is saying is that laws whose whole intention is to restrain and protect, may sanction 'population extermination' in the event of war.

It will surprise nobody that the British Foreign Office pours brandy on this funeral pyre. When I raised questions about British policy towards the 1977 Additional Protocol 1, David Owen passed on my enquiry to the Foreign Office. The reply of the Minister of State, Douglas Hurd, contains some interesting comments: 'The Government's decision to sign was intended as a demonstration of goodwill towards the principles contained in the Protocols and enabled Ministers to embark on serious preparations for eventual ratification.'[1]

Douglas Hurd does not consider that the reservation added by the British to exclude nuclear weapons 'invalidates their effect overall'. He concludes by saying that 'the laws of war are, of course, a part of military training'. This illustrates the jumble of contradictions which is British official interpretation of the law on this issue. What kind of demonstration of goodwill is it which negotiates extensive laws and then declares that in the event of a war for which Britain's military strategy is designed, they will be inoperative? If this does not 'invalidate their effect overall', what would? The so-called 'serious preparations' for ratification are no more serious than the rest of this solemn pantomime, judging by their lack of result seven years after signing. As for the final line about military training, we have already seen how the British Army does its best to teach these minimum laws of war, emphasizing that non-combatants must not be the object of attack. It is the Government's incitement to break these laws by threats of nuclear mass destruction which criminalizes its armed forces.

The Foreign Office contains an Arms Control and Disarmament Research Unit, which might be expected to show some interest in upholding the law, despite its Cinderella status. Yet it has nothing to say about these vitally important issues other than that nuclear weapons must be lawful because 'there is no general multilateral convention outlawing nuclear weapons'.[2] This ignores entirely the elementary fact that most law deals in principles of behaviour rather than specific weapons, including domestic law forbidding murder. The Unit does not reply to questions about laws protect-

[1] Letter from Douglas Hurd MP to David Owen MP, 29 September 1982.
[2] Letter to author, 6 September 1984.

ing non-combatants. It refers to the Government's binding obligation to disseminate the laws of war to the widest public, civilian and military, and draws attention to publications available at Her Majesty's Stationery Office shops. This last news should be understood in the context of a massive publicity campaign which dispenses free Ministry of Defence publications to schools and other institutions all over the country, extolling NATO's virtues. The laws of war remain almost unknown to those whom they most concern, ordinary citizens. It is the job of our campaign to correct this lack of awareness.

The British Attorney-General also uses the absence of a treaty specifically banning nuclear weapons as their main justification in law: 'There is no specific prohibition on the use or possession of nuclear weapons under international law. None of the international instruments which you list contains such a prohibition nor can such a prohibition be derived indirectly from these instruments in the way you suggest.'[1]

This rationalization of nuclear threats of mass destruction ignores the simple fact that international law, in purpose and detail, forbids attacks on non-combatants. It evades the fact that British soldiers are specifically warned not to attack non-combatants. It contradicts in spirit and in fact what the chief British prosecutor at Nuremberg, Sir Hartley Shawcross QC, had to say on this theme: 'There is no rule of international law which provides immunity for those who obey orders which – whether legal or not in the country where they are issued – are manifestly contrary to the very law of nature from which international law has grown. If international law is to be applied at all, it must be superior to State law in this respect, that it must consider the legality of what is done by international and not by State law tests. By every test of international law, of common conscience, of elementary humanity, these orders were illegal . . . . '

There was a further warning to our present rulers: 'murder does not cease to be murder merely because the victims are multiplied ten millionfold', and the 'principle war crime . . . with which these men are charged is the violation of the most firmly established and least controversial of all the rules of warfare, namely, that non-

---

[1] Letter from Legal Secretary, Attorney-General's chambers, to author dated 8 March 1984.

combatants must not be made the direct object of hostile operations'.

It is a measure of the nazification of nuclear policies that such clear, humane principles are brushed aside by today's leaders as of no account. What we have gained from these communications with nuclear authority is an accurate map of its mind. Law has been taken hostage by its minders, and is being used in the way that a gunman uses a hostage, as a shield to ward off attack.

Our campaign approached the last stage of this investigation of nuclear authority, its symbol of integrity, the Queen of England. She was asked to investigate allegations of law-breaking, against the British Government and its main agents. Petitions to this effect were signed by thousands of British citizens from many parts of the country. The response was a note to say the complaint had been forwarded to the appropriate ministry, Defence. The circle of evasion was complete.

We now know that every major British institution colludes either directly or indirectly with unlawful weapons of mass murder. While this scandal persists there is only one way forward which is neither violent nor futile. It is up to the individual citizen to uphold and enforce the law against mass murder and the final pollution of life on earth. A first step is to seek a court summons against the Prime Minister, on the grounds of conspiracy to commit mass murder, in violation of the 'law of nature from which international law has grown', of specific binding commitments to protect the helpless, of orders given to British soldiers and of the common conscience of mankind.

A summons of this kind may be stopped in its tracks by a magistrate, or later by the Director of Public Prosecutions whose job is to oversee the prosecution of serious crime. Such obstruction, if it occurs, will mean that the entire machinery of the law has been closed to us. We will find ourselves finally in the situation of the citizen under Hitler, where everyday law enforcement continued more or less normally, as a cover for official crime. What is left is the right to approach each agent of nuclear crime, one by one, at work or home, with a personal warning of complicity. If that final civic right is denied we will indeed become the concentration camp victims we so nearly are. We will be in our nuclear Auschwitz, under guard by people whose schizophrenic patriotism leads them to regard mass murder as a solemn duty, if required as a final solution.

The contagious evil of the nuclear nightmare which we have
endured in these pages is so overwhelming that it becomes tempting to pretend that we at least are immune. But the cold snake we
have by the neck has each of us by the neck, too.

An American soldier met a French security officer in Marseilles
at the end of the Second World War. He described in his diary how
the latter interrogated a French girl who had fallen in love with a
German Gestapo officer. He joked and laughed with her before
signing a secret report to the civil authorities recommending that
she be shot: 'When I remonstrated with him about such callousness, he made clear to me that he regarded himself as an army
officer in a quite different way from himself as a human being . . . .
As a human being, he was capable of kindness, even gentleness,
and within limits he was just and honest. In his capacity of
functionary, he could be brutal beyond measure without ever
losing his outward amiability and poise. I observed precisely the
same qualities in the Fascist and Nazi politicians and police with
whom it was my fate to deal.'[1]

The polluted river of twentieth-century crime flows through our
bloodstream and mingles with our thoughts. It is not only the
Polaris crew, the cossetted heirs of Eichmann, who have adopted
the concentration camp survivor's motto: 'If you don't see evil it
may not see you!' It is not only the Hiroshima survivor who says:
'Don't feel.' We only need to look in the mirror to observe the same
defences. In a profound sense, the Third World War is already
being fought, in our mind and soul. The Cold War is our nuclear
winter.

By daring to confront the full extent of our nightmare we can
re-discover the fact that spring lies waiting, even within this winter
of the dead. The situation is far worse than we admit, yet we are far
better people than we imagine. By feeling this unique strength we
can throw off the curse exposed by the Austrian poet, Grillparzer:

> To strive half-heartedly, by half measures,
> To bring about half of what must be done.

The weapons of 'population extermination' are not half-hearted
but absolute. Our response must be no less complete. We are not
obliged to tolerate the token dissent of those who denounce the

---

[1] J. Glenn Gray quoted in Falk et al. (ed.), op. cit.

nuclear idol while grovelling for its bribes. The law will not provide the hard floor of a revitalized civilization if it is left to the lawyer who told me on 13 December 1983: 'You are looking at actions that lawyers can't necessarily do because it would not be politically or legally advisable, like serving a summons on the Prime Minister.'

The time is ripe to spit out the poisonous logic which weighs so heavy on us, exemplified by a retired British Air Vice-Marshal, Stewart Menaul: 'What Britain needs is a theatre nuclear force capable of attacking military targets in the Soviet Union under a realistic strategy but with the ability to attack cities and industrial complexes if the situation so demanded.'[1]

Sickened at last by murderous criminality masquerading as defence, we can answer the desperate appeal of Rilke, during the First World War, from Munich: 'Can no one prevent it and stop it? Why are there not two, three, five, ten people who would unite and cry out in the market-places: Enough! ... Why is there not one person who will endure it no longer, who refuses to endure it – if he cried but for a single night in the midst of the false beflagged city, cried and would refuse to be silenced, who would dare call him liar?'

The German poet sensed that once the 'universal misery and sadness' of war was rejected, the 'confused survivors' would once more 'resume the discarded laws of their inner being.' He speaks for us, the confused survivors of two world wars, searching for discarded law in a sad graveyard.

We know the necessary law exists and must be used. Law enforcement against nuclear death is a condition of human survival. What we want is not utopian love but something as simple and natural as a glass of clean water, a minimum respect for life. Only then will we be fit to live.

To those who ask, what if the Soviet Union scorns the law, even if we obey it? – tell them that the people of the Soviet Union are much like us, walking on two feet, breathing air and trapped in the same nightmare. They are fellow-inmates of nuclear industrial society, have allied with us before and can do it again. The risk of recognizing their humanity is nothing to the risk of denying it.

We have glimpsed a path in the fog, and have taken the first steps. We can find enough life in our fragmented selves and

---

[1] *The Times*, 26 February 1982.

societies to lay the foundations of a post-nuclear civilization. We will be doing something which has challenged the human spirit for thousands of years. When Theseus entered the gloomy labyrinth of Knossos, lair of a half-man, half-bull Minotaur, he was testing nightmare projections of evil. For us in the West today it is a Soviet Minotaur which haunts us, inciting crime on a suicidal scale.

Theseus relied on a thread of feminine insight to guide him out of his dead end. So must we. As I examined the solemn ruins of that ancient palace in Crete I wondered about Ariadne's saving part in the drama. These two figures of mythology remind us that only when masculine and feminine are one can we emerge into the daylight and begin to live without the shackles of sub-human fantasy.

The law which we seek to enforce is the floor of new life. It is also a frontier between dream and nightmare which runs right through us.

Appendix

THE CITIZEN
versus
NUCLEAR CONSPIRACY

The way towards prosecuting nuclear crime

Alone or in combination, religion, morality, reason and political ideology have failed to stem the flood of modern destructive power. Civilization's finest ideals have been hijacked by the agents of nuclear militarism, generating a false and neurotic security based on threats of mass murder.

We have seen in detail how this corrupting process has spread through the mind and sinews of the twentieth century, finally invading every corner of our lives. Brave efforts by earlier generations to bind violence within humanitarian law have failed, not because the law is too weak but because its guardians have betrayed it. The threat of extinction now demoralizes and terrifies humanity, violating the most elementary values and laws.

In the face of this acute threat there is both widespread apathy, and the first signs of violence against military installations. But there is a more positive response, to enforce the law as an 'emergency brake' on our runaway arms race to extinction. Not law cynically subservient to the nuclear status quo and its agents, but law rooted in common sense humanity which outlaws cruelty and wanton violence.

INLAW (International Law Against War), a network of people determined to enforce minimum law, is now promoting a world-wide citizens' prosecution of the main agents of nuclear crime. The first prosecution took place on 13 February 1985 (the anniversary of the bombing of Dresden), in the town of Bedford, England. The indictment used at Bedford Magistrates Court has since been used

by other citizens in the local courts of England, Wales and
Scotland.

Related initiatives in other countries indicate, even at this early
stage, that the patience of ordinary people around the world with
nuclear tyranny is wearing very thin. When the will exists to arrest
nuclear crime, nothing can stop it. The foundation stone of a just
world will have been laid.

The courts and the lawyers are astonished by this democratic
invasion of their temple, some even alarmed by it. But it is the right
and duty of every citizen to bring suspected criminal activity to the
attention of the police, or the courts. The Bedford indictment does
this, not in legal jargon, but in everyday language. The allegations
are serious and simple. Nuclear defence strategy involves a threat
to exterminate, poison and injure the enemy population, thus
violating the most basic principles of international and domestic
law. The indictment contains several pages of evidence and legal
interpretation, which can be made available by INLAW to any
reader.

A copy of the front page of the Bedford indictment appears on
page 353.

Governments have for many years kept these laws at bay, by a
double bluff. They pretend that domestic courts cannot handle
such problems—a tactic which was dismissed with scorn at
Nuremberg when it was used by Nazi defendants. And they invoke
the special status of 'national security', as if matters of national
survival are outside the law. This ploy too was thrown out by the
judges of Nuremberg.

The Nuremberg Trial confirmed that there is no legitimate
hiding place for law-breakers, whatever their status. Government
leaders who break the laws of military restraint must be tried and
punished, in a national or international court. The Bedford
indictment brings the law down to earth, relating international
law-breaking to national law-breaking, by charging three British
leaders with specific violations requiring prosecution in British
courts. By pursuing nuclear policies beyond their lawful authority
they are liable to be charged as ordinary criminals. Threatening the
lives of defenceless people in the Soviet Union (the old, the sick,
children) who are protected by law, makes these leaders liable to a
charge of conspiring to commit murder.

Recent evidence in support of this allegation comes from the case

INDICTMENT FOR CONSPIRACY AND INCITEMENT

MARGARET THATCHER, Prime Minister; MICHAEL HESELTINE, Minister of
Defence; SIR GEOFFREY HOWE, Foreign Secretary.

PART ONE

     WE, THE UNDERSIGNED BRITISH CITIZENS, RESIDENT IN
...... *Bedford* ....IN THE COUNTY OF . *Bedfordshire*...
ALLEGE THAT THE ABOVE MEMBERS OF THE BRITISH GOVERNMENT HAVE ABUSED
THEIR HIGH OFFICE BY PROMOTING NUCLEAR DEFENCE POLICIES WHICH
VIOLATE THE MOST FUNDAMENTAL PRINCIPLES OF INTERNATIONAL AND
BRITISH LAW.

WE ALLEGE   I. THAT THEY HAVE BASED BRITISH SECURITY ON THREATS OF
NUCLEAR ANNIHILATION AGAINST THE SOVIET UNION AND ITS PEOPLE, THUS
THREATENING THE LIVES AND HEALTH OF COUNTLESS MILLIONS OF PROTECTED
PERSONS, INCLUDING THE OLD, SICK, WOUNDED, AND WOMEN AND CHILDREN.

     SUCH A POLICY DIRECTLY VIOLATES LAWS FORBIDDING INDISCRIMINATE
DESTRUCTION BY ANY MEANS. BY MOVING OUTSIDE THE LAWFUL AUTHORITY OF
THE STATE THEY HAVE CONSPIRED TO VIOLATE BOTH THE LAWS OF WAR AND
BRITISH LAWS AGAINST THREATS OF MURDER.

     2. THAT THEY, IN THE COURSE OF PROMOTING THIS UNLAWFUL
POLICY, HAVE INCITED MEMBERS OF THE BRITISH ARMED FORCES TO BREAK
INTERNATIONAL, MILITARY AND DOMESTIC LAW, THUS BETRAYING THEIR OATH OF
ALLEGIANCE TO THE CROWN AND THEIR PROFESSIONAL CODE OF CONDUCT.

     3. THAT THEY HAVE CONSPIRED TO MISLEAD THE BRITISH PEOPLE
BY LEADING THEM TO BELIEVE THAT THREATS OF NUCLEAR MASS DESTRUCTION
ARE A NECESSARY AND LAWFUL BASIS OF NATIONAL SECURITY.

     4. THAT AT THE CORE OF THIS CRIMINAL OFFENCE LIES A
CONSPIRACY TO COMMIT SIMPLE MURDER AGAINST AN UNNAMED, PROTECTED
CITIZEN OF MOSCOW.

TO THE MAGISTRATE OF.... *Bedford* .... *13 February 1985*
WE ASK THAT A FULL AND THOROUGH INVESTIGATION BE MADE OF THESE
SERIOUS ALLEGATIONS. THE LAW FORBIDS MURDER, THE THREAT OF MURDER, AND
ALL FORMS OF INDISCRIMINATE DESTRUCTION. WE ASK THAT IT BE ENFORCED.

         (see attached signatures and supporting evidence)

of a young British soldier convicted of murder while on duty in Northern Ireland. He shot and killed a civilian man during a routine city patrol and was jailed for life on 14 December 1984, by a West Belfast criminal court. He had exceeded his legitimate powers as a soldier and was tried as a common criminal. The three accused British leaders have similarly exceeded their legitimate authority, by promoting a nuclear policy which threatens the murder of non-combatants.

Furthermore, it is alleged that an illegal defence policy incites military personnel to do what they are expressly forbidden to do, prepare to commit war crimes.

British magistrates courts handle minor cases, but can refer a major criminal prosecution to a crown court if they are satisified that there is a case to answer. When two of us appeared at the Bedford Magistrates Court to request a hearing of our indictment, it was clear that our arrival was anticipated. We were at once asked to go to a specified court and wait. A local newspaper had already phoned the courts to ask how we would be received.

After a one-hour wait, when the Court Usher took our names and apologized for the delay while 'various odds and ends' of outstanding cases were dealt with, we were invited into court. There was a buzz of interest amoung court officials and reporters. The Bench of three Magistrates looked solemn, even apprehensive. We all looked at each other, nobody knowing quite what to expect. It may have been the first time in any country that national leaders were being accused in court by ordinary citizens of major crime.

Following a few preliminary questions the Magistrates and Chief Clerk retired to read through and consider our indictment. After forty-five minutes they returned, to announce that they could not act on the evidence before them although they shared our concern about nuclear war. They were polite, almost apologetic. It was evident that they found the whole experience somewhat unnerving, so remote was it from their normal case-work.

When I asked if I could put a question to them there was consternation. Meaningful looks were quickly exchanged between the Chairman of the Bench and the Chief Clerk. Yes, said the latter, but only if I addressed my question to him. So I asked if we could take our case to a higher court. He replied that we could ask the High Court for a writ of 'mandamus', a judicial ruling which would compel the Magistrates to act on our evidence and investigate our complaint.

Since then the Bedford indictment has been used in local courts in England, Wales and Scotland, sometimes with minor modification. The intention is to build on this experience so that a concerted, nationwide and then worldwide citizens' prosecution can be organized.

Experience suggests that there is much to be gained from this project. It costs nothing. Even an appeal to the High Court involves minimal costs, if it is argued without paid legal help. Local media show a strong interest in such an unusual initiative. Those who present the indictment gain in confidence by learning about their fears and discovering their courage. They learn how to take the first steps in using the law on behalf of their most deeply held values. They learn that it will be a hard struggle to recapture the law from those who pervert it for reasons of established privilege and power.

Magistrates, court officials and police become aware that there is a dimension of the law beyond their experience which is vital to the survival of their society. As they begin to explore this new ground they will begin to put pressure on Government authorities to justify their policies.

The general public learns from these local cases that the law is relevant to issues of war and peace. It is not hard to understand that laws forbidding attacks on non-combatants are violated by weapons which threaten the existence of entire cities. Peace groups can give a sharp focus to their concerns, instead of relying on symbolic marches described by one activist as 'amiable groups of sauntering victims with a grievance'. The assertion of basic rights and laws means that vitality can begin to creep back into the roots of democratic life.

Lawyers who are used to a narrow, legalistic interpretation of victory and defeat are beginning to understand that the law must play a positive role in providing a firm foundation for social justice and legitimate defence. Citizens' prosecutions remind them that stale ritual is no substitute for common humanity. Under pressure from concerned and determined citizens, the judiciary of the nuclear States will rediscover their primary responsibility to enforce laws safeguarding civilization.

In Europe and the United States, too, initiatives are under way to challenge nuclear illegality in the courts. Political parties have begun to express interest in the legal issues, for the first time. Our aim is to extend and develop this active concern to every part of the world. There is something of value which everyone can do to further this campaign.

For further information please write to: *INLAW, 90 Gladstone Street, Bedford, England, MK41 7RT*.

George Delf
May 1985

Bibliography

Adler, Bill (ed.), *Letters from Vietnam*, New York 1967
Akehurst, Michael, *A Modern Introduction to International Law*,
   London 1984
Best, Geoffrey, *Humanity in Warfare*, London 1980
Bowen, C. D., *Francis Bacon*, Boston 1963
Builder and Graubard, *The International Law of Armed Conflict;
   Implications for the concept of Mutual Assured Destruction*, USA
   1982
Calvocoressi, Peter, *Nuremberg*, London 1947
Carver, Field-Marshal Lord, *A Policy of Peace*, London 1982
Cortright, David, *Soldiers in Revolt*, New York 1975
Dicey, *Law of the Constitution* (8th ed.), London 1923
Driver, Christopher, *The Disarmers*, London 1964
Dyson, Freeman, *Disturbing the Universe*, New York 1979
Eichmann Interrogated, London 1983
Estey and Hunter (ed.), *Violence*, Boston 1971
Falk, Richard, *et al* (ed.), *Crimes of War*, New York 1971
Fénelon, Fania, *The Musicians of Auschwitz*, London 1977
Gentili, *De Jure Belli Libri Tres* (Book II), 1612
Gowing, Margaret, *Independence and Deterrence*, London 1974
Gray, Tony, *Champions of Peace*, New York 1976
Green, L., *Superior Orders in National and International Law*,
   Netherlands 1976
Griffith, J. G., *Politics of the Judiciary*, London 1981
Grotius, Hogo, *De Jure Belli ac Pacis*, 1625
Hailsham, *Hamlyn Revisited*, London 1983
Hart, Kitty, *Return to Auschwitz*, London 1981
HMSO, *Trial of Major War Criminals*, London 1946
—*International Military Tribunal* (trial transcript), London 1946
—*British Manual of Military Law* (Part 3), London 1956
Hesse, Hermann, *If the War Goes On*, London 1972
Horne, Alistair, *The Price of Glory*, London 1962

Howard, Michael, *War in European History*, Oxford 1976
—(ed.), *Restraints of War*, Oxford 1979
Institute of World Order, *War Criminals, War Crimes*, New York
    1974
Irving David, *The Destruction of Dresden*, London 1974
Jung, Carl, *Collected Works* (Vol. II), London 1968
Kafka, Franz, *The Trial*, London 1973
Kaminskaya, Dina, *Final Judgment: My Life as a Soviet Defence
    Lawyer*, London 1983
Karsten, Peter, *Law, Soldiers and Combat*, USA 1978
Kennan, George F., *The Nuclear Delusion*, London 1984
Lane, Mark, *Conversations with Americans*, New York 1970
Lang, Daniel, *Incident on Hill 192*, London 1970
Laing, Ronald, *The Politics of Experience*, New York 1967
Leahy, William D., *I Was There*, New York 1950
Leber, Annedore, *Conscience in Revolt*, New York 1957
Levy, Charles, *Spoils of War*, USA 1974
Milgram, Stanley, *Obedience to Authority*, London 1974
Millis (ed.), *Forrestal Diaries*, New York 1951
Muir, Edwin, *Collected Poems*, London 1960
Neave, Airey, *Nuremberg*, London 1978
Paine, Thomas, *The Rights of Man*, London 1958
Polner, Murray, *No More Victory Parades*, New York 1971
Post, van der, Laurens, *Dark Eye in Africa*, London 1955
—*Testament to the Bushmen*, New York 1984
Prins, Gwyn (ed.), *The Choice: Nuclear Weapons versus Security*,
    London 1984
Rottman, L. (ed.), *Winning Hearts and Minds*, New York 1972
Schindler and Toman, *The Laws of Armed Conflicts*, The Hague
    1981
Scholl, Inge, *Six Against Tyranny*, London 1955
Schwarzenberger, Georg, *The Legality of Nuclear Weapons*,
    London 1958
Scott, J. B., *The Hague Conventions and Declarations of 1899 and
    1907*, London 1915
Shirer, William L., *The Rise and Fall of the Third Reich*, London
    1964
Sereny, Gitta, *Into that Darkness: From Mercy Killing to Mass
    Murder*, London 1974
Smith, Bradley F., *Reaching Judgment at Nuremberg*, London 1977

Steiner, George, *Language and Silence*, New York 1967
Stern, J. P., *Hitler, the Führer and the People*, London 1975
Telford Taylor, *Nuremberg and Vietnam*, USA 1970
Thoreau, Henry, *Walden*, New York 1980
Trevor-Roper, Hugh, *The Last Days of Hitler*, London 1947
United States Army Field Manual, USA 1956
Walzer, Michael, *Just and Unjust Wars*, London 1980
Webster and Frankland, *The Strategic Air Offensive Against Germany 1939/45* (3 vols.), HMSO, London 1961
Williams, Francis, *A Prime Minister Remembers*, London 1961
Yass, M., *Hiroshima*, New York 1971

Index